CURRENT ISSUES IN
THEORETICAL PSYCHOLOGY

ADVANCES
IN
PSYCHOLOGY
40

Editors

G. E. STELMACH

P. A. VROON

NORTH-HOLLAND
AMSTERDAM · NEW YORK · OXFORD · TOKYO

CURRENT ISSUES IN
THEORETICAL PSYCHOLOGY

Selected/Edited Proceedings of the Founding Conference of
The International Society for Theoretical Psychology
held in Plymouth, U.K., 30 August–2 September, 1985

Edited by

William J. BAKER
University of Alberta
Edmonton, Alberta, Canada

Michael E. HYLAND
Plymouth Polytechnic
Plymouth, United Kingdom

Hans VAN RAPPARD
Free University
Amsterdam, The Netherlands

Arthur W. STAATS
University of Hawaii at Manoa
Honolulu, Hawaii, U.S.A.

1987

NORTH-HOLLAND
AMSTERDAM · NEW YORK · OXFORD · TOKYO

ISBN: 0 444 70120 6

Publishers:
ELSEVIER SCIENCE PUBLISHERS B.V.
P.O. Box 1991
1000 BZ Amsterdam
The Netherlands

Sole distributors for the U.S.A. and Canada:
ELSEVIER SCIENCE PUBLISHING COMPANY, INC.
52 Vanderbilt Avenue
New York, N.Y. 10017
U.S.A.

PRINTED IN THE NETHERLANDS

PREFACE

As a consequence of informal discussions among academics with an explicit interest in theoretical issues in psychology (primarily from Britain, The Netherlands, Canada, and the United States), it began to appear, in the early 1980's, that some sort of international society might be useful to formalize and focus such discussions, as well as to broaden their base. To explore this, a questionnaire was circulated to various individuals in 1984 to elicit opinions about the nature of theoretical issues and the feasibility of such an organization.

Response to the questionnaire was encouraging and suggested two broad areas of concern: metatheory, and the development of new theory. In due course, a founding conference was organized for August, 1985 at Plymouth, England. The papers in this book resulted from the efforts which this first conference attracted. These papers display the kind of kaleidoscopic effect one ought to expect since what constitutes 'theoretical psychology' is quite an open-ended issue. No attempt was made - nor should it have been - to force these initial offerings into any particular mold. Consequently, the results are offered here in simple alphabetical order, by author, even though certain possibilities for grouping begin to emerge. The International Society for Theoretical Psychology which was founded at this conference, and which will hold its second biannual meeting in Canada in 1987, should serve to further clarify some of this.

Of course, the newly formed organization simply reflects an area of interest which has evolved over many years. In 1951, Koch suggested that progress towards adequate theory in psychology could only be achieved by:

> ... the pursuit of *theoretical psychology* as defined by a set of modest objectives, geared to a realistic estimate of the status of our knowledge.

He saw these objectives to be:

(a) Education in the methodology and logic of science.

(b) Analysis of methodological or foundational problems that are more or less unique to psychology. These include the nature of psychological prediction and related questions concerning the optimal characteristics of our units of causal and descriptive analysis; the relations between psychology and physiology; the roles of quantitative procedures.

(c) Internal systematization of suggestive, but formally defective, theoretical formulations.

(d) Intertranslation and differential analysis of conflicting theoretical formulations.

(e) Construction of new theory.

The objectives described by Koch are interrelated. For example, the construction of new theory is enhanced by objectives earlier in the list. This relation between the different activities of theoretical psychology comes across more clearly in the description of theoretical psychology given initially by Bergmann (1951) and which was developed more fully by Madsen (1959, 1985).

Madsen suggests a hierarchical arrangement within theoretical psychology:

Philosophy of Science

Metatheory

Theory

Analysis at the level of philosophy of science includes prescriptive arguments about sciences such as the way psychology should proceed as a scientific (or, indeed, non-scientific) discipline. Analysis at the level of metatheory includes analysis of key concepts and groups of theories. At the level of theory, there is an attempt to improve or develop new metatheory.

The papers in this book fall within the accounts of theoretical psychology proposed by Koch and Madsen. For example, the papers by

Parker and by Shotter fall into the category of philosophy or logic of science, as both papers are critiques of the assumptions on which scientific psychology is based. Other foundational and methodological papers include those by Thorngate and by De Wit. The paper by van Geert corresponds to Madsen's level of metatheory or Koch's intertranslation and differential analysis. Papers contributing to the construction of new theory include those by Hezewijk, Davies, and Corcoran and Mehmet. The history of psychology is important for our understanding of theory since history informs our understanding of theoretical development. The papers by Lovie and McGuire are examples of the historical emphasis within theoretical psychology.

Another emphasis within theoretical psychology is the unifying effect of theory, an idea which formed the focus for the first Banff conference in theoretical psychology in 1969 (see proceedings in Royce, 1970). Some, such as Koch (1981), believe that unification is not possible. Others believe that unification, integration, or systematization is possible and that it constitutes an important goal in psychology. Many papers in this book include an integrative emphasis. The paper by Staats argues specifically for the value of unification.

The International Society for Theoretical Psychology is just one more step toward greater institutionalization of theoretical psychology, although the institutional basis for it has been with us for many years. The Center for Advanced Study in Theoretical Psychology was officially approved by the University of Alberta, Canada, in 1965, and it started operating two years later. "The major idea behind the Center," wrote Royce (1970, p. 3), "is to bring theoretical psychology into clearer focus, to meet an urgent need within the discipline - a need to advance our understanding of behavior by conceptual analysis and integration, and to train a small, select group of potential theoreticians to continue such efforts." In Europe, theoretical psychology is largely practiced as foundational research with a heavy emphasis on the history of psychology. Units of theoretical psychology exist in many universitites in the Netherlands and at Heidelberg in Germany.

In conclusion, then, it appears that theoretical psychology, as a specific focal point in its own right, is beginning to have an increasing role within the discipline of psychology. The papers in this book stem from contributions to the founding conference for the International Society for Theoretical Psychology. The papers were selected by the organizers on the basis of quality and intent rather than specific topic area. To that extent, then, they represent an example of current work and thinking in the theoretical domain.

Wm J. Baker, Canada
Michael E. Hyland, England
Hans Van Rappard, The Netherlands
Arthur W. Staats, U.S.A.

June, 1986

References

Bergmann, G. (1951). The logic of psychological concepts. *Philosophy of Science, 18,* 93-110.

Koch, S. (1951). Theoretical psychology, 1950: an overview. *Psychological Review, 58,* 295-301.

Koch, S. (1981). The nature and limits of psychological knowledge: lessons of a century qua 'science.' *American Psychologist, 36,* 256-269.

Madsen, K. B. (1959). *Theories of motivation.* Copenhagen: Munksgaard. (4th ed., 1968).

Madsen, K. B. (1985). Psychological metatheory. In Madsen, K. B. & Mos, L. P., (Eds.) *Annals of Theoretical Psychology.* Vol. 3. New York: Plenum.

Royce, J. R. (1970). *Toward unification in psychology: the first Banff conference on theoretical psychology.* Toronto: University of Toronto Press.

ACKNOWLEDGEMENTS

This volume was prepared using the facilities and resources of the Center for Advanced Study in Theoretical Psychology at the University of Alberta. Mrs. Evelyn Murison, Center secretary, entered the text, prepared the author index and, together with Mr. Casey Boodt, assisted in editorial work and the searching of references. Preparation of the text for this volume was accomplished through the facilities provided by Computing Services at the University of Alberta. The editors are grateful to the text-formatting consultants who assisted, patiently and competently, in educating the first editor (WJB) in how to make it work! We thank all of these people who were essential in the production of this work.

TABLE OF CONTENTS

Current Issues in Theoretical Psychology
Wm J. Baker, M.E. Hyland, H. Van Rappard, A.W. Staats (Editors)
© Elsevier Science Publishers B.V. (North-Holland), 1987

A CHANGE OF PERSPECTIVE FOR COGNITIVE SCIENCE

G. P. Corcoran and A. Mehmet

University of Bradford
West Yorkshire, England

SUMMARY: Recent work concerning cognition has concentrated upon the computational or information-processing approach. Classical conditioning theory is now generally considered inappropriate for explaining such complex internal psychological processes. This paper seeks to resurrect an interest in classical conditioning as a possible rival to the computational theory.

Introduction

The recent literature would have us believe that there is an area of academic enterprise called Cognitive Science which is on the upsurge (cf. Dennet, 1978; Fodor, 1980, 1981, 1983, 1985; Pylyshyn, 1980). Psychologists, philosophers, linguists, and computer scientists are supposedly in fruitful collaboration, combining the resources of their respective disciplines, tackling crucial questions concerning human mentality. To what extent this idea holds true is difficult to determine. The suspicion is that matters are at least improving. In this paper attention will focus on preparatory work designed to provide a basis for an alternative to the influential computational theory of cognition (Fodor, 1980) which, on recent evidence, seems unable to give plausible accounts of the enduring relations which obtain between the human subject and the environment.

Churchland & Churchland (1983) state:

A completed computational psychology is nonetheless a radically incomplete theory of how humans work. For if it has nothing whatsoever to say about how representational systems represent features in the world, it has left out a crucial part of the theory. (p. 11)

and also:

The point is that it seems brains do what they do in virtue of the referents of their assorted states, inasmuch as there

is a stupendously good fit between representational systems
and the world. (p. 11)

The naturalistic alternative seeks an account of this 'stupendously good
fit' as a basis for the construction of a rich cognitive theory.

Two Strategies for Cognitive Theory

Broadly speaking one can follow one of two strategies when re-
searching and developing cognitive theory. *Cognitivism* is the view that
behavior is to be explained by a psychological theory which holds there to
be an inner mental structure, comprised of mental processes defined over
mental representations in a rule-governed manner. Mental states such as
belief and desire are taken to be relations between the subject and appropriate representations (Fodor, 1975).

Typically, representations are assumed to be sentence-like entities
encoded in an inner 'language of thought' which has a structure and elements isomorphic to those of the natural languages used to report and
talk about such things as mental states (Fodor, 1975; Stich, 1983). Consequently, cognitive activity is best described in terms of the processes of
transition which occur between sentences in the 'language of thought.'
The nature of the relations involved in cognitive activity is specified by
the logical relations which hold among sentences in a natural language.
Characterized in this general way, cognitivism has an additional fundamental principle. It is the *content* of the representations which puts constraints on the type of logical relations which may obtain (Churchland &
Churchland, 1983; Fodor, 1975; Stich, 1983). The inability to say precisely what *content* consists of has proved a persistent worry, and it has
caused cognitive theorists to posit a restrictive, computational theory
which, in trying to avoid semantic problems such as *content,* has left itself
open to the charge of being either an *incomplete* theory, as in Churchland
(1983), or totally inappropriate, as in Searle (1980).

Naturalism (Churchland, P. M., 1979, 1980, 1981; Churchland, P.
S., 1980a, 1980b, 1980c; Churchland & Churchland, 1983), as the alternative research strategy, supports different fundamental principles. The reliance upon almost wholly semantic or linguistic accounts of inner representation and subsequent cognitive activity is relinquished, and the close
relation between a system and its environment is acknowledged and
emphasized. Brains have been so acted upon by the process of evolution
that it is possible to receive information from the environment via perceptual systems, store it as a representation, transform it, and act upon

it, in ways which provide a whole array of behaviors typically appropriate for the detected situation, yet also in a way which allows rehearsal of *possible* responses to future events. Insofar as humans have evolved from non-verbal organisms, such complex *information-processing* must not in principle be of a *radically* different nature to that of intelligent non-verbal organisms (Churchland, P. S., 1980c). The required theory would seek to account for the enduring and consistent relation between environment, changes in states of the brain, and consequent behavior.

The fundamental naturalist observation is:

> In some manner, devolving from Evolution's blind trials and blunders, densely crowded packets of cells inevitably come to represent the world. The conglomeration which is the human brain standardly evolves an awesomely complex world-representation in short order and on the basis of scanty input ... But how can a brain be a world represent- er? How can brains change so that some of their changes consist in learning about the world? How are representa- tions used by a brain such that the output yields purposive and intelligent behavior? (Churchland & Churchland, 1983, p. 5)

Even if these basic questions can be answered and basic principles agreed upon, it still seems a long way from excitable packets of cells to semantic aspects of mental representations, but attempts are being made to chart a route, now that the issues are being seriously raised.

The Primacy of Cognitivism

Cognitivism is the most influential general thesis in modern cogni- tive psychology, and its plausibility stems, in part, from the fact that the representations, states, and processes it postulates are recognized by 'folk' or 'common sense' psychology. We all hold a sophisticated psychological theory involving the ascription of beliefs and desires and so forth to oth- ers, which aids us in making sense of, and predicting, behavior. This theory typically relies on the assumption that individuals represent states of affairs internally and that they have cognitive states in virtue of some relation to those representations. Thinking involves the systematic ma- nipulation of such representations. Cognitivism actually attempts to pro- vide an account of the systematic manipulations that occur in these epi- sodes. Folk psychology asks, "I wonder what he has on his mind?" Cog- nitivism looks to provide a theory which can at least suggest what sorts of processes and representations may be involved.

Cognitivism retains the terms involved in 'folk' psychology yet makes some ontological claims concerning the internal machinations that may give rise to psychological states such as belief and desire. As such states are typically identified by the linguistic sentences used to talk about them, the resources of the logical theories regarding sentences can, as has been indicated, be transferred to the *internal* sentences. This provides an already existing, coherent, and rich framework on which to build a cognitive theory.

The naturalistic approach has to start from a far more impoverished framework. Scientific investigation of psychological phenomena based on the resources of neuroscience, psychophysics, and perceptual theory, for instance, seems a far more daunting prospect. However, this particular tension between cognitivism and naturalism is merely symptomatic of the more general tension between the two meta-strategies within cognitive theory research, the top-down and the bottom-up approach. The details of this tension are well documented, and need not directly concern us here. Relevant to our discussion, the *top-down approach*, emphasizing as it does the most general cognitive capacities as a starting point for theory construction, is very much the received doctrine of cognitive science and any position, such as *cognitivism*, which is embedded in the meta-strategy will receive its 'patronage.'

Computational Theory of Mind

Fodor (1980) identified a form of cognitivism which he called the computational theory of mind (CTM). This particular theory has become the single most powerful and pervasive weapon of the cognitivist cause. Fodor has argued that the difficulties encountered in trying to provide a semantics for mental representations in any *direct* sense may prove insurmountable. Far better to approach this goal obliquely. The first step in this approach is to render semantic aspects of mental representations irrelevant to the causal processes of cognition. CTM states that our behavior is the outcome of mental processes defined over mental representations in a rule-governed way in virtue of the *formal aspects* of those representations. It is the requirement that processes apply to formal machines in so far as they operate on symbols in virtue of formal or intrinsic aspects of the symbol rather than with regard to how the symbol may be semantically interpreted. Fodor (1980) states:

If mental processes are formal, then they have access to

the formal properties of such representations of the environment as the senses provide. Hence they have no access to the *semantic* properties of such representations, including the property of being true, of having referents or, indeed, of being representations of the environment. (p. 65)

The *formality condition* within CTM says that any two or more representations can be treated as type-distinct only if there is a formal difference between them that will be detected by the system, and which causes the system to implement different computational processes. Methodological solipsism says that system *will* be provided with formal properties only because no semantic information from the environment can be represented in a way recognizable by the computational system other than formally.

In wishing to approach semantics at a tangent Fodor required a causal process which could map input into output in a way which was wholly constrained by the formal character of the intermediate states. Semantics enters the picture only inessentially insofar as it must be formally characterized for the operating system, but may be interpreted semantically by us. A computational theory seemed the only plausible option. The crucial question *which remains unanswered* (Fodor, in press), is how do humans, if they are computational systems, come to interpret their formal states semantically, that is, as having some relation to external states of affairs. It may be that the questions will never be answered if cognitivism generally, CTM specifically, continues to draw upon the semantic aspects of natural language sentences in order to illuminate *possible* isomorphisms with sentences or representations within cognitive systems.

Naturalism and Classical Conditioning Theory

Churchland has correctly observed that naturalism also honours the formality condition. This is not surprising when we consider that the brain deals in small millivolt signals entering along afferent and identical physical signals leaving along efferent nerves. Admittedly these signals occur in great numbers, complexity, and frequency, yet these are purely formal considerations in themselves.

What naturalism has over CTM is a desire to show that such formal aspects may be interpreted semantically by the system through constant interaction with specific types of environmental events and monitoring the appropriateness of the behavior generated to deal with the events. The picture to be sketched here is a preliminary study; the details are to be filled in at a later date, but it seems to suggest that a change of perspective should be considered in something like a serious manner.

Gibson (1966) points out that the environment is a rich source of information and systems such as humans have been acted upon by the processes of evolution to pick out ecologically important information via environmentally attuned perceptual systems. Such information is represented in the system, usually by means of changes in the brain. When the resultant behavior is appropriate to the environmental event which yields the informational input, the relation between that input, the representation, and the behavior, assumes a new significance. Subsequent instantiations of this situation serve to refine and make concrete this relation. In future a *particular* aspect of the complex environmental event may be sufficient to 'activate' the representation and subsequent behavioral repertoire which has on previous occasions been appropriate to the events containing this type of *particular* aspect. The informational input is potentially so rich (Miller, 1956) that the system has to be selective, and the automation of the environment-representation-behavior relation would be a simplifying procedure. The activity of a particular representation within the system comes to mean that a particular environmental event has occurred and that the appropriate behavior is required. The relation between environmental event and behavior may be described via classical conditioning theory; what is more difficult is to show the role of internal mental events in mapping the input onto output insofar as classical conditioning is not supposed, in a traditional sense, to treat such problems. The crux of the problem is that this picture seems plausible for relatively simple and straight forward behaviors. In humans there seems to be a crucial leap in complexity of behavior and cognitive power. How could such regular correlations act as the basis for cognition?

Behavioral plasticity may occur firstly, when low level event-representation-behavior relations operate in an unconscious or automatic fashion, leaving consciousness to monitor 'novel' situations, or to modify the relation between an already represented event and subsequent behavior when that relation becomes no longer appropriate. And secondly, when a relation can occur between events which exist only internally as representations of potential states of affairs. It is this factor that may allow for the rehearsal of possible behavioral responses based on previous experience. Quite simply it allows us to look before we leap.

If we are to suggest a theory of the mind based on the close relation between the environment, the system's ecological niche in that environment, and behavior then we may find it useful to adopt a classical conditioning paradigm. In the picture outlined here the relation in question is, crucially, mediated by representations in the brain, something which is beyond the normal scope of conditioning. The real interest comes when we try to *internalize* the conditioning paradigm and suggest that the relations and processes obtaining between mental representations may be amenable to such an *experimental* treatment. The experiments to be described seek to show that such mental representations, the relation between them and environmental events or other mental representations along with appropriate emitted behavior, are amenable to the classical conditioning process.

In the traditional Pavlovian paradigm classical conditioning was seen as a process which would bring about the elicitation of a response to a particular stimulus which previously would not have done so. Thus by successive pairings of stimulus A with stimulus B (which produced some response C), the situation would arise such that presentation of A alone would elicit response C.

The majority of research carried out involving conditioning has employed the exteroceptive paradigm, i.e., the conditioned stimulus (CS) and unconditioned stimulus (UCS) have been real external or public events. Razran (1961, 1971) has reviewed many studies from both the East and the West employing the interoceptive conditioning paradigm, i.e., either the CS or UCS or both are presented to parts of the subject's internal anatomy, where they may give rise to either behavioral changes or responses without being available to consciousness. The experimental methodologies employed in the studies to be discussed here differ from both of those mentioned above in that the CS and/or the UCS employed exist only in representational form as a private event in the mind of the subject; such events will hereafter be referred to as Ideational.

Pavlov (1932) believed that with the advent of language a new principle of neural action was formed; this he termed the Second Signalling System. There are two ways in which language or language components (words) can be viewed as CS's:

1. As an acoustic pattern: in this sense a word would be no different from any other auditory stimulus or visual stimulus if the word was presented via that modality. In this use consideration is directed at the physical configuration of the stimulus.

2. As a symbol for its referent: this second mode of action is of far more interest. It, of course, subsumes 1 above but stimulus configuration is less important than the semantic component of the said stimulus.

Volkova's (1953, reported in Razran, 1961) work on the meaning of words used as CS's is well known in this field. She conditioned a thirteen year old boy to increase salivation on hearing the Russian word 'khorosho' meaning good or well, and to decrease salivation on hearing the word 'plokho' meaning bad or poorly. She found that the conditioned salivatory response generalized to sentences which expressed the same sentiments as the original CS words but did not contain them. The sentences were semantically equivalent with the CS words but were very different in terms of configuration. Should this experiment be repeated using a non-Russian speaking subject it would be anticipated that no difference in salivatory response to either type of sentence would be observed. However, such differences may be evident on CS word presentation as discrimination may occur on the basis of stimulus configuration, not word meaning.

Volkova's work demonstrates quite clearly that semantic generalization occurs. It is, however, still derived from real exteroceptive cues, i.e., the presentation of the CS word. Acker and Edwards (1964) work, using vasoconstriction as the conditioned response to the words 'good' and 'bad,' found results which supported those of Volkova's. Hunter and Hudgins (1934) were able to induce contraction and dilation in the irises of their subjects by presenting the words 'contract' and 'relax' respectively. Once the response had been established, it was sufficient for the subjects to merely think of the word to elicit the response. Impressive though this might seem, it is little more than an investigation of stimulus generalization, but in terms of mode of presentation rather than configuration.

The experiments to be described here go beyond those mentioned above in seeking to demonstrate that involuntary physiological responses can be brought under the control of a conditioned stimulus which exists only as a 'thought' in the mind of the subject, i.e., it has never actually been presented in verbal, pictorial, or symbolic form. As the CS is generated by the subject, not the experimenter, the second part of the first one of the experiments was designed as an attempt to establish the effective range of generalization of the CS as it was by no means certain apriori just how specific the CS would be. As such, this portion of the experiment could be viewed as a crude (in its present form) assessment of the generalization gradient of a thought.

Methodologies

All studies were carried out in a sound attenuated and RF screened room. The subjects were required to sit in a comfortable chair facing a screen approximately two meters away, except for the subjects in Experiment 4 who were required to look into a six-field tachistoscope. All subjects were informed that the purpose of the experiment was to measure palmar sweat gland activity in relation to various auditory and visual stimuli.

Experiment 1

Twenty subjects were used. The experimental group were given 32 presentations of slides depicting simple arithmetic problems. Of these problems, 16 produced the answer '8' and these 16 slides were randomly arranged throughout the series of 32. The actual digit '8' did not appear in any of the slides. Subjects were informed to look at the screen and solve the problems shown without verbalizing the answer. All slide presentations had a six-second duration. When the slide being shown produced the answer '8,' a 115dB tone at 1000Hz, which acted as the UCS, was delivered to the subject via headphones for .5 seconds, 4 seconds after slide on-set. The subjects in the control group (10 in all) were presented with the same series of slides but with 16 randomly associated pairings of the UCS. Skin conductance responses (SCR's) were measured throughout the experiment but only those from the test phase were subjected to analysis.

The test phase consisted of the presentation of another 32 slides similar to those in the learning phase but with the inclusion of the digit '8,' the word *eight*, and anagrams of the word eight, e.g., *htegi*, eight randomly spaced lines, an outline octagon, the Roman numeral for eight, an eight-dot pattern that would be seen on two dice, and an otherwise blank clock face with the hands showing eight o'clock. Non-eight equivalents of all the above slides were also presented.

An independent group 't' test, comparing experimental and control groups' responses to slides with some property of eightness showed that the experimental group's responses were significantly greater than those of the control group (p<.0005). This result shows that conditioning of an autonomic response using an ideational CS, i.e., the thought of eight, was possible and that once the CR to 'thought of eight' was acquired, the response would generalize to other stimuli which had some property of eightness.

Experiment 2

This was a reversal of Experiment 1 in that the CS used was both real and external (a slide of an outline star), but the UCS was ideational, i.e., the thought of an electric shock.

Twenty subjects were used (10 in both the experimental and control group). Subjects in the experimental group were given a consent form to read and then sign, those who did not sign took no further part in the study. On signing the form, two 4cm^2 shocking electrodes were attached to their non-preferred upper forearm. They were then given the written instruction: "An electric shock will follow some presentations of the star." If they made any enquiry as to the nature and severity of the shock they were simply told that it would not be permanently damaging. The subjects were then presented with a series of 18 slides consisting of six stars, six squares, and six circles arranged in a random order. The control group underwent the same procedure except that they were not given the written instructions regarding possible shock contingency. Instead, they were told to relax and watch the screen after having signed the consent form and had the shocking electrodes fitted. Comparison between the experimental and control groups' SCR's showed that the experimental group produced significantly greater responses than the control group (p<.001).

The results of this study show that conditioning is also possible when the UCS is in ideational form. Earlier studies by Davies and Mehmet (1985) also indicate the CR's produced using the ideational paradigms outlined are amenable to related conditioning procedures such as pre-conditioning and higher order conditioning.

Experiment 3

The aim of the third study was to produce a conditioned autonomic response derived from the association of an ideational CS and UCS, i.e., via the operation of a relationship between two mental representations. Twenty subjects were used. The 10 experimental subjects were given 10 pairings of some simple arithmetic problems yielding the answer eight followed by the presentation of an outline star. Each numeric slide was shown for six seconds followed by a half-second of blank screen after which the outline star was presented for half a second.

The experimental group then underwent the same procedure used for the experimental group in the second study, i.e., they were given a consent form to read and sign followed by written instructions regarding possible shock contingency. The control group received no such instruction.

During the test phase subjects in both groups were presented with a series of 16 slides consisting of 4 outline stars, 4 with some property of eightness, and 8 neutral slides (2 squares, 2 circles, and 4 non-eight equivalents). Comparisons between the experimental and control groups SCR's to slides of stars and slides with some property of eightness showed that the experimental group's responses to both cases were significantly greater than those of the control group (p<.0005).

What must be emphasized is that at no point during Experiments 2 and 3 were any electric shocks actually delivered. The subjects were merely led to believe that they would be shocked. Experiment 3 shows that conditioning can be demonstrated when the CS and UCS exist as private ideational events in the subject. Furthermore, responses to CS1, i.e., the outline star, can generalize to pre-conditioned associations, i.e., slides of simple arithmetic problems yielding the answer eight. It was also possible to show that the preconditioned associations would generalize to stimuli with some general property of eightness, e.g., an octagon, the word eight, the Roman numerals for eight, etc.

Having demonstrated that there are ways in which mental phenomena can be used within the conditioning paradigm, it also becomes necessary to show that such a process can occur at an unaware and automatic level. That is to say, conditioned associations can be made without recourse to such higher mental or cognitive processes such as Contingency Learning (Dawson, 1973) or Expectancy (Mandel & Bridger, 1973). Both the above authors suggest that classical conditioning cannot occur without the subject being consciously aware of the CS-UCS relationship. Experiment 4 was designed so that conditioning could be carried out using a CS which was presented below the level of the subject's awareness, i.e., the stimulus was presented subliminally. Presentation times were set such that on five successive presentations the subject could not report when or what was presented.

Experiment 4

Eleven subjects were used, each acting as their own controls. Once the presentation thresholds had been determined they were told to watch

the centre of the tachistoscope screen (on the pretext of reducing artifac-
tual SCR's) and wait for the randomly presented tones (115dB at
1000Hz). Each subject received 15 subliminal CS presentations which
were either of squares, triangles, or circles, and the tonal UCS.

They were then given 9 subliminal presentations of different CS's,
three of which had already been paired with the UCS. No tones were
presented during these 9 presentations. Following this series another 3
slides were shown. One was CS+, i.e., it had previously been paired with
the UCS. Each slide had a presentation duration of 1 second.

Analysis of SCR responses to the test phase indicated that subjects
produced significantly greater responses to their respective CS+'s than to
CS's which were not paired with the tone at both the sub- and supralim-
inal levels ($p < .001$). This clearly indicates that conditioning is possible
in the absence of conscious awareness. However, it must be said that
some level of awareness is required for such associations to be made and
stored.

The experiments outlined here suggest that the relations and processes obtaining between mental representations as described in the earlier
part of this paper are amenable to the classical conditioning process.
These experiments could be seen as charting the first steps along the route
to developing a 'whole' theory which could account for the enduring and
consistent relation between environment, changes in brain state, and consequent behavior.

References

Acker, L. E., & Edwards, A. E. (1964). Transfer of vasoconstriction over a bipolar dimension. *Journal of Experimental Psychology, 67,* 1-16.

Churchland, P. M. (1979). *Scientific realism and the plasticity of mind.* Cambridge: Cambridge University Press.

Churchland, P. M. (1980). In defence of naturalism. *Brain and Behavioural Sciences, 3,* 74-75.

Churchland, P. M. (1981). Eliminative materialism and the propositional attitudes. *Journal of Philosophy, 78,* 67-90.

Churchland, P. S.(1980a). A perspective on mind-brain research. *Journal of Philosophy, 77,* 185-207.

Churchland, P. S. (1980b). Neuroscience and psychology: Should the labour be divided? *Behavioural and Brain Sciences, 3,* 133.

Churchland P. S. (1980c). Language, thought and information processing. *Nous, 14,* 147-169.

Churchland, P. S., & Churchland, P. M. (1983). Stalking the wild epistemic engine. *Nous, 17,* 5-19.

Davies, P., & Mehmet, A. (1985). Ideational conditioning. Annual Conference, British Psychological Society. Abstract in *Bulletin of the British Psychological Society, 38,* May 1985.

Dawson, M. B. (1973). Can classical conditioning occur without contingency learning? A review and evaluation of the evidence. *Psychophysiology, 10 (10),* 82-86.

Dennett, D. (1978). *Brainstorms.* Bradford: M.I.T. Press.

Fodor, J. A. (1975). *Language of thought.* New York: Crowell.

Fodor, J. A. (1980). Methodological Solipsism considered as a research strategy in cognitive psychology. *Behavioural and Brain Sciences, 3,* 225-253.

Fodor, J. A. (1981). *Representations.* Bradford: M.I.T. Press.

Fodor, J. A. (1983). *The modularity of mind.* Bradford: M.I.T. Press.

Fodor, J. A. (1985). Fodor's guide to mental representation: An intelligent aunts vade mecum. *Mind, XCIV(373),* 76-101.

Fodor, J. A. Psychosemantics: Or, where do truth-conditions come from. (Unpublished manuscript).

Fodor, J. A. Banish discontent. (Unpublished manuscript).

Fodor, J. A. The persistence of the attitudes. (Unpublished manuscript).

Gibson, J. J. (1966). *The senses considered as perceptual systems.* Boston: Houghton-Mifflin.

Hunter, W. S., & Hudgins, C. V. (1934). Voluntary activity from the standpoint of behaviorism. *Journal of General Psychology, 10,*

198-204.

Mandel, I. J., & Bridger, W. H. (1973). Is there classical conditioning without cognitive expectancy? *Psychopharmacology, 10 (1),* 87-90.

Miller, G. A. (1956). The magical number seven, plus or minus two: some limits on our capacity for processing information. *Psychological Review, 67,* 81-97.

Pavlov, I. P. (1932a). Physiology of higher nervous activity. *Priroda,* Nos. 11-12, 1139-1156. In G. Razran, *Mind in evolution: An East-West synthesis of learned behaviour and cognition.* Boston: Houghton-Mifflin.

Pylyshyn, Z. (1980). Computation and cognition: Issues in the foundations of cognitive science. *Behavioural and Brain Sciences, 3,* 111-132.

Razran, G. (1961). The observable unconscious and the inferable conscious in current Soviet psychophysiology: Interoceptive conditioning, semantic conditioning, and the orienting reflex. *Psychology Review, 68*(2), 81-147.

Razran, G. (1971). *Mind in evolution: An East-West synthesis of learned behaviour and cognition.* Boston: Houghton-Mifflin.

Searle, J. (1980). Minds, brains, and programs. *Behavioural and Brain Sciences, 3,* 417-424.

Stich, S. (1983). *From folk psychology to cognitive science: The case against belief.* Bradford: M.I.T. Press.

Current Issues in Theoretical Psychology
Wm J. Baker, M.E. Hyland, H. Van Rappard, A.W. Staats (Editors)
© Elsevier Science Publishers B.V. (North-Holland), 1987

IS PHYSICS REDUCTIONISTIC?[1]

G. J. Dalenoort

University of Groningen
Haren, The Netherlands

SUMMARY: It is argued that properties of systems and processes can be defined such that no fundamental difference needs to be discerned between physical properties and psychological properties, apart from our private experiences. In this way of defining properties, all properties become emergent, although in a somewhat different sense than the term is used traditionally. The basic point is that all properties are considered to be the result of interactions, and that the assignment of properties to systems is an abstraction. In this approach the traditional problems of scientific reduction become obsolete. Scientific reduction is just one way of representing relations between different levels of aggregation, going from the parts to the whole. For complete understanding of a system the complementary representation, starting from the whole, and going to the parts, is also needed.

The doctrine of scientific reduction holds it possible to explain high-level properties from low-level properties, and to explain phenomena at one level of description in terms of general principles and laws at the same level of description. To be more precise, reduction is often considered as a process of logical deduction of statements or theories from other statements or theories at different levels, or at one level of description (see e.g., Nagel, 1961). There is a widespread opinion that psychological properties, and biological properties as well, cannot be explained from properties at lower levels of aggregation. In contradistinction, disciplines like physics and chemistry are considered as being reductionistic. With respect to psychology, the term physicalism is often used as more or less synonymous with scientific reductionism.

In this paper I shall argue that physics is as little reductionistic as biology and psychology and that the view that it is, is based on an erroneous view of the epistemology of physics. I shall argue for a unified epis-

---

[1]I am grateful to Michael Hyland who, by his misunderstanding of an earlier version, demonstrated the inadequacy of that first representation of the problem. I thus decided to rewrite the paper completely. He also proposed many linguistic improvements in the second version.

temology that can accommodate the way properties are explained in phys-ics as well as in psychology, and, in fact, in all sciences. Of course, this claim does not imply that there are no qualitative differences between the properties studied in the different disciplines, on the contrary. First I shall describe globally the way explanations in physics are given, and then how this approach can be reinterpreted in a manner that is also suitable for the explanation of psychological and biological properties.

Let us ask what the actual practice of physics is, in comparison to, or even in contradistinction to what the *doctrine* states. How,in physics, are phenomena, and the properties of systems, explained in what is tradi-tionally called a reductionistic approach.

In physics, there are general equations of emotion. The classic ex-ample is Newton's equation which states that the acceleration of an ob-ject due to the application of a force is proportional to that force. The constant of proportionality is the mass. This equation is the basis for classical mechanics, which comprises the motions of cars, bicycles, and the solar system. From Newton's equation it is possible to derive Keppler's laws for the orbits of the planets around the sun: their elliptic shape and corresponding parameters, and the variation of the velocities along the orbit. Another classic example is Schroedinger's equation, which describes the behaviour of systems at the atomic level.

Both equations express in mathematical form the relations between the variables of the systems involved, and how they develop in time. Thus, given the state (the values of a complete set of variables) at one time, it is possible to compute states in the future and, in some cases, also in the past (important for astronomy). The variables represent the properties of the systems involved, properties that can be directly ob-served, like position and velocity, and properties that are constructed, like the charge of the electron, and the mass of the planet Mars.

In psychology, there are no equations of motion with a status com-parable to that of the equations of physics. Only some very simple mo-dels can be expressed in terms of mathematical equations, the solutions of which are not easy to test empirically. There are several reasons for this state of affairs. One reason is the difficulty, or even impossibility to measure variables at the psychological level, as well as at the underlying levels, physiological, chemical, and physical (e.g., EEG). A second rea-son is the number of variables involved. A third reason is our ignorance of the relations between the variables corresponding to our ignorance of the nature of the interaction between the corresponding subsystems. A fourth reason is the seeming qualitative difference between the properties at the higher level of aggregation and those at the lower level. In physics such differences are less strong or even absent. Qualitatively there is no difference between the velocity of a part of the system, and that of the system as a whole. Even for the velocity of the electrons in atoms, we can draw an analogy with the velocity of the planets around the sun, although quantum mechanics demonstrates the restrictions of such a comparison. In some way we can project physical properties onto objects; we can externalize them, and we can have the illusion that they have, to some extent, an objective status. A second kind of properties are physical properties that seem to be more elusive, but that we can still project onto the world around us, independently of our experience, although their roots lie in our experience. Examples are the light of the sun, the warmth of the sun, the sound of a bell. The third kind of properties are consciousness, and sensory experiences like the perception of colours, smells, shapes by touch, sound, the meaning of a sentence, the beauty of a piece of music. They are, on one hand, more certain; we have the most direct and first experience of them, but they cannot be projected onto the world. They have their locus in ourselves, and we can only construct the same properties as being present in other people on the basis of observations of their behaviour and of what they say. Here I do not mean the systematic analysis of these phenomena, but the subjective experience that I can only *describe*, but not demonstrate. Perhaps the difference between both types of properties lies mainly in the *way* we can demonstrate them.

It must have been this difference between physical properties on one hand, and psychological properties on the other hand, that has given rise to the doctrine of emergent properties. Nagel discusses several forms of this doctrine and a number of aspects were described by Oatley (1978). For the present purpose it is sufficient to take the meaning of 'emergent properties' as properties that are the result of interactions between two or more systems that each on themselves do not show those properties, or are in no way able to do so. There are also abstract properties that have a similar status. For example, Fodor (1981) claims that the concept of money can in no way be derived from any physical properties or process, be it coins, cheques, or credit cards, or even the knowledge in a community of who is the owner of some objects. (Such ownership can be changed in a transaction by making known who the new owner is.) I can agree with this point of view, but I do not contrast it with the interpretation of physical properties in the same way Fodor seems to do. My claim is that we can also interpret physical properties as the result of interactions, and that our assignment of properties to objects is an abstraction. We have direct experience of some physical properties, which are the result of an interaction between an object and an observer. For other properties we only have indirect experience, where we project onto the subsystems of a system on the basis of our interaction with the system as a whole.

We observe many objects and systems directly, which we have also observed before, or will observe afterwards, functioning as parts of a larger system. Often, the properties we observe in isolation take on a new meaning in the light of our experience of the function of the object in the larger system. This demonstrates that our perceptions, and also our understanding of properties of objects and systems, are strongly influenced by our experiences at higher levels or of composite systems. For example, our knowledge and understanding of cogwheels would be much poorer if we had never seen one in interaction with other cogwheels.

Let us follow this line of reasoning further. Consider a child that continues to ask "why is ....", and let us adopt its attitude towards physical questions. If we explain the behaviour of a hydrogen atom from the Schroedinger equation, in terms of the masses and charges of electron and proton, it is legitimate to ask how these basic properties themselves are explained. A physicist might answer that these properties are being explained in terms of the properties of quarks and their interactions, but the child continues to ask: "how are the properties of quarks explained?" No satisfactory answer is available; the properties of quarks cannot be explained, they are postulated. If that leads to a good theory, which produces predictions in agreement with the results of experiments, the postulates are accepted, otherwise they are rejected or modified. In fact, physicists might even come to believe they *understand* quarks from the postulated theory, and that quarks *explain* the properties of electrons, protons, and other elementary particles. This would be turning around matters. Physicists construct quarks, or rather the concept of quarks, from their knowledge gained before, and they try to predict new phenomena. They thus perform a complex process of reasoning upwards and downwards. Finally the origins of their reasoning must be traceable to primitive concepts that originally were the product of direct sensory experiences. The conclusion is that every chain of explanation must come to an end, that of primitive properties. Some of these properties are the concepts of object, of motion, of colour, of time.

We cannot explain primitive properties; we can only analyze, for example, the physical and physiological conditions under which a person will perceive the colour of red. We cannot explain his experience. These primitive properties emerge from the interactions which we can describe at the physical level and the physiological level. We can thus describe the conditions at lower levels of aggregation that must be fulfilled in order that a high-level property will emerge.

My claim is that it is possible to state that all properties emerge from interactions. The expression 'emergent properties' then becomes a tautology. The assignment of properties to objects is a constructive process; it refers to potential interactions, formalized in mathematical equations, from which we may conclude which phenomena are actually observable. All physical properties can be considered to be the result of interactions between objects and, finally, of systems of objects with an observer. Assignments of properties may be considered as statements about potential interactions, as statements about actual interactions, or as statements about constructs. The same holds for psychological and biological systems, although the formalization is far less easy.

Physical properties and psychological properties are similar in this respect, with the difference that disciplines like physics and chemistry have been more successful in stating the conditions that must be fulfilled at the lower level in precise, mathematical form, as in the equations of motion described before. Partly this is due to the fact that the systems of physics are simpler, partly to the fact that we, as observers, have a less direct influence on the systems measured, or an influence that can be well described (quantum mechanics). As stated, our only measurement of consciousness is purely subjective, and our assignment of this property and related properties to others remains a construction.

We cannot explain why certain equations of motion are successful. We may be able to derive them from more general equations, like Keppler's equations for the orbits of the planets from Newton's equation, but the general equations are postulated. The equations that express interactions are constructs. Their validity as models follows from the correspondence with the results of experiments.

The usual way we define properties that are constructs is from observable phenomena. This process of definition can go 'down' to microscopic objects, or 'up' towards cosmic objects. These properties can then in turn be used to construct models which serve to predict other directly observable properties. We then build a network of directly observable properties and constructs. If the network involves different levels of aggregation we may say that we 'reduce' complex phenomena and properties to more basic ones, but it must be kept in mind that the original starting point was the observation at the higher level, the 'whole.' Thus, this view of reduction is completely compatible with the adage, 'the whole is more than the sum of its parts.'

The network of concepts may be construed in many ways, and simplifications of it, corresponding to specific models, can be of many kinds. These models may concern parts or aspects of the network. An important criterion for the way we build such models concerns what Ernst Mach (1919) has called "the economy of thought." There is a pay-off between making concepts more complex and relations simple, or the other way round. This pay-off is also found in the way concepts are decomposed into simpler ones. We want the final conceptual construction to be as parsimonious as possible, with sufficient explanatory power. This power must be understood as the possibility to formulate general principles and equations of which particular relations are examples. They may relate variables and phenomena at one level of description, or at different levels. Whether it is possible to do so in a completely logical framework is doubtful. For example, it is not (yet?) clear where our logic abilities come from (cf. Johnson-Laird, 1983). Are they just the result of biological evolution, do they have survival value? It seems likely that logic reasoning will have to go together with intuition, private experience, heuristic insight. The problem does not become less interesting for that reason.

We may also view the reductionistic approach as a representation that is complementary to a top-down approach in which we explain the role of the parts from their function in the whole. Both representations are necessary for full understanding: for understanding the whole we must know the parts, for understanding the parts we must know the whole (Blaise Pascal). This thesis has been elaborated in another paper, also in relation to self-organization of systems (Dalenoort, 1985).

References[2]

Dalenoort, G. J. (1985). Representations of cognitive systems. *Cognitive Systems, 1-1,* 1-16.

Fodor, J. (1981). *Representations, philosophical essays on the foundations of cognitive science.* Brighton: Harvester Press.

Johnson-Laird, P. (1983). *Mental models.* Cambridge: Cambridge University Press.

Mach, E. (1919). *Die Leitgedanken meiner naturwissenschaftlichen Erkenntnislehre und ihre Aufnahme durch die Zeitgenossen.* Leipzig: (see also his *Analysis of sensations.*).

Nagel, E. (1961). *The structure of science.* London: Routledge & Kegan Paul.

Oatley, K. (1978). *Perceptions and representations.* London: Methuen.

---

[2]This list of references is only a minor selection of what has been written on these topics. It reflects the somewhat idiosyncratic knowledge of the author. They were chosen to illustrate some specific aspects of the problem of scientific reduction.

Current Issues in Theoretical Psychology
Wm J. Baker, M.E. Hyland, H. Van Rappard, A.W. Staats (Editors)
© Elsevier Science Publishers B.V. (North-Holland), 1987

CONDITIONING, THE BASIS OF ALL PSYCHOLOGICAL ACTIVITY

Peter Davies

University of Bradford
Bradford, England

SUMMARY: Conditioning, including both operant and classical varieties, is considered as the behavioural concomitant, and intellectual determinant, of phyletic ascent. The role of conditioning in breaking the 'informational bottleneck' imposed by our information processing capacity is discussed together with such issues as free will and determinism and the predictability of behaviour. It is argued that conditioning develops phylogenetically, underpins perception and consciousness, and accounts for cognition. Selective attention is regarded as the product of the ecological imperative for individual survival and previous predictive utility embodied in established conditioned responses. Behaviour, at all levels, is therefore determined but open to modification through experience. It is also unpredictable given the limitations on information processing capacity. The approach taken here seeks to demystify consciousness, eliminate "free will" as mere arbitrary choice, and to provide a behavioural account of all higher cognitive function.

The law of parsimony requires the simplest level of explanation that will account for the facts that have to be explained. Clearly psychological activity covers a very wide range of facts indeed and the purpose here is to indicate the possibility that conditioning is the fundamental process underlying all psychological action. In order to fulfill this demanding role all types of conditioning, and conditioning-like behaviours, have to be invoked. However, major consideration here will be given to classical conditioning as, hitherto, this has received less attention than operant conditioning as a determinant of human behaviour. It should be stressed that both forms of conditioning are relevant; however, the role of operant conditioning is so well established that it seems reasonable to devote the limited space available to other considerations.

Phyletic Ascent and Conditionability

The extent to which any organism can be conditioned is determined by its position on the phyletic scale. The more advanced the organism, the greater its ability to form conditioned responses and the more complex the range of stimuli that may be effective. At the very lowest levels of this hierarchy of behaviour we may observe sensitization and habituation which are the very cornerstones of learning. As brain size and weight, and consequently neuronal complexity, increase, the range of conditionability increases through simple associative conditioning to compound and configured conditioning, with humans exhibiting semantic conditioning. It could, of course, be argued that this ascent only parallels cognitive development but acceptance of such an argument must raise the question as to what purpose is thereby served. If it is believed that this increase in conditionability is a mere accidental consequence of increasing neuronal complexity this would be tantamount to saying that an ability had been developed in the absence of any function. If this were true, many organisms should possess abilities which were non functional. Of course, it could be argued that higher animals utilize this ability so that at each level of phyletic ascent we should find an increased range of conditioned behaviours. These behaviours could automate routine responses and so allow more scope for higher mental processes.

Such a view is almost undoubtedly over simplistic. To start with, all organisms at all levels of evolution have basic routine requirements if they are to survive. These requirements preclude cognitive control in that the lowest organisms do not possess a brain and hence cannot be sentient beings. All basic life supporting behaviours such as respiration and digestion must take place for all organisms without any cognitive control. Thus all organisms already possess innate behaviour patterns which support the fundamentals of living. Increased conditionability can confer no advantage here.

The argument advanced is that it is the increasing range of conditionability that is the behavioural manifestation of phyletic ascent. It is not a coincidental parallel, but the actual ascent itself. For this to be the case conditioning must be fundamental to all the behavioural repertoire other than the basic life supporting activities which are carried out inflexibly and automatically for so long as any animal lives. Hence it is to be argued that conditioning is the mechanism upon which our intellectual ascendancy rests, and that our higher mental functions are conditioned. Those who ascribe to Skinner's views (Skinner, 1985) will no doubt protest that too much is included. They will no doubt accept the view that conditioning, especially operant conditioning, provides a total explanation of behaviour while continuing to deny that cognition and feelings have existence other than as figments of the cognitive scientist's imaginations. In some sense the present argument seeks to reconcile the differences between these behaviourist views and cognitive science by suggesting that higher mental processes are conditioned responses. This issue is discussed elsewhere in this volume by Corcoran & Mehmet, and some recent experiments bridging the cognitive behaviourist divide are outlined there. On the other hand to many the suggestion that most of our behaviours, thoughts, and feelings are conditioned will seem an affront to human dignity and a denial of common sense. The suggestion will probably seem especially inappropriate for "the mind of the possessor" though less so for "mind as it appears to the onlooker." (Hobhouse, 1901). This is because people cherish the notion that they themselves possess free will while expecting behvioural regularity from others. Conditioning does imply determinism. Nevertheless, even casual observation reveals a diversity of behaviours, but normally only within limits. Only occasionally do we observe behaviour which is truly abnormal in the sense that it violates all expectations. The case to be advanced will seek to show that the regularities of conditioning, and the determinism this implies, will account also for the diversities of behaviour which may be observed.

Determinism and Reflexivity

From the point of view of psychology itself it is necessary to assume determinism. In seeking to explain behaviour the psychologist is making the tacit assumption that behaviour is subject to some law which he seeks to discover through his inquires. This is not usually seen as posing any problem for the general case of free will as it is frequently assumed that one might find laws of memory, or attention, or vision without denying free will. The problems arise only when psychologists seek to explain all behaviours including *reasoning*. As has been argued cogently, "if it (psychology) is to proceed with any hope of ever being able to propound general propositions about the nature of these mental processes, it must be prepared to face the paradoxes of self-reference." (Oliver & Landfield, 1962, p. 115).

The customary view is that higher cognitive functions represent the apogee of evolutionary ascent and are not constrained by anything other than the whims and intellect of the person carrying them out. However, this cannot be so, for if any aspect of behaviour were to be truly arbitrary, then no other aspect of behaviour could possibly be lawful. To be explicable, all behaviours must be lawful. If it is lawful, it must be determined; and if behaviour is determined, people cannot have free will; and though they may well have such a belief, this belief itself must be determined. If this position is accepted, one of the major arguments against conditioning as the basis of cognition has been met. A determined process could be responsible for what we erroneously believe to be an untrammelled activity. It should be added that *laws* are empirically deduced from observations, which in themselves are probabilistic. Space limitations preclude a full discussion of the nature of laws, especially the *laws of chance*, as these are largely axiomatic, and the implicit assumptions of probability implied in *determinism*. For the purposes of the present argument it is assumed that the determinism is of the same order as that implied in physics or chemistry, where processes are explained rather than the behaviour of individual molecules or atoms.

Special Specificity and Stimulus Selection

How then can diversity be explained? To start with I shall consider the regularities of behaviour in terms of an ecological imperative. Organisms exist to propagate their kind, and to do this they have to ensure their individual survival as the aggregate of individual survivals is species survival. If an organism is to survive, it must shape its behaviour in a way which maximizes its chances of survival. Assuming it is physiologically sufficiently advanced to be able to receive a variety of environmental inputs, it must select those which are most relevant to its survival as the basis of its response. Repeated presentations of irrelevant stimuli, those with no behavioural consequences for good or ill, soon habituate and cease to evoke responses. It should be noted that some stimuli, which may be specific to a single species or even a single individual as a consequence of individual experience, never habituate as they are always potentially relevant.

The physiological structure and functional architecture of an organism's brain reflect the types of stimuli of greatest relevance to that organism. The majority of the sensory system may be given to vision, audition, or olfaction at the expense of other sensory systems. Despite their complexity, brains are finite structures and one area can only be over represented at the expense of another. Moreover, it is not sufficent to just receive sensory information. It must be processed and selections must be made as to what is processed. Even the most advanced of brains, the human brain, can only cope with 7 ± 2 bits of information according to Miller (1956). This is woefully little when we consider the amount of information potentially available to us. Clearly, not all this information is of equal importance. In the majority of cases the presence of an approaching motor car is of more importance than its make or colour. Given limited processing abilities, we are well advised to process some information before other information. The visual system is neuronally organized in just this way in that form and movement are processed before colour information. Experiments in auditory selective attention have revealed similar hierarchies in that only gross characteristics of the non-attended messages are processed to the level of consciousness. In every circumstance, and in every modality, the input exceeds our ability to handle it. In order to account for our abilities Miller concludes that we are not restricted to *bits* of information but, "By organizing the stimulus input simultaneously into several dimensions and successively into a sequence of chunks, we manage to break (or at least stretch) this informational bottleneck." (Miller, 1956, p. 95).

While not doubting that *chunking* takes place, it seems to add nothing to our understanding of the underlying problems. Without a knowledge of how chunking takes place and what rules govern this process we are no further advanced. However, it is possible that preconditioning, and compound and configured conditioning are manifestations of the chunking process. Here at least we do have the advantage of knowing something of the conditions under which such conditioning occurs even though the neural substrate of learning remains to be discovered.

The Range of Conditionability

The simplest form of classical conditioning relates to the situation where a previously neutral or ineffective stimulus is paired repeatedly with an unconditioned stimulus which already evokes a response. After an adequate number of pairings the previously neutral stimulus comes to evoke reliably the response previously associated only with the unconditioned stimulus. Where the response to the unconditioned stimulus is innate, the conditioning is indeed simple. Where the response to the unconditioned stimulus is itself learned, the above description would fit higher order conditioning. In practice it is quite difficult to say what the status of the original response is. For example, Anton Snarksy, a student of Pavlov, showed that some apparently innate responses have to be learned. He found that a dog would show no salivary response to the smell of aniseed until aniseed had been placed in its mouth a few times. "Later experiments by one of Snarksy's successors showed that a dog hitherto fed only on milk similarly displayed no reaction to the smell of meat until it had experienced meat-in-the-mouth," (Boakes, 1984, pp. 120-121). Thus it is quite possible that many apparently simple classically conditioned responses are, in fact, higher order responses.

Once conditioning has been established it is possible in higher organisms, especially humans, to extend the responses to preconditioned and higher order conditioned stimuli. In the former case the association between the preconditioned and the conditioned stimuli is established, and without any undue significance being attached to either stimulus or their associations, by pairing them before the conditioned stimulus acquires its new role as the effective stimulus for the conditioned response. In higher order conditioning new associations are established once the conditioned stimulus is effective. In humans, words may be used as conditioned stimuli not only as acoustic patterns but also semantically in terms of their meanings. Recent work (Davies & Mehmet, 1985) has shown that the subjects' own thoughts may also act as conditioned or unconditioned stimuli or even as both. It is possible to associate two cognitions, one playing the role of the conditioned stimulus and the other the role of the unconditioned stimulus, to establish a psychophysiological response. It is upon these complex and advanced forms of classical conditioning that the claim is advanced for the role of conditioning in the establishment of even the most complex of human behaviour.

The Nature of Perception

For the purpose of argument it will be assumed that we are conscious only of what has been, is, or might be perceived and that our responses and interactions with the world are determined by our conscious and unconscious perceptions of it. If this is accepted, perception assumes a key role in all our doings. Like the Gestaltists before me, I accept that perception differs from reception in that not-immediately-present influences enter into it and that "the whole is more than the sum of the parts." However, rather than invoke some mysterious innate predisposition to 'wholeness' or 'meaning', I would suggest that experience, i.e., previous encounters plus memory, offers a perfectly adequate explanation when this experience is encapsulated within the brain as an operating system. Once notions of direct access to the world, and eidola based theories of perception, are abandoned, one is forced to accept that man is not stimulus bound. As Neisser put it, "Whether beautiful or ugly or just conveniently at hand, the world of experience is produced by the man who experiences it." (Neisser, 1967, p. 3.). This notion runs through Associationism, Probabilistic Functionalism, Directive State Theory, and the present argument which is congruent with Taylor's Behavioural Basis of Perception (Taylor, 1962) while resting heavily upon Helmholtz's concept of 'unconscious inference.' All the arguments go against stimulus-binding. Organisms transform the input chemically and neurologically, process it and draw upon experience in some form or another before perceiving the world. Furthermore, all the evidence suggests that the resulting percept is based upon only a limited selection from the potentially available input; limited processing and selective attention capacity dictate this.

Helmholtz, in his *Founder's Day Address* at Berlin University, argued the symbolic nature of sensations. Symbols gain their function from their reliable association with their referent, not from any identity nor similarity with it. Their value lies in an invariant relation to the object symbolized. The symbolic basis of perception was fundamental to that other great concept of Helmholtz, the principle of unconscious inference which he sometimes called unconscious conclusion. In his *Lectures on Conditioned Reflexes,* Pavlov pointed out that, "Evidently, what the genius Helmholtz referred to as 'unconscious conclusion' corresponds to the mechanism of the conditioned reflex ..., from this hardly contestable point of view, the fundamental facts of the psychological part of physiological optics is physiologically nothing else than a series of conditioned reflexes." (Pavlov, 1928, reprinted in Warren & Warren, 1968, p. 18).

Nearly all theories of perception accept that certain stimuli form invariant parts of environmental sequences. The average text book on perception devotes its sections to how such stimuli provide the bases for size, distance, form, and colour perception. But, if we take it that one or more of these invariants is all that is required to determine a survival oriented behavioural sequence, then the remainder of the environmentally originating sequence is redundant. If we have already learned the response to the stimulus sequence then we can invoke that response once we have identified the invariant stimulus. Our limited information processing capacity need only be burdened with the processing of this stimulus and our memory with the recognition of the pattern of which it is a part. In short, we have an alternative description of the basic classically conditioned response. It will be recalled that the symbol enjoys its status only through the invariance of its relation with its referent. Should it lose this, it ceases to be a symbol. Should a stimulus lose its invariant referent, it too will lose its status as predictor of the total pattern and as determinant of the perceptual response, i.e., the behaviour, or percept, will undergo extinction.

Clearly, in many situations, more than a single stimulus is involved in an invariant relation with a single referent. Let us assume that a particular situation is uniquely specified by three such stimuli and that each of these could also be components of other situations. In such a case confusion would reign, as a single stimulus could predict either of two situations, and two stimuli could predict any of three situations. Studies of configured conditioning, which are extensive (Razran, 1971, notes "Soviet laboratories have yielded approximately 750 experiments ... containing significant data on configuring" pp. 207-208), reveal how such confusions are finally resolved. Over trials, configuring develops. In the early stages the various elements of a compound stimulus configuration are effective both individually and in sub-combinations, but increasing exposure to the compound over trials results in a unique response to the complete configuration only. When the compound is simultaneous, i.e., the stimuli occurring together, the response is more quickly learned than when they occur in succession. Moreover, the ability to achieve compound conditioning is related to phyletic ascent as it is within the capacity of birds and mammals but beyond the abilities of fish. Within mammals the number of trials required to develop a reliable response to a compound stimulus varies as expected with baboons being superior to dogs who are superior to rabbits (cf. Razran, 1971, pp. 207-213).

Conditioning and Perception

Limitations of space preclude more detailed discussion of conditioning in general. However, as the earlier argument rested largely upon perception underpinning consciousness, it is necessary to consider the evidence for perception being conditionable. It is not possible to demonstrate that perception is nothing more than conditioning. Even if it could be shown that all percepts could be conditioned this would still not constitute evidence that all normal percepts are conditioned. However, it is necessary to show that percepts may be conditioned if the present thesis is to have any validity whatsoever. There is surprisingly little hard evidence because the experiments are, on the whole, difficult and tedious to carry out. If we were to use a visual stimulus to evoke a visual response our subject would report a visual percept. An auditory stimulus will likewise produce the sensation of hearing, and a tactile stimulus sensations of touch. As nobody doubts that these types of stimuli give rise to these types of sensations we should not have advanced the case at all. On the whole the only satisfactory evidence comes from cross-modal conditioning in which light stimuli give rise to auditory percepts or vice versa, though it is possible to produce an intra-modal response that exceeds the stimulus input. One of the earliest experiments was of this type. Swindle (1917) was able to condition a human subject to report the sensation of many nail points when but a single point was applied to his forearm. However, as the principles of conditioning were but poorly understood in the West at this time, Swindle's experiments are open to criticism, though not on the grounds of lack of originality. (The same paper describes the conditioning of a cockatoo to beat the air with its leg whenever the experimenter played the Jew's harp, and provides an explanation based on visual conditioning to account for sightings of ghosts.)

Far better evidence is provided by cross-modal conditioning. Ellson (1941a; 1941b; 1942), in studies of what he referred to as conditioned hallucinations, demonstrated that an auditory response could be obtained to light. The basic paradigm was to pair a tone with indeterminate onset and offset with a visual stimulus. Over some 60 to 80 trials the visual stimulus became adequate to evoke the auditory response. This finding has been replicated, but only in recent years (Warburton, Wesnes, Edwards & Larrad, 1985; Davies & Charlton, 1985).

Howells (1944) demonstrated what he termed *colour-tone synesthesia* by pairing a high and a low tone with red and green lights. After several thousands of such pairings subjects came to report the hue of desaturated lights according to the tone which was presented rather than the hue of the light. In a subsidiary experiment the subjects would, using a colour comparator, match the perceived hue according to the tonal, rather than the visual, stimulus. In this experiment the conditioned response was strong enough to over-ride the response to the conflicting (but weak) physically presented visual stimulus.

In the early 1950's the Popovs reported a series of classical conditioning experiments in which the response of visual afterimage was evoked by a variety of stimuli ranging from tones and musical notes to the words *light-light*. In addition to establishing conditioned visual afterimages, they also compared the effects of both alcohol and caffeine upon both normal and conditioned visual afterimages (Popov & Popov, 1953). In over a decade of my own research I have conducted experiments similar to those of the Popovs and their Georgian successor, Bzhalava, who devised an extremely effective conditioning paradigm for the establishment of this response (Bzhalava, 1966). A description of one of my own experiments serves to illustrate Bzhalava's paradigm. The subject is isolated from the experimenter in a totally dark room where a tone is repeatedly paired with a brief visual presentation of a geometric target (circle, square, or triangle). The tone starts 20-30 seconds (held constant for each individual subject) before the light is presented, and is maintained until 10 seconds after the subject stops reporting afterimages. Trials are spaced 4-7 minutes apart with 10 trials in each session. After some 200 to 300 pairings the tone evokes strong images of the target which last several seconds (Davies 1974a; 1974b) or, in a few cases, for as long as the tone sounds (up to the maximum tested which was 10 minutes when imagery ceased 3 seconds after the tone offset (Davies, 1976)). It has proved possible, really I should say 'surprisingly easy,' to precondition, second-order condition, and third-order condition this basic response (Davies, Bennett & Davies, 1983).

The above summary covers most of the experimental evidence for the conditioning of percepts. Experiments which involved manipulations such as hypnosis of the subjects are not included as it is arguable that the observed results could be as attributable to the hypnosis as the conditioning. On the whole hypnosis does not seem to facilitate conditioning (Platanov, 1959; Sarum & Slagle, 1972) but it can, in the absence of any conditioning, produce negative hallucinations (not seeing objects which are physically present), or positive hallucinations (or distortions of reality). Thus the case must rest upon the non-controversial experiments which show that visual and auditory percepts may be conditioned.

Conditioning and Cognition

Now if the argument, raised earlier, that cognition is dependent upon actual and possible perceptions is accepted, it follows that the extent to which perception is conditionable is that to which cognition is conditionable. In the perceptual conditioning experiments it is not the eye nor the ear that is conditioned. They continue to work normally while the brain itself is conditioned to produce perceptual responses to *inappropriate* stimuli on the basis of an experimentally established regularity of relation.

One of the striking features about all the experiments cited is the abnormally large number of trials required. The Popov, Davies, and Bzhalava experiments involved some hundreds of pairings of stimuli while Howells needed some 5000 trials per subject. However, such regularities are as nothing to the world outside the laboratory when smoke being associated with fire, coolness with marble, and sweetness with sugar, etc., are encountered with unfailing regularity on innumerable occasions. For these basic responses in our perceptual world *nature* provides more than an adequate number of acquisition trials and no (or certainly insignificantly few) extinction trials. There is certainly enough direct and indirect evidence to suggest that perceptions may be conditioned.

In his book, *The Behavioural Basis of Perception*, Taylor (1962) argued that all perception is conditioned, largely without reference to the above evidence, on the basis of studies of perceptual adaptation to abnormal conditons such as the wearing of inverting or bicoloured spectacles. Because of the way he chose to couch his theory in set notation it is difficult to read although it is a rigorous, and testable, theory. It is in no way at variance with the evidence presented above.

Where then does this leave us? The main strands of argument advanced have been that we cannot process all the information that is potentially at our disposal and that all processing takes time. Conditioning, which is a formalization of the more general term *experience*, provides both a mechanism of selective attention and a process for minimizing the informational load. Conditioning of perception has been demonstrated and it is probably the basis of all learned aspects of perception. It was argued that perception both limits and determines the contents of consciousness. If all these arguments are accepted it follows that conditioning is the fundamental behavioural process that controls all aspects of our behaviour from environmentally provoked reflexes through to higher mental processes and that all our behaviour is determined and lawful. The model does not exclude wide variations in behaviour either between individuals nor within one individual at different times. The informational processing limitation ensures that only a subset of information is used at any one time and this subset will be dependent upon many factors such as stimulus strength, temporal order, and ecological utility, as well as the size of the informational processing system. Thus we can confidently anticipate that another person's behaviour and cognitions will never be fully predictable to an observer, though we can assert with confidence that the other person is behaving in a lawful and determined manner. The same rules apply even to our subject's assertion that he is exercising his free will!

References

Boakes, R. (1984). *From Darwin to behaviourism.*Cambridge Cambridge University Press.

Bzhalava, I. T. (1965). *Perception and set.* Tbilisi: Metsniyerba.

Davies, P. (1974a). Conditional after-image: I. *British Journal of Psychology, 65(2),* 191-204.

Davies, P. (1974b). Conditional after-image: II. *British Journal of Psychology, 65(3),* 377-393.

Davies, P. (1976). Conditioning afterimages: a procedure minimizing the extinction effect of normal test trials. *British Journal of Psychology, 67,* 181-189.

Davies, P., Bennett, S., Davies, G. L. (1983). Semantic generalization investigated using second-order conditioned visual afterimages. *Perceptual and Motor Skills, 57,* 703-709.

Davies, P., Charlton, E. (1985). *Conditioned auditory hallucinations.* Paper presented to the First Scientific Meeting of the Psychobiological Section, British Psychological Society.

Davies, P., & Mehmet, A. (1985). *Ideational conditioning.* Annual Conference British psychological Society. (Abstract in Bulletin of the British Psychological Society, 38, May 1985).

Ellson, D. G. (1941a). Hallucinations produced by sensory conditioning.*Journal of Experimental Psychology, 28,* 1-20.

Ellson, D. G. (1941b). Experimental extinction of an hallucination produced by sensory conditioning. *Journal of Experimental Psychology, 28,* 350-361.

Ellson, D. G. (1942). Critical conditions influencing sensory conditioning. *Journal of Experimental Psychology, 3l,* 333-338.

Hobhouse, L. T. (1901). *Mind in evolution.* Macmillan: London.

Howells, T. H. (1944). The experimental development of colortone synesthesia. *Journal of Experimental Psychology, 34,* 87-103.

Miller, G. A. (1956). The magical number 7, plus or minus two: some limits on our capacity for processing information. *Psychological Review, 63,* 81-97.

Neisser, U. (1967). *Cognitive psychology.* New York: Appleton-Century-Crofts.

Oliver, W. D. , & Landfield, A. W. (1962). Reflexivity: an unfaced issue of psychology. *Journal of Individual Psychology, 18,* 114-124.

Pavlov, I. P. (1928). *Lectures on conditioned reflexes.* (W. H. Gantt, Trans.) New York: Liveright.

Platanov, K. I. (1959). The world as a physiological and and therapeutic factor. In K. I. Platanov (Ed.), *Problems of theory and practice of psychotherapy on the basis of the theory of I.P. Pavlov*

(D. A. Myshne, Trans.) Moscow: Foreign Languages Publishing House.

Popov, N. A., & Popov, C. (1953). Contribution a l'étude des fonctions corticales chez l'homme par la methode des reflexes conditiones electrocorticaux. II. De la modification par l'alcool des couleurs de images consecurives et des images consecutives conditionees. *Compte Rendus hebdomanaire Academie des Sciences, 237,* 14939-41.

Razran, G. (1971). *Mind in evolution.* Boston: Houghton Mifflin.

Romanes, G. J. (1904). *Animal intelligence.* London: Kegan Paul, Trench, Trubner & Co. Ltd.

Sarum, T. R., & Slagle, R. W. (1972). Hyponosis and psychophysiological outcomes. In E. Fromm, R. I. Shur (Eds.), *Hypnosis research developments and perspectives.* Chicago: Aidine-Ahterton.

Skinner, B. F. (1965). Cognitive science and behaviourism. *The British Journal of Psychology, 76,* 291-301.

Swindle, P. F. (1917). Visual, cutaneous, and kinaesthetic ghosts. *American Journal of Psychology, 28,* 349-372.

Taylor, J. G. (1962). *The behavioural basis of perception.* New Haven & London: Yale University Press.

Warburton, D. M., Wesnes, K., Edwards, J., & Larrad, D. (1985). Scopolamine and the sensory conditioning of hallucinations. *Neuropsychobiology* (in press).

Warren, R. M., & Warren, R. P. (1986). *Helmholtz on perception.* New York & London: John Wiley & Sons, Inc.

Current Issues in Theoretical Psychology
Wm J. Baker, M.E. Hyland, H. Van Rappard, A.W. Staats (Editors)
Elsevier Science Publishers B.V. (North-Holland), 1987

ON THE METHODOLOGY OF CLARIFYING CONFUSION

Han F. De Wit

Vrije Universiteit
Amsterdam, The Netherlands

SUMMARY: Based on developments within cognitive psychology, this paper reviews the concepts of experience and of methodology. Cognitive psychology has brought back the old Kantian theme that our ways of cognizing or perceiving the human world (environment) are permeated by our ways of thinking or conceptualizing (about it). The conceptual relativity of experience implies that experience - the touchstone of empirical science - is to some extent not independent of the researcher. This conclusion calls for the construction of a generalized or *relativized* methodology and epistemology. To that aim, the conventional view on methodology, according to which it outlines methods to acquire knowledge, is abandoned and an alternative view is adopted which outlines methods for clarifying confusion and for eliminating ignorance. The relativized methodology is based not on a theory of knowledge but on a particular *anepistemology*, a theory of ignorance and confusion.

The Conceptual Relativity of Experience

Research in cognitive psychology as well as in cultural anthropology has shown that our ways of cognizing or perceiving the world are permeated and influenced by our ways of thinking about it. Our perceptions are in fact conceptualized experiences, that is, experiences are relative to the way we conceive or conceptualize them. Within the philosophy of science the conceptual relativity of experience, already mentioned by Kant, has been discussed under the heading of the theory-ladenness of observables (see e.g., Hanson, 1958; Hesse, 1970; Koch, 1964). Within psychology the idea of conceptual relativity has lead to an increasing interest in the study of mental activity and to the development of a terminology, e.g., *schema* (Neisser, 1967), *prototype* (Rosch, 1977), *mental model* (Johnson-Laird, 1983), that would be fit to take the conceptual relativity of experience into account.

However, the concept of conceptual relativity is much broader than the concept of theory-ladenness. Conceptual relativity refers to the fact that our perceptual activity is almost continuously conjoined with and influenced by the activity of thinking. However, the content of thought

could be, but need not be, about what is perceived. In both cases, thinking activity mixes with perceptual activity and thereby modifies conceptualized experience in a certain way. Thinking might structure or direct our
perceiving, it might add to or distract from our perceptions, and it might
even block out conscious perception. Theory-ladenness, however, is restricted to the idea that observables are theory laden because the thoughts
we have are about them.

What are the methodological implications of assuming that experience - the touchstone of empirical science - is conceptually relative? The
implication seems to be that some generalized psychological methodology
is needed, a methodology that would be based on and exploit the conceptual relativity of experience. The psychological epistemology that should
come with it should therefore both avoid *and* explain the realism-idealism
controversy that, under various modern disguises (e.g., the presentationalism vs. representationalism controversy in cognitive psychology discussed in Shaw, Turvey & Mace, 1982), lurks behind it. I will address the
methodological and the epistemological issues here, beginning with a preliminary remark on the role of thought.

The Double Epistemic Role of Thought

I will use the term *thought* as a catch-word for *any* mental activity,
but in particular for the epistemic modalities of mental activity that play
a part both in the perception of the *world as we know it* and in our
theories *about* that world. This statement already points towards the
double role of thought or thinking activity.

The first role that thoughts seem to play is the role I mentioned before; thoughts permeate and intermingle with other (sensory based)
aspects of experience, thus providing us with conceptualized experience.
The second role refers to the fact that our thoughts also seem to be *about*
experience, which suggests that thoughts or knowledge hold some kind of
meta-position and, as such, are separate from experience or rather, I
should say, separate from conceptualized experience. These two highly
interdependent roles relativize both the concept of experience and the concept of knowledge, for they reflect a dual relationship between knowledge
(thought) and experience: we can experience our thought and we can
think about experience. Let me clarify this key-point.

A very common epistemological attitude among laymen and among
quite a few researchers in psychology is that reality, or the empirical, is a
given, not a question. Therefore the epistemological emphasis is exclu-

sively on the second role of thought, that is, on thinking in the role of thinking *about*. From this perspective, the empirical or the experientially given seems independent from and not contaminated by the theories or conceptual structures that one conceives *about* it. Knowledge is here supposed to be some kind of commentary or story-line that one formulates 'back-stage,' so to speak, whereas the empirical is what happens 'on-stage,' unencumbered by our scientific whisperings in the back.

However, although we might imagine ourselves to be back-stage philosophers of science, from the other perspective in which thoughts play their first role, this back-stage does not exist. Or more precisely put, this back-stage has only relative existence, in the sense that it is 'part of a larger stage' on which the drama of the intermingling of thoughts and other experience happens. On this larger stage our so-called 'back-stage' thoughts are noticed just in the same way as the other so-called 'on-stage' aspects of experience are noticed, as well as their way of inter-mingling which constitutes the play of conceptualized experience.

To claim that our thoughts happen back-stage, that is, somewhere away from experience, is a metaphor for the perspective that limits the act of thinking to the act of thinking *about* experience. To state that the back-stage is part of a larger stage is a metaphor for the fact that we also can and do eperience our thoughts. So our thoughts have a *dual relationship* to experience: we can think about experience and we can experience our thoughts. Thoughts can be *about* experience and they are *part of* our experience at the same time. Therefore the concepts of knowledge and experience are relative concepts, dependent upon each other in a different way than realistic or idealistic epistemologies deny or defend. Let me point out two implications of this.

First, the dual relationship relativizes the presentationalism vs. re-presentationalism controversy in cognitive psychology. For viewing thoughts (mental events) in their back-stage role of *conceptual representations of on-stage experience* does not exclude viewing them also as *part of the presented* larger stage of experience. In my view, representational-ism and presentationalism are based fundamentally on two different but compatible epistemic modalities or propositional attitudes; the 'back-stage' representational propositional attitude of 'knowing that' and the 'on-stage' presentational propositional attitude of 'noticing that.' These attitudes are related to two different strategies or cognitions, the 'conceptual strategy' and the 'awareness strategy' respectively (cf. Section 5 below and De Wit, 1985).

Second, the dual relationship also indicates that there is no such thing as 'pure experience,' that would provide for an absolute or solid empirical domain, free from our conceptions about it, and there is no need to look for it either. When we think about (theorize) and explore the empirical domain we, in fact, think about and explore conceptualized experience, relative experience of which our thoughts are part. So from this point of view, freeing the empirical domain from our conceptions about it for the sake of creating 'pure experience' would be just a form of reductionism if it would be possible to do this at all. But accepting our 'natural' conceptualized experience as a pure or solid base for psychology would be extremely naive, as it denies the existence of experiential confusion and ignorance.

The Methodology of Clarifying Confusion and Ignorance

Within the conventional scientific tradition of psychology the aim of science and its methodology is often defined as the acquistion of (theoretical) knowledge (cf. Braithwaite, 1955; De Groot, 1969) which presupposes some a priori definition of knowledge. However, if the status of knowledge is relative, so are the methodological rules that specify how to acquire it. Therefore the relativity of the concept of knowledge calls for a generalized methodology: a methodology that takes both conceptualized experience and the dual relationship between thinking and experienceing into account. Such a methodology neither can be based on a particular preconceived concept of knowledge nor can it apply preconceived concepts of acquiring knowledge. But if we let go of the idea that psychological science aims at acquiring (a particular a priori defined type of) knowledge, what other options do we have?

Looking again at actual research behavior, we could view the purpose of methodology not so much to be to outline methods of how to acquire empirical knowledge, but rather to outline methods of how to clarify confusion and to eliminate ignorance. Viewed in this way research methodology is the formalized and systematized expression of human inquisitiveness triggered by the experience of confusion and ignorance and of the attempt to be free from it.

Confusion, ignorance, and their elimination seem to be concepts prior to and much broader than the concept of (empirical) knowledge and its acquisition. Therefore they might provide a promising starting point for the development of a truly psychological epistemology and methodology. Instead of trying to save one's self from the ocean of confusion by first imagining and then dwelling upon an epistemologically perfect island of knowledge, it might be promising to plunge into unknown waters. In order not to drown however one needs a life belt which consists of a theory of confusion and ignorance. With reference to the Greek 'an-epi-stemoon' meaning 'being without knowledge or not aware' I will call this theory 'an-epistemology'.

Outline of an An-epistemology

Of course there are many aspects to confusion and ignorance, but for now only methodological aspects are relevant. Going back to the key concepts of 'thought' and 'experience' and keeping their dual relationship in mind, it seems well to distinguish between experiential confusion and ignorance, and between conceptual confusion and ignorance. That gives us four categories (see Table 1) that I will discuss briefly.

Conceptual Confusion. This could be defined (on the syntactic level) as the result of entertaining inconsistent theories or thoughts and (on the semantic level) as the result of entertaining theories that are incompatible with experience. Put differently conceptual confusion results from *inconsistent conceptual information* or *wrong information* about reality or the empirical, that is from conceptual misrepresentation.

Conceptual Ignorance. This refers to the *absence* of conceptual information, to the absence of (right or wrong) conceptual representations. So conceptual confusion and ignorance both refer to thinking in its 'back-stage' role of thinking *about* experience. It seems to me that conventional empirical science defines confusion and ignorance primarily as *conceptual* confusion and ignorance.

However there are other forms of confusion and ignorance that are neither the result of entertaining empirically wrong or inconsistent theories nor the result of lacking conceptual structures. This brings us to experiential (or perceptual) confusion and ignorance.

Experiential Ignorance. This refers to ignorance resulting from not being aware of one's actual experiential situation, from not noticing what's going on. We are all familiar with this type of ignorance (or ignoring) both from our daily life experience and from psychological research on attention. However, identifying non-awareness as a source of ignorance implies that awareness is not only a psychological issue, but that it is also methodologically relevant.

Table 1

An-epistemology: a Methodology for Eliminating
Confusion and Ignorance

CC: Conceptual Confusion	EC: Experiential Confusion
Caused by wrong information about Conceptualized Experience (CE).	Caused by functional non-awareness of CE.
CI: Conceptual Ignorance	EI: Experiential Ignorance
Caused by lack of information about CE.	Caused by material non-awareness of CE.
Conceptual Strategies	Awareness Strategies
•Theory construction counteracting CI. •Empirical research counteracting CC. •Logical analysis counteracting CC and CI.	•Techniques of mindfulness counteracting EI. •Techniques of functional awareness counteracting EC.

The meaning of terms like 'awareness' and 'consciousness' are notoriously multifarious (cf. Natsoulas, 1978). As to meanings that are methodologically relevant, there are two of them that I would like to mention briefly, material awareness and functional (or formal) awareness (De Wit, 1985).

Material Awareness. This refers to what is often called 'attention' or 'mindfulness' in psychology; it refers to being aware or conscious of the actual content or configuration of one's experience. Simply put, it is noticing *what* you experience as opposed to noticing *that* you experience.

Functional Awareness. This refers to being aware of the actual mode of one's experience. It is noticing that you experience, being aware that you see, hear, think or dream.

Let me clarify the meaning of both aspects of awareness with an example. When we dream, we are materially aware of the dream content, but we are only by exception functionally aware that we dream. When we are lost in our thoughts, we are often only materially aware of their content, but not functionally aware of our thinking activity. Looking at a movie, we often lose functional awareness of our looking at a movie. So the cause of experiential ignorance seems to be primarily material non-awareness. Although functional non-awareness is also a cause of experiential ignorance, its effects are more prominent in the category of experiential confusion.

Experiential Confusion. This refers not so much to perceptual ambiguities or distortions resulting from peculiarities or defects of the sensory apparatus, but to experiential 'illusions' or 'mistakes' resulting from mistaking a thought (conceptual representation) *about* reality (the represented) for reality itself. Experiencing a snake while stepping on a rope, mistaking a bush in the distance for a man waving at us, or seeing an enemy or friend approaching us where, in fact, a human being is approaching us, are all familiar examples.

Functional non-awareness is a condition for the appearance of experiential confusion. For confounding a thought about an experience with the experience that the thought is about is based on not being functionally aware of one's thought as thought. It is a case of confounding different modes of experience with each other. Or, said in terms of a well known analogy, the map is not the landscape. To confound the map with the landscape is a case of functional non-awareness of the map as a map. When we are not functionally aware of the experience of a thought, but only materially aware of its content, we might mistake (or misplace) its content for a non-mental (or non-conceptual) experience. For instance, not being functionally aware, one might experience a man approaching as 'an enemy approaching.' If one were functionally aware, however, one would experience a man approaching and at the same time experience the thought *there is an enemy.*

So functional awareness is a discriminating awareness that separates out the conceptualized quality of conceptualized experience and thereby clarifies the experiential confusion that might be contained in it. Functional awareness penetrates the emulsion of thoughts and experience that

makes up conceptualized experience, leaving no room for experiential confusion. Because conceptualized experience might contain experiential confusion, and also might be the object of experiential ignorance, functional
and material awareness become relevant issues for a methodology of clarifying confusion and ignorance. Let me summarize the an-epistemology
outlined here in Table 1, and then discuss methodology.

A Methodology of Clarifying Confusion

What are the methodological implications of the an-epistemology
outlined above? Two sources of confusion and ignorance have been identified: first, a conceptual source that provides wrong conceptual information resulting in conceptual confusion, or one which provides no information resulting in conceptual ignorance; second, a source of non-awareness
resulting in experiential ignorance and experiential confusion. Both
sources have their effects on the way one thinks about and is aware of
one's conceptualized experience. Therefore, a generalized methodology
should outline strategies of how to discover and systematically eliminate
both conceptual and experiential confusion and ignorance.

The Conceptual Strategy. The conventional methodology and practice of science appears to be a strategy well suited for and in fact aiming
at the elimination of *conceptual* confusion and ignorance. This strategy
could therefore be called a *conceptual strategy* (De Wit, 1983; 1985). The
main tools of the conceptual strategy are experimental research and logical
analysis of theories. Primarily, these tools eliminate *conceptual confusion*.
Also, this strategy includes the creative use of intellectual abilities to develop new theories that could both remove *conceptual ignorance* and *clarify conceptual confusion*. Generally speaking the conceptual strategy aims
at improving thinking (or theorizing) in its 'back-stage role' of thinking
about experience.

The Awareness Strategy. As non-awareness is another source of
confusion and ignorance, a generalized methodology should also outline
awareness-strategies (De Wit, 1983, 1985), that is, methods that are
suited for eliminating material and functional non-awareness. Generally
speaking awareness-strategies aim at improving awareness of one's experience, the experience of thought included. So this strategy focusses on
thinking (theorizing) in its 'on-stage role,' aiming at improving one's
conscious experience of one's thoughts and improving one's awareness of
how one's thoughts intermingle with other aspects of one's experience.

Conventional methodology, however, does not explicitly contain anything like awareness-strategies. Its emphasis is on the conceptual strategy only, which is related to its reliance upon and preoccupation with the concept of knowledge. Based on the correspondence theory of truth, its concept of knowledge accounts primarily for thinking in its representational role of 'thinking (theorizing) about.' It views the other role of thinking that leads to conceptualized experience primarily as a psychological phenomenon and not as a methodological issue.

Conventional methodologists might even contend that a researcher should 'of course' be aware of his experience and of his 'personal ideas' about it and leave it at that. But that is as naive as saying that one should 'of course' only hold on to thoughts and theories that are true. For it is precisely the function of a methodology to outline methods that increase our ability to do exactly that; singling out *both* consistent, possibly empirically 'true' theories *and* separating out experiential confusion and ignorance within one's conceptualized experience. Simply trying to eliminate *experiential* confusion and ignorance by means of *conceptual* strategies alone does not work. Conceptualizing afterwards (or back-stage) what it was that (on-stage) has escaped one's attention does not remove the cause of experiential confusion and ignorance. At best, it removes the symptoms. At worst, the use of a conceptual strategy here might even add to experiential confusion and ignorance.

If awareness-strategies are not included in the conventional methodologies of our psychological tradition, where can we find them? If we cannot find them anywhere, we need to create and develop them, for they are methodologically necessary. Fortunately there are some traditions, although they are not part of our scientific tradition, that do contain awareness-strategies of sorts and they might give us a clue. I hope it is not too shocking to mention that the contemplative traditions of most world religions, and in particular the buddhist tradition with its mindfulness/awareness practice, do contain systematic methods and practices that aim at sharpening one's awareness. The emphasis of these methods appears to be primarily on sharpening the material and functional awareness of one's thoughts and of other (sensory mediated) experiences and of how they intermingle into conceptualized experience, creating the world as we believe it to be (cf. Kochumuttom, 1982). Training in these methods initially takes place in a standardized set-up. In this set-up, sensory mediated experience is kept more or less constant so that the only movement left is the movement of one's thoughts. As awareness tends to be drawn to what moves, otherwise unnoticed habitual thought patterns begin to draw our attention.

Usually a technique is introduced (cf. Wayman, 1978) that has proven to prevent or detect moments in which our attention or awareness degenerates into material awareness without functional awareness. So, day-dreaming or being lost in thoughts, however sophisticated our thoughts might be, is not the idea. Noticing and investigating our day-dreaming on the spot and therefore developing some familiarity with these mental activities that shape our experience is the epistemic purpose of these methods. It might therefore be worthwhile for the development of a truly psychological epistemology and a generalized methodology to investigate the nature and function of the awareness-strategies that the contemplative traditions contain.

Conceptual and Awareness Strategies Working Together. As a closing remark I would like to emphasize that a generalized methodology of the social sciences not only needs to contain, in an explicit form, both the conceptual strategy and the awareness-strategy, but also these strategies need to be applied together. These strategies in fact need each other. Why is that?

On the one hand the conceptual strategy provides us with conceptual information, empirical theories, conceptual structures, or whatever one likes to call it. However, if we (believe to) *know* in a certain situation what is going on, it seems we could afford not to be *aware* of what is going on. We know already and we might easily substitute (and therefore confound) our presumed knowledge about what is going on for (with) awareness of what is actually going on. The non-awareness involved then leads to experiential confusion and ignorance. So the conceptual strategy, when used on its own, allows for, and possibly even creates room for non-awareness. What we believe or know about reality (or about the empirical domain) then becomes reality to us. Therefore the awareness-strategy is needed to make this kind of subjectivity and lack of realism visible and to cut through it.

On the other hand awareness-strategies when used on their own have shortcomings as well. Foremost, they have no language because of their non-conceptual nature. Conceptualizing and the use of language are closely connected. Therefore, conceptual strategies provide communicable theories, but awareness-strategies do not, by themselves, result in *communicable* insights. They are in need of application of conceptual strategies for their results, just as conceptual strategies are in need of application of awareness strategies for their conceptual results.

It is only when we apply the awareness strategy on the results of conceptual strategies that the 'on-stage role' of our conceptual knowledge becomes clear. For the awareness strategy has as its result the experiential clarification of whatever plays on-stage: our sights, sounds, smells, tastes, touch, and thoughts, our conceptual knowledge and the intermingling of all this. However, because this clarification has no language, we subsequently and conversely need to apply 'back-stage' the conceptual strategy on the results of the awareness strategy as well. For only by conceptualizing its results, do they become conceptually clear and communicable.

So both strategies in fact complement each other because they counteract each others shortcomings. Therefore training in both types of strategies amounts to training in a methodology that takes the dual relationship between thinking and experiencing into account. Such a generalized methodology accepts conceptualized experience as its field of empirical research and thereby it seems preeminently suited for research in the field of psychology.

References

Braithwaite, R. (1955). *Scientific explanation.* Cambridge University Press.

De Groot, A. D. (1969). *Methodology: Foundations of inference and research in the behavioral sciences.* The Hague: Mouton.

De Wit, H. F (1983). *Ervaren, Denken en Bewustzijn.* Report to the organization of Pure Scientific Research (ZWO). Amsterdam: Vrije Universiteit Press.

De Wit, H. F. (1985). Methodologie in Contemplatief perspectief. In L. K. A. Eisenga e. a. (Ed.), *Over de grenzen van de psychologie.* Amsterdam: Swetz & Zeitlinger.

Hanson, N. R. (1958). *Patterns of discovery.* Cambridge: Cambridge university Press.

Hesse, M. B. (1970). Is there an independent observation language? In R. G. Colodny (Ed.), *The nature and function of scientific theories (pp. 35-78).* Pittsburg: University of Pittsburg Press.

Johnson-Laird, P. N. (1983). *Mental models.* Cambridge: Cambridge University Press.

Koch, S. (1964) Psychology and emerging conceptions of knowledge as unitary. In T. W. Wann (Ed.), *Behaviorism and phenomenology (pp. 1-42).* Chicago: University of Chicago Press.

Kochumuttom, Th. A. (1982). *A Buddhist doctrine of experience.* Delhi, Varanasi, Patna: Motilal Banarsidas.

Natsoulas, T. (1978). Consciousness. *American Psychologist, 33,* 906-914).

Neisser, U. (1967). *Cognitive psychology.* New York: Appleton-Century-Crofts.

Rosch, E. (1977) Human categorization. In N. Warren (Ed.), *Studies in cross-cultural psychology* (pp. 3-50). New York: Academic Press.

Shaw, R., Turvey, M. T., & Mace, W. (1982). Ecological psychology: the consequence of a commitment to realism. In W. B. Weimer & D. S. Palermo (Eds.),*Cognition and the symbolic processes.* Hillsdale, NJ: Erlbaum.

Wayman, A. (1978). *Calming the mind and discerning the real.* Delhi, Varanasi, Patna: Motilal Banarsidas.

Current Issues in Theoretical Psychology
Wm J. Baker, M.E. Hyland, H. Van Rappard, A.W. Staats (Editors)
© Elsevier Science Publishers B.V. (North-Holland), 1987

"THERE IS NOTHING MORE PRACTICAL THAN A GOOD THEORY" (KURT LEWIN) - TRUE OR FALSE?

H. J. Eysenck

Institute of Psychiatry, University of London
London, England

SUMMARY: An attempt is made to consider what constitutes a 'good theory' in the light of recent discussions by philosophers of science, and in the light of the writer's suggestion that there is a historical development from weak to strong theories, and that the requirements may differ depending on the stage reached. The suggested criteria for a good theory are discussed in relation to various experimental paradigms, and it is concluded that 'good' theories are distinguished by being part of a progressive and advancing research programme, while 'bad' theories are associated with a regressive research program.

Lewin's statement about the usefulness of a good theory has become famous in psychology, and few would probably disagree with him. However, his statement is more honoured in the breach than the observance; there is little evidence in their actual work that most psychologists pay much attention to theory, and some explicitly disassociate themselves from the search for theory and adopt a Baconian or pre-Baconian, purely inductive approach. Indeed, the lack of a proper *paradigm* in the social sciences generally, and in psychology in particular, noted by Kuhn (1962) and Barnes (1982), can be identified with a lack of accepted theories in these fields. Disagreement with the request and need for theories is not often voiced explicitly, or defended philosophically; it forms one of the unverbalized axioms underlying much of psychological thinking.

Even where the need for a good theory is not only explicitly acknowledged, but also forms part of a given psychologist's research philosophy, there still remains the question of when a theory is 'good,' and when it is not. For many psychologists, to give but one example, Freudian theories are regarded as 'good' because they are believed to be full of 'insights', and to touch on vital questions of motivation, mental disorder, psychotherapy, memory, and other human concerns. To others, like Popper (1959, 1974a, 1974b), Eysenck (1985a), Grunbaum (1984), Rachman (1963), Zwang (1985), and many others psychoanalysis appears to be the prime example of a bad theory. Clearly we need criteria as to what constitutes a 'good' theory, and this in turn would seem to demand some kind of answer to the demarkation dispute about science and pseudo-science.

There has been much philosophical argument on this topic; Achinstein (1965), Bergmann (1951, 1954, 1957), Bergmann and Spence (1941), Carnap (1966), Feyerabend (1975), Hanson (1958), Hempel (1952, 1965, 1966), Krige (1980), Lakatos (1968), Lakatos and Musgrave (1970), Putnam (1962), Quine (1962), Suppe (1974), Tarski (1941, 1956), Toulmin (1953), and many others have attacked the problem without reaching agreement. Eysenck (1985) has given a detailed survey of the present position; the only point of agreement among modern philosophers appears to be that the theory of 'logical positivism' associated with the Viennese school, usually the only theory known to and considered by psychologists, is definitely out of favour, and regarded as obsolete.

Perhaps the most relevant solution to the problem, and the one most closely related to this specific question of what constitutes a 'good' theory, may be related to a suggestion made by Lakatos (1968; Lakatos & Musgrave, 1970). His view, which is an advance on Popper's well known 'falsification' criterion, is widely accepted amongst philosophers of science. It aligns a 'good' theory with an advancing and *progressive* research programme, while a 'bad' theory is associated with a *regressive* research programme, i.e., one which, instead of predicting and discovering new facts, is concerned with explaining away failures and anomalies. On this basis, clearly, psychoanalysis is a 'bad' theory, because it has failed to predict and discover new facts, and has rather been forced to explain away failures and anomalies. Examples are the failure of psychoanalysts to cure neurotic and psychotic illnesses more decisively than do other methods of psychotherapy and behaviour therapy (Rachman and Wilson, 1981; Smith, Glass and Miller, 1980; Strupp, Hadley, and Gomes-Schwartz, 1977); the fact that behaviour therapy successfully cures the 'symptoms' of neuroses, but does not lead to relapse or symptom substitution (Kazdin & Wilson, 1978; Schorr, 1984); and the fact that the experimental study of Freudian theories has been almost entirely negative (Eysenck & Wilson, 1973; Kline, 1981; Eysenck, 1985a). In spite of the strong evidence that psychoanalytic theory is in fact a 'bad' theory, which could be documented at much greater length were it considered necessary, it is still widely accepted by many clinical psychologists, an obvious proof of our assertion that theories may be accepted or rejected for reasons other than their 'goodness' or 'badness.'

If we are willing to accept Lakatos' proposal of aligning a 'good' theory with an advancing and progressive research programme, we are still left with certain problems. One of these is the distinction between 'strong' and 'weak' theories, first discussed in detail by Eysenck (1960), and later made a central part of his discussion of the place of theory in a world of facts (Eysenck, 1985b). It is characteristic of weak, as opposed to strong theories that "only few observations, and these of doubtful accuracy, are available. Few quantitative or even qualitative laws, universally established, are available in sub-fields. The nature of the phenomena in question is by no means clear-cut or well understood. Mathematical relations are often very complex, and predictions are neither straight-forward nor precise" (Eysenck, 1960, p. 304). This type of theory is clearly differentiated from a strong theory, like Newton's theory of gravitation, or Einstein's theory of relativity.

Eysenck (1976) has suggested that there is a historical development from weak to strong theories, related to the changing criteria for scientific acceptability. Figure 1 shows this relationship. At an early stage of development, we have hunches based on observation and induction. Slowly we graduate to hypothesis formation and the verification criterion of the Vienna school. Hypotheses develop into wide-ranging and more specific theories, and Popper's falsification criterion is now apposite. Finally, we reach a stage where general laws become possible, and these may only be challenged by the statement of alternative theories leading to Kuhnian revolutions. Clearly psychology is still at an early stage, where induction and verification are primarily relevant, and where weak rather than strong theories are the rule. This imposes important restraints on our experimentation, theory development, and theory testing. What, it may be said, is the use of weak theories? The answer, I believe, can be found in the words of the famous physicist, J. J. Thomson: "A theory in science is a policy rather than a creed." This statement indicates the heuristic nature of theories, particularly weak theories; the value of such a theory lies in the fact that it directs attention to those problems which repay study from a systematic point of view; in Thomson's words, it defines a policy of action and research. It is by giving rise to worthwhile research, rather than by necessarily being right, that a weak theory makes its greatest contribution to science.

A good example of the usefulness of weak theories in pointing in the right direction is the work of John Dalton (Greenaway, 1966) on the atom. All that Dalton said about atoms, apart from the effect of their existence, which was not novel, was wrong. They are not indivisible nor of unique weight, as he thought; they need not obey the laws of definite

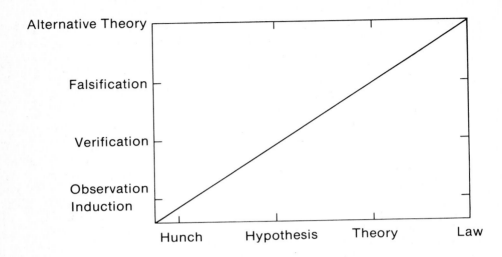

Fig. 1. Stages in the development of scientific theories from weak to strong.

or multiple proportions, as he believed; and in any case his values for relative atomic weights and molecular constitutions were for the most part incorrect! Yet, for all that, John Dalton, more than any other single individual, was the man who set modern chemistry on its feet. His theory is a good example of Lakatos' "advancing and progressive research programme;" it is a weak theory, because very little was in fact known about atoms at the time, but it led to the elaboration of experiments and theories which in fact created modern chemistry, and they were also fundamental for much in modern physics.

The distinction between strong and weak theories is an important one, because psychologists are often impatient with the failure of theories to predict accurately and to explain exhaustively all the known facts. This is a fundamental failure to understand the nature of science. All theories, even the stronger theories in the most advanced physical sciences, are full of anomalies when tested experimentally. Newton's theory of gravitation appeared full of exceptions and errors, and for 300 years scientists were busy trying to iron out these anomalies, attempting to explain the observed deviations from theory, and generally carrying out what Kuhn calls "the ordinary business of science," i.e., the solving of puzzles created by discrepancies between theory and fact. Weak theories, of course, suffer even more from these difficulties, and even more patience is required. Psychologists often reject theories impatiently when they fail to give 100% accurate predictions and explanation; this is unreasonable. Had physicists and chemists proceeded with the same abandon, it is safe to say that no physical or chemical theories would have been made in the hard sciences. We must take seriously the proposition that "a theory is a tender growth, naturally imperfect when first proposed, and only likely to become acceptable after many years and possibly centuries of experimental work to explicate its complexity, and theoretical efforts to improve it and make it more precise and accurate. It must be given time to do these things, otherwise it will die of neglect" (Roley, 1959).

From the point of view of metatheory, we have drawn attention to two features of scientific theories. In the first place, they are 'good' when they lead to an advancing and progressive research programme, and in the second place they are likely to be 'weak' in the early stages of a science, and to grow 'strong' only later, through a great deal of experimental research and theory development. It may be possible to make a little more precise the distinction between weak and strong theories. In testing a given theory (H), many assumptions (K) must be made in order to make the testing of the theory possible. Failure of the experiment may indicate not that H was erroneous, but that some of the assumptions under K were incorrect. In weak theories the part played by K, and general ignorance about K, is much larger than in strong theories; hence the testing of H is very much more difficult, and H should not readily be abandoned simply because H + K can be shown to be falsified by actual experiment (Cohen & Nagel, 1936). Let us put the logic of this argument in the following form: if H and K, then P. If our experiment shows P to be false, then either H is false or K (in part or complete) is false. If we have good grounds for believing K is not false, H is refuted by the experiment. Nevertheless, the experiment really tests both H *and* K. If, in the interest of the coherence of our knowledge, it is found necessary to revise the assumptions contained in K, the crucial experiment must be reinterpreted, and need not then decide against H. The difference between weak and strong theories lies in the reliance we may place on K; far more is known about K in the case of strong than in the case of weak theories.

This discussion leads quite logically to a consideration of the importance of parameter values. Consider Eysenck's (1967) prediction that introverts would show eye-blink conditioning more rapidly and more strongly than extraverts. This was indeed found to be so when weak intensity UCSs were used, but the reverse was found when more intense UCSs were used (Eysenck, 1981). In this case it was not H that was responsible, but K; the intensity parameter is clearly implicated, and proper predictions can be mediated by the use of Pavlov's law of transmarginal inhibition, which states that the relation between intensity of stimulus and strength of conditioning is not linear, but curvilinear. Many other examples of a similar kind are given in Eysenck (1981). Ideally, the general theory should always state the parameter values under which it can operate, but in weak theories this inevitably forms part of a research programme and is not normally included in the statement of the original weak theory. It is only by discovering the requisite parameter values that the weak theory can become a strong one.

It might be said that to explain a 'good' theory in terms of it being linked with a progressive research programme is tautological, unless a 'progressive research programme' can be defined more precisely. The literature on the philosophy and history of science suggests that there are five criteria which may be used in order to formulate such a judgement, and I will try to state these at the same time as giving examples taken from psychological research. The first criterion, and one which is universally admitted, is the power of the theory to *predict new facts*. It is, of course, desirable, and it may be essential, that these facts should not be predictable in terms of any other theory, and if the facts go counter to common sense expectation, so much the better. Such predictions are particularly impressive when the new facts contradict existing scientific and/or common sense views. As an example, consider enuresis. Here, as Morgan (1978) points out, there are two behaviouristic theories, one a classical conditioning paradigm, the other an avoidance learning paradigm. Both make similar predictions, however, and may therefore be considered together. In either case, the theory declares enuresis to be the result of a failure to learn the connection between the US (the enlargement of the bladder) and the response (waking up and urinating in the toilet). The bell-and-blanket method provides the missing link, the ringing of the bell being the CS needed to provide the required conditioning. This theory contrasts with the psychoanalytic theory, which regards enuresis as a consequence of anxiety and other emotional states of the individual, and declares that symptomatic treatment is useless because it will only exacerbate the underlying emotional conflicts.

Predictions made from the learning theory model are as follows: (1) enuresis should be abolished in more subjects (other than those suffering from certain physical disabilities, infections, etc.) by means of this technique than any other. (2) There should be a fair degree of relapse, because conditioning stops the moment the criterion is reached. (3) The *intensity* of the US should be related to the success of the treatment and the lack of relapse. (4) Intermittent reinforcement should prove superior to 100% reinforcement in preventing relapse. (5) Over-learning should be effective in preventing relapse. These are quite specific predictions, often counter-intuitive, but all following directly from well-known learning theory principles. As Morgan has demonstrated, the evidence is very much in line with these predictions. In addition it appears that a sixth prediction is also borne by the facts, namely (6) that the patients' anxieties and other mental symptoms would markedly decrease once enuresis had been eliminated. All this goes completely counter to the Freudian position.

This evidence suggests that learning theory is a *progressive,* and hence a 'good' theory, whereas psychoanalysis which has to rely on trying to argue away these very critical findings in some way, is *regressive,* and hence a 'bad' theory. A much more detailed discussion of behaviour therapy and learning theory, on the one hand, and psychoanalysis on the other, is given elsewhere (Eysenck, 1985a).

The second virtue of a good theory is its ability to *explain* what previously appeared to be anomalies. As an example, consider the anomalies which have arisen since Urbantschitsch (1883) put forward the hypothesis that the perception of visual, auditory, tactile, pressure, pain, olfactory, and gustatory stimuli can be facilitated by simultaneous heteromodal sensory stimulation. The hypothesis essentially states that the arousal produced by more intense heteromodal stimulation lowers sensory thresholds for other types of stimulation. The experimental evidence in many studies has been contradictory, some of it being positive, some of it negative, and some neutral (Eysenck, 1976). Shigehisa and Symons (1973; see also Shigehisa, Shigehisa, & Symons, 1973) put forward the theory that (a) the regression should be curvilinear, following Pavlov's law of transmarginal inhibition, and (b) that in line with Eysenck's (1967) theory relating extraverion-introversion to cortical arousal, the transition from decreasing to increasing thresholds should take place earlier in introverts than in extraverts. In a whole series of studies they managed to demonstrate that the regression was indeed curvilinear, and related to personality in the manner posited. In this way it was possible for Eysenck's personality theory to clear up anomalies in the experimental literature which were completely inexplicable before. This is an important function of a 'good' theory.

The third sign of a good theory is that it may act as a *criterion* between different interpretations which, in the absence of a good theory, could not be empirically separated. As an example, consider the long-lasting controversy concerning Spearman's general factor of intelligence, *g*. There have been many attempts to solve the problem of its existence by means of factor analytic studies, but it became obvious that the way in which variances were distributed by means of the rotations implicit in factor analysis could not be determined objectively. Thurstone's 'simple structure' seemed at first to present a useful criterion, but it soon became obvious that the two criteria suggested, namely 'simple structure' and 'orthogonality of axes,' were opposed to each other. Given the typical factor analysis of a matrix of intercorrelations between a large number of intelligence tests, it was possible *either* to reach simple structure and abandon orthogonality, or to preserve orthogonality, and abandon simple structure. Thurstone (1967) abandoned simple structure. Clearly there is no statistical answer to this problem, and both interpretations are still very much alive in the literature.

An answer to this problem has been suggested by Eysenck (1982), who advocated taking seriously Galton's original theory that intelligence had a biological foundation, and that measures of intelligence should directly address this physiological basis. Using the event-related potential on the EEG as a measure of this underlying physiological basis of individual differences in intelligence (Eysenck & Barrett, 1985), it was found that a very high correlation of .83 existed in a group of 219 15-year old school children between the AEP (Average Evoked Potential) and the Wechsler IQ. This clearly suggested that the advocates of *g* were right and those denying it were wrong. This is highly indicative, but not conclusive. A more conclusive deduction can be made possible by using Eysenck's method of criterion analysis (Eysenck, 1950).

The particular form this method takes in this connection might also be called the *proportionality criterion*. If we take the 11 sub-tests of the WISC on this sample, intercorrelate them and extract the first or general factor, the factor loadings indicate to what extent each test measures that which is common to them all, i.e., *g* according to our theory. Again, if we correlate the AEP score with each test separately, then, if we assume that the AEP is a direct measure of *g*, then each such correlation indicates the extent to which each sub-test of the WISC correlates with *g*. If both these hypotheses are correct, then clearly the two sets of values should be *proportional*, and consequently should show a very high correlation. In actual fact the correlation was found to be .95, which is not significantly different from unity. This result is impossible to interpret along the lines of a theory which denies the existence of *g*, and hence the theory helps us to decide between two interpretations of a large body of empirical data, namely that furnished by factor analytic investigations carried out over the past 75 years.

The theoretical considerations underlying this argument can be applied in many ways, and are fundamental in deciding between many interpretations of empirical data. Another example in which it has been used is the application of criterion analysis to the theory that there exists a continuum between normality and psychiatric abnormality, i.e., neurosis and psychosis, and that these two continua are essentially independent. The evidence indicates that the theory is essentially correct, and thus enables us to to make firm affirmations concerning large numbers of data and observations which previously had not been looked at from this particular theoretical point of view.

The fourth advantage of a 'good' theory is its ability to unify apparently separate disciplines. Experimental psychology and correlational psychology have in the past pursued rather divergent courses, and have had little to do with each other. Cronbach (1957), in his famous presidential address to the APA talked about the "two disciplines of scientific psychology," and argued that we would never succeed in establishing psychology as a basic science if we did not bring these two disciplines together. Eysenck (1967) has argued very much along similar lines. The question, of course, is how this can be done, and it may be suggested that a personality theory which explains individual differences, and the dimensions created by these individual differences, along the lines of concepts worked out by experimental psychologists, may be the answer to this question (Eysenck & Eysenck, 1985).

Such a theory, e.g., that of explaining differences in extraversion-introversion in terms of differences in cortical arousal, mediated by the ascending reticular formation, extends even beyond the limits of psychology proper. As an example, consider psychopharmocology, where Eysenck (1983a, b) has suggested that a classification of drugs which alter human behaviour can best be made in terms of the major dimensions of personality (psychoticism, extraversion, neuroticism). A great deal of evidence is cited in these studies to demonstrate the viability of this suggestion.

Eysenck (1983c, 1984) has suggested that by linking the two disciplines of scientific psychology, it is possible to create a paradigm in personality research, and that a theory which is thus capable of uniting a great number of divergent approaches has certain advantages which set it apart from competing theories. The ability to generate a paradigm of the Kuhnian type would certainly be an index of a good theory, and this ability to unify apparently separate disciplines characterizes a far-reaching paradigm.

In direct line with Lewin's statement is a fifth criterion, namely, the *practical application* of a given theory. Scientists who stress the differences between pure and applied science are often hostile to statements of this kind, and prefer the 'purity' of research unemcumbered by application. In philosophical discussion it is possible to argue the two sides to this question, particularly with reference to the physical sciences, but in psychology I would submit that such a debate would be quite irrelevant.

The reason for this lies in the particular character of psychology as a science. The hard sciences (with certain exceptions, like astronomy) rely on experiment rather than on observation, and the main characteristic of such experiment is the limitation and exclusion of variables which affect the outcome of the experiment. What is aimed at is a simple functional statement of the kind: $a = f(b)$, i.e., a is a function of b. Usually a mathematical statement of the type of function is looked for. Novel experimental techniques and analyses may be needed before it becomes possible to investigate directly any such functional relationships, but this analytic work is the essence of experimental physics.

The difficulty in psychology, of course, is that we are dealing with *behaviour,* which implies an intact *organism.* In the organism, functional relationships of the kind mentioned above are always complicated by the fact that other variables which also determine the occurrence of a cannot be excluded, so that the formula has to read: $a = f(b, o)$, where o denotes the organism, i.e., a multiplicity of influences which act upon the dependent variable, and make it impossible to study the independent variable in isolation.

It is one of the major errors of experimental psychology when it assumes that by isolating an individual in the laboratory, one can exclude unwanted influences residing in the organism. This is clearly impossible. It is well known that differences in intelligence, differences in attitude, differences in degrees of anxiety, and other such variables inevitably determine a person's reaction to experimental manipulations, and may be even more powerful than the independent variables selected by the experimenter. This is now so widely agreed that there is little need to substantiate these statements.

Although the experimental situation enables us to exclude or minimize certain independent variables, it also imposes upon us certain restrictions which are related to moral and ethical problems. If we wish, for in-stance, to study strong emotions as the independent variables in our de-sign, we are unable to do so in the laboratory because we cannot arrange matters in such a way that our experimental subjects experience devastat-ing anxieties, suicidal depressions, etc. That means that these variables can only be studied *outside* the laboratory, and again ethical considera-tions make it necessary that they should be so studied in the context of a therapeutic endeavour. This immediately means that we cannot study strong emotions other than in a practical setting, which alone enables us to test theories of the origin, preservation, and extinction of such emo-tions through some kind of therapeutic endeavours (Eysenck, 1985b). We can, of course, to some extent address the issue by working with animals, but convincing evidence regarding the place of emotion in human conduct cannot easily be supplied by *only* working with animals. Animal experiments have been important in suggesting to us theories and hypo-theses in conditioning and learning which have been extremely valuable in creating modern behaviour therapy, but such theories always require ap-plication to human conduct before they can be accepted and that means inevitably that we must apply them in a therapeutic setting.

Much the same might be said about intelligence testing. As Jensen (1984) has pointed out, divergent notions about the generality or specific-ity of intelligence can with advantage be tested in the applied field. As he says: "If the specificity notions of test validity that prevail through fed-eral enforcement agencies lead to unnecessary and costly validity studies, or to greatly relaxed selection standards, or to quotas, or to abandoning the use of tests altogether in an organization, it would seem important to estimate the actual monetary consequences of these alternatives. If tests are abandoned or replaced by less valid selection techniques, such as in-terviews, there is bound to be a decline in the overall quality of those hired, and lower-performing personnel mean a loss in productivity" (p. 107). According to *Time*, the rate of productivity growth in the U. S. A. has declined, since 1970, from 3.5% to 1%, and Schmidt (1979) has suggested that this decline is due in part to a reduced efficiency in al-locating people to jobs because of governmental obstacles put in the way of using tests and optimal selection model.

Some figures may be of interest. It has been estimated that the total annual savings in training costs to the armed forces as a result of test selection classification of enlisted personnel was 442 million dollars (Jensen, 1984). Hunter, Schmidt, and Rauschenberg (1984) have im-proved on earlier statistical methods for cost estimates of the consequence of different selection strategies for various jobs, and have shown that employee differences in job proficiency correspond to considerable differences in the actual dollar value of their performance. In a study of budget analysts, Schmidt and Hunter (1980) have estimated, for instance, that the dollar value productivity of superior performers was 23,000 dollars per year *greater* than that of low performers; this value should, of course, be multiplied by the number of persons employed. In a study of the Philadelphia police department, with 5,000 employees, Hunter (1979) has estimated that abandonment of general ability tests for the selection of police officers would cost a total of 180 million dollars over a ten-year period. The estimated gain in productivity resulting from one year's use of a more valid selection procedure for computer programmers in the federal government ranges from 5.6 to 92.2 million dollars for different sets of estimation parameters, and for the whole federal government, with 4 million employees, Hunter and Schmidt (1980) conservatively estimated optimal selection procedures would save 16 billion dollars per year. Hunter and Schmidt (1982) have also estimated the cost effectiveness of using tests for job selection on a national scale. The differences between not using and using tests for the allocation of the work force to jobs they calculated at about 169 billion dollars! If general ability tests, to the extent that they are currently used in selection, were to be abandoned, the estimated loss in national productivity would be about 80 billion dollars per year. Many other similar figures are available, but these are reasonably sufficient to indicate the practical usefulness of intelligence tests as selection devices in actual practice.

In conclusion, let me state certain points which seem to arise from the discussion. (1) Theories are an essential part of science, including psychology. (2) It is possible to distinguish 'good' from 'bad' theories. (3) 'Good' theories are distinguished by being part of a progressive and advancing research programme, while 'bad' theories are associated with a regressive research programme. (4) There are five major criteria by which to judge a given theory, and to decide whether it is part of an advancing and progressive, or a regressive research programme. Psychologists should take theories and their assessments more seriously than they do at present, and might, with advantage, apply the standards and criteria suggested.

References

Achinstein, P. (1965). The problem of theoretical terms. *American Philosophical Quarterly, 2,* 193-203.

Barnes, B. (1982). *T. S. Kuhn and social science.* London: Macmillan.

Bergmann, G. (1951). The logic of psychological concepts. *Philosophy of Science, 18,* 93-110.

Bergmann, G. (1954). *The metaphysics of logical positivism.* New York: Longman, Green.

Bergmann, G. (1957). *Philosophy of science.* Madison: University of Wisconsin Press.

Bergmann, G., & Spence, K. (1941). Operationism and theory in psychology. *Psychological Review, 48,* 1-14.

Carnap, R. (1966). *Philosophical foundations of physics.* New York: Basic Books.

Cohen, M. R. , & Nagel, N. (1936). *An introduction to logic and scientific method.* New York: Harcourt, Brace & Co.

Cronbach, L. J. (1957). The two disciplines of scientific psychology. *American Psychologist, 12,* 671-684.

Eysenck, H. J. (1950). Criterion analysis: An application of the hypothesis - deductive method to factor analysis. *Psychological Review, 57,* 38-53.

Eysenck, H. J. (1960). The place of theory in psychology. In H. J. Eysenck (Ed.), *Experiments in personality* (Vol. 2, pp 303-315). London: Routledge & Kegan Paul.

Eysenck, H. J. (1967). *The biological basis of personality.* Springfield, Ill.: C. C. Thomas.

Eysenck, H. J. (1976). *The measurement of personality.* Lancaster, Eng.: MTP.

Eysenck, H. J. (1981). *A model for personality.* New York: Springer.

Eysenck, H. J. (1982). *A model for intelligence.* New York: Springer.

Eysenck, H. J. (1983a). Drug as research tests in psychology: experiments with drugs in personality research. *Neuropsychobiology, 10,* 29-43.

Eysenck, H. J. (1983b). Psychopharmacology and personality. In W. Jahuke (Ed.), *Response variability to psychotropic drugs.* (pp. 127-154). New York: Pergamon Press.

Eysenck, H. J. (1983c). Is there a paradigm in personality research? *Journal of Research in Personality, 17,* 369-397.

Eysenck, H. J. (1984). The place of individual differences in a scientific psychology. *Annals of Theoretical Psychology. 1,* 237-285.

Eysenck, H. J. (1985a). *Decline and fall of the Freudian empire.* London: Viking Press.

Eysenck, H. J. (1985b). Psychotherapy to behaviour therapy: A paradigm
    shift. In D. B. Fishman, F. Rotgers, & C. M. Franks (Eds.),
    Paradigms in behaviour therapy: Present and promise. New York:
    Springer.
Eysenck, H. J. (1985c). The place of theory in a world of facts. In
    K. B. Madsen & L. P. Mos (Eds.), *Annals of theoretical psychol-
    ogy.* (Vol. 3, pp. 17-72). New York: Plenum Press.
Eysenck, H. J., & Barrett, P. (1985). Psychophysiology and the measure-
    ment of intelligence. In C. R. Reynolds & V. Wilson (Eds.), *Me-
    thodological and statistical advances in the study of individual dif-
    ferences.* New York: Plenum Press.
Eysenck, H. J., & Eysenck, M. W. (1985). *Personality and individual dif-
    ferences.* New York: Plenum Press.
Eysenck, H. J., & Wilson, G. D. (1973). *The experimental study of
    Freudian theories.* London: Methuen.
Feyerabend, P. K. (1975). *Against methods.* London: New Left Books.
Greenaway, F. (1966). *John Dalton and the atom.* London: Heinemann.
Grünbaum, A. (1984). *Foundations of psychoanalysis.* Berkeley: Univer-
    sity of California Press.
Hanson, N. R. (1958). *Patterns of discovery.* Cambridge: Cambridge
    University Press.
Hempel, C. G. (1952). *Fundamentals of concept formation in empirical
    science.* Chicago: University of Chicago Press.
Hempel, C. G. (1965). Aspects of scientific explanation. In
    C. G. Hempel (Ed.), *Aspects of scientific explanation and other es-
    says in the philosophy of science.* New York: Free Press.
Hempel, C. G. (1966). *Philosophy of natural science.* Englewood Cliffs,
    NJ: Prentice-Hall.
Hunter, J. F. (1979). *An analysis of validity, differential validity, test
    fairness and utility for the Philadelphia Police Officers selection ex-
    amination.* Philadelphia: Report to the Philadelphia Federal Di-
    strict Court, Alverez vs. City of Philadelphia.
Hunter, J. E., & Schmidt, F. L. (1980). Noncompensatory aspects of the
    utility of valid personality selection. Unpublished manuscript cited
    by Jensen, 1984.
Hunter, J. E., & Schmidt, F. L. (1982). Fitting people to jobs: The im-
    pact of personnel selection on national productivity. In
    M. P. Dimutte & E. A. Fleishman (Eds.), *Human performance
    and productivity: Human capability assessment* (Vol. 1). Hillsdale,
    NJ: Lawrence Erlbaum Associates.
Hunter, J. E., Schmidt, F. L., & Rauschenberger, J. (1984). Methodo-
    logical, statistical and technical issues in the study of bias in psy-
    chological tests. In C. R. Reynolds & R. T. Brown (Eds.), *Per-

spectives on bias in mental testing (pp. 41-100). New York: Plenum Press.

Jensen, A. R. (1984). Test validity: g versus the specificity doctrine. *Journal of Social and Biological Structures, 7*, 93-118.

Kazdin, A. E., & Wilson, G. T. (1978). *Evaluation of behavior therapy.* New York: Ballinger.

Kline, P. (1981). *Fact and fantasy in Freudian theory.* London: Methuen.

Krige, J. (1980). *Science, revolution and discontinuity.* Sussex: Harvester Press.

Kuhn, T. S. (1962). *The structure of scientific revolutions.* Chicago: University of Chicago Press.

Lakatos, I. (Ed.).(1968). *The problem of inductive logic.* Amsterdam: North-Holland.

Lakatos, I., & Musgrave, A. (Eds.). (1970). Criticism and the growth of knowledge. Cambridge: Cambridge University Press.

Morgan, T. T. T. (1978). Relapse and therapeutic response in the conditioning treatment of enuresis: A review of recent findings on intermittent reinforcement, overlearning, and stimulus intensity. *Behaviour Research and Therapy, 16*, 273-279.

Popper, K. R. (1959). *The logic of scientific discovery.* London: Hutchinson.

Popper, K. R. (1974a). *Conjectures and refutations.* London: Routledge & Kegan Paul.

Popper, K. R. (1974b). Replies to my critics. In P. A. Schilpp (Ed.), *The philosophy of Karl Popper.* La Salle: Open Court Publishing Co.

Putnam, H. (1962). What theories are not. In E. Nagel, P. Suppe, & A. Tarski (Eds.), *Logic, methodology and philosophy of science.* Stanford: Stanford Press.

Quine, W. V. O. (1962). *From a logical point of view.* Cambridge: Harvard University Press.

Rachman, S. (1963). *Critical essays in psychoanalysis.* London: Pergamon Press.

Rachman, S., & Wilson, T. (1981). *The effects of psychological therapy.* New York & London: Pergamon Press.

Roley, T. B. (1959). An opinion on the construction of behaviour therapy. *American Psychologist, 14*, 129-134.

Schmidt, F. L. (1979,Jan/March). Poor hiring decisions, lower productivity. *Civil Service Journal.*

Schmidt, F. L., & Hunter, J. E. (1980). *Personnel Psychology, 33,* 41-60. (Quoted by Jensen, 1984.)

Schorr, A. (1984). *Die Verhaltenstherapie.* Weinheim: Beltz.

Shigehisa, T., & Symons, J. R. (1973). Effect of intensity of visual stimulation and auditory sensitivity in relation to personality. *British Journal of Psychology, 64,* 205-213.

Shigehisa, P., Shigehisa, T., & Symons, J. (1973). Effects of intensity of auditory stimulation on photopic visual sensitivity in relation to personality. *Japanese Psychological Research, 15,* 164-172.

Smith, M. L., Glass, G. V., & Miller, T. I. (1980). *The benefits of psychotherapy.* Baltimore: The John Hopkins University Press.

Strupp, H. H., Hadley, S. W., & Gomes-Schwartz, B. (1977). *Psychotherapy for better or worse: The problems of negative effects.* New York: Jason Eronson.

Suppe, F. (1974). *The structure of scientific theories.* Chicago: University of Illinois Press.

Tarski, A. (1941). *Introduction to logic and to the methodology of deductive sciences.* New York: Oxford University Press.

Tarski, A. (1956). *Logic, semantics, metamathematics.* Oxford: Clarendon Press.

Toulmin, S. (1953). *The philosophy of science.* London: Hutchinson.

Thurstone, L. L. (1938). *Primary mental abilities.* Psychometric Monographs, No. 1. Chicago: University of Chicago Press.

Urbantschisch, V. (1883). Über den Einfluss von Trigeminus Reizen auf die Sinnesempfindungen insbesondere auf den Gesichtssinn. *Archiv für die gesamte Physiologie, 30,* 129-175.

Zwang, G. (1985). *La statue de Freud.* Paris: Robert Laffont.

Current Issues in Theoretical Psychology
Wm J. Baker, M.E. Hyland, H. Van Rappard, A.W. Staats (Editors)
© Elsevier Science Publishers B.V. (North-Holland), 1987

POWER RELATIONS IN PSYCHOANALYTIC PSYCHOTHERAPY[1]

Stephen Frosh

Birkbeck College
London, England

SUMMARY: This article explores the links between power relations and psychotherapy, using as a case study some post-Freudian psychoanalytic theories. The approaches of 'classical,' Kleinian, and 'object relations' theories to psychoanalytic psychotherapy are compared, and particular attention is paid to the 'image' of the analyst that they convey. Criticisms are presented of the denial of power relations in the classical approach, and of the unquestioning acceptance of a 'maternal metaphor' in object relations theory. Kleinianism, while sharing some of these difficulties, presents more radical possibilities through its attitude towards destructiveness and its advocacy of a thoroughgoing restructuring of the underlying structure of personality during analysis. The article concludes with a reference to the subversive possibilities to be found in Lacanian therapy.

In recent years, the tendency of radical critics to regard psychotherapy as a form of bourgeois self-indulgence has been challenged by a recognition of the significance of feelings and personal perceptions in social life. In particular, the 'New Left' and feminist movements have drawn attention to the way social assumptions may be internalized, to appear as ideological structures which heavily influence a person's experience of themselves and others. This has combined with a growing awareness of the difficulties of bringing about personal change - the limitations of 'consciousness raising' - to encourage a renewed interest in psychoanalysis, both as a theory of how individuality becomes constructed, and as a form of therapeutic practice. Some of the work on psychoanalysis as a general theory has been extremely interesting and very sophisticated (e.g., Coward and Ellis, 1977; Gallop, 1982), but writing on psychoanalysis as radical therapy has been far more limited. This is partly because of the difficulties involved in developing a convincing 'political' account of what is in essence a private activity (cf. Banton, Clifford, Frosh, Lousada, & Rosenthall, 1985), but it is also because of the rather limited use that is generally made of the complexity of the existing literature on therapy. In the context of psychoanalysis, for example, there is a tendency to neglect consideration of the wide range of different analytic theories that bear on therapy; these are often opposed to one another in their substance or in

---

[1]This paper is based on Chap. 9 of the author's forthcoming book, *The politics of psychoanalysis*, to be published by Macmillan. Used here with permission.

their implications. Instead, psychoanalysis is either referred to in a gen-eralized way, as if it were a unitary entity, or one psychoanalytic theory is employed in an argument as if it represents the whole, or it is presented as the only 'correct' approach. Often this latter tendency is made worse by a discussion of psychoanalysis which completely omits all post-Freudian developments. The truth is, however, that psychoanalytic theories are very various, and they differ importantly on many matters, including their approach to therapy. This article is founded on the belief that these differences connect significantly with the general issue of the relationships between therapy and power, an issue which is at the centre of the renewed radical enterprise in psychology. Taking post-Freudian psychoanalytic ideas on the therapeutic process as its focus, this chapter attempts to clarify these relationships and hence to contribute to the in-vestigation of the 'political' significance of psychological encounters.

There is a considerable technical literature in psychoanalysis, but this is not the place to attempt to evaluate differing approaches in terms of their therapeutic effects. In this article, the implied power relations of the therapeutic encounter will be explored through an investigation of the images of the analyst that are produced by the various accounts of the basic components of therapy. The major comparisons used here are among 'classical,' Kleinian' and 'object relations' theories, beginning with a discussion of the positions taken by the first two theories on the con-cepts of transference and interpretation.

Transference and Interpretation

Given the centrality of transference in the theory and practice of psychoanalysis, it is perhaps surprising to realize that there are substantial differences even of definition. Sandler, Dare, and Holder (1973), after distinguishing between the 'treatment alliance' (based on the client's wish to co-operate) and transference, define the latter as:

> a *specific illusion* which develops in regard to the other person, one which, unbeknown to the subject, represents, in some of its features, a repetition of a relationship to-wards an important figure in the person's past. (p. 47)

It is seen as more than a general tendency to repeat past relationships; rather, transference represents "a concentration of a past attitude or feel-ing, inappropriate to the present, and directed *quite specifically* towards the other person or institution" (p. 47). This is quite different from the conception of transference advanced by Kleinians, who have extended the concept to refer to *all* aspects of the client's communication with the analyst - the "totality of all intrapsychic components of the patient's fantasies about and reactions to the analyst" (Langs, 1976, p. 57). In this formulation, it ceases to be possible to distinguish realistic aspects of the therapist-client interaction from imaginary ones, for all reality is read through a fog of phantasy, and is half constructed as it is perceived. The analytic relationship becomes a field of phantasy; any discrimination between internal and external worlds is made fragile and unconvincing.

The differing definitions of tranference relate to some important differences in accounts of the nature of the mechanism by which transference operates. At the core of the classical view is the notion of transference as a form of *displacement*; feelings that properly belong in one relationship, directed towards some particular person or persons, instead become concentrated onto the analyst. Because this assumes the possibility of forming relatively coherent relationships, classical theory makes transference the product of a fairly late period in the child's life, when the ego is well developed and there is a clearly established sense of self and of the boundary between self and others. The therapeutic focus is consequently on an autonomous individual psyche which has become fixated in certain ways, but which is basically capable of forming relationships and of distinguishing between phantasy and reality - hence the reluctance of classical analysts to treat psychotics, who supposedly lack these capabilities. The analyst's task is to aid the process of reality testing by helping the client identify conflicts as they are expressed in the transference, and, through interpretations, refine her/his knowledge of their origin and the way they distort contemporary relationships. The analyst in this scenario is in many respects outside the interaction: the passive recipient of, or 'sounding board' for, the client's impulses and phantasies, relatively unaffected by them but commenting upon them in order to sort out their sense. Hence, although the analyst's refusal to accept the phantasy role given to her/him by the client is seen as one of the major techniques for revealing repressed material, there is no necessary consideration of the real interpersonal aspects of the therapeutic encounter; rather, all that is changed occurs inside the client's head.

The emphasis in classical theory on the distanced stance of the analyst is also reflected in the account it gives of interpretation, defined by Sandler et al. (1973) as:

> all comments and other verbal interventions which have the
> aim of immediately making the patient aware of some
> aspect of his psychological functioning of which he was

not previously conscious. (p. 110)

This broad definition has its roots in the idea that therapy operates by communicating a form of knowledge to the client's ego. The assumption behind it is that this knowledge will somehow strengthen the ego and give it more power to control the demands of unconscious forces, or to allow conflicts to be dealt with in consciousness. The strategy by which this takes place is a gradualist one, in which interpretations move from surface to depth, from anxieties and impulses that are relatively near to consciousness to those that lie far beneath. In the classical approach, this means working in an order that reverses the developmental stages: from reasonably integrated genital concerns to more distorted and primitive anal and then oral ones; from interpretation of defences to uncovering of unconscious content (Zetzel, 1956). The rationale behind this is that the analytic procedure can only be helpful if the ego can be protected against being flooded with anxiety generated by primitive impulses. As defences, anxiety and emotions are interpreted at each level, the underlying conflicts which they reveal can be dealt with under the gaze of a gradually strengthened ego, freeing psychic energy and making it possible to move deeper. In all this, the support offered by the analyst is a significant prop to the ego, allowing it to cope even with destructive emotions. Gradually, impulses become more controllable, and more basic conflicts are ready to be faced.

Langs (1976) points to a limitation of the conventional classical form of analysis: that it avoids regressive and primitive processes and ignores preverbal responses. Too easily, the slow work of supporting a gradually strengthening ego can slide into the conformist adaptationism which makes social adjustment the final therapeutic goal. It is also possible that this mode of work is in part the product of defensiveness amongst analysts - fear of dealing with destructive material that might bring up uncomfortable feelings. For instance, the politically progressive feminists, Eichenbaum and Orbach (1982), are opposed to early interpretations that expose the client's vulnerability and can "sound like an attack" (p. 52); it may be that this is due to their understandable desire to offset the patronizing and punitive elements involved in much therapy, but it could also represent a rationale for steering clear of painful emotions. Elaboration of interpretations that "sound like an attack" may in fact be an appropriate procedure for investigating the ways in which the client's psyche is, or has been, under attack from powerful and painful forces. In many respects, this is precisely the argument used by Kleinians in their thoroughgoing critique of traditional views on the appropriate structuring of the therapeutic process.

The contrast between the classical and Kleinian views can be concentrated into one distinction: whereas in the classical view the analyst
functions as a mirror onto which the client displaces her/his impulses,
Kleinians describe the analyst as a receptacle *into* which internal figures
and the feelings that surround them are projected (Segal, 1981, p. 82).
The crucial word here is 'projection,' especially as it is linked with the reformulation of developmental theory by Klein which makes projection
and introjection into fundamental mental processes. Thus, Klein (1952)
notes the connection between what occurs in therapy and what takes place
in early life in the following terms:

> I hold that transference originates in the same processes
> which in the earliest stages determine object relations.
> Therefore, we have to go back again and again in analysis
> to the fluctuations between objects, love and hatred, ex-
> ternal and internal, which dominates early infancy. (p.
> 53)

This view has a number of important implications. First, it is directly responsible for the widening of the concept of transference so characteristic
of Kleinian thought. If transference is based on mechanisms which are
fundamental in mental life, which form the foundations upon which all
mental functioning is based, then every aspect of the client's communication must be in some way linked to transference and hence to primitive
material. Hence, Kleinian technique centres on the interpretation *as
transference phenomena* of the varied material produced by the client. In
itself this is simply an extreme version of an approach common to many
psychoanalysts, although different schools vary in the exact weight given
to transference. However, where the peculiarities of the Kleinian approach assert themselves most is in the *content* of transference interpretations, which focus upon the elucidation of primitive material. This stance
arises from two considerations. First, the Kleinian position that transference operates through projective mechanisms which are fundamental to
mental life leads to a concern with primitive anxieties and with splitting
processes otherwise found in early infancy. Secondly, Kleinians argue
that in order for unconscious material to be acceptable to consciousness,
the anxiety that it generates has to be lessened at the same time as the defences are removed. Hence, they place at least as much emphasis on the
interpretation of basic anxieties as on the interpretation of defences, and
do not follow the sequence from genital to anal to oral described earlier.
Rather, they hold that because the phantasies that give rise to transference are constituted by early anxieties and object relationships, interpretation of primitive unconscious contents and defences is crucial from

the start of analysis.

Another directive of Kleinian practice arises from their insistence on the destructive aspects of early life, leading to a focus on the *negative* transference, the complex of hostile feelings which the client may bring to bear on the analyst. Klein (1957) argues that the fundamental task of analysis is to enable integration of the personality to occur through over-coming splits in the psyche which are perpetuated by unresolved primitive conflicts. The method employed is to analyze both sides of the early love-hate conflict as they are replayed in the positive and negative trans-ference. Destructive and loving feelings can by this means gradually be brought together in the presence of the security provided by the good analytic object, laying the foundation for improved stability and integra-tion. In all this, Klein emphasizes the intensity of the resistance encoun-tered and the fragility of change.

Much of what has been described above comes together in the Kleinian concept of projective identification, which seems to have become acceptable as an explanation of the process of therapy to many analysts who would not otherwise hold with Kleinian concepts. In its 'pure' form, projective identification seems to be a wholly negative phenomenon; it is defined by Laplanche and Pontalis (1973) as "a mechanism revealed in phantasies in which the subject inserts his self - in whole or in part - into the object in order to harm, possess or control it" (p. 356). In thera-peutic parlance, this notion is often modified to include positive as well as negative insertions, opening the way for consideration of how it can have beneficial effects. In the analytic situation, projective identification in-volves interpolating into the analyst aspects of the client's inner world, thereby influencing the analyst's emotional state. It is:

> a means by which the patient induces in the analyst all
> sorts of feelings, such as helplessness, rejection and lack of
> understanding, based on the fact that the patient has pro-
> jected into the analyst the child part of himself, with all of
> the related feelings. (Langs, 1976, p. 470)

As well as changing the analyst, however, the projected parts of the client also undergo alterations while held by the other. These are then re-experienced by the client through a parallel introjective mechanism, whereby parts of the analyst (which may originally have been projected by the client) are internalized and alter significant aspects of the client's psychic world. In this way, the client not only internalizes the analyst as a 'good object' who can make possible the integration of destructive and loving feelings but also takes back aspects of her/himself which have been contained and altered through the analytic experience. All this makes the representation of the analyst very complex in Kleinian thought: as Langs (1976) points out, the analyst can represent parent figures, as in classical theory, but also internal objects and part objects or even aspects of psychic structure, such as the id or super-ego. Consequently, the analysis of transference leads not just to an unearthing of past relationships, but also to an exploration of the "current dynamic state of the patient's internal objects and unconscious fantasies" (p. 57). Overall, this also results in a much firmer focus on the interpersonal components of therapy than in classical theory: the therapeutic situation is a ground on which the interplay of projection and introjection operates in relation to the presence of the analyst, who acts as the container and transmuter of feelings and parts of the client's psyche, rather than just as a mirror to help the client see her/himself more accurately.

The Kleinian approach contrasts with that of classical analysis in a number of ways. At the most schematic level, there is a difference in the focus of analysis. Where classical analysis concentrates on uncovering defences, on ego analysis, Klein's is very much an 'id psychology,' dealing directly with primitive unconscious emotions, and employing the analyst as an object to be introduced into the client's unconscious world. The therapeutic mechanisms are projection, introjection, and projective identification; change does not come about through increased knowledge becoming available to the ego, which can then control conflicts more effectively, but through repairing splits at an unconscious level, aided by the internalization of the analytic object. Hence, the value of interpretations is that they feed back to the client the projected elements in her/his personality, invested with the qualities of the analyst; the process of change is one of identification and integration, not just greater control over impulse. Other analysts have often criticized Kleinian work on a number of grounds: for example, that its emphasis on interpretation of primitive feelings often operates to the exclusion of anything else, including recognition of the occurrence of real events; or that the manner in which it launches into depth interpretations at the earliest possible moment can lead to overwhelming anxiety or the raising of destructive defences which can then not be overcome. Kleinian analysts often seem to present themselves as omniscient and rigid, using the same techniques for the analysis of all problems, as everything is seen as referring back to basic infantile anxieties. In practice, many of these criticisms ring true, but where Kleinian theory repeatedly reveals its superiority is in its recognition of painful feelings, its refusal to turn away from despair and destructiveness, and its insistence that if one is able to face squarely up to this in an interpersonal encounter allowing modification of unconscious structures, it becomes possible to build a new integrity and stability. But the central political radicalness of Kleinianism is revealed in a statement of Segal's on psychoanalytic insight:

> It involves conscious knowledge of archaic processes, normally inaccessible to the most intuitive person, through reliving in the transference the very processes that structured one's internal world and conditioned one's perceptions. (1981, p. 79)

The Kleinian approach to analysis emphasizes reworking the basic structuring principles of the personality, focussing particularly on the projective mechanisms which underlie the transactions between the infant's internal and external world. In so doing, it directly confronts the 'socializing' forces which construct the organized psyche and lead not just to psychological distress, but to the specific forms of psychic organization prevalent within any social environment. In contrast to the neutral, commentating stance of classical theory, Kleinian therapy aims at being a process of re-creation.

Schizoid Phenomena and Human Relationships

The classic Freudian patients were hysterics and obsessional neurotics - people with relatively clearly differentiable symptoms who could be understood to be suffering from too much repression. They functioned on the ordinary human level which required recognition of reality and the ability to form relationships; in psychoanalysis, treatment was by uncovering repressed material through the medium of the transference. The end point of therapy referred to something like freeing the client's ego from domination by unconscious forces, so that everyday life could be made smoother and richer. These classical neurotic patients, whose pathology was held to derive from Oedipal conflicts, were the bases upon which psychoanalytic theory was formulated and have dominated cultural images of analysis from the start, as well as dictating the therapeutic techniques employed. But over the post-Freudian period there has been a gradual shift in the nature of the typical analysand, from someone needing to liberate her/himself from unconscious conflicts, to someone desperately seeking for a secure core of self.

> For perhaps fifty years, reports of analytic work have referred increasingly to patients who do not present with well organized neurotic symptomatology, nor with the massive

disturbance of overt psychosis. Their malaise is profound but diffuse. Khan (1966) says: 'The schizoid character disorders are distinguished by the fact that the symptom lies in the way of being.' (Richards, 1984, p. 125)

The reasons for this change are debatable, and the terminology used to refer to the new type of patient is variable, from 'narcissistic' to 'borderline' to 'schizoid.' However, the realization by analysts that they were working with people with fundamental difficulties in the construction and maintenance of the self and of relationships with others has led to some profound alterations in analytic practice. Although examples could be culled from many sources, Winnicott and Guntrip provide the clearest points of comparison, the former suggesting a new set of procedures for use with schizoid patients, the latter reformulating the entire therapeutic process.

In Winnicott's view, the goal of therapy with schizoid clients is radically different from the conventional analytic work of exposing and sorting out conflicts under the aegis of a relatively integrated ego; instead, it is more like remothering, taking a fragmented ego and providing the conditions of support and worth which allow it to begin to grow. Winnicott's (e.g., 1955) term for this process is 'management,' which actually means doing very little: a minimum of interpretation is provided, referring to the client's basic sense of unrelatedness, but refraining from interrogatory or threatening comments. Instead, the focus is on the boundaries and consistency of the session: the presence of the analyst, reliable and accepting, who can begin through her/his predictability to make up for the absences and frustrations of the severely regressed client's early life. Regression itself is seen as a productive mechanism under these circumstances; not only does it refer to the fundamental state of the client's true self, but it also represents a normal healing process whereby the early 'failure situation' is returned to and repaired.

The regressed state of the client also means that everything that occurs in the analysis is experienced as if it were here-and-now reality; that is, analysis with such clients is not a process of making links between current emotions or perceptions and past experiences, but instead is a matter of *reliving* the past, of encouraging the client to accept the security of the analyst's reliable presence to release, tentatively and with setbacks, the hidden 'true self' or regressed ego that has never been allowed to live. This approach also produces a new attitude towards resistances, which are not analyzed in terms of the client's pathology, as they would be with neurotics. Instead, with schizoid clients, the analyst must interpret resistance as a sign that s/he has made a mistake, and must allow articulation of the reality of that error, so that the client can experience realistic anger in the context of a relationship that continues to be secure.

The 'negative transference' of classical analysis is thus replaced by objective anger about the analyst's failures; expression of this anger within the safety of the carefully managed setting allows integration of the self to begin to occur. Throughout all this, the metaphor of the maternal 'hold' is visible: the analyst supplies a safe and caring environment in which the client can experiment with relationships, shaping her/his self in the light of the analyst's successes and failures, with the analyst offering support for the client's gradually developing ego processes. Finally, Winnicott makes it clear that 'holding' of this kind is by no means passive; not only does it normally require careful monitoring and acute sensitivity to the client's response to the setting, but with very severely regressed clients it can involve actively seeking out contact. In opposition to all traditional analytic practices, Winnicott (1955) states, "In the extreme case the therapist would need to go to the patient and actively present good mothering, an experience that could not have been expected by the patient" (pp. 281-282).

Winnicott presents his 'replacement therapy' as an addition to classical analytic technique for use with a special kind of client thought to be otherwise unreachable; his emphasis on the significance of the analytic setting also has the virtue of opening out for consideration a large range of interpersonal factors that might otherwise go neglected. But there are some important dangers with this kind of corrective work. First, it alters the stance of the analyst from that of critical ironist, revealing underlying conflicts, to that of rescuer and ideal object. In addition, its use of the maternal frame, both in theory and in practice, not only runs the risk of reducing to a procedure of attributing blame to 'not-good-enough' mothers, but also propagates a phantasy of omnipotence, that the analyst can be 'good enough' to make up for all the slings and arrows of fortune, however early they begin, however widespread they may be. Finally, there is a danger in all approaches that emphasize the supportiveness of the therapeutic relationship above its content, that there will be a drift away from exploration of the wider sources of an individual's pain, to a humanistic 'growth' encounter that submerges everything in an optimistic, but unrealistic, therapeutic 'love.' To see this more clearly, it is useful to briefly consider Guntrip's views on the centrality of human relationship in therapy.

Guntrip takes up the Winnicottian notion of the analytic situation as a reparative one, emphasizing forcefully its parenting components, the sense in which it is 'replacement therapy.' The therapeutic task with schizoid clients is "how to start off the growth of an ego which has not yet properly begun to be" (1968, p. 359); this is linked to the client's need for a relationship with someone "who *in loco parentis* will enable him to grow" (p. 350). The analyst has to develop that sense of empathy with the client that mothers have with their babies, that "parental love which the Greeks called *agape* as distinct from *eros,* the kind of love the psychotherapist must give his patient because he did not get it from his parents in an adequate way" (p. 357). Although this is similar in formulation to Winnicott's ideas, Guntrip extends the emphasis on relationship further than just the schizoid situation, and develops an harangue of the traditional psychoanalytic concern with technique. He is explicit on this point: classical analysis of transference can be helpful, but it often simply reveals the schizoid despair underneath, and anyway the active component of analytic treatment is always the relationship and not the techniques employed. Technique is itself a dirty word in the Guntripian lexicon; not only is he critical of the 'objective' stance of traditional interpretative psychoanalysis because its unresponsiveness to the client repeats the emotional traumas that presumably spark off schizoid conditions in the first place, but he is against the antihumanist *sound* of the word. Technique refers to what the analyst *does*, but what matters is what the analyst *is* in the relationship with the client:

> Terms such as 'analysis' and 'technique' are too impersonal. They remind me more of engineering than of personal relations. One can teach a technique, but cannot teach anyone how to be a therapeutic person. (1973, p. 183)

In this view, therapy is the opposite of something technical, mechanical; it is the entry into a deeply empathic relationship which enables the client to feel valued and held, perhaps for the first time, intuitively known and hence supported enough to allow change to be risked. Interpretation is "simply the medium of an understanding relationship" (p. 188); there is, in fact, *nothing special* about psychotherapy; it is simply "the application of the fundamental importance of personal relationships, in the sense of using good relationships to undo the harm done by bad ones" (p. 194). Entwined in this is a notion of how the therapist must become 'real' in the relationship with the client: the analyst must genuinely care for the client and be unafraid of a truly personal relationship with her/him; that is, the analyst must be a good object in reality and not just in phantasy. Sometimes what Guntrip means by 'real' seems to be empathy, but mostly he is referring to a relationship that is not built around the distance and phantasy-manipulation of other forms of analysis, but which represents the meeting together of two people in an ordinary, if intensely caring, way. The client has needs of the therapist which go further than the interpretation of infantile feelings, and which involve a necessity for support in the real, everyday world. It may be that transference relations have to be worked through first, but these should eventually give way so that therapist and client "can at last meet mentally face to face and know that they know each other as two human beings" (1968, p. 353). Whether the analyst should give advice or not is left open to the dictates of common sense; how much other active involvement in the client's life is required is never specified.

Much of Guntrip's argument is familiar from other branches of psychotherapy, particularly the humanistic school of workers such as Carl Rogers. In the humanists, too, there is an emphasis on the total personal encounter which allows the client to retrieve parts of her/himself that have been submerged by painful or neglectful experiences in the past, thence to begin a process of 'personal growth.' Guntrip's discussion of 'reality' is also present in humanistic psychology, and has been taken up in some progressive ways, for example, in feminist psychotherapy where there is specific attention paid to dealing with the power aspects of the situation and with offering continuing support after the end of therapy (Eichenbaum & Orbach, 1982). There are substantial criticisms to be made of both these aspects of his work, however. Langs (1976) puts his finger on one of them in criticizing the concern of Guntrip's mentor, Fairbairn, for the relationship between analyst and client over and above technique: Langs argues that Fairbairn's focus on surface interaction leads to a neglect of the influence of unconscious phantasies and an avoidance of the analysis of basic intrapsychic conflicts (p. 232). This tendency is particularly noticeable in Guntrip's valorizing of the 'reality' aspects of the relationship, especially as they are supposedly contextualized in wholly supportive and positive behaviour on the part of the analyst. Psychoanalytically, it is difficult to see how the painful feelings that the object relations theorists emphasize as being at the root of schizoid phenomena can be properly exposed and integrated if they are perpetually avoided - which is what appears likely to happen in relationships that prioritize here-and-now reality over phantasy, positive support over the analysis of destructive feelings. Politically, there are also dangerous assumptions in this approach to therapy, most of all because it seeks to institute a replacement for the pains of the world in the rarefied situation of analysis, where it claims that a 'real' relationship is possible and that human love can overwhelm the damage of the past. This is neglectful of the structuring of political relationships: there is no 'real' interpersonal encounter existing independently of the distortions induced by specific social forms. There is also no way in which the destructiveness brought about through relationships embedded in certain social structures can be made good by a 'love' that stands outside them, and to suggest that such an artificial love can make up for the activities of the world is politically reductionist. If Lasch (1979) and other critics are correct in their linking of the increase of narcissistic character formations with changes in the social sphere, then to suggest that therapy can provide some *absolute personal* relationship is to argue that it can stand outside of society, offering something which is pure and whole, uncontaminated by all of the rest of the world. Whatever therapy at its best can do, it cannot do that.

Mummy, Daddy, Lacan

The discussion of variations in classical, Kleinian, and object relations approaches to therapy provides insights into their different versions of the 'image' of the analyst - the metaphorical position given her/him and the political implications that surround this. All forms of therapy involve power relations: however supportive and egalitarian the therapist, the relationship is always an unbalanced one, its structure suggesting that the 'expert' therapist can deal with the client's pain, can know more about the client than the client does. Classical psychoanalysts have traditionally claimed that they approximate in their sessions to a 'blank screen' onto which the client displaces her/his underlying conflicts, and emphasize the importance of the analyst's distance and neutrality. This is congruent with Freud's 'rule of abstinence' which, as Ingleby (1984) points out, makes the relationship between client and analyst less than a reciprocally human one. The rule is that according to which:

> the analytic treatment should be so organized as to ensure
> that the patient finds as few substitutive satisfactions for
> his symptoms as possible. The implication for the analyst
> is that he should refuse on principle to satisfy the patient's
> demands and to fulfill the roles which the patient tends to
> impose upon him. (Laplanche & Pontalis, 1973, p. 2)

Whether it is intentional or not - and it is hard to believe that there is no element of intention involved - this emphasis on neutrality and distance actually has the effect of enormously accentuating the power asymmetries present in the therapeutic encounter. The structure of the classical psychoanalytic situation is not simply one in which one person unavoidably has some power over another; everything that is done therein serves to in-

crease that power. The analyst remains mysterious while the client dis-
closes the most intimate recesses of her/himself; the analyst is silent while
the client speaks; the client is observed and the analyst invisible; and
everything that the client says is scrutinized for hidden meanings, so that
even criticism of the analyst is interpreted as belonging elsewhere. The
analyst can never be confronted, s/he epitomizes that subtle power that
slips away, unspoken but dominant. In theory, as everything that occurs
between client and analyst is analyzed, the uses of power may itself be examined; but this is always in the terms defined by the arc of psychoanalysis itself. All this suggests that the apparent non-interference of the traditional analyst is a charade built upon a denial of politics: being neutral,
passive, reflective is in many ways a means of avoiding articulation of the
actual power relations that psychoanalysis produces and thrives upon.

The alternative images of the analyst in the theories·discussed here
mostly represent her/him as a form of parent. As implied by all their
metaphors of holding and 'management,' object relations theorists concentrate on the role of the analyst as a maternal figure. Winnicott, in
particular, provides an account of therapy as utilization of an intuitive
personal knowledge of the client's needs that parallels the mother-infant
relationship, or is even a deliberate imitation of the 'natural' response of
a mother for her child. The analyst, acting as a 'good mother,' makes it
possible for the client to take into her/himself those split-off, projected
aspects of the psyche that are experienced as uncontrollable. Guntrip
(1968) formulates this idea in line with his own emphasis on the reality
aspects of therapy:

> 'Analyzing' is a male function, an intellectual activity of
> interpretation, but based on the female function of intui-
> tively knowing experienced ... through identification.
> Ultimately 'being there for the patient' in a stable and not
> a neurotic state is the female, maternal, and properly
> therapeutic function, which enables the patient to feel real
> and find his own proper self. (p. 360)

The assumptions in this passage concerning the essential differences between masculinity and femininity are fairly obviously ideological: that
maleness is intellectual and analytic, while female means maternal, containing, loving. Therapy, already defined as a process of remothering, is
also a 'female function,' this being both a term of approbation and a use
of conventional gender imagery. Leaving these assumptions unquestioned
feeds into the creation of an analytic practice which supports patriarchal
categories, even if the simple identity of these 'masculine' and 'feminine'

attributes with actual men and women is avoided. It also, through a specious division of labour between male and female, avoids confronting the actual patterns of domination that appear inside and outside analysis. Nevertheless, this kind of language is taken up by many therapists without much consideration, particularly by those troubled by the power elements of classical analysis described above. So Eichenbaum and Orbach (1982) emphasize the reality context of therapy as a way of reducing power imbalances, and also describe how the 'process of feeling that the little girl inside is accepted, understood and loved by the therapist is an extremely important part of the healing process' (p. 62). This kind of unquestioning modelling of therapy on an idealized maternal nurturance is presumably what Klein (1957) is referring to when criticizing analysts who fail to interpret their client's longing for reassurance and appreciation and instead respond to it through identification with the client's desire, with the result that they rush in and attempt immediately to alleviate anxieties instead of working with them. Nevertheless, Kleinians also use a maternal image of the analyst, albeit in a different way. Klein (1957) refers to the significance of "repeated experiences of the effectiveness and truth of the interpretations given" as an analogue of happy infantile experiences of being fed and loved, both of them leading to the internalization of the analyst/mother as a good object. More generally, the Kleinians' emphasis on projection and projective identification in therapy is an exact replication of their description of infantile development in the context of the interaction with the mother. It is not, however, that the analyst *replaces* the mother, as in object relations therapy, but that the processes exploited in analysis are the same as those in the infantile world, and act to install the analyst and, retrospectively, the mother as good internal objects. The analyst-as-mother is more than a metaphor, but less than reality.

Oddly, despite Freudian patrocentricity, there is a far weaker theoretical tradition of 'analyst as father' than 'analyst as mother.' In practice, the history of the psychoanalytic movement itself attests to the sway of authoritarian figures over acolytes of all schools, but it has proved much more difficult to construct an image of the analytic role around maleness than around the more acceptable (in object relations theory) or basic (Kleinian) foundation of mothering. Rieff (1966) suggests the importance of having an 'exemplary figure' with whom to identify if cure of any kind is to be forthcoming; the dangers of authoritarianism are overt in his argument. However, in general, it is not the explicit figure of a father that hovers over the analyst, but the implicit patriarchy involved in the manifestations of power present in the therapeutic setting. The way in which this infiltrates the classical notion of analyst as distant, neutral interpreter of psychic conflicts has already been described; the law-making paternal role provides an unarticulated substratum to this mode of practice. There is, in addition, a pattern by which analyst and client perpetuate this patriarchal power by leaving it unquestioned, un-analyzed. Fromm (1970) describes the "gentlemen's agreement" that often operates between client and therapist so as not to challenge existing relations or bring up any substantially new experience, while Gear, Hill, and Liendo (1981) suggest that the power relations inherent in 'thera-peutic' relationships have a sado-masochistic structure in which each partner needs the other to continue in their respective roles. Ingleby (1984) expresses this clearly: after noting the asymmetries of the power relations present in therapy, he suggests that it is an imbalance built into the very nature of psychoanalysis, which operates imperialistically on the values of the client:

> What the patient submits to is not the rule of the analyst,
> but the rule of *analysis*, to which the analyst is every bit as
> subject. The real authoritarianism of psychoanalysis lies,
> not in the domination of patient by analyst, but in the
> domination of both by analytic doctrine. (p. 51)

Too simple, perhaps, and it lets the actual person of the analyst off the hook too lightly. Perhaps not surprisingly it is from feminism that the most astute attack on the paternal analyst comes. Gallop (1982) provides a dazzling critique of the authority structure of analysis, arguing that at every point that it becomes fixed in a claim to dominance or 'mastery,' it also becomes patriarchal. She describes the French analyst Irigaray's op-position to the imposition of a definite 'grammar' of psychoanalysis, for instance as stated by Lacan, on the grounds of its colonization of the client's own speech:

> Irigaray's suspicion is that Lacanian discourse functions as
> some fundamental referent which any analysand's dis-
> course can only 'translate,' approximate to in some secon-
> dary, inadequate way. (p. 97)

In opposition to the perpetuation of the 'mastery' of analysis by the fath-er (Lacan, previously Freud), Gallop asserts the continually subversive nature of the unconscious, the way in which no-one can be its master; the analyst's position must always be undermined. Schneiderman (1980) places this argument in a more practical context by showing how in the practice of Lacanian analysis, the analyst is "a subjective participant in the experience of the transference," influencing what is said even though her/his intention is to let the analysand "speak what had heretofore been unspeakable - to find her/his own voice." This recognition itself moves some way towards demolishing analytic claims to truth: the analyst is not listening to the 'real' desire of the client, but is participating in its creation. The Lacanian enterprise is thus directed towards subverting its own authority, revealing the manner in which there are no absolute answers to the client's questions, no way of meeting her/his desire. Analysis in these terms has, indeed, the structure of patriarchy: there is mastery and phallocentrism, there is obedience to the word of Lacan. But it also contains, at times explicitly, a model for rebellion which asserts that the end of therapy is the recovery of a voice for the client's desire, and the dismantling of all claims to absolute authority. In this way, it recognizes the authority structures of analysis and intervenes in them directly, and in doing so provides a commentary on the linkages between power and change that operate in all therapeutic contexts.

References

Banton, R., Clifford, P., Frosh, S., Lousada, J., & Rosenthall, J. (1985). *The politics of mental health.* London: Macmillan Press.

Coward, R., & Ellis, J. (1977). *Language and materialism.* London: Routledge and Kegan Paul.

Eichenbaum, L., & Orbach, S. (1982). *Outside in...inside out.* Harmondsworth: Penguin.

Fromm, E. (1970). *The crisis of psychoanalysis.* Harmondsworth: Penguin.

Gallop, J. (1982). *Feminism and psychoanalysis.* London: Macmillan Press.

Gear, M. C., Hill, M. A., & Liendo, M. (1981). *Working through narcissism.* New York: Jason Aronson.

Guntrip, H. (1968). *Schizoid phenomena, object relations and the self.* London: The Hogarth Press.

Guntrip, H. (1973). *Psychoanalytic theory, therapy and the self.* New York: Basic Books.

Ingleby, D. (1984). The ambivalence of psychoanalysis. *Radical Science 15,* 39-71.

Klein, M. (1952). The orgins of transference. In M. Klein, *Envy and gratitude and other works.* New York: Delta.

Klein, M. (1957). Envy and gratitude. In M. Klein, *Envy and gratitude and other works.* New York: Delta.

Langs, R. (1976). *The therapeutic interaction, Vol. II.* New York: Jason Aronson.

Laplanche, J., & Pontalis, J-B. (1973). *The language of psychoanalysis.* London: The Hogarth Press.

Lasch, C. (1979). *The culture of narcissism.* London: Abacus.

Richards, B. (1984). Schizoid states and the market. In B. Richards (Ed.), *Capitalism and infancy.* London: Free Association Books.

Rieff, P. (1966). *The triumph of the therapeutic.* Harmondsworth: Penguin.

Sandler, J., Dare, C., & Holder, A. (1973). *The patient and the analyst.* London: Maresfield (Reprints, 1979).

Schneiderman, S. (1980). The other Lacan. In S. Schneiderman (Ed.), *Returning to Freud.* New Haven: Yale University Press.

Segal, H. (1981). *The work of Hanna Segal.* New York: Jason Aronson.

Winnicott, D. W. (1955). Clinical varieties of transference. In D. W. Winnicott, *Through paediatrics to psychoanalysis.* London: Hogarth Press.

Winnicott, D. W. (1956). Primary maternal preoccupation. In

D. W. Winnicott, *Through paediatrics to psychoanalysis.* London: The Hogarth Press.

Zetzel, E. R. (1956). Current concepts of transference. *Journal of Psychoanalysis, 37,* 369-376.

Current Issues in Theoretical Psychology
Wm J. Baker, M.E. Hyland, H. Van Rappard, A.W. Staats (Editors)
© Elsevier Science Publishers B.V. (North-Holland), 1987

SYSTEMS, CAUSALITY, AND TIME: A FRAMEWORK FOR THE INTEGRATION OF THEORIES OF SCHIZOPHRENIA

John Gosling

Hatfield Polytechnic
Hatfield, England

SUMMARY: This paper deals with the integration of theories expressed in different theoretical languages. Brief details of a conceptual schema for the classification of theories with different explanatory functions are presented and this is then applied to the special case of theories of schizophrenia. Certain abstract properties of theoretical languages are discussed and the paper concludes with a consideration of differences in the temporal characteristics of theoretical languages.

In recent years, a number of distinct hypotheses have emerged with regard to the causation of schizophrenia. Firstly, several studies have provided convincing evidence that there exists a hereditary basis for the disorder (Heston & Denny, 1968; Kety, Rosenthal, Wender, & Schulsinger, 1968). Secondly, research in neurochemistry and pharmacology has pointed to the role of the neurotransmitter dopamine. The current hypothesis is that the clinical state of schizophrenia is associated with raised levels of activity in the dopaminergic regions of the brain (Iverson, 1978). Thirdly, there is evidence that in roughly half the cases of new admissions for schizophrenia, the onset of the illness is preceded by a major change in the life circumstances of the patient (a life event) occurring within the three weeks prior to admission (Birley & Brown, 1970; Leff & Vaughn, 1980). Finally, a growing number of studies have shown that the emotional characteristics of the patient's immediate family are very strongly related to relapse after an earlier episode of the disorder. The probability of relapse for patients whose relatives are critical, hostile and emotionally overinvolved (i.e., high on *expressed emotion*) is significantly higher than for patients whose relatives are less emotional (Brown, Birley, & Wing, 1972; Vaughn & Leff, 1976). Furthermore, the most recent work in this field indicates that high expressed emotion in the families of adolescents is associated with subsequent schizophrenic diagnoses in later adult life (Doane, West, Goldstein, Rodnick, & Jones, 1981; Valone, Norton, Goldstein, & Doane, 1983).

These distinct hypotheses may be conceived of as different asser-
tions as to the causation of schizophrenia. That they are different asser-
tions does not, however, imply that they are incompatible with one
another. They deal with different types of causal influence and each in
its own way may be relevant to an eventual understanding of the disorder.
The first problem faced by the theoretical psychologist is therefore to find
a means of describing the relationships between these different theoretical
approaches and to specify, in a precise manner, how each may contribute
to an integrated theory of schizophrenia. The second problem which must
be dealt with is that of the incommensurability of the theoretical languages in which the different hypotheses are expressed. The languages
differ in their semantics and in their syntax and there exists no obvious
set of rules by which causal relations expressed in one language may be
re-expressed in terms of other languages.

If integration between theoretical languages is to be achieved, some
such set of translation rules will clearly be needed. However, the development of translation rules must be founded upon a clear understanding
of the differences which exist between the explanatory functions of the
theories characteristically associated with each theoretical language. That
is, a *classificatory* schema is required into which existing substantive
theories may be placed. The purpose of the schema should be to enable
the role of any given psychological theory to be precisely specified in relation to a given psychological context. As a result of such contrasts, the
task of relating causal phenomena which are characteristically expressed in
different languages (for instance, the task of explaining the influence of
life events on subsequent dopaminergic functioning in schizophrenics) will
be considerably simplified.

The following section will present in outline the details of such a
classificatory schema. Due to limitations of space, only a brief description is possible. A more complete account may be found in a previous
article (Gosling, 1985).

A General Schema for the Classification of Psychological Theory

It should firstly be emphasized that the schema to be presented is
no more than a schema. That is, it asserts nothing; neither in psychological nor in philosophical terms. It is, rather, a set of suggestions for the
organization of theories about systems and is designed particularly to apply to theories about systems which change in their manner of functioning
over time. It is therefore especially relevant to theories in the biological
and social sciences.

The schema centres on the concept of *mechanism*. The term mechanism in this context should not necessarily be taken to refer only to *mechanistic* mechanisms (i.e., structures defined in terms of some mechanical analogy). The term is to be understood in its most general sense and could therefore be as easily applied to the psychological mechanisms of humanistic psychology as to the mechanisms of cognitive psychology. Examples of *mechanisms* that might figure in a theory are mechanisms for regulating blood-sugar level, mechanisms for preserving cognitive consistency, or mechanisms for defending the *ego* against the *superego*.

In general terms, a mechanism might be defined as a feature of a system which permits a wide but finite range of system behaviour, both internal and external. The characteristics of a mechanism may be considered in terms of those which are constant over the life of the system and those which are variable. The constant characteristics of a mechanism are those which distinguish it from other mechanisms within the system and which give rise to a particular class of system behaviours. To take a mechanical example, the constant features of the carburetor of a motor car are those which (a) distinguish it from the fuel pump and the alternator and (b) which, among other things, govern the rate of fuel delivery to the engine and various consequent aspects of engine performance.

The variable characteristics of a mechanism are those which permit the mechanism to function in different *modes*. The mechanism may be *set* in different ways and different settings will enable different subclasses of system phenomena to occur. In the case of the carburettor, for instance, each setting will be associated with a particular set of relationships between the operating conditions (e.g., depression of accelerator pedal, position of choke control, etc.) and the performance of the engine. The modes of a mechanism are therefore the several distinct manners in which that mechanism may operate.

If a system may be described in terms of the mechanisms which govern its internal and external behaviour, then the state of the system at any point in time will be given by a description of the modes in which each of its mechanisms is currently operating. We may therefore refer to the *mode-state* of a system. A mode-state may be thought of as a state of the system which is associated with a particular manner of system functioning.

Coming now to the question of theory construction, the mechanisms of the system must be described in terms of a theoretical language, that is, a *mechanism language* (L_M) must be adopted. To some extent, the choice of theoretical language is arbitrary: the theorist may choose whichever language most obviously suits the problem at hand or is most in line with his or her theoretical inclinations. However, it is also the case that particular characteristics of a given language may impose restrictions upon its adequacy as a mechanism language. This point will be discussed in more detail below. For the present, the languages of cognitive psychology or biological psychology may be taken as typical examples of mechanism languages.

Once a mechanism language has been chosen, a theory about the system may then be cast in it. This may be referred to as the *mechanism theory*, or Θ_M, and its purpose is twofold. Firstly, it should describe, in terms of the given language, the mechanisms which underly system behaviour (both internal and external), and the means by which inputs to the system give rise to particular system behaviours. The precise details of the mechanism theory are not relevant to present concerns since these will be determined, on the one hand, by experimental data and, on the other, by the ingenuity of the theoretician. The second purpose of the mechanism theory will be to provide a description of the possible modes in which each mechanism may operate. In other words, it will provide an account of the range of possible modes of functioning of system mechanisms and thus of the range of possible behaviours of which the system is capable.

As it stands so far, the *mechanism theory* provides all that is required to describe system functioning in any given mode. However, it provides no means of describing system development and change. A second type of theory is therefore required to go alongside Θ_M and this may be referred to as a *system development theory*, or Θ_{SD}. Θ_{SD} will be expressed in mechanism language L_M and its purpose will be to describe the mechanisms by which mechanism modes may change. Θ_{SD} therefore describes higher-order mechanisms which enable the switching of the modes of lower-order mechanisms. Furthermore, it should also provide a list of both external (i.e., input) and internal system phenomena which are hypothesized to initiate transitions between mode-states of the system.

Θ_M and Θ_{SD}, taken together, constitute a general theory for the system. The theory is *general* in that it will explain the range of possible behaviours of the system. It is also general in that it is not expressed in relation to any particular set of circumstances. However, for many purposes in psychology, we have need of *particular* theories rather than general ones: that is, theories which describe how a particular course of system development will arise from a particular set of circumstances. This is especially the case in clinical psychology where theories of aetiology play an important role. Aetiology is the study of the development of psychiatric disorder. The intention of an aetiological theory is to relate a particular set of pathogenic circumstances to a particular sequence of changes in a person's functioning. An aetiological theory is therefore a theory about particular transitions between particular states of the system (person). Each transition will, in principle, be relatable to a particular set of pathogenic circumstances. To incorporate aetiological theories (and other similar theories of particular system development) into the schema, a further general type of theory must be defined.

This new type of theory should describe transitions between mode states of the system and may be referred to as a *mode-state sequential stage theory,* or M-SST for short. The theory describes a sequence of stages of system development, each characterized by a transition from one mode state to another (see Figure 1). The most important point to note about the M-SST is that system development is described in terms of the same set of theoretical principles as used for the general description of system functioning. System functioning is described in terms of system mechanisms and system development is described in terms of the transitions between the different modes of functioning of system mechanisms. The particular relevance of this point to the integration of different types of causal theories of schizophrenia will be discussed below. For the moment, it will suffice to emphasize that the special characteristics of the M-SST are rarely, if ever, to be found in existing aetiological theories. For instance, the *life event* theory of schizophrenia mentioned earlier states merely that Event X (a life event) occurring at some point in the patient's recent experience gives rise to State Y (schizophrenia) at some later point in time. To offer theoretical respectability to the assertion, life event theorists have interposed the loosely defined construct of *arousal* between X and Y; that is, life events are said to increase the arousal level of the patient and this in turn causes the onset of an acute episode of schizophrenia (see Sturgeon, Kuipers, Berkowitz, Turpin, & Leff, 1981). But in no sense does this offer an *explanation* of the effects of life events on system functioning.

A truly explanatory account would require that the influence of the event on the system be firstly construed in terms compatible with the theoretical language used to describe mechanisms. The life event would be, as it were, *translated* into a form suitable for input to the theoretical system which is used to describe system functioning. The application of the general theories, Θ_M and Θ_{SD}, would then enable a description of the ensuing course of development of the system until some ultimate schizo-

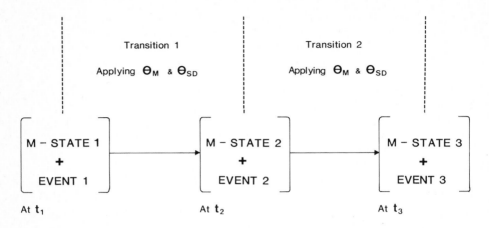

Figure 1. The form of a mode-state sequential-stage theory. (The theory describes two mode-state transitions: from Mode-State 1 to Mode-State 2, and from Mode-State 2 to Mode-State 3. Θ_M = Mechansim Theory, Θ_{SD} = System Development Theory.)

phrenic state were reached. The latter would be described in mechanism language (e.g., in terms of current abnormalities in biochemical or cognitive functioning) and would be correlated with clinical observations of schizophrenic symptoms. The general point to be made here is that by noting what would be required by the general classificatory schema, existing theories may be judged in relation to the specifications of the schema and their deficiencies or limitations become more readily apparent.

Returning now to Figure 1, the diagram appears to suggest that transitions between states can be explained entirely in terms of environmental inputs. However, the schema may be elaborated to deal also with the effects of internal phenomena which are ultimately explainable in terms of genetically determined individual differences. Due to limitations of space, only a brief outline of this can be given and further details may be found in Gosling (1985). The elaboration of the general schema presumes that Θ_M, the theory for describing system mechanisms, will vary slightly for each individual. Thus, Θ_{M1} is the theory which describes how mechanisms operate for Person 1, and Θ_{M2} is the theory which describes how system mechanisms operate for Person 2. Such person-specific mechanism theories are, of course, all very similar for members of the same species. The point is that, when comparing individuals, the ground rules of system functioning will be found to differ. That is, people are genetically different. If, however, individual differences are ignored, as is the case in much of psychology, Θ_{M1}, Θ_{M2} ... Θ_{Mn} will be assumed to be equivalent and all equal to Θ_M. This is the assumption that psychological mechanisms are the same for all people and can be described by a single general psychological theory.

Another issue arising from Figure 1 is that of whether the M-SST should describe each and every state of the system in the course of its development. In an aetiological theory of schizophrenia, for instance, this would clearly not be necessary. Theories are selective. They describe what has to be described and no more. The problem for the theorist is to describe the development of the system from one point in time to another point later on. Each stage in the description may be likened to a series of stepping stones; the question of which stones we happen to place our feet on is, to some extent, a matter of choice. To put this another way, there is no need for an M-SST to be pedantic. The theory describes only what is necessary for a given purpose. By the same token, it is equally unnecessary for an aetiological theory to describe the mode of functioning of each and every mechanism within a given mode-state of the system. In any actual M-SST, the mode-state description will be limited only to the description of those mechanisms which are relevant to the theoretical problem at hand.

The Characteristics of a Developmental Theory of Pathology

Turning now to the requirements of an integrated theory of schizophrenia, what should such a theory contain? Firstly, the theory should provide a description of the schizophrenic state: that is, a description of how the schizophrenic system (or schizophrenic person) functions. It should describe the behaviour (both internal and external) of the system and should explain how those behaviours can be understood in terms of system mechanisms. The description of the schizophrenic state need not be exhaustive. It will be necessary to describe only those mechanisms which are operating in ways specific to schizophrenic systems and which underly specifically schizophrenic behaviours. In the terms of the general schema, an *M-state description* for schizophrenia is required. The M-state description will be selective, only describing what is necessary to enable us to understand why schizophrenics are different from non-schizophrenics. This selective M-state description will, in effect, be a description of *current system abnormalties* or, in terms of conventional psychiatric terminology, a *theory of pathology*.

Given a description of the pathological state, the theory will then need to describe the particular course of system development which gave rise to that pathological state. In other words a theory of aetiology is required. To avoid metaphysical explanation, it must be presumed that some set of discrete events (either internal or external to the system) have, at their time of occurrence, modified the *then-current* state of the system. Furthermore, it must be presumed that the states of the system at all future points in time will be at least partially determined by these historical influences. In theory, therefore, it should be possible to describe a progression of states, beginning at a point in time when the individual was considered normal and continuing to a point in time at which he or she is considered schizophrenic. An aetiological theory cast in this form might be referred to as a *developmental theory of pathology* (see Figure 2). The intention of such a theory is to follow the development of pathology through each of its stages by observing the gradual change in the functioning of the system.

The theoretical relationship between external pathogenic factors and the end-state will not merely be a simple correlational or predictive one. Rather, *the effects of such factors will be described in terms of their immediate influence upon system functioning.* The developmental theory of pathology has of course the form of an M-State Sequential-Stage Theory (M-SST). Each description of system functioning in the diagram corresponds to an M-State description and, as is the case for any M-SST, the influence of external events in triggering transitions between mode states will be described in terms of the *same* set of principles which are used to describe normal system functioning, viz., the principles of Θ_M and Θ_{SD}

The developmental theory of pathology provides a blueprint for at least two levels of integration. Firstly, the traditional distinction between aetiology and pathology has now been removed. Secondly, the developmental theory describes the manner in which a simple correlational aetiological theory may be translated into the language used for the main description of system functioning (the mechanism language, L_M). For instance, a theory which states that phenomenon X leads to psychiatric disorder Y is now translatable into a more general theory of developmental changes in, say, cognitive or biological functioning. Figure 3 illustrates the distinction between the relatively simplistic means of accounting for the effects of life events mentioned earlier and the form of explanation used by the developmental theory of pathology. The hypothetical construct, *arousal*, which is linked in an unspecified manner to the correlated observations is replaced in the developmental theory by a truly explanatory sequential-stage theory.

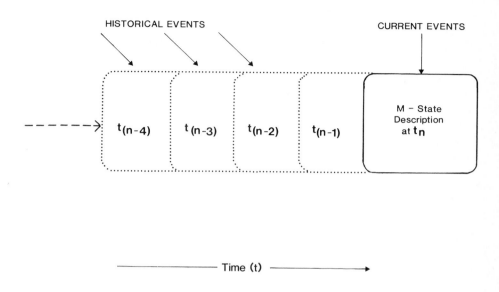

Figure 2. The form of a developmental theory of pathology. (The theory describes both the influence of historical pathogenic events upon system development and the influence of current events upon current pathological functioning.)

In one respect the discussion of aetiology has been oversimplified. Just as the earlier discussion of M-SST's made no reference to genetically determined individual differences, neither have these been considered in relation to the developmental theory of pathology. However, since the latter has essentially the form of an M-SST, the solution is in principle identical. Θ_M is assumed to be identical for all individuals. If individual differences are to be taken into account, then Θ_M must be stated in slightly varying form for each individual (e.g., Θ_{M1} for Person 1, etc.). In other words, the way one person's mechanisms work is slightly different from the way another person's mechanisms work. Furthermore, the idiosyncratic features of mechanism functioning in a subgroup of the population at large may be taken to be responsible for the predispostion of the members of that group to the development of schizophrenia, given that they are subsequently exposed to appropriate environmental circumstances.

Predispositions are of course not only genetically but also environmentally determined. A predisposition may be thought of as a particular tendency to react to a given set of circumstances in a particular manner.

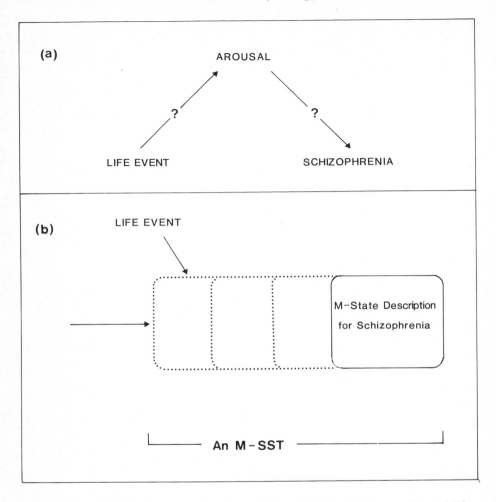

Figure 3. Figure 3(a) illustrates a simple correlational aetiological theory. Figure 3(b)
illustrates how the construct of Arousal in the correlational theory is replaced in the developmental theory of pathology by a mode-state sequential-stage theory (M-SST).

Such a tendency will be a reflection of a particular mode of functioning,
or particular mode-state, of the system at the time of occurrence of those
circumstances. Current mode-state will be determined jointly by the particular history of environmental circumstances experienced by the system
and the genetically determined idiosyncracies of functioning of the system

in question as expressed in the system-specific general theories, Θ_{Mi} and Θ_{SDi}. The latter will determine the particular nature of mode-state transitions for the given system in response to the given set of environmental circumstances. There is insufficient space to discuss this in detail, but further details of how the schema tackles genetic-environmental interactions in the determination of predispositions may be found in Gosling (1985).

Characteristics of Theoretical Languages

It is all very well to argue that external pathogenic factors such as life events should be related to ongoing system functioning in some ideal theory of schizophrenia. But, in practice, such a task might initially seem quite impossible, given the current limited state of our knowledge. However, a consideration of the nature of theoretical language used in psychology may provide one or two clues as to how to proceed.

Considering firstly the biological languages of psychology (such as the languages of psychophysiology, physiological psychology, neuropsychology and neurochemistry), these appear to be largely oriented to the description of structure and system processes of relatively brief duration. Consequently, they are well suited to the description of mechanisms, in the sense in which this term has been used above. On the other hand, the biological languages are generally rather poor at describing transitions between different modes of functioning. The operation of mechanisms *within* modes can be handled relatively easily but the higher-order mechanisms governing transitions between modes are less easily dealt with. One reason for this may be that the biological sciences deal largely with equilibrium states of living systems. In such states, much of the activity of the system is cyclic and repetitive. It is only when the state of equilibrium is radically disturbed that a *new form* of equilibrium must be found by the system; and the setting up of a new equilibrium state will in many cases correspond with what has been described above as a change in the mode-state of the system. The system will have made the transition to a new mode of functioning. For these reasons, the biological languages of psychology are excellent languages in which to cast mechanism theories, but they do not lend themselves so easily to system development theories which describe transitions between different modes of functioning.

Much the same can be said of the languages of cognitive psychology. As with the biological languages, they describe structures and the mechanisms arising from those structures; although, in this case, both the structures and their associated mechanisms are analogical in nature. Consequently, these languages are also well adapted to the description of mechanisms.

Very different from the cognitive and biological languages is the language of learning theory. Firstly, learning theory contains no description of mechanisms. This is obviously the case. Learning theories have arisen from the tradition of *behaviourism* and it is antithetical to that tradition to describe mechanisms of any sort whatsoever (although the more recent cognitive versions of learning theory, for instance, those of Bindra, 1978 or Bolles, 1979, are exceptions to this general rule). However, learning theory does contain a sort of system development theory, but one which is difficult to recognize in terms of the description of Θ_{SD} given earlier. A system development theory, it has been argued, should describe the mechanisms by which mechanism-mode transitions occur. The learning theory concept which is closest to that of *mechanism-mode* would be a particular stimulus-response association, and the term *mode-state* would correspond to the entire set of associations characteristic of the organism's behavioural repertoire at any point in time. The learning theory version of Θ_{SD} would therefore state that *certain special types of input will lead to certain particular changes in mode-state.* A special input might be *CS+US simultaneously presented,* and the theory would further explain that inputs of this particular sort will cause a mode-state transition such that, in the new state, the probability of CR, given CS, is slightly greater than in the previous mode-state. The learning theory version of Θ_{SD} therefore states the circumstances under which mode-state transitions will occur but offers no explanation of these transitions in terms of the mechanisms which govern the general behaviour of the system.

In contrast, therefore, to the biological languages, learning theory is relatively rich in developmental constructs but possesses very few constructs for dealing with system structure and functioning. It is thus particularly well suited for describing the effects of events located at discrete points in time upon external system behaviour at later points in time.

This contrast between the language of learning theory and the languages of biological psychology illustrates that in relation to the earlier proposed *ideal* form for a theory of schizophrenia (viz., the developmental theory of pathology) they each have advantages and disadvantages. Learning theory is an excellent aetiology language and provides a ready explanation for how traumatic conditioning experiences, for instance, can lead to phobias in later life (cf. Little Albert!). But lacking any account of mechanisms, it fails badly in the description of end-state pathology.

Biological and cognitive languages, on the other hand, provide excellent theories of end-state pathology (cf. the dopamine theory of schizophrenia) but have little to offer in the explanation of aetiology.

A related issue is that of the differing temporal characteristics of theoretical languages. Certain groups of languages, particularly the biological and cognitive languages, employ what might be called *microdimensions* of time. In other words, these languages are used to describe processes which have characteristically brief durations, often measurable in only fractions of seconds. On the other hand, languages such as those of social psychiatry and learning theory tend to employ *macrodimensions* of time. These languages generally describe relationships between phenomena which are separated by intervals of minutes, hours or years. Microdimensions, on the whole, tend to be associated with mechanism theories which describe the general manner of functioning of a system within any given mode-state. Macrodimensions tend to be associated with mode-state sequential stage theories which describe transitions over time between different modes of functioning. To some extent, this issue is related to a further one; that of the *construability* (in the Kellian sense) of an event in relation to a given theoretical language. Events may be considered as either *normal* or *extraordinary* in relation to a particular language. For instance, events occurring at the synapse can be easily construed within the language of biochemistry, but are not at all construable within the language of social psychiatry. We might say that such events are normal with respect to biochemical language but extraordinary with respect to the language of social psychiatry.

The problem of theoretical integration in the field of schizophrenia will be to some extent a problem of dealing with the relationships between the microdimensions associated with descriptions of pathology and the macrodimensions which are associated with descriptions of aetiology. Furthermore, it will be necessary to find a means of developing theoretical devices which will enable the translation of events which are extraordinary with respect to a particular language into a form in which they become normal with respect to that language. For instance, if a theory of the effects of life events in schizophrenia is to be related to a theory of biochemical dysfunction, it will be necessary to use theoretical devices by means of which a life event description may be translated into a form in which the event, or its consequences for the system, become interpretable in terms of the language of biochemistry. However, a discussion of such devices is beyond the scope of this paper.

References

Bindra, D. (1978). How adaptive behaviour is produced: a perceptual-motivational alternative to response-reinforcement. *The Behavioural and Brain Sciences, 1,* 40-49.

Birley, J. L. T., & Brown, G. W. (1970). Crises and life changes preceeding the onset or relapse of cases of acute schizophrenia. *British Journal of Psychiatry, 116,* 327-333.

Bolles, R. C. (1979). *Learning theory* (2nd ed.). New York: Holt, Rinehart and Winston.

Brown, G. W., Birley, J. L. T., & Wing, J. K. (1972). Influence of family life on the course of schizophrenic disorders: a replication. *British Journal of Psychiatry, 121,* 241-258.

Doane, J. A., West, K. L., Goldstein, M. J., Rodnick, E. H., & Jones, J. E. (1981). Parental communication deviance and affective style: predictors of subsequent schizophrenia disorders in vulnerable adolescents. *Archives of General Psychiatry, 38,* 674-685.

Gosling, J. (1985). The classification of theory in psychology: a prerequisite for theoretical integration. Manuscript submitted for publication.

Heston, L. L., & Denny, D. (1968). Interactions between early life experience and biological factors in schizophrenia. In D. Rosenthal & S. S. Kety (Eds.), *The transmission of schizophrenia* (pp. 363-376). New York: Pergamon Press.

Iverson, L. L. (1978). Biochemical and pharmacological studies. In J. K. Wing (Ed.), *Schizophrenia: towards a new synthesis* (pp. 89-116). London: Academic Press.

Kety, S. S., Rosenthal, D., Wender, P. H., & Schulsinger, F. (1978). The types and prevalence of mental illness in the biological and adoptive familes of adopted schizophrenics. In D. Rosenthal & S. S. Kety (Eds.), *The transmission of schizophrenia* (pp. 345-362). New York: Pergamon Press.

Leff, J. P., & Vaughn, C. E. (1980). The interaction of life events and relatives' expressed emotion in schizophrenia and depressive neurosis. *British Journal of Psychiatry, 136,* 146-153.

Sturgeon, D., Kuipers, L., Berkowitz, R., Turpin, G., & Leff, J. (1981). Psychophysiological responses of schizophrenic patients to high and low expressed emotion relatives. *British Journal of Psychiatry, 92,* 399-407.

Valone, K., Norton, J. P., Goldstein, M. J., Doane, J. A. (1983). Parental expressed emotion and affective style in an adolescent sample at risk for schizophrenia spectrum disorders. *Journal of Abnormal Psychology, 92,* 399-407.

Vaughn, C. E., & Leff, J. P. (1976). The influence of family and social factors on the course of psychiatric illness: a comparison of schizophrenic and depressed neurotic patients. *British Journal of Psychiatry, 129,* 125-137.

Current Issues in Theoretical Psychology
Wm J. Baker, M.E. Hyland, H. Van Rappard, A.W. Staats (Editors)
© Elsevier Science Publishers B.V. (North-Holland), 1987

PSYCHOLOGY AS DISCOURSE: TOWARDS A GENERAL

PARADIGM FOR PSYCHOLOGY THEORY[1]

Richard Hammersley

University of Strathclyde
Glasgow, Scotland

SUMMARY: Psychology has sought a single, objective base from which to develop scientifically. Such a base is impossible, as there can be no privileged observation methods providing unquestionable facts. There are only real observation tools which can be used to observe other real things. Observations depend upon both the nature of the tools employed and the nature of the things so observed. As the subject matter of psychology is primarily symbolic, psychology theories (including observation tools) and individual psychology are both symbolic. This means that theory and the individual can exchange symbols and thereby affect each other. In this sense, psychology cannot be objective, for the nature of the observation tools used can change the system being observed in non-trivial ways. Instead, psychology can be considered to be discourse between the observer or theorist and the subject. Such discourse could become a paradigm for psychology theory.

Theoretical change in modern psychology has typically been destructive, the adoption of a new research program leading to the abandonment of the old one by some and its increasingly entrenched defense by others without any serious attempt at synthesis. The last century has included a variety of attempts to create or discover a fundamental grounding for psychology; an absolute and objective base which would enable the systematic and scientific development of the discipline. Candidates for this base have included introspection, behavior, logical structure, phenomena, and linguistic analysis. Assuming that psychology could be a unified discipline, in Kuhn's (1962) terms, psychology is preparadigmatic and psychologists have tended to imagine that a paradigm would provide them with some set of facts, or methods which would become the buil-

[1]The ideas herein were first developed in my PhD thesis while MRC scholar at the Applied Psychology Unit in Cambridge. Most of this paper was developed at the University of Lethbridge while I was in receipt of a grant from the Alberta Law Foundation. Many people's thoughts are rewritten into this work, but I would like to especially thank Keith Humphrey, John Morton, Nick Radin, and John Vokey, also Arthur Staats for many editorial suggestions.

ding-blocks of psychology.

There has been considerable debate over the nature of paradigms which has passed by most psychologists, especially the more empirically-oriented ones who view theory primarily as a means for enabling observation. These empiricists view theory as a means of deriving methodology and, putting the cart before the horse, tend to loosely refer to methods as paradigms. When more abstract theoretical ideas are discussed at all, the utility of the empiricist's favorite methods in generating observational data is used as validation of the theory underlying those methods. In practice, there are many different methods for making observations and this leads, as Bhaskar (1979) has stated, to excessive tolerance of divergent theories which in turn - in the absence of any reason to change - leads to conservative preference for well-known theories coupled with whimsical changes of theoretical fashion. For example, I recently (to be reported in Hammersley, in preparation 1) attempted to survey the changing use of some cognitive technical terms ('image,' 'schema,' 'association,' and 'rehearsal') over a period of five years, but I could not find any authors whose vocabulary repeatedly included such terms, never mind whether they were used consistently. Yet, the information-processing approach is generating a vast amount of research which is in itself supposed to serve as an index of the approach's vitality and progress. There must be an alternative to such sheer proliferation of findings and ideas. Paradigms do not unify at the level of methodology, but at a more abstract level. Operating within a paradigm allows scientists to make diverse findings coherent and often implies new methods rather than validating old ones. Psychology is rich in methods and deficient in paradigms.

What this paper initiates is a paradigm for psychology. Psychology's current diversity is due to the search for a paradigm being confused with the search for a fixed and objective domain of psychological facts. That is, psychologists have sought methods of treating their subjects as objects. This attempted *objectivism* can be found in writers as diverse as Husserl (1977), who equated phenomenological life with objective facts, Watson (1977/1944), who equated behavioral observations with objective facts, and Fodor (1980), who equated the subject's internal structure with objective facts. In each case, the observer (or the observational method for phenomenology) is somehow separated from the observations made and is usually ignored or regarded as entirely passive. In contrast, this paper will propose that it is the very relationship between observer and subject which can provide us with a paradigmatic framework for understanding psychology in general. In consequence, we must abandon any hope of being able to treat our subjects as objects.

Realism

A viable alternative to objectivism has already been proposed. The realists (e.g., Bhaskar, 1978, 1979; Harré & Secord, 1972) have argued that objectivism is impossible because the Humeian model of inference cannot work (see Bhaskar, 1978, for a proof of this) and also because the idea of 'objective' facts presupposes some observer of those facts. As the observer must be outside the facts, the observer cannot be reduced to objective facts. Rather than ending up with a single, scientific realm of observable and verifiable facts, objectivism ends up with two separate realms, one observable and 'objective' and the other 'subjective' and therefore closed to scientific study. Oddly enough, a behavioral objectivist and a phenomenological objectivist directly disagree about which realm is which, experiential states being subjective to the former and objective to the latter. Similarly, there is still a debate in philosophy of science over whether theory determines the observations which can be made (as in Kuhn's 1962 paradigms) and everything is subjective (Feyerabend, 1975), or whether the observations determine the theory (as in Popper, 1963) and observations are objective but theories are conjecture. Historically, neither of these positions is correct (Krige, 1980). The realists seek to provide an account of science which replaces two or more realms with a single real world. According to Bhaskar (1978), the fact that science is possible suggests that there is a real world with determinable properties, but those properties are not to be confused with any single class of observables. To summarize realism, real properties belong to the real world, not to our observations of the world. For example, hardness is a property of rocks which can be measured with the correct equipment. Hardness is not a property of the measurement. However, the measurement, being equally real, has its own properties. What is measured depends upon both the rock and the measuring tools used ('tools' here include both material and conceptual devices). If all we have is a hammer and the rock is too hard to damage then we cannot measure its hardness. For an objectivist this would mean that the rock's hardness is not a fact. For a realist this means that the rock is hard, but that this property (or *power* to use Harré's (1970) term) cannot be measured. Science often assumes that unmeasurable powers really exist, as when some of the heaviest and most unstable periodic elements were postulated prior to their discovery on the basis of the powers of known elements.

The realists argue that science, whatever individual scientists believe, cannot operate in an objectivist manner. In particular, prediction of an inductive sort is never possible. When 'predictions' are seemingly made these are consequences of the nature of the real world, rather than of the nature our hypothetico-deductive system. Using the example of the periodic table again, the postulation of the heavier elements was due to a belief in the real powers of the elements and not to a valid sequence of inferences. For Harré (1970), the term 'prediction' is saturated with the concept of induction and should therefore be abandoned. However, the realist approach allows something akin to prediction, but on the basis of a model of reality rather than on the basis of induction. In general, such anticipation is possible because of our expectation that real things have stable powers, although this does not mean that things will always interact with our observation tools in the same way. When prediction (from here on used in the realist sense of anticipation rather than formal prediction) is possible it is because we are observing in a closed system. A closed system is one where we have control of or means of compensating for all powers. Closure requires a model of the system being observed and a model of the tools being used in observation. Predictions realized in this manner are one important aim of science, but they cannot be used to automatically validate the model which was used to generate them. In fact, there are no automatic validation procedures.

In summary, the realists have argued that objectivism is unworkable because it depends upon the existence of the subjective. Realism denies that there is any distinction between objective and subjective and assumes that there is one reality which can be modelled and observed.

Observation Systems

Implicit in the realist position is the notion of an observation system where observations are relative to the tools used, the observer's model of the material to be observed, and the observer's less coherent assumptions. In contrast, objectivist observations are taken to be objective data and, in consequence, the roles of the observer and observation tools are relegated to the status of 'methodological problems' which must be solved rather than incorporated into theory.

Observation systems can be both open and closed. In a closed system, the combination of the model and tools allows control or compensation for all relevant powers. Closure varies depending upon what one is trying to observe. For example, although the solar system can be treated as closed for many astrophysical observations, it remains open when trying to account for eccentricities in the orbits of the outer planets. Bhaskar (1979) argued that in social science observation systems are rarely closed, because the people being observed themselves have control over what is observed. Attempts to construct closed observation systems in psychology are all too often invitations for the subjects to knowingly mimic the powers which we are trying to observe in a closed system. For example, it is possible that conditioning in adult humans does not occur without the subjects being aware of the contingencies involved (Brewer, 1974). Alternatively, closing a psychological observation system may impose such constraints on the subjects that they can only behave in the manner expected. The most common way of doing this is to 'test' one's model against an absurd, if not impossible, null-hypothesis. For example, any effects of stimulus structure whatsoever have been interpreted as evidence for memory schemata (Alba & Hasher, 1983). The only acceptable support for the null-hypothesis would be subjects performing entirely at random with respect to the stimulus.

A more detailed example should clarify the concept of a closed system: To prevent rehearsal in memory experiments, it is conventional to make subjects count backwards in threes from some large number during the delay period. Counting backwards is supposed to be an observation tool which prevents rehearsal and thereby allows us to study the powers of memory without rehearsal. However, ignoring subjective reports, counting backwards is an uncalibrated observation tool, for the only evidence that it actually prevents rehearsal is a subsequent reduction in memory performance. This reduction is what we wanted to study in the first place, so the total observation system is circular. This circularity means that it is closed, but it remains a serious problem to decide whether what was found inside this system will apply outside it. Notice that in this example closure is dependent on the cooperation of the subjects (if they refuse to count backwards then the results will change). Notice also that there is no independent means of determining whether the observation system is really closed or not.

In order to decide whether a specific observation system is closed or not we at least require a model of the observation tools which has been developed independently of whatever it is we are observing. The well-known refusal of skeptics to look through Galileo's telescope was based on a serious doubt that it could show them anything reliable (Krige, 1980). By now, telescopes are understood and observations made with them are not normally explained away by postulating some unknown properties of telescopes. However, if the objects observed are UFOs or other inexplicable objects then skeptics may well prefer to question the veracity of the observation tool rather than to modify their beliefs about what is possible.

There is no independent and objective model of counting backwards, or of many other psychological observation tools. Yet, such tools
are still used. If these tools have not been objectively validated, then how
can they be used? In practice psychologists do not operate as objectivists.
The reason for believing that counting backwards hinders rehearsal is that
there are our own and our subject's reports to go on. Unfortunately,
these reports have never been made into a theory of counting backwards
as an observation tool, because subjective reports as data are usually considered scientifically embarrassing and tend to be excluded from 'archival'
psychology journals even if they are admitted in less formal forms of discourse. In general, because of the lip-service paid to objectivism,
although subjective ideas are essential to psychology they are only retained in the most sloppy and unsystematic way. The ultimate rationale
for many theoretical concepts appears to be that they are subjectively
convincing to the theoretician. The normal piece of trickery used to justify the subjectively convincing is to assume that whatever is convincing is
objectively real. For example, in psycholinguistics, everything from single
vocable features to entire bodies of discourse have been regarded as physically present stimuli whose nature can be objectively determined. Such
manoeuvers create apparently closed observation systems by including
subjective concepts disguised as objective ones.

In short, a closed observation system should consist of a model of
the observation tools and a model of what is being observed. Although
these models may be more or less separate, it is always possible to explain
observations by changing our model of the tools rather than our model of
the observed. It might be better to regard closed observation systems as
closable systems, for closure is never effortless nor absolutely certain. In
psychology, observation systems are often closed by circular definitions of
the observation tools and equating the observer's model of what is observed with 'reality.' Parts of the observer's model are usually subjective
and for this reason (which is not a good reason) neglected or disguised.
From a realist approach, there is nothing fundamentally unsound about
subjective concepts, for they are real, so theories should be explicit in
their subjective assumptions.

Open Systems

According to Harré and Secord (1972) and Bhaskar (1979), open
systems are the opposite of closed ones. Despite the importance which
these authors ascribe to open systems in social science, they tend to discuss them in terms of the properties they lack. Translating into this
paper's terminology, an observation system is open if any or all of the

following are true:

1. There are no available observation tools (even if such tools exist elsewhere). For example, without a thermometer we cannot observe the boiling temperature of water to be 100 degrees centigrade. As a psychological example, we cannot directly measure percepts, but can only use some report or report-like index of perception (see Lian, 1981).

2. The observation tools are such that their use alters the system being observed in ways which are not themselves understood or possible to compensate for. For example, the pattern of breakage in a flawless pane of glass (i.e., one which only has flaws which are too minute to measure) cannot be predicted except by breaking the glass (Bateson, 1979). As a psychological example, psychotherapy may, while 'uncovering' underlying mental traumas, make the client resemble the therapuetic model (Lacan, 1978), while any attempt to independently record what the client would have been like without therapy may change the client in other ways.

3. There is no model of what is to be observed which allows closure. Pure Baconian observation is open, because there are no expectations and therefore no control over what may happen. This is quite rare in science. More common is that the model which is supposed to allow closure transparently fails to do so. For example, the debate over the spontaneous generation of living things seemed irresolvable until it was shown that temperatures higher than boiling were sometimes required to sterilize material (see Conant, 1961). In psychology, if we allow that ESP exists then its nature is currently unestablishable: Clairvoyance would theoretically permit a subject access to *any* information anywhere, rendering controlled experiments impossible prior to some model of the control of ESP.

Whatever the reason a system is open, in an open system everything is subject to change. A theory of social behavior may change society to accord with that theory. A model of mind, like the computational model, can change the way people think about their thoughts (Turkle, 1984) and will probably change the way they think as well. If teachers follow a specific theory of reading, then the children they teach may end up reading in accord with the theory. Bhaskar (1979), Gergen (1982), and Harré (1984) give further examples.

Although these authors attempt to draw a more-or-less rigid distinction between open and closed systems, our exploration of the nature of closable systems suggests that no such distinction can be drawn.

Whether a system is open or closed is determined historically, but not in principle. It remains true that in contemporary psychology most systems are open and changeable. Although open systems occur in the natural sciences, in the social sciences they are much more common. Gergen (1982) has argued that the subject matter of social science is symbolic. It is obviously also true that scientific models are symbolic. Therefore, unlike natural science, social science is concerned with the symbolic representation of things which are already symbolic. This is a major reason for psychology being mostly open, especially as the nature of symbol systems is often poorly understood. Models of psychology are confused with 'reality,' as in psycholinguistics when the 'text' is treated as a physical stimulus, and the subject's symbolic construal of events is either ignored altogether (as 'subjective') or treated as objective data (as the measure of text comprehension).

The Symbolic Content of Psychology

People have their own accounts of their activities in ways in which rocks or rats do not. These accounts are symbolic, whether they are linguistic or non-linguistic. People's activities are also symbolic (Eco, 1976; Goffman, 1981; Harré, 1984) even when the people suppose that what they do is entirely determined by the 'concrete' situation they are in. Such 'concrete' situations are of people and cultures' own making and are not 'objectively' real. To a realist, they are none the less real, because symbols can have effects on other real things (Bhaskar, 1979). Beliefs in ghosts are real, in that they can influence people's behavior, but ghosts may not be real in any other sense. Objectivists' attempts to reduce symbolic behaviors to objective entities are in fact translations from one symbol system to another. There is nothing especially real about psychological modes of discourse like psychophysics or behaviorism. They are attempts to describe other real structures but this does not mean that they are not symbolic. For example, emotions are classified culturally (Harré, 1984), which makes it unlikely that English emotion-terms have fundamental neurological correlates. Whatever connections there are between emotion-terms and neurological structure are themselves symbolic.

One consequence of both subject-matter and theory being symbolic is that in principle the two systems can exchange symbols, just as a word from one language can be adopted into another. As in normal translation (see Steiner, 1975), this adoption may lead to an alteration in the meaning of the adopted word and/or an alteration in the host language.

If a psychologist is observing a person's behavior then there are three symbol systems to consider: first, the theorist's model of the behavior; second, the tools for observing behavior (both apparatus and design) and the data gathered with those tools; third, the subject's account of the behavior. For example, Gibson (1966) showed that the optic flow patterns resulting from one's own movement and the movement of external objects are different and that people use that information to move about the world. People do not spontaneously report optic flow patterns, nor are they necessarily able to report the adjustments they make as a result of variations in optic flow. So, we have the psychological model - optic flow - the observed behavior - adjustments - and subjects' reports. All of these are real and, importantly, all can exchange symbols. For example, people can be taught to attend to their optic flow patterns and make optic flow part of their self-descriptions. Similarly, a person could point out some feature of their behavior which would become part of the psychological model. Two kinds of confusion frequently arise from failing to appreciate that all three of these systems are equally real and equally symbolic. First, there is the objectivist mistake we have already discussed of assigning real status to only one system. For example, a radical behaviorist believes that behavioral observation tools lead to real data, while the subject's account of that behavior is somehow less real. Both are real, and the validity of data depends upon the validity of the tools. Facile conceptualizations or inadequate measuring devices lead to inadequate data, however statistically significant they may be. Casual use of subjective reports leads to equally inadequate data.

Secondly, there can be *location errors,* where symbols are believed to have come from a system other than the one they really came from. For example, debate continues over whether Gibsonian invariants like optic flow are 'really' part of people's cognitive representation of the world or not. More generally, the normal form of the location error in psychology is to believe that any adequate formal account of a subject's behavior must be contained in the subject in order for the behavior to have taken place. For example, Vokey and Brooks (in press) have shown that subjects behaving grammatically do not possess, know, or have the 'requisite' grammar. Location errors also take other forms, like believing that a subjective observation was actually a part of 'real' behavior.

The psychology of open systems must try to avoid these confusions by being clear about the status of different systems and also deal with the possibility that psychological concepts will change the psychology of the people being studied. Attempting to construct any theory of psychology with a fixed and non-symbolic content is a mistake.

Psychology as Discourse

Instead, we can consider both observer and subject to have equal status in that either can alter (transfer symbols - ideas - to) the other. Such an exchange between symbol systems is discourse (Pask, 1980). Discourse includes, but is not limited to, conversation. Any situation where two systems can both affect the other can be considered as discourse. In psychological observation we have the observer, consisting of observation tools and a model of what is to be observed, and the subject, consisting of parts which can currently be observed and parts which cannot. Observation is a kind of discussion, with presentation by the subject, comprehension (or incomprehension) by the observer leading to re-presentation by the subject and so on. What can or cannot be discussed depends upon history and upon both the observer's and the subject's skill and ingenuity. For example, with a film camera it is possible to observe behavior which could not be observed before. Conversely, a novelist, writing out of personal experience can add ideas to our culture. Such observations and ideas can be incorporated into observers' models and into subjects' accounts of themselves. None of this can occur without discourse. This paradigm emphasizes the symbolic content of psychology and makes theory relative to the observation tools and model used. Elsewhere (Hammersley, in preparation 2), I will argue that successful psychology theory already has these characteristics, although they are usually considered to be methodology rather than theory and often mistakenly considered to lead to absolute or objective data.

Conclusions

While this brief paper has undoubtedly raised more problems than it has settled, there are some things which can be concluded about the nature of a valid and general psychology paradigm.

1. Psychology must abandon the distinction between subjective and objective information. So-called objective information is constructed by the individual theorist or the psychology community at large and remains a subjective, symbolic system. The subject's system may be less articulated and less accurate than a good psychological model, but both are equally real.

2. Such symbolic systems are usually open in psychology because they can change the psychology of the people being studied. Psychology theory needs to take this into account, rather than being formulated as if the subject-matter of psychology was unchanging.

3. Psychology must be clear about the source of its ideas. At the moment objectivism leads to considerable confusion between properties of theories, of subjects, and of observables. This confusion contributes to a profusion of observations and theories with little evaluation.

4. A paradigmatic framework for psychology can be found in the concept of discourse, where there are two parties involved in some form of exchange, rather than there being a 'subject' and a separate 'observer.'

To paraphrase Bhaskar (1978), it is not so much that our research must change as that our beliefs about the knowledge we gain from our research must change. The search for an objective psychological data base is futile, but this should not prevent psychology from proceeding as a science.

References

Alba, J. W., & Hasher, L. (1983). Is memory schematic? *Psychological Bulletin, 93,* 203-231.

Bateson, G. (1979). *Mind and nature.* London: Wildwood House.

Bhaskar, R. (1978). *A realist theory of science.* Brighton: Harvester Press.

Bhaskar, R. (1979). *The possibility of naturalism.* Brighton: Harvester Press.

Brewer, W. F. (1974). There is no convincing evidence for operant or classical conditioning in adult humans. in W. B. Weimer & D. S. Palermo (Eds.), *Cognition and symbolic processes.* Hillsdale,NJ: Erlbaum.

Conant, J. B. (1961). *Science and common sense.* New Haven, CT: Yale University Press. (paperbound)

Eco, U. (1976). *A theory of semiotics.* Bloomington, Ind.: Indiana University Press.

Feyerabend, P. (1975). *Against method.* London: NLB.

Fodor, J. A. (1980). Methodological solipsism considered as a research strategy in cognitive psychology. *The Behavioral and Brain Sciences, 3,* 63-109.

Gergen, K. J. (1982). *Towards transformatin in social knowledge.* New York: Springer-Verlag.

Gibson, J. J. (1966). *The senses considered as perceptual systems.* Boston: Houghton Mifflin.

Goffman, E. (1981) *Forms of talk.* Pennsylvania: University of Pennsylvania Press.

Hammersley, R. H. (in preparation 1). Closable systems: A theory of the psychology experiment.

Hammersley, R. H. (in preparation 2). Intentionality, indeterminacy and intersubjectivity: a theory of intention and a theory of theories of intention.

Harré, R. (1970). *The principles of scientific thinking.* Chicago: University of Chicago Press.

Harré, R. (1984). *Personal being.* Cambridge, MA: Harvard University Press.

Harré, R., & Secord, P. F. (1972). *The explanation of social behavior.* Oxford: Blackwell.

Husserl, E. (1977) *Phenomenological psychology.* The Hague: Martinus Nijhoff.

Krige, J. (1980). *Science, revolution and discontinuity.* Brighton: Harvester Press.

Kuhn, T. S. (1962). *The structure of scientific revolutions.* Chicago: University of Chicago Press.

Lacan, J. (1978). *The four fundamental concepts of psycho-analysis.* New York: Norton.

Lian, A. (1981). *The psychological study of object perception.* London: Academic Press.

Pask, G. (1980). Developments in conversation theory - 1. *International Journal of Man-Machine Studies, 13,* 357-411.

Popper, K. R. (1963). *Conjectures and refutations.* London: Routledge & Kegan Paul.

Steiner, G. (1975). *After Babel.* Oxford: Oxford University Press.

Turkle, S. (1984). *The second self: computers and the human spirit.* New York: Simon and Schuster.

Vokey, J. R., & Brooks, L. R. (in press). Taming the clever unconscious: analogic and abstraction strategies in artificial grammar learning. *Cognition.*

Watson, J. B. (1967/1914). *Behavior: An introduction to comparative psychology.* New York: Rinehart & Winston.

Current Issues in Theoretical Psychology
Wm J. Baker, M.E. Hyland, H. Van Rappard, A.W. Staats (Editors)
© Elsevier Science Publishers B.V. (North-Holland), 1987

MODULARITY, MENTAL MODELS, AND TERTIARY QUALITIES

René van Hezewijk

Department of Psychonomics
Utrecht, The Netherlands

SUMMARY: Theoretical psychology is about the non-empirical aspects of psychology as an empirical science. There are good reasons to think that every theory has both empirical and non-empirical consequences. Experimental and empirical psychologists are more concerned with the former, theoretical psychologists are more concerned with the latter. I will give an example of what I mean by discussing a non-empirical issue in cognitive psychology. I will take some non-empirical aspects of two theories of mind: J. A. Fodor's Representational Theory of the Mind, as he interprets it in his recent Modularity View; and P. N. Johnson-Laird's Theory of Mental Models. It is shown that both imply non-empirical consequences that are problematic.

A short account of the main points of both theories is given. Then it is made plausible that theories do have non-empirical consequences and should not be judged only according to empirical evidence. Some ways are suggested to evaluate the non-empirical aspects of a scientific theory. Then the non-empirical consequences of Fodor's and Johnson-Laird's theories are identified, as well as what is problematic about them. Next, another metaphysical interpretation is suggested that seems to overcome at least some of the problems. In the conclusion, reasons are given to adopt the proposed metaphysical interpretation.

Fodor's Theory

One of the more interesting theories in cognitive psychology is J. A. Fodor's. It has two aspects: the 'representational' theory of mind (RTM for short) and the so-called 'modularity' view of the mind. RTM is about propositional attitudes, i.e., entities such as *beliefs, desires*, etc. It:

> ...purports to explain how there *could be* states that have the semantical and causal properties that propositional attitudes are ... supposed to have. (Fodor, 1985, p. 78)

So it should answer the question: What are propositional attitudes?

If I understand him rightly, Fodor's answer can be summarized as follows:

1. Fodor is a *realist*: there (really) are beliefs, desires, etc., i.e., propositional attitudes. They cannot be reduced to other mental states (such as 'experiences') or material events or things.

2. Fodor is a *functionalist*: beliefs, desires, and other propositional attitudes are not purely mental states. Beliefs and desires could be identified according to their function, which is their causal role in the mental life of an organism. To have a belief supposes one or another physical event.

Yet it is not necessary, or even possible, to specify which physical event is the counterpart of a specific propositional attitude. As a functionalist, Fodor is partly a *token physicalist*: propositional attitudes can be realized in quite different, non-typical, physiological ways; they can also be represented by mechanical and electronic devices.

In other words: we do have mental representations (propositional attitudes) that can be identified according to their function; and we do have some brain events that go with them; but we cannot identify the one by looking at the other.

3. Fodor is a *logicist,* as I would like to call it. Mental representations are symbols with both formal and semantic properties. They have their causal roles in virtue of their formal properties and they inherit their semantic properties from those of the mental representations that function as their objects (Fodor, 1981a).

So a mental representation is seen as a token in relation to a propositional attitude. Besides that, Fodor says:

> what can't be doubted is this: the causal roles of mental states typically closely parallel the implicational structures of their propositional objects; and the predictive successes of propositional-attitude psychology routinely exploit the symmetries thus engendered. (Fodor, 1985, p. 90)

In other words: trains of thoughts, and mental processes in general, are transformations of mental representations that look very much like logical transformations in arguments.

Apart from RTM Fodor has given an interesting account of the architecture of the mind. According to the:

- function of cognitive mechanisms; and
- the subject matter of cognitive mechanisms; and
- the computational character of cognitive mechanisms;

one can distinguish two kinds of cognitive processes, Modular Input Systems and Central Systems, characterized as follows:

	Modular Input Systems	Central Systems
Function	Input Analysis	Fixation of Beliefs
Subject Matter	Domain Specific	Domain Neutral
Computational Character	Encapsulated	Quinean & Isotropic

Inputs we receive from the senses (transducers) are first analyzed in mental modules. They abstract from very detailed inputs to outputs that represent specific aspects of environmental states. They are syntactically of one form only (something like: 'there is now something with characteristics x, y, z, in range'). These outputs are used at the central cognitive level for the fixation of beliefs, e.g., perceptual beliefs (like 'there's a horse coming down the road') and relational beliefs (like 'healthy horses sleep in an upright position').

Second, modules are domain specific. They have a limited range in their receptability and in the range of properties they can report about. There must be modules for colour analysis, for shape analysis, for grammatical analysis, for melody, for rhythmic structure, etc. Central systems, on the other hand are domain neutral. They can transform diverse outputs of the modules into perceptual beliefs. ("There is a black horse coming down Penny Lane singing 'she came in through the bathroom window,' but she doesn't keep time.")

Third, modular processes are cognitively impenetrable. There is limited access from central processes to the mental representations that input systems compute at the modular level. So everything an input analyzer computes is mandatory (For instance: the Müller-Lyer illusion remains an illusion *for the eye* even though the mind knows it is illusionary. We cannot help but see the one line as a longer one.) Besides, modules are encapsulated: relatively little information is *consultable* that is available at the central cognitive level. So according to Fodor, modules (or input analyzers) are also fast, and have shallow outputs, in *natural kinds* that are innate. They also are supposed to have a fixed neural architecture, to exhibit characteristic and specific breakdown patterns, and to have a characteristic pace and sequence of ontogenetic development.

Central cognitive processes differ in function, subject matter and architecture from the modular processes. Belief fixation resembles hypothesis formation in science. Fodor concludes from this that central processes, contrary to modular ones, are Quineian and isotropic. By Quineian, he means that because they can (and do) make use of properties of the entire belief system one possesses, every belief is sensitive to changes in any one or some beliefs anywhere else in the system. So any change in one or the other can be disastrous:

> the degree of confirmation assigned to any given hypothesis [in science or belief formation] is sensitive to properties of the entire belief sytem; ... the shape of our whole science [central system] bears on the epistemic [cognitive] status of each hypothesis [belief]. (Fodor, 1983, p. 107)

By isotropic Fodor means that facts relevant to the fixation of a belief (like facts relevant to the confirmation of a hypothesis) may be drawn from anywhere in the field of other beliefs (or hypotheses). This makes it unpredictable which of many possible beliefs will be fixed. So Fodor believes that there are propositional attitudes (realism), that there are nonreducible functions of matter (functionalism), and that for every function there is some (non-typical) physical (and mostly physiological) realization (token physicalism), except for a few functions, which do have typical realizations (modules). Besides, Fodor thinks that there is a mental logic that has a strong resemblance to propositional logic and that the mental logic has, in virtue only of its syntactical properties, both semantic and causal functions (logicism).

Cognitive processes - especially the *higher* ones - run strongly in parallel with hypothesis formation in science (scientism). As in science, it is hardly possible that we learn from experience alone (anti-empiricism and anti-associationism). This forces Fodor to conclude that almost all concepts are innate (nativism). Fodor's First Law of the Non-Existence of Cognitive Science: Quineianism and isotropism of central processes lead to the impossibility of a scientific psychology of higher cognitive processes. (Why he *has* to conclude to Nativism and the First Law I will show later on).

Johnson-Laird's Theory of Mental Models

Fodor's basic problem is: how do we explain the facts of mental life? Johnson-Laird (1983) sees this as his central problem too. He concentrates on *central processes*, and also questions himself: Is psychology possible? There are similarities between Fodor and Johnson-Laird: both are *functionalists;* both take cognitive processes to be computational in character. Yet Johnson-Laird's theory is in conflict with Fodor's on the issue of the supposedly strong resemblance of the language of thought with logic. "An inference," he states (1983, p. 23), "is a process of thought that leads from one set of propositions to another." But though human beings are capable of forming and following formal deductions by which truth is transmitted from premise to conclusion, we do not have a logic in the personal mind. There are a number of problems with the hypothesis since we do make too many fallacious inferences. It is hard to see which logic could be the logic of the mind or how we acquire it. Why are we sensible to the content of premises, when logic is a purely syntactically operating system?

From his experiments Johnson-Laird (1983) concluded that we form mental models of solutions to formal reasoning problems. In reasoning with propositions, for instance:

> ... people reason by constructing a representation of the events described by the premises. This mental model is based on the meanings of the premises ... and also on implicit inferences of general knowledge. (p. 53)

On this account, then, - unlike Fodor's suggestion - we do not reason in abstract p's, q's, r's and formal implication rules or truth rules. We reason with concrete examples, like artists, bee-masters, and chemists travelling from Paddington Station to Plymouth. And we do not reason with an infinite number of possible p's and q's, but with small samples. According to Johnson-Laird:

> reasoning is not a matter of recovering the logical forms of the premises and then applying rules of inference to them in order to derive a conclusion. ... The heart of the process is

interpreting premises as mental models that take general
knowledge into account, and searching for counter-examples
to conclusions by trying to construct alternative models of the
premises. (1983, p. 54)

We make use of a number of mental rules that are not equivalent
to logical rules of inference (deduction). They are much simpler and
much more stupid - as it were. Yet they are adequate most of the time
for drawing the conclusions we need in everyday life. Mental modelling
produces results that imitate what the formal analysis would give. The
more complex and/or the more abstract the formal logical problem, the
worse the results of this mental procedure, and the slower we *think*. But
in everyday life we manage quite well. So one could speak of 'the cun-
ning of mental modelling,' to paraphrase Hegel.

Theories Have Empirical and Non-Empirical Consequences

Both theories conflict in a number of aspects, especially where
higher cognitive processes are concerned. Both produce empirical results
that are in line with their theories. Johnson-Laird, in particular, did experiments that corroborate his theory, and that refute Fodor's First Law.
And yet, as I will make clear now, theories cannot always be judged by
their empirical evidence alone.

Theoretical psychologists and scientists in general will by now be
familiar with K. R. Popper's most important axiom: the falsifiability
principle. Statements are scientific if they can be falsified by empirical
facts (Popper, 1934/1959). Popper and some of his co-workers and students have worked out some consequences of this principle. They are as
important as the falsifiability principle, but less well known. To begin
with, Popper's principle, in the original formulation in which it is known,
should be refined. What Popper had meant to say was, according to
Bartley (1968), that the empirical aspects of the scientific theories are
falsifiable in principle. This implies that scientific theories contain
non-falsifiable statements, i.e., that science is partly metaphysical.

Watkins (1957; 1958) made it clear that in science there must be
four kinds of statements. They can be characterized according to the two
questions cross-tabulated in Table 1. There it is obvious that statements
like (1) and (3) have much to do with science. Yet Watkins (1957; 1958)
thought that metaphysical statements were influential too as guidelines for
research. He later showed that they are embedded in every empirical scientific theory (Watkins, 1975; 1978; 1984). They are logical consequences

Table 1

Watkins' Four Kinds of Statements in Science

		Is the statement falsifiable?	
		Yes	No
Is the statement verifiable?	Yes	$\exists(x)_{p,t}$ (1) Basic statements E.g., "There is now a lion in the conference room."	$\exists(x)$ (2) Existential statements E.g., "There is a monster of Loch Ness."
	No	$\forall(x)$ (3) Universal statements E.g., "All hungry lions eat people."	$\forall(x)\ \exists(x)$ (4) All & Some statements E.g., "For every lion there is a mother lion."

that are non-falsifiable. That is, every theory has infinitely many empirical consequences (basic statements); but they also have non-empirical consequences, which are by definition metaphysical. They can be identified in any formal theory by the method of quasi-ramseyfication. I want to stress that these so-called metaphysical components are logical consequences. They are not necessarily assumptions we are conscious of, or which we choose to entertain. They follow from entertaining a falsifiable theory, and they have the form of purely existential statements or of all-and-some statements.

One of the most important tasks of theoretical psychologists is to discover those metaphysical presuppositions in scientific theories, but not in order to eliminate them, as the positivists intended but failed to do, for then we destroy theories, i.e., knowledge. We want to find them in order to have more ways of criticizing theories, that is, of eliminating error.

Empirical criticism by experimental test still is, of course, one important way to discover falsity in science. But as we saw, not every statement in science is empirically falsifiable, though it can be false. (It is probably false that there is a Loch Ness Monster, but every Scotsman can answer the claim you never saw one with this reply: 'You have not searched enough.')

But we need not despair of the metaphysical. There are ways to criticize metaphysical statements. Bartley (1964/1984) suggested three:

1. check of the problem: does the metaphysical component solve the problem it is supposed to solve?

2. check of logic: is the theory consistent, especially when the metaphysical components are taken in consideration?

3. check of theories: are the metaphysical components compatible with other scientific theories and with the metaphysics they imply?

In addition Watkins (1975) suggested another one:

4. check of systematic interdependence: has the metaphysical component an essential, indispensable function in the theory?

The Metaphysics of Fodor's and Johnson-Laird's Theories

Earlier I concluded that Fodor's theory presupposes not only *functionalism, physicalism, and logicism,* but also *nativism, Quineianism,* and *isotropism.* Fodor explicitly mentioned them, but what he has not stated anywhere, to my knowledge, is that the latter three are consequences of the former.

Nativism is the metaphysical thesis that:

1. there is an innate mental logic;

2. for (almost) every word in the natural languages there is an innate concept;

3. for (almost) all concepts there is a primitive internal structure that is innate.

(Statement (1) is an existential statement; (2) and (3) are all-and-some statements).

In debate with Piaget, Fodor (1980) sided with Chomsky, and defended *nativism* aggressively. The difference between empiricism and rationalism (or associationism and nativism) is that the empiricists do not accept that (almost) all concepts are inborn (Fodor, 1981a). Non-sensory, lexical concepts need only to be triggered by experience.

Fodor's motive for accepting *nativism* is that the empiricist-cum-associationist position is logically impossible and that nativism is the only alternative available. I think he is wrong. First of all it is implausible that concepts like *university, graduate, isotropism, unemployment benefit* are innate. It would be incompatible with biology, unless one is a Lamarckian. Fodor may be right, we do not learn them from experience, but I don't accept his conclusion that we therefore must have them in a triggerable state, as it were, from birth.

Johnson-Laird's solution to this problem is much more attractive. He suggests that a limited number of our concepts are primitive: they are inborn and have internal structure. Words like *travel, possess, see,* refer to those primitive concepts. Other, non-primitive concepts can be constructed by a few innate semantic operators, operating on the limited number of primitive concepts. They resemble Kant's categories and *Anschauungsformen.* For instance: time, space, possibility, permissibility, causation, and intention can operate on the concept *see* to construct *new* concepts like *sight, glimpse, show, spy, view, scrutinize, watch.*

Yet, because of the metaphysical character of this issue, empirical tests alone will never be able to decide between empiricism and rationalism. Johnson-Laird hints at a third solution later on. But first I will offer an explanation of why Fodor propagates *nativism.* It is because of his *anti-empiricism* in combination with *(token) physicalism. Token physicalism* demands that concepts we use have some physical counterpart somewhere and thus must have a matter-like realization (Shannon, 1984). Like Plato (Meno), Fodor concludes that it is plausible that conceptual knowledge is innate.

The thesis that there is a mental logic that resembles some formal logic and which is purely syntactical in its causal functions, leads to *nativism* also. The mental logic is supposed to connect concepts with each other to form propositional attitudes, but due to its syntactical effects it doesn't contribute in any way to the content. So the content must be innate.

Johnson-Laird's semantic operators are richer, in this respect. They do contribute to transforming the semantic content of primitive concepts into non-primitive ones. Besides they are more or less optional.

So Fodor's and Johnson-Laird's theories both propose solutions to the problem of concept acquisition. They arrive ex aequo. But Fodor's theory does worse at another problem, the explanation of higher cognitive processes. Fodor's First Law is the result of the supposed *Quineianism* and *isotropism* of belief fixation. *Quineianism* and *isotropism* are consequences of logicism, anti-empiricism, and his view of science as the confirmation of hypotheses. The problem is that, whereas in his theory the modular processes are supposed to be constrained in several, connected ways (domain specificity, encapsulated, fixed neural architecture, limited penetrability), the central cognitive processes are not constrained enough. There are only logical-syntactical constraints to belief fixation, but modular processes are bounded externally by the outside world and internally by what is innate. As in science every hypothesis is always *underfixated* by inputs and other beliefs. That makes them vulnerable to instability (*Quineian*) and makes them too powerful in respect to other beliefs (*isotropic*).

Johnson-Laird's experimental work offers support for the counter thesis. There is a corroborated theory about higher cognitive processes. But this experimental work does not refute Fodor's claim of *logicism*. Fodor will reply, like the Scotsman, by advising to make more of an effort to find it. As for his First Law, it seems refuted by Johnson-Laird's experimental work, but this has no severe effect on the metaphysical components the First Law is the consequence of. For these components cannot be refuted empirically, they can only be verified.

Yet, non-empirical evaluation suggests that Johnson-Laird's theory is the more plausible one. It does not contradict the experimental facts; it offers a solution to both the acquisition problem, to the problem why people reason badly but mostly adequately, and to the problem of the possibility of cognitive science. It is consistent, as far as I can see, and it is compatible with other theories in and outside psychology (biology, for instance), but at least one important question remains unanswered.

One Remaining Problem: The Status of Things Modelled Mentally

The remaining metaphysical problem Johnson-Laird has not solved satisfactorily is this:

What is the status of the propositions, meanings, concepts, etc., we make mental models of?

Most answers to this question are dualistic. Matter on the one side, mind on the other. And mind is taken as the mental, be it conscious or not, functionalistic or *really* mentalistic. From Descartes to Fodor and Johnson-Laird, in almost all varieties of dualism, knowledge is interpreted as something possessed completely by a knowing subject, as a relation between a knower and an object.

Johnson-Laird (1983) also poses the question of status in a way. Chapter 9 is called: 'What is meaning?' He rejects both *realism* of the Fregean kind and *psychologism*, an example of which he recognizes in Fodor's *nativism. Psychologism* cannot be true because some nouns are analytic: their meanings "comprise ... set(s) of essential conditions that support necessary truths" (1983, p. 196). Other nouns are natural kind terms and so are primitive in that "their true intensions are unknown, and their mental representations consist of schemata specified by default values ..." And "[s]till other nouns like home, chair, and melody, have [what he calls] a 'constructive semantics.' The intensions of these words are mental constructions, imposed upon the world ..."

But what, then, are mathematical entities, numbers, logical principles, etc.:

Modern mathematicians tend to be Realists and to assume that numbers exist and that their nature is independent of the operations of the mind. ... Yet the invention of mathematics and the apprehension of numbers must depend on the properties of the mind. If we accept Realism, we are committed to an extraordinary Platonic domain of numbers whose existence is mysterious. ... If we reject Realism, we seem to have a problem in explaining the objectivity of mathematics. It's proofs endure for all time, and this fact seems hard to explain if mathematics is merely the product of the mind. It was for just such reasons that Frege launched his attack on Psychologism... There is, however, a third possibility, which is to revive and to revise Intuitionism. (Johnson-Laird, 1983,

p. 445)

Fodor (1981a, p. 117-121) also rejects *Platonistic realism*. He advocates *epistemic idealization*, whereby not propositions and other abstract
entities are idealized, but the bearer of mental representations. This point
of view resembles Chomsky's ideal native speaker. In this respect Fodor
is committed to Brouwerian *intuitionism* too, like Chomsky (Gil, 1983).
Elsewhere, Fodor (1981b) rejects the *Platonistic* version of *realism*, because "... deep down, nobody is remotely interested in it." (I do not
need to argue against this position, if it is arguable at all.)

Intuitionism, however, doesn't solve the problem either. In fact, it
is a kind of *psychologism* too. *Psychologism* is the twin sister of *logicism:*
the doctrine that logic describes the way we think, and that the laws of
logic are laws of thought. *Intuitionism* states that abstract objects are
mental constructions. They are made 'in the mind' and remain there, and
after that event they can be formulated; we can prove them, talk about
them or write about them, but only after we have constructed them in our
personal mind. In the last analysis they are mental constructions.

That may not be too objectionable. But what Brouwer did with it,
and what Johnson-Laird repeats, is to confuse the mind as a source of
this kind of *objects* with the mind as the foundation or justification of
them. Surely intuitions can be sources of inspirations for mathematical
conjectures, propositions, concepts, etc. But they are not thereby the
infallible legitimization of them.

Johnson-Laird follows Brouwer in this view, at least as far as
meanings are concerned:

> Language embodies no particular metaphysics; it embraces
> both Realism and Psychologism. However, psychology has
> the last word. Whatever the semantics of a term, its relation
> to the world depends on human cognitive capacity.
> (Johnson-Laird, 1983, p. 204)

This position resembles both Chomsky's *transformational generative
grammar* and the *intuitionism* of Brouwer and Heyting. Gil (1983, p.
236) observes that "while Chomsky confidently asserts that linguistics is
part of psychology, biology or natural science in general, intuitionists
generally view mathematics not as an empirical science but rather as an
empirically based human activity. The fundamental parallel is thus between intuitionistic mathematics and language, not linguistics." So to

quote Brouwer: "... the construction of intuitive mathematics in itself is an action and not a science; it only becomes a science ... in a mathematics of the second order ..." (Brouwer, quoted by Gil, 1983, p. 236). Both are "mentalistic disciplines," according to Gil, that study the mathematical and the language faculties in an idealized way. So Johnson-Laird's position implies *psychologism* just as well.

Of course, one must admit that human cognitive capacity influences:

1. meanings, propositions, mathematical and logical principles, etc., that we construct individually and initially;

2. the mental models we, as individuals, can have of these abstract objects.

But our initially mental constructions, once they are published or made in another way accessible to others, acquire a life of their own. They have logical consequences - their content - that are objective, that is, independent of the cognitive capacity of their (re)constructor. We can construct, at a certain time, an object, be it a theory or an artefact, which has consequences that no one will foresee at that moment, not even the creator. This can remain so for 100 years or more. So how could this potential logical content be there as an intuition only? Intuitions die with the individual having them. Especially in logic and mathematics it is clear that a subjective source and legitimization will not do.

Secondly, we discover new aspects of abstract objects because we make mental representations of them. But that does not mean a mental representation contains the whole lot of logical consequences. The logical content of an abstract object is not limited to the accidental cognitive capacity of the representing individual. Human cognitive capacities constrain the mental models of abstract objects. But mental representations and logical contents are not equivalent.

And, thirdly, there are constraints going out, as it were, from the contents of abstract objects: meanings, syllogisms, propositions themselves. The meaning, that is, intension, of *chair* was a mental construction of someone, some time. But it became objective, that is, mind-independent, so that we now make chairs that you and I sometimes ask ourselves of whether they should not carry a government health warning. Still other concrete objects can be seen as or used as chairs though the maker would never have thought of that.

Tertiary Qualities

Abstract objects like meanings, propositions, numbers, and logical principles certainly were mental constructions at some time. But that does not imply they are still in minds and minds only. In matters like these there is a third position which might offer a solution: *Platonism*, but only a *Platonism* of sorts.

Three kinds of *Platonism* can be distinguished: Plato's, Frege's, and Popper's. Plato's *Platonism* is propogated by J. J. Katz (1981, 1985) in our days, as far as the status of linguistics is concerned. Frege's *Platonism* is discussed in theoretical psychology, in philosophy, and in the philosopy of linguistics and of psychology (e.g.: Barwise & Perry, 1983; Jorna, this volume).

Hardly discussed in psychology is Popper's secularized version of *Platonism*. Yet it could solve many problems in cognitive psychology in general, and for the interpretation of mental models theory and RTM in particular. And it solves some of the problems I have sketched above.

Platonism is the metaphysical view that there are abstract, objective entities. More specifically, that there is a realm or class of objective entities, independent of individual minds, that are not directly sensible, yet conditionally intelligible for human beings.

Plato's *Platonism* was meant to solve the problem: what makes similar objects look similar to us. Plato said that there were objective, abstract *ideas* or *forms*, for instance of *horse-likeness*, that make us see any horse as a horse. So, in fact, it was a theory of the taxa of the visible. But there were also ideal *forms* of invisible, abstract qualities, like the *good,* the *beautiful*, and the *just*.

Frege did not differ in some respects from Plato. In his third realm there are thoughts, numbers, meanings. They are objective, eternal, true and immutable. Yet Plato considered the *forms* to be divine, but according to Frege they were not divine, but only abstract. Besides, they were graspable, that is, individuals could understand their nature and their consequences.

Plato's ideal *forms* and Frege's inhabitants of the third realm both had the same function: to justify other aspects of Plato's philosophy, and Frege's theory of meaning and of mathematics, respectively (Popper, 1972; Currie, 1980). They needed it in order to have a foundation for other parts of their system, because they thought that a belief or assertion or idea or judgment or perception is only rational if it is justified. The senses cannot offer enough justification for non-observable ideas, so they declared the *forms*, respectively *thoughts*, to be eternal, true, and immutable.

Popper, on the other hand, is not a justificationist. Rational belief, rational knowledge and rational action is criticizable belief, knowledge, action; *not* justified or justifiable belief, knowledge, action. Popper makes a distinction between *World 1*, the world of physical objects and physical processes as such, and *World 2*, the province of subjective experience and psychological processes in general. The latter includes endosomatic entities like thinking as a subjective process, Frege's ideas, conscious and subconscious experiences and - I would suggest - Johnson-Laird's mental models. *World 3*, is the class of the exosomatic products of the human mind. It's inhabitants include:

- Artefacts, cultural and technical objects, like paintings, chairs, cars, machines, and tools, and also computers as symbol manipulating machines - physical objects designed by human beings for specific purposes.

- Historical entities and processes, and social institutions. They are the planned or unplanned effects of human activities, in virtue of the fact that they have objective, person-independent consequences.

- Abstract entities: numbers, geometrical figures, classes, concepts, propositions, values, and norms, and most important, theories and problems, as well as logical principles.

What characterizes *World 3* objects most is the fact that they have content, that they have logical consequences objectively, without interference of specific individual minds. One could call these tertiary qualities. We can think out something subjectively and act upon it, or publish the results of our thinking, without fully knowing what the logical consequences of it are. "Knowledge is a product not fully known to its producer," as Bartley (1984) puts it. I will give one dramatic example of this tertiary quality. Einstein published his special *relativity theory* in 1905, but when, in 1939, Szilard told him it was possible to make a very powerful bomb (the A-bomb) on the basis of 'his' theory, Einstein had to say: "Daran hab' ich gar nicht gedacht!" (I've never thought of that). It wasn't Einstein's theory anymore, and - as we may conclude from Einstein's opposition to the production of A-bombs - it had never been completely 'his.'

Plato, as well as Frege and Popper, agrees that the third realm influences us. Logical consequences 'kick back,' they can hurt us. Plato understood that we try to get a glimpse of the heavenly ideal *forms* by way of the intellectual intuition. We use references to the *ideas* in order to explain concrete events and appearances, as well as to justify certain actions. (Think of the power the *philosopher king* is given in the Politeia.)

Frege said his 'Thoughts' (Gedanke) have a kind of reality, or better, actuality, "... they are capable of acting upon things we accept as real; the mind and, by way of the mind, the physical world. Thoughts are 'actual' (wirklich) because they can 'act' (wirken) upon things" (Currie, 1980, p. 235). The mind can grasp a *thought*, that is, come to stand in a representational relation to it.

In both interpretations then, the third realm could influence our mental representations only in so far as true (and eternal and immutable) *ideas* or *thoughts* are concerned. These interpretations are much less convincing than a Popperian interpretation, in which not only true theories, propositions, logic, mathematics, can influence our subjective thoughts and actions, but false theories, and problems, and contradictions as well. It is especially the mind-independent feedback function that is interesting for cognitive psychology. This makes cognitive science in part a science of *World 3*.

On the other hand: cognitive psychology is interesting for philosophers and theoreticians of science too. Just as theories of perception suggest and explain observation biases, theories of mental representation suggest and explain our imperfect ways of understanding reality, apart from our theories of reality.

Popper does not pay much attention to his *World 2*, as is often observed. Unintentionally Johnson-Laird's theory of mental models fulfills this purpose very well, when one accepts the Platonic metaphysical component that is implicit in his theory. His theory will be the more fruitful by acknowledging the partly autonomous existence of the products of individual minds that have what I called tertiary qualities: logical consequences which are smuggled in but are not foreseen by their producers. Objective qualities of the things modelled, as well as psychological qualities of the minds modelling them, constrain each other.

This interpretation changes some other metaphysical components of both Fodor's and Johnson-Laird's theories. Extreme nativism is not necessary anymore: we have *World 3* as the class of abstract, cultural objects, historical events, societal institutions with their logical consequences. We now have an exosomatic store as it were, that contains all consequences and contents we will never be able to keep in mind. In this metaphysics it is possible to have a partial model of, for instance, the meaning of a word, and still communicate with others. We sometimes say more than we mean, because words can mean more than we understand.

Besides, this interpretation solves the problem of Quineianism and isotropism, by acknowledging that our higher cognitive processes are not only constrained by modular inputs and by what is already believed, but also by what is objectively possible to believe, and by what is globally known to be true or false to the best of human knowledge. An explosion of logical possible statements in *World 3* need not trouble us as persons, because we do not have direct access to *World 3*. We have only selective models of the tertiary objects; we made the Quineian and isotropic aspects exosomatic. And we do not need *logicism* either, because a more *primitive* but mostly adequate way of mentally modelling logical processes will do in everyday life.

This metaphysical interpretation also saves culture for cognitive psychology. It suggests how to think about the way our incomplete mental models of existing *World 3* objects create new problems and new ideas. My interpretation is, perhaps, a bold conjecture, born out of a mistaken mental model of the metaphysical theory of Popper. But it might be promising to trace its logical consequences.

References

Bartley, W. W., III, (1964). *The retreat to commitment.* La Salle: Open Court. (2nd rev. ed. 1984).

Bartley, W. W., III, (1968). Theories of demarcation between science and metaphysics. In I. Lakatos & A. Musgrave (Eds.), *Problems in the philosophy of science.* (pp. 40-64). Amsterdam: North Holland.

Bartley, W. W., III, (1984). Knowledge is a product not fully known to its producer. In K. R. Leube & A. H. Zlabinger (Eds.), *The political economy of freedom.* (pp. 17-45). Munich/Vienna: Philosophia Verlag.

Barwise, J., & Perry, J. (1983). *Situations and attitudes.* Cambridge, Mass. : MIT Press.

Currie, G. (1980).Frege on thoughts. *Mind, 89,* 234-248.

Johnson-Laird, P. N. (1983). *Mental models.* Cambridge: Cambridge University Press.

Fodor, J. A. (1980). Fixation of belief and concept acquisition. In M. Piatelli-Palmarini (Ed.), *Language and learning.* (pp. 143-160). London: Routledge and Kegan Paul.

Fodor, J. A. (1981a). *Representations.* Brighton: The Harvester Press.

Fodor, J. A. (1981b). Some notes on what linguistics is about. In N. Block (Ed.), *Readings in philosophy of psychology.* (pp. 197-207) Cambridge, Mass. : Harvard University Press.

Fodor, J. A. (1983). *The modularity of mind.* Cambridge, Mass. : MIT Press.

Fodor, J. A. (1985). Fodor's guide to mental representations: The intelligent Auntie's Vade-Mecum. *Mind, 94,* 76-100.

Gil, D. (1983). Intuitionism, transformational generative grammar and mental acts. *Studies in the History of Science, 14,* 231-254.

Katz, J. J. (1981). *Language and other abstract objects.* Oxford: Basil Blackwell.

Katz, J. J. (1985). An outline of Platonist grammar. In J. J. Katz (Ed.), *The philosophy of linguistics.* (pp. 172-203). Oxford: Oxford University Press.

Popper, K. R. (1959). *The logic of scientific discovery.* London: Hutchinson.

Popper, K. R. (1972). *Objective knowledge.* Oxford: Oxford University Press.

Shannon, B. (1984). Meno - a cognitive psychological view. *The British Journal for the Philosophy of Science, 35,* 129-147.

Watkins, J. W. N. (1957). Between analytic and empirical. *Philosophy, 32,* 112-131.

Watkins, J. W. N. (1958). Confirmable and influential metaphysics. *Mind, 67,* 344-365.

Watkins, J. W. N. (1975). Metaphysics and the advancement of science. *The British Journal for the Philosophy of Science, 26*, 91-121.

Watkins, J. W. N. (1978). Minimal presuppositions and maximal metaphysics. *Mind, 87,* 195-209.

Watkins, J. W. N. (1984). *Science and scepticism.* London: Hutchinson.

Current Issues in Theoretical Psychology
Wm J. Baker, M.E. Hyland, H. Van Rappard, A.W. Staats (Editors)
© Elsevier Science Publishers B.V. (North-Holland), 1987

SYMBOLS IN THE MIND: WHAT ARE WE TALKING ABOUT?[1]

R. J. Jorna

University of Groningen
Groningen, The Netherlands

SUMMARY: The notion of mental representation is fundamental in recent cognitive psychology. Furthermore, it is presumed that mental representations consist of mental symbols and that internal mechanisms operate on mental symbols. In explaining problem solving, reasoning, thinking, etc. cognitive psychologists have suggested various forms of mental representations. In this paper it is proposed that one way of comparing the various mental representations is by analyzing the syntactic and semantic features of mental symbols. This analysis has first been made by Goodman in the case of external symbols. In this paper Goodman's analysis is applied to the mental symbols, which constitute pictorial representations (Kosslyn) and propositional representations (Anderson).

Introduction

Two very important notions in recent cognitive psychology are those of symbol and mental representation. Previous discussions have concentrated on the question of how one form of mental representation (for example, pictorial) can be based on another form (for example, propositional) (Anderson, 1983; Kosslyn, 1980; Pylyshyn, 1984). However, because it is very difficult to define the features of propositional (or semantic) representations and because mental imagery seems to be very real, some cognitive psychologists (Anderson, 1983) have defended the view that two (or more) mental representations are equivalent. Although a lot of experiments have been done, still no decision has been made concerning whether some mental representations are equivalent or not. In my opinion, a contribution to the solution of this problem not only consists in doing experiments, but also in trying to elucidate the basic assumptions of mental representations and the stuff of which (mental) representations are made, namely, symbols.

---

[1] Preparation of this paper was supported by Grant 560-269-009 (Psychon) from the Dutch Organization for Scientific Research (Z.W.O.). For comments, not always in agreement with my views, I thank A. Bax, J. A. Michon, and S. Silvers.

If cognitive psychologists intend to make comparisons between mental representations, a starting point for doing so is to examine the notions of (mental) representation and symbol. The reason why we have to examine symbols is that, according to Newell (1982), Pylyshyn (1984) and Simon (1978), the things we, as natural information-processing systems, have in common are representations, constituted out of symbols.

Before going on, let me first explain what I mean by symbols. I endorse the assertion of Goodman (1968), who says:

> 'Symbol' is used here as a very general and colorless term. It covers letters, words, texts, pictures, diagrams, maps, models, and more, but carries no implication of the oblique or the occult. The most literal portrait and the most prosaic passage are as much symbols, and as 'highly symbolic,' as the most fanciful and figurative. (p. XI)

So, my paper has two main themes. The first theme is: what can we say about the features of symbols. The second is, does an analysis of symbols contribute to a comparison of various mental representations? In the first section I discuss the meaning and reference of words and pictures, conceived as symbols. In the second section a survey of mental representations, formulated in recent cognitive psychology, will be given. In the third and fourth section I will go into the details of propositional and pictorial representations. In Section Five I will return to symbols and because I will defend the point of view that comparisons are only possible if the things compared have something in common, I will go into the details of symbols. For that reason I want to examine an approach to a theory of symbols proposed by Goodman (1968, 1984). Goodman distinguishes several features of symbols, and in the final section I will try to apply these features to propositional and pictorial mental representations.

Meaning, Reference, and Symbols

For a long time, meaning, sense, and reference have been hard nuts to crack in philosophy. Since Frege's pioneering work in logic and the philosophy of language these concepts are clear in so far as one can defend the positon that (proper) names may have the same reference but different senses, or may have the same sense but different references. For example, 'morning star' and 'evening star' have different senses (Sinn), but the same reference (Bedeutung), whereas Socrates (the Brazilian football player) and Socrates (the teacher of Plato) have different references, but the same sense (Salmon, 1982).

Problems concerning meaning, sense, and reference in philosophy and logic are currently of great interest in cognitive psychology. This interest arises because, when we ask what is the meaning (in Frege's terms 'sense') and reference of words, pictures, and photographs, we should also ask what is the meaning and reference of so called words and pictures in our mind. Prior to dealing with the details of this question I wish to make a few preliminary statements.

When I discuss the reference of a word or a picture, I mean a word or picture denoting something; for example 'morning star' refers to or denotes an object, namely Venus. In the case of meaning I have in mind the concept of a word; for example, the meaning of 'bachelor' is 'an unmarried man.' Now two questions arise.

The first question is whether aspects of words, pictures, and photographs in the normal situation can be compared to the so called words, pictures, and photographs in the mind. Three possible answers can be given to this question.

The first possible answer is a simple one. There is no relation between the words and pictures on paper and the so called words and pictures in our mind. When in cognitive theory we speak about the mental alphabet or the aspects of mental pictures, then that has nothing to do with the real form of our thinking. I do not think any serious cognitive psychologist could advocate this answer, because to do so terminates cognitive psychology as the science of the mind.

The second possible answer is that the only way of characterizing the process of thinking is by propositions, pictures, etc. That is, metaphors are used as modes of expression of the internal processes. The use of words, pictures, etc., is not arbitrary, because some sort of mapping between symbolization inside and outside our mind must hold.

The third possible answer is that a cognitive theory literally expresses what happens inside the mind. A cognitive theory that formulates thinking as propositional is consistent with the thesis that what is expressed in the external symbolization is the same as what happens inside our mind.

I think it does not matter whether one gives the second or the third possible answer. Examples of both positions can be found in cognitive psychology and, from my point of view, both positions are acceptable. The first possible answer however eliminates cognitive psychology. Some

workers in artificial intelligence have advocated this position. But there is
no reason why cognitive psychologists themselves should join artificial intelligence in rejecting a science of the human mind. Let us now examine
the second question.

The second question is whether pictures and photographs can have
reference and meaning in the same way as words and sentences? This
question can only be answered if I say something more about meaning
and about what words and pictures have in common.

Price (1953) has emphasized that the word 'meaning' can be used
in two ways: meaning in the *sign*-sense and meaning in the *symbol*-sense.
When we say: *dark clouds mean rain* (a) meaning functions as sign, while
when we say *'rain' means rain* (b) we have the symbol in mind. Clearly
Price does not distinguish between the sense and the reference of the symbol, as for example Frege (1892) did. In the example of *'rain' means
rain* we are relating to reference, while for example in *'rain' means 'water
that is falling down in the form of drops'* (c) we are regarding the sense
of the symbol. These distinctions can be illustrated in the following set
of relations where 'rain' can be a sign (in a), a symbol (in b), or a concept (in c):

(a)   Natural Reference   →   Sign

(b) Conventional Reference   →   Symbol   ←   Denotation

(c)   Concept   ←   Connotation
                                                                          (Sense)

In these statements, the arrows should be read as "is indicated by."

The reason why I will discuss signs is that cognitive psychology
concentrates on (mental) symbols, by which they also mean - and that is
rather confusing - concepts. As stated before, the notion of symbol is
one of the central notions in current cognitive psychology and according
to Pylyshyn (1984): "The notion of a discrete atomic symbol is the basis
of all systems of thought, expression or calculation for which a *notation* is
available" (p. 51). All thinking, all the modes of expression and all computations are made with the help of or in the form of symbols.

I return now to the problem of comparing aspects of words and
sentences with aspects of pictures and photographs. If we say that the
mind is a symbol operating system and if we say that we can think in pic-

tures, words, etc., then we can state that words as well as pictures consist of symbols. This, of course, is not to say that words, pictures, etc., consist of the same symbols: on the contrary. If we say that humans have thoughts in their mind, they are processing information. In cognitive psychology this means that humans have and operate upon mental representations, which in turn consist of symbols. So, before we can look at the features of symbols in general, we have to review what cognitive psychology has formulated concerning mental representations.

Mental Representation in Cognitive Psychology

Representation simply means that one entity stands for another entity (Palmer, 1978). In the case of mental representation this means that what goes on within our mind has a certain relationship with internal mechanisms as well as with the state of affairs outside our mind. Here, the first opportunity for confusion arises because in cognitive psychology the mental mechanisms as well as the internal entities are called mental representations. Generally stated, mental representations consist of symbols under the interpretation function of beliefs, goals, and expectations, which - and this really makes things complicated - can also consist of symbols. Thus, if cognitive psychologists say that thinking consists of the calculation of mental representations, they in the first place mean that representations are symbols and in the second place that calculation is identical to the manipulation of symbols and thereby to the execution of computations on internal symbols. In Figure 1 I have given the interconnectedness of several mental representations, which I will discuss below (see also Rumelhart & Norman, 1983). In this figure, the double-headed arrow indicates "considered as contrary to."

There are semantic representations which start from the principle that the meanings of words consist of sets of verbal associations, structured in the shape of networks. Propositional representations consist of statements with a truth value which can be formulated in a logical calculus. Pictorial representations use the analogy with visual perception and start from the assumption that representations retain configural information when mentally represented. Episodic representations are composed of events and episodes which are stored in memory without any internal solid structure. The only structure present is the time dimension according to which things have happened. The temporal string representations reflect the sequential structure of events. It is not clear how this representation can be distinguished from episodic representations. Anderson (temporal string) and Tulving (episodic) seem to deny that they are talking about the same thing, mainly because the episodic representations

Mental Representations as: Mental Elements
                            Internal Mechanisms

Procedural   Declarative
Representation   ↔ Representation
_____

                Pictorial   Propositional
                Representation   ↔ Representation
                _____

                        Semantic   Episodic
                        Representation   Representation

    Episodic Representation   ↔   Temporal String Repr.

        Analog Representation ↔   Digital Representation

        Discrete Representation ↔   Continuous Representation

Fig. 1. An overview of the interrelatedness of mental representations.

contain an internal hierarchy. All representations mentioned before are
classified under the term: declarative representations. What matters here
is knowledge of something; the way in which knowledge is represented is
important. Declarative representations are explicit, the knowledge is
accessible immediately.

    In the literature, procedural representations are contrasted with de-
clarative representations. In procedural representations it is stated how
the system has extended certain processes; furthermore, the functional architecture is not immediately accessible, it is encapsulated (Fodor, 1983),
or as Pylyshyn (1984) says, it is cognitively impenetrable. Two further
distinctions are between analog and digital representations and the distinction between discrete and continuous representations. The first distinction is based on the criterion of resemblance or similarity between the
representing and the represented entities, while the second distinction is

based on the degree of continuity in physical reality which is represented inside. Though this last distinction does not exhaust the varieties of mental representations, I think I have named the most important ones that can be found in cognitive psychology. Furthermore, I want to state that the enumeration does not mean that representations exclude each other. There is a lot of overlap and subordination, for example, between analog, pictorial, and continuous representations and between digital, discrete, and propositional representations (Rumelhart & Norman, 1983).

Propositional Representations

As I stated before, the problem is to define or reconstruct the nature and structure of the mental symbols that can be found in the arguments for propositional, pictorial, and other mental representations. After this reconstruction, a comparison of representations is fertile. This comparison, among others, has the following benefit. In cognitive psychology, the problem nowadays is that authors do little more than defend their own view (and form) of mental representation and denounce other viewpoints (and forms). To give an impression of the way I think this problem can be solved, I will first discuss briefly some aspects of two of the most widely defended theories of mental representation, namely propositional and pictorial representations. The former has been defended in one way or another by Pylyshyn (1984), Anderson (1983), and Newell (1982), whereas the latter has been defended by Kosslyn (1980), Shepard and Chipman (1970), and Paivio (1971). After that I will discuss the tool I use for the comparison.

Propositional representations are mental representations of verbally expressible propositions, that are characterized by the truth values, true and false; a propositional representation is the representation of a function from states of affairs to truth values (Johnson-Laird, 1983). Propositional representations are abstract and show a similarity to ordinary sentences; according to Pylyshyn (1984) they are "symbolic expressions in an internal, physically instantiated symbol system sometimes called 'mentalese' or 'the language of thought'" (p. 194).

In this view, everything a human being knows can be stated in a list of propositions and, with the help of rules of inference, new and valid propositions can be deduced. These inference rules mirror, for the greater part, the procedures in the predicate and propositional calculus. So, if someone hears the sentence "John was hit by Bill," he will decompose the sentence into its component parts and will subsequently store the proposition in his memory. This means that propositional representations must have a structure, a category system, and a set of properties. In the proposition of John and Bill it is not important what sort of clothes they wear, neither is the precise form of the sentence of importance. But the stored proposition contains information, in most cases implicitly, about the fact that John and Bill are male and that to hit is a verb that takes two arguments. In cognitive psychology, propositional representations have been elaborated in several, so called, semantic representation systems; see, for example, the theories of Anderson & Bower (1973), Lindsay & Norman (1972), and Kintsch (1974).

Pictorial Representations

Pictorial representations can best be illustrated by referring to visual perception. In one way or another the information present in visual perception is stored in the cognitive system. For example, the painting that I have seen, can be remembered in a pictorial way two days later. In cognitive psychology, the question is, which aspects of the object are presented in the pictorial (mental) representation and, furthermore, how does the cognitive system proceed in using these aspects?

Kosslyn (1980), the strongest defender of pictorial representations, thinks that in the case of pictorial representation, one should distinguish two aspects of this process. The first aspect, to be called surface representation, has a close resemblance with a visual image and is executed in a spatial medium which has the following properties: first, the distances between the parts of the visual image are proportionally preserved in the pictorial representation; second, the pictorial representation is sensitive to the size of the visual image; the spatial medium can overflow. Further, like a photograph, the image has a so called grain-size; the possibility of resolution has its boundaries. Details are lost when the image has been blown up too much. Finally, pictorial representations need refreshing from time to time, or, as Kosslyn remarks, pictures tend to fade away.

But there is a second aspect, the so called deep representation which, as Kossyln (1980) says:

> is the information in long-term memory from which the surface image is derived. ... The long-term memory medium is structured to contain sets of lists of propositions. These lists are stored in files in the model. Lists are named, and the names indicate both the contents and format of the encodings." (p. 139-145)

As a matter of fact, both surface and deep representations co-operate in the production and experience of pictorial representations.

Much research on pictorial representations has been done in experimental psychology which has shown the following: pictorial representations function in a spatial medium of restricted size; the time required for making a pictorial representation depends upon the number of objects in the visual field; it takes more time constructing a representation of a large object than one of a small object; and, finally, the field in which the pictorial representation appears is circular. So, one of the tasks, for example, Kosslyn has set for himself, is to determine the visual angle of the mind's eye.

One could have the impression that Kosslyn thinks that pictorial representations look like photographs and pictures not outside, but inside the head. In principle I think this is right. His claim is that the experience of an image resembles the experience of seeing the referent of the image (Block, 1981, p. 154). Within the information processing both pictorial representations and visual images have roughly the same format and use the same operations.

One last argument in favor of the existence of pictorial representations is the experience of human individuals. Suppose one has to answer the question: can you tell me how many doors there are in your living room? Subjects seem to (mentally) scan a pictorial representation of the room and then give the answer.

Anderson (1983) summarizes the properties of pictorial representations as follows: in encoding they keep the configural information; storage and retrieval of image entities is an all or none process. The matching process in memory is, concerning the degree of matching, a function of the distance and the configurations, and concerning the salient properties, a matter of distance, direction, and overlap. New structures are constructed by synthesis of the existing images and by rotation.

Features of Symbols and Goodman's Analysis

The problem of representation is in fact a problem of symbolization or notation, and it seems clear to me that the nature and structure of symbols can be taken as a guiding principle in the conceptual analysis of mental representations. Goodman, in his *Languages of Art* (1968), has made a first start with a theory of symbols and I will try to apply his enumeration of features of symbols to propositional (semantic) and pictorial representations.

In the following a coherent set of symbols is called a symbol
scheme, that is to say, every symbol scheme consists of characters: a set
of marks. A symbol scheme defines the well-formedness (the syntactic
aspect) of each symbol and each symbol string. In the case that symbols
also have, implicitly or explicitly, a domain of reference, we speak of a
symbol system. In fact, a symbol system is a symbol scheme with a semantics (a reference system of the symbols).

Goodman has defined the syntactic and semantic aspects of symbols
as follows. Syntactic features are: syntactic disjointness and syntactic
finite differentiation. Syntactic disjointness means that the same characters of a symbol scheme are replicas or copies of each other. It is an impossibility for a mark to belong to more than one character. Let me give
an example. In the English alphabet the $\wp$ is not a character in the symbol scheme, whereas the mark Q is a character in this symbol scheme. If
the (right) stick of the character can be clearly seen, the symbol scheme
is syntactically disjoint. But if the character is of the form Θ, confusion
arises, because Θ can be a replica of a Q or an Θ, and so the symbol
scheme is not syntactically disjoint.

The other syntactic feature is finite differentiation, which Goodman
(1968) defines as follows:

> For every two characters K and K' and every mark m that
> does not actually belong to both, determination either that
> m does not belong to K or that m does not belong to K' is
> theoretically possible. (p. 136)

A symbol scheme that is not finitely differentiated is called syntactically
dense; this means that infinitely many characters are ordered in such a
way that between each two a third is possible. Examples of symbol
schemes with the features of syntactic disjointness and syntactic finite
differentiation are the alphabet of the natural languages, the
morse-alphabet, the musical notation, and the symbol scheme of ones and
zeros.

Semantic features of symbols are unambiguity, semantic disjointness, and semantic finite differentiation. Unambiguity means that one
expression does not have more than one extension. Goodman's own example is as follows: "In sound-English, for example, 'c' is naturally regarded as ambiguous since some 'c's are soft and others hard" (1968, p.

148).

Semantic disjointness means that the symbols in the symbol scheme are not redundant. No two characters in a symbol scheme have any extension in common, says Goodman. (This feature is missing in natural language.) The last semantic feature is semantic finite differentiation. This means that aspects of reality can be divided in such a way that an object or property is placed in the one or in the other category. A symbol system that is not finitely differentiated is semantically dense. Semantically dense means that between two extensions of predicates, for example, orange and red, new extensions, in this case shades of colors in reality, can always be inserted. if a symbol scheme and a symbol system consist of all the here mentioned syntactic and semantic features, then it can be called a notational system.

Earlier (in the Section on meaning, reference, and symbols) I mentioned the problem of the reference and the meaning of non-linguistic symbols and now I will return to this problem. It seems that only linguistic symbols can refer, that is to say, they refer from expression to state of affairs. Pictorial and other non-linguistic symbols do not seem to refer, but instead depict and imitate because, as opposed to linguistic symbols, pictorial symbols seem to be defined by a degree of similarity between symbol and that which it symbolizes. However, similarity is neither a necessary nor a sufficient condition for representation. So, all symbol systems in one way or another refer, without taking into account similarity or resemblance, because almost anything can stand for almost anything. As Elgin (1983), discussing Goodman, says: "... a name denotes its bearer; a variable its value; and a portrait, its subject." (p. 19)

The most interesting point on the reference of symbols is not whether they refer, but it is the direction of their reference. In the case of the reference from the word 'snow' to snow the direction of reference is simply from term to object. But consider now a picture painted by Picasso, for example 'Guernica,' and let us say that 'Guernica' indicates the cruelty of war, then the direction of reference is from object - the picture - to term - 'cruelty.' Goodman calls this instance of reference 'exemplification.' Take another example. When we say that green denotes grass, then green refers to grass. But when we say that grass exemplifies green, the grass refers to green. In both cases there is reference, but the direction of the relation is different.

Application and Conclusion

In this section I will apply the features of symbols to propositional and pictorial (mental) representations. To make things clear, I will take as examples two descriptions of a certain area, namely the area of Cornwall and Devon. At least two descriptions of this area (and others) are possible. The first is a description by (natural) language, whereas the second is a description by using a map. Suppose I have read a book with detailed explanations about Cornwall and Devon and suppose further I have also profoundly studied a map of the same area. After six months I try to remember whether the river Tamar is in Devon or in Cornwall and whether Penzance is on the south coast or on the north coast.

The cognitive psychological problem in this case is what sort of mental entities I use in answering both questions. If I give the answer by remembering the map, I use a pictorial (mental) representation, whereas by remembering the passage in the book (or its propositional counterpart), I use a propositional representation.

The last thing I have to do, before comparing the entities which constitute the propositional and pictorial representations, is to determine the symbols in both cases. In the case of propositional (and semantic) representations, the letters of the alphabet and the words in the sentences are the symbols. In this case it does not matter whether we speak of a natural language or of a language of thought. In the case of the pictorial representation - that is to say the representation of the map (of Cornwall and Devon) - the lines, circles, icons, and colors are the symbols which constitutue a mental image. Given the mental representations and the symbols which constitute them we now can try to apply the features of symbols, as defined by Goodman. Broadly speaking it looks as follows.

The symbol scheme of propositional representations is syntactically disjoint and also syntactically finitely differentiated. Within 'the language of thought' the characters that constitute the representation have to be replicas of each other. Besides that, it is possible to distinguish whether a certain mark belongs to the one or to the other character. The 'language of thought,' as a symbol scheme, must syntactically have an explicit structure. A structure that looks like a case-grammar, a subject-predicate grammar or whatever, but may also be modelled after syllogisms, the predicate or propositional calculus, or a mixture of these.

Concerning the pictorial representations, the symbol scheme is not syntactically disjoint. Inside the internal spatial medium, the characters that constitute the (map) representations are not replicas of each other. The symbol scheme is finitely differentiated, because one cannot decide whether a certain mark belongs to the one or to the other character. For instance the length of a line indicating a distance is not syntactically finitely differentiated; in the symbol *scheme* it is rather difficult to determine whether a symbol is a replica of a line of length 0.001 cm. or of a line of length 0.0009 cm. The same is true with colors, circles, etc. For the time being we may ascertain the fact that pictorial representations are syntactically dense. In my opinion Johnson-Laird's (1983) suggestion to work with mental models can be seen as an attempt to place the features of different symbol schemes in a new symbol scheme, called 'mental model.' A mental model concentrates on propositional representation, but tries to integrate the pictorial representation.

Concerning the semantic features, propositional representations are not semantically unambiguous, since representations can refer to various referents. But we have to be careful in this case, because, if propositional representations take the form of semantic representations, the semantic feature of unambiguity does not hold, whereas if propositional representations are connected with truth values, the representation can only refer to true and false and not to both. A similar problem exists with the semantic disjointness of the symbol system, that is to say, propositional representations are not disjoint and so semantically dense. This also depends on their connection with either truth values or with semantic representations. Furthermore, propositional representations are not semantically finitely differentiated; they are semantically dense, because there will always be an entity or part of it in reality that does not belong to the one or to the other character. If propositional representations are connected with truth values, the direction of reference is from representation to truth value. But in the case of the one or the other sort of semantic representation, the direction of reference is from representation to state of affairs; (in the case of the language description of the area of Cornwall and Devon, from representation to area).

Concerning the semantic features, pictorial representation as symbol system seems to be unambiguous, but this depends on the level of enlargement. Very accurate images can only refer to one referent so a pictorial representation on a certain level of image-formation can only have one extension. The feature of semantic disjointness also seems to hold, but this again depends on the level of image-formation. On the most accurate level, one extension has only one representation. In short, pictorial representation as symbol system is not redundant.

	Propositional Representation of an Area	Pictorial Representation of an Area (Map)
Syntactic Disjointness	Yes	No
Syntactic Finite Differentiation	Yes	No
Semantic Unambiguity	No	Yes
Semantic Disjointness	No	Yes
Semantic Finite Differentiation	No	Yes
Direction of Reference	Language → Area	Map → Area

Fig. 2. Syntactic and semantic features of propositional and pictorial representations.

These two features probably explain the power of this sort of symbol system, namely the possibility of focusing and reducing; a positive result of the lack of syntactic disjointness. Further, pictorial representations are semantically finitely differentiated, because, given the level of enlargement, an object or part of an object will always belong to the one or to the other character.

It is difficult to determine the direction of reference, because some cognitive psychologists think pictorial representations presuppose visual images (Paivio, 1971), while others (Kosslyn, 1981) think pictorial representations presuppose deep representations. This difference in opinion has consequences for the direction of reference, which is in the first case from visual image to pictorial representation and in the second case from deep to pictorial representation. In our example of the area of Cornwall and Devon the direction of reference is from (mental) map to area. In Figure 2 I have summarized the syntactic and semantic features which the propositional and pictorial representations presuppose in our memory of the area of Cornwall and Devon. The yes and the no in the figure indicate whether I think the feature holds.

Finally, I will say a few words about the procedure I have adopted, which I think has at least three advantages. The first is that I have suggested a tool for comparing the various mental representations. It gives a way of reducing the various mental representations that have been suggested in the cognitive psychology literature by analyzing the features of the mental symbols. Not every new mental representation, as assumed in cognitive psychology, is really a new mental representation and by using the features of symbols we can discover why. The second advantage is that I think this tool can be effective in the development of new theories of mental representation which can be tested in experimental research on human cognition. In other words, when we suppose that human cognition functions on the basis of (internal) symbols, then knowledge of the features of the various symbol systems gives us an indication of the aspects of the transducibility and of the development of mental symbols inside the cognitive system of one human individual. The third advantage is that the features of symbol schemes and symbol systems can be useful in defining the domain of entities in mental representations, so we finally can have some idea of what we are talking about in determining the real units and quantities of human cognition.

References

Anderson, J. R. (1983). *The architecture of cognition.* Cambridge: Harvard University Press.

Anderson, J. R., & Bower, G. H. (1973). *Human associative memory.* Washington: Winston and Sons.

Block, N. (Ed.). (1981). *Readings in the philosopy of psychology* (Vol. 2). Cambridge: Harvard University Press.

Elgin, C. Z. (1983). *With reference to reference.* Indianapolis: Hackett.

Fodor, J. A. (1983). *The modularity of mind.* Cambridge: MIT Press.

Frege, G. (1892). Uber Sinn und Bedeutung. *Zeits. f. Philos. u. philos. Kritik, 100,* 25-50.

Goodman, N. (1968). *Languages of art.* Indianapolis: Bobbs-Merrill.

Goodman, N. (1984). *Of mind and other matters.* Cambridge: Harvard University Press.

Johnson-Laird, P. N. (1983). *Mental models.* Cambridge: Cambridge University Press.

Kintsch, W. (1974). *The representation of meaning in memory.* Hillsdale, NJ: Erlbaum Associates.

Kosslyn, S. M. (1980). *Image and mind.* Cambridge: Harvard University Press.

Lindsay, P. H., & Norman, D. A. (1972). *Human information processing.* New York: Academic Press.

Newell, A. (1982). The knowledge level. *Artificial Intelligence, 18,* 1, 87-127.

Palmer, S. F. (1978). Fundamental aspects of cognitive representation. In E. H. Rosch, & B. B. Lloyd (Eds.), *Cognition and categorization.* Hillsdale, NJ: Erlbaum.

Paivio, A. (1971). *Imagery and verbal processes.* New York: Holt, Rinehart & Winston.

Price, H. H. (1953). *Thinking and experience.* London: Hutchinson.

Pylyshyn, Z. W. (1984). *Computation and cognition.* Cambridge: MIT Press.

Rumelhart, D. E. & Norman, D. A. (1983). Representation in memory. La Jolla, California: Cognitive Science Laboratory.

Salmon, N. U. (1982). *Reference and essence.* Oxford: Basil Blackwell.

Shepard, R. N., & Chipman, S. (1970). Second-order isomorphism of internal representations: shapes and states. *Cognitive Psychology, 1,* 1-17.

Simon, H. A. (1978). On the forms of mental representation. In C. Wade Savage (Ed.), *Minnesota Studies in the Philosophy of Science.* (Vol. IX). Minneapolis: University of Minnesota Press.

Current Issues in Theoretical Psychology
Wm J. Baker, M.E. Hyland, H. Van Rappard, A.W. Staats (Editors)
© Elsevier Science Publishers B.V. (North-Holland), 1987

ETHNOGRAPHIC DISCOURSE ANALYSIS AND J. B. WATSON:

THE BEHAVIOURIST AS PROPAGANDIST

A. D. Lovie

University of Liverpool
Liverpool, England

SUMMARY: In 1913, J. B. Watson published two key papers in the history of behaviourism. Versions of these articles formed the first chapter of Watson's 1914 book on the same topic. The present paper compares the articles with the book, and finds a large number of significant and consistent differences between them. This provides evidence for the thesis that Watson systematically reworked the papers to give the impression, in the book, that behaviourism was a monolithic and conceptually coherent movement, subscribed to by an intellectually self-conscious group of behaviourists, in contrast to the picture revealed by the papers themselves. These differences are accounted for in terms of an elementary model of the communication process, the one developed by Hymes for ethnographic discourse analysis. This finding is used to explain, in part, the paradox that while most contemporary opinion (particularly in cognitive psychology) has behaviourism dominating psychology from 1913 onwards, the historical evidence points in quite the opposite direction, at least up until the 1930's. The paper ends with a brief discussion of the general value of discourse analysis in historical research, particularly with its power to uncover the driving presuppositions behind past research in psychology.

The Resistible Rise of John Broadus Watson

One of the more persistent (and pernicious) myths in the history of psychology could be termed "The (Spurious) Triumph of Behaviourism." Promulgated in an entirely uncritical and repetitive fashion by cognitive psychologists from the mid-1960's onwards, this view maintains that Watsonian behaviourism killed off any research on attention, thinking, problem-solving, imagery, and certain aspects of memory from about 1910 (or so) until the 1950s when Broadbent's work on attention began to have an impact on experimental psychology.

Although such a version of events can be seriously faulted on the internal consistency of its collective wisdom (a quick review of the quoted start dates of the Watsonian purge, for example, reveals a range from

1890 to 1930, with a somewhat smaller spread, 1940 to 1960, for the rise of modern cognition), the major problems arise when we examine (a) work on cognitive psychology actually carried out over the period 1910 to 1950 and (b) the real success of behaviourism over this time. For the former, I have found (Lovie, 1983, 1984) ample evidence of work on attention, problem-solving, thinking, etc. over this time; while other, more contemporary accounts, for example, Bruner and Allport (1940), have revealed little diminution in experiments using normal adult human subjects over the period 1890 to 1940 (typically over 40% of all studies), although they also point to the sharp rise in animal based research over the same time. Further, anecdotal evidence either from this period itself, or later on from people active at the time, shows the comparative vigour of work in cognitive psychology over the period. C. H. Graham's declaration in 1951 that the 1920s were "the heydey of work on attention" is typical.

As far as point (b) is concerned, we have only to consult Franz Samelson's mammoth investigations into behaviourism during the 1910s and 1920s (1981, 1985) to see just how small an impact the movement actually had on main stream psychology prior to the 1930s. Of course, this latter decade saw the rise in animal based experiments and animal based thinking, but even as late as 1958 Skinner's radical behaviorism found the going hard indeed. Krantz (1972), for example, points out that the first issue of the Journal of the Experimental Analysis of Behavior (1958) nearly did not appear because of a lack of suitable material.

We therefore have the paradox that, on the one hand, modern cognitive psychology believes in the Triumph of Behaviourism, while, on the other, historical research into the actual position from 1910 to 1950 reveals a much more complex and, to a marked extent, contrary picture of the success of the movement. Why should this be? Although it is not the purpose of this paper to provide a final answer (indeed I suspect that this lies sometime in the future when the real impact of Watson and others has been properly assessed), I believe that part of it lies in the presentation of the behaviourist position, particularly the version provided by J. B. Watson. Of course, as will be made clear later, my paper has other purposes beyond the historical ones. In particular, it can be treated as a demonstration of the value of Hymes' ethnographic approach to discourse analysis (1962) where parallel spoken and written texts are available for comparison. However, the major aim of the work is to discuss the presentation of behaviourism as a historical force.

Watson 1913-1914

In the latter part of 1912, J. B. Watson, who was then Head of the Department of Psychology at Johns Hopkins and editor of the Psychological Review, was asked by J. McKean Cattell to give a series of lectures at Columbia University on his behaviouristic views. Although there is some ambiguity about the actual dates of the lectures, compounded by Watson's own contradictory account of events (see also Samelson, 1981), there is enough external evidence to suggest that the two lectures that will be dealt with in this paper were given on March 24th, 1913 (*Psychology as the Behaviorist Views It*) and April 13th of the same year (*Image and Affection in Behavior*). These were the only two papers to appear in the public domain, the first published in Watson's own journal. The former paper (1913a) is, of course, the most widely cited of Watson's oeuvre and, because of his perceived position in the history of psychology, one of the most widely cited papers in psychology. The other paper (1913b) is, however, of equal historical importance since the two formed the basis of the first chapter of Watson's 1914 text: *Behaviorism, the Study of Comparative Psychology.*

The received view of the relationship between these two papers (1913a, b) and the first chapter of the book (1914) by Watson is that the latter is no more than a slightly changed version of the former (see, for example, Boring, 1950; Samelson, 1981; Boakes, 1984; Murray, 1983). Some of these writers state that only 1913a was recycled in 1914, while others have realized (correctly) that both 1913a and b were used by Watson.

My thesis can be simply stated: Watson self-consciously and consistently reworked the two papers into a form (the book chapter) which could with some justification be described (as Watson's colleague Harvey Carr did in 1914) as propaganda for the behaviourist movement. In particular, I will present results from a comparison of the texts that shows that Watson changed the papers from a personal, qualified, and problematic statement of behaviourism into an impersonal, unproblematic, and unqualified version of his position for the book. This, in turn, has implications for Watson's subsequent writings and for later historical views of his work. That these changes to Chapter 1 were Watson's own responsibility can be inferred from the Preface to the book (pp. v-vi) where apparently only Lashley contributed specifically to the text, and even there not to Chapter 1. It is true that Watson does acknowledge the help of various people in the Preface (pp. vi), from Lovejoy to Yerkes, but this is couched in the most general terms, while the publishers themselves seemed to have exercised no control at all over the contents of the book.

Before presenting this evidence, however, I would like to describe the ethnographic discourse analysis that I am using to account for the differences between the texts. Hymes (1962) has produced a useful way of capturing the whole of a communication situation. Basically, this is done by enumerating a plausible list of the components of such a process, including the purpose of the communication, and then assuming that changes to part of the process have implications for the others. Hymes himself has listed a knowledge of the speaker, the audience, the code used by the speaker, and the setting of the communication as essential parts of the process, but others have elaborated these components and added others (see Brown & Yule, 1983, for more details).

The application of these ideas to the relationship between Watson's papers and the book is as follows: Watson had the same purpose in giving the talks (and in writing the papers based on the talks) and in publishing the book. This was to persuade the psychological community of the force of his radical behaviourist message. However, the audiences and, to a lesser extent, the forms of expression were different. The papers were a record of spoken material given before an audience of Watson's peers and interested and experienced students, while the book was a written account of behaviourism designed exclusively for beginning students. It is these similarities and differences which, I believe, are enough to account for the bulk of the changes that Watson made to the papers when rewriting them for the book chapter.

The Changes

I have found some 182 alterations, deletions and additions in a comparison of the two papers and the chapter. These three types of change I have classified into (a) Personal to Impersonal and (b) Qualified (Problematic) to Unqualified (Unproblematic). I have also attempted a further subdivision of the changes in (a) into (1) Non-stylistic Personal to Impersonal and (2) Stylistic Personal to Impersonal. There are also a small number of changes (about 12% of the total) that can be classified as purely stylistic, while a final twenty changes cannot be classified within the present scheme. Finally, where instances of an obvious overlap between Personal-Impersonal and Qualified-Unqualified existed, these were placed, for convenience, in the Qualified-Unqualified part of the results. In other words, the number of Personal to Impersonal alterations listed below somewhat underestimates the figure that I found in the comparison. Finally, the thinking behind the Deletions and Additions classifica-

tion is that here Watson has either removed a personal or qualified statement or has added an impersonal or unqualified one. The results of my
analysis (which I believe has detected nearly all of the changes) is presented in Table 1.

A qualifying point to make about the results in Table 1 is that they
actually belie the extent of the changes in that they do not show their
size. In other words, although the bulk of the changes were confined to
single words or short phrases, there was a considerable number of much
more lengthy alterations and insertions. Indeed, Watson greatly amplified
many aspects of the two papers in the latter part of the book chapter. I
have, therefore, included examples of both brief and extensive changes in
this paper.

Other points from the figures in Table 1: most of the changes are
of the personal to impersonal type, with a considerable overlap with the
other main class. The major change can be classified as an alteration,
particularly the non-stylistic one. However, the stylistic personal to impersonal alteration (where, for example, all the personal pronouns in an
illustration have been changed to either their plural or impersonal equivalents) are also well represented in the texts.

First then, examples of the short changes (mainly personal to impersonal; note that the dates refer to the appropriate publications by
Watson):

1913a/b	1914
I do not accede...	We do not accede...
I doubt...	It is doubtful...
I call attention...	Attention is called...
I firmly believe...	One must believe...
If I did not...	If we did not...

Such short but systematic changes make up the bulk of the alterations made by Watson to the texts. Clearly, I have only been able to
quote a tiny percentage of them. However, I believe that those I have
cited are representative of the range and style of the changes wrought by
him.

Table 1

Breakdown of the Various Changes to Watson 1913a and b
in Watson 1914

Type	Alterations	Deletions	Additions
Personal-Impersonal	64	8	1
Stylistic Pers-Impers	33	0	0
Qualified Unqualified	21	12	1
Overlap Pers-Qual	13	11	1
Stylistic Only	17	3	2
Unclassified	8	5	7

Further, just in case it might be argued that these changes are purely stylistic, it should be noted that there are many instances where both the 1913a/b and 1914 texts share the same (stylistically appropriate) plural pronouns, for example, 'we,' 'the behaviorists,' 'psychologists,' and 'experimenters.' In other words, while Watson was careful, in 1913, to differentiate between his personal (and highly qualified) views and those held more generally by psychologists, he abolished this distinction in the 1914 book. Consequently, what were presented exclusively as his own opinions in the earlier texts were now put into the mouths of a much larger group in the book.

The next part of the paper will be devoted to examples of the longer quotations mentioned earlier. these will be given without a gloss, apart, that is, from headings that relate to the entries in Table 1.

Alterations: Personal to Impersonal

1913a. I must confess that these arguments had weight with me when I began the study of behavior. I fear that a good many of us are still viewing behavior problems with something like this in mind...

1914. Such arguments have weight with the neophyte, but as time goes on and the horizon of animal work broadens, he becomes less and less convinced of their weight. Many of us are still viewing behavior problems with something like this in mind...

1913a. I used to study over this question ("what is the bearing of animal work upon human psychology?"). Indeed it always embarrassed me somewhat. I was interested in my own work and felt that it was important, and yet I could not trace any close connection between it and psychology as my questioner understood psychology. I hope that such a confession will clear the atmosphere...

1914. With psychology based on its present premises such a question is necessarily embarrassing for the reason that no answer is open to the man who uses animals for subjects. The behaviorist has found it convenient in the past to cultivate a repressed attitude when talking of his work before orthodox psychologists. He is interested in his work and believes firmly in its intrinsic value, albeit he is unable to trace its bearing upon psychological theory. Such a confession it is hoped will clear the atmosphere...

1913a. The psychology which I should attempt to build up would take as a starting place...

1914. A psychology of interest to all scientific men would take as its starting place...

1913b. If I did not perceive certain signs of weakening on the part of the garrison, I think I should agree with Professor Cattell that I am being too radical...

1914. If we did not perceive certain signs of weakening on the part of the garrison, it would seem best to agree with Professor Cattell that the position of the behaviorist is too radical...

1913b. ...lead to my principal contention, viz. that there are no centrally initiated processes.

1914. ...lead to our principal contention, viz. that there are no centrally initiated processes.

Alterations: Qualified to Unqualified

1913a. View

1913a. I do not wish to criticize psychologyy. It has failed signally, I believe, during the fifty-odd years of its existence as an experimental discipline to make its place in the world as an undisputed natural science.

1913b. I may have to grant a few sporadic cases of imagery...

1913b. My own view - which I advance as a theory, not as something introspectively ascertained or introspectively verifiable - may be stated as follows. I agree with Stumpf and Woolley in holding that affection is an organic sensory response.

1914. Theory

1914. Psychology has failed signally during the fifty-odd years of its existence as an experimental discipline to make its place as an undisputed natural science.

1914. There are probably in most cases kinaesthetic substitutes for imagery.

1914. The Stumpf-Woolley view may be modified and stated in more definite terms. Every stimulus which calls out either overt or delay response arouses concomitantly (reflexly) a definite and complex group of afferent impulses from tissue not specified definitely by the authors.

Deletions: Personal to Impersonal

Note that many of these examples overlap with the Qualified to Unqualified category. The examples consist of the material deleted from the original paper, thus making that part of Chapter 1 more impersonal.

1913a. There remains, to be sure, the practical difficulty, which may never be overcome, of examining speech movements in the way that general bodily behavior may be examined. (Omitted, 1914)

1913a. Will there be left over in psychology a world of pure psychics, to use Yerkes' term? I confess I do not know. The plans which I most favor...

1914. Will there be left over in psychology a world of pure psychics, to use Yerkes' term? The plans which we most favor...

1913a. In concluding, I suppose I must confess to a deep bias on these questions. I have devoted nearly twelve years to experimentation on animals. It is natural that such a one should drift into a theoretical position which is in harmony with his experimental work. Possibly I have put up a straw man and have been fighting that....Certainly the position I advocate is weak enough at present and can be attacked from many standpoints. Yet when all this is admitted I still feel that the considerations which I have urged should have a wide influence upon the type of psychology which is to be developed in the future....Certainly there are enough problems in the control of behavior to keep us all working many lifetimes... (Omitted, 1914)

1913b. I have been trying to find out whether any of the spoken phonographic records can be read by experts in that work. I have not been able to ascertain this information, but I am sure there is nothing inherently difficult about the problem. Records of laryngeal movements could likewise be read directly. (Omitted, 1914)

1913b. For years to come, possibly always, we shall have to content ourselves with experimental observation and control of explicit behavior. I have a very decided conviction, though, that not many years will pass before implicit behavior will yield to experimental treatment. Possibly the most immediate result of the acceptance of the behaviorist's view will be the elimination of self-observation and of the introspective reports resulting from such a method.

1914. The result of our examination into the nature of both image and affection seems to indicate that after all the behaviorist can bring them into his general scheme of work without in any way weakening his position. It would thus seem that there is no field which an introspective psychology legitimately can call its own.

Discussion

The picture of behaviourism that Watson reveals in his 1914 book is that of a relatively unproblematic, widely held, and conceptually mature subject. As we can see from the papers, however, this was not actually the case, at least as far as the unbonnetted Watson was concerned. Indeed, the lineaments of a most painful intellectual journey can be discerned in the frankness of many of his remarks and asides. On my ethnographic analysis, however, such apparent candidness was in part dictated by the audience that Watson faced, and not by a weakening of any commitment to his own position. On the contrary, it is clear that Watson was as determined in 1913 as at any other time in his life to persuade his listeners to adopt his position. However, the means by which this was to be accomplished was tailored to the audience whom Watson judged would find such a heavily qualified and personal approach more acceptable than the one pursued in the book. There is also the possibility, hinted at in his letters of the period (see Cohen, 1979, pp. 72-73), that Watson considered his message to be so revolutionary that a more cautious approach was indicated when giving his paper before an audience of his peers. Either consideration would, of course, point him in the same presentational direction and would have been determined by the composition of his audience, and the nature and purpose of his message.

In a comparable fashion, therefore, one can also appreciate the forces that shape the book chapter since the audience now was not composed of his peers but of his intellectual inferiors (students) for whom the message was less ambiguous, more magisterial and, indeed, more pugnacious. Although it is not my purpose to examine Watson's later writings in any detail, it is worth noting that all of his subequent major works (and a not inconsiderable number of his minor ones as well) adopt the same confident and robust style of his 1914 text. In addition, all of them include early sections which echo the same attacks on introspectionist psychology and the same forthright and unqualified statement of his own position (see Watson 1919, 1924, 1928). It is my contention, therefore, that it is these latter self-confident and unproblematic versions of behaviourism that modern writers on cognitive psychology have taken to be the actual state of psychology at the time and not the much more cautious and, in the event, more accurate version contained in the two papers. Of course, by the late 1920's the influence of behaviourism had grown both on theorizing and experimental practise in psychology, with the consequent gain in credibility of some of Watson's views, but it is still the case that his position in 1913 was very much a minority view even though he attempted to suggest otherwise in his book. A further, somewhat speculative, point also suggests itself here which is that although recent writers in cognitive psychology religiously cite Watson 1913a, their views have actually been conditioned by Watson 1914. Perhaps it is the case of reading only one version but citing its (apparent) source. Alternatively, such modern commentators have only read highly selective secondary sources, particularly those that have also been convinced that 1913a/b and 1914 are identical.

There is other evidence, although not as clearcut as the present parallel texts, that Watson tailored his views to his audience. Take, for example, his opinions on Freud. In his 1928 book, based on a series of articles originally published in Harpers Magazine, he writes that Freud "resorted to voodooism instead of falling back upon his early scientific training" when he put forward the idea of the unconscious (p. 94), although it is also true that he praises Freud for his recognition of "the role sex plays in the lives of all" (p. 95). Further, his robust prediction that "...20 years from now an analyst using Freudian concepts and Freudian terminology will be placed on the same plane as a phrenologist" (1924, p. 297) reveals the direction of his published views on psychoanalysis. These quotations should, however, be contrasted with the transcript (one of the few extant) of a radio broadcast made by Watson in 1933 where he praised Freud as "... a great teacher ... [who] ... deserves to go down in history with Mahomet and Confucius" (see Cohen, 1979, p. 255).

In a similar vein, Jill Morawski, in a forthcoming historical survey of Yale's Institute of Human Relations, has noted how Watson's self-doubts seemed to surface only in his correspondence, not in his public writings. In other words, Watson's utterances, whether written or spoken, can be divided into statements delivered cathedra or ex-cathedra, that is, the official line as against the off-the-record remark. Which of these actually represents Watson's "true" position is perhaps difficult to say, but is anyway a less interesting aspect of his work than the realization that his remarks are very much a function of the audience to whom they were directed and the medium in which they were given. Here indeed do we see the future advertising copy-writer's view of science and its presentation!

Finally, it should be realized that there are many more uses for discourse analysis in the history of psychology beyond its value as a device to dissect a communication process. There is, for example, its role in uncovering a worker's conceptual presuppositions, that is, their personal scientific dictionary (to borrow Enrico Bellone's useful phrase; see his *A*

World on Paper, 1980). Watson is a particularly easy writer here, since one can differentiate (in the parallel texts) between statements containing approving self-references ("I am quite sure that if the idea of the image...") and more general ones that he either agreed with ("The enormous number of experiments that we have carried out upon learning has likewise contributed little to human psychology") or repudiated ("Unless our facts are indicative of consciousness, we have no use for them..."). In addition, I am aware that the extensive set of quotations that I gave earlier can be analyzed in much more detail than I have attempted, while there are the texts still to be dissected. There is, for instance, an interesting change from the 'association' between responses to their 'connection,' suggesting, perhaps, that Watson was refining (or acquiring) his technical vocabulary on the topic of conditioning during the time that he was writing the book. In spite of the incomplete state of my current work, therefore, I hope that this paper has demonstrated the value of discourse analysis in the study of the history of psychology.

References

Bellone, E. (1980). *A world on paper*. Cambridge: MIT Press.

Boakes, R. B. (1984). *From Darwin to behaviourism*. Cambridge: Cambridge University Press.

Boring, E. G. (1950). *A history of experimental psychology*. New York: Appleton Century Crofts.

Brown, G., & Yule, G. (1983). *Discourse analysis*. Cambridge: Cambridge University Press.

Bruner, J. S. & Allport, G. W. (1940). Fifty years of change in American psychology. *Psychological Bulletin, 37*, 757-776.

Carr, H. (1914). Review of Watson, J. B. *Behavior, an introduction to comparative psychology*. New York: Holt. *Psychological Bulletin, 12,*, 308-312.

Cohen, D. (1979). *J. B. Watson, the founder of behaviourism*. London: Routledge & Kegan Paul.

Graham, C. H. (1951). Visual perception. In S. S. Stevens (Ed.), *Handbook of experimental psychology*. New York: Wiley.

Hymes, D. (1962). The ethnography of speaking. In T. Gladwin & W. C. Sturtevant (Eds.), *Anthropology and human behavior*. Washington, DC: Anthropological Society of Washington.

Krantz, D. L. (1972). Schools and systems: the mutual isolation of operant and non-operant psychology as a case study. *Journal of the History of the Behavioral Sciences, 8*, 86-102.

Lovie, A. D. (1983). Attention and behaviourism-fact and fiction. *British Journal of Psychology, 74*, 301-310.

Lovie, A. D. (1984). Paper presented at the British Psychological Society's London Conference, December.

Morawski, J. G. (forthcoming). Organizing knowledge and behavior at Yale's Institute of Human Relations. *Isis*.

Murray, D. J. (1983). *A history of western psychology*. Englewood Cliffs, NJ: Prentice-Hall.

Samelson, F. (1913-1920). Struggle for scientific authority: the reception of Watson's behaviorism. *Journal of the History of the Behavioral Sciences, 17*, 399-425.

Samelson, F. (1985). Organizing for the kingdom of behavior: academic battles and organizational policies in the Twenties. *Journal of the History of the Behavioral Sciences, 21*, 33-47.

Watson, J. B. (1913a). Psychology as the behaviorist views it. *Psychological Review, 20*, 158-177.

Watson, J. B. (1913b). Image and affection in behavior. *Journal of Philosophy, Psychology and Scientific Methods, 10*, 421-428.

Watson, J. B. (1914). *Behavior, an introduction to comparative psychol-

ogy. New York: Holt.

Watson, J. B. (1919). *Psychology from the standpoint of a behaviorist.* Philadelphia, PA: Lippincott.

Watson, J. B. (1924). *Behaviorism.* New York: Norton.

Watson, J. B. (1928). *The ways of behaviorism.* New York: Harper.

Current Issues in Theoretical Psychology
Wm J. Baker, M.E. Hyland, H. Van Rappard, A.W. Staats (Editors)
© Elsevier Science Publishers B.V. (North-Holland), 1987

THEORETICAL PSYCHOLOGY:

A DEFINITION AND SYSTEMATIC CLASSIFICATION[1]

K. B. Madsen

Royal Danish School of Educational Studies
Copenhagen, Denmark

SUMMARY: This paper presents a proposal for a definition of the discipline of *theoretical psychology* and a systematic classification of its different sub-disciplines. I shall summarize the various published definitions of theoretical psychology in this way: *Theoretical psychology can be defined as the metascientific study of psychological theories and theory-problems.* After the definitions I shall present a rough classification of the different papers presented at the founding conference for the International Society for Theoretical Psychology and reproduced in this volume.

A Concept of Science

Before we define metascience it would be convenient to have a definition of *science*. This is a major problem and some people would prefer to postpone the formulation of such a definition until after a long metascientific exposition. But we prefer to start with a preliminary definition which may later be revised. Our conception of science contains the following three components:

Empirical Research. For most scientists and philosophers the word *science* means first and foremost empirical research, the results of which are descriptions of observations. Some philosophers of science believe that the concept of science should be exclusively identified with empirical research and its descriptions. This was especially the case with the nineteenth-century philosophers of science including August Comte and the continental positivists, as well as John Stuart Mill and the English empiricists. After the First World War, however, this restrictive conception of science was enlarged by the logical empiricists (neopositivists) such as Bertrand Russell, Ludwig Wittgenstein, Rudolf Carnap, and other

---

[1]The main part of this paper is selected from K. B. Madsen, Psychological Metatheory: An Introduction to Volume 3. *Annals of Theoretical Psychology* (Vol. 3). New York: Plenum Press, 1985. Republished with permission.

members of the Vienna circle.

Theoretical Thinking. The logical empiricists added theoretical thinking to empirical research as one of the components of science. The role of theoretical thinking should be to produce theories, which were conceived of as sets of testable hypotheses along with explanatory models. Therefore, according to this conception, there are two scientific processes: empirical research and theoretical thinking, which produce two kinds of scientific expositions: descriptions and theories. This conception of science was dominant in the western world until after the Second World War, when a new enlarged conception of science was developed by Karl Popper and his many - more or less critical - followers, such as Mario Bunge, Norwood Russell Hanson, Thomas S. Kuhn, Imre Lakatos, Michael Polanyi, Stephen Toulmin, Håkan Törnbohm, Gerard Radnitzky, and others.

Philosophical Thinking. These new philosophers of science added philosophical thinking to theoretical thinking and empirical research. The role of philosophical thinking is to produce a philosophical background or frame of reference, called *paradigm* by Kuhn and *metaphysical research program* by Popper. The present author has used the term *metalevel* including sets of *metatheses*, for this philosophical part of a scientific text. The metalevel may be divided into two subparts (see Figure 1).

1. *Philosophy of the world* includes ontological (metaphysical) *world-hypotheses* and the overall *metamodel.* These philosophical world-hypotheses must be distinguished from scientific hypotheses. Scientific hypotheses, which belong to the hypothetical level of the scientific text, are testable, whereas philosophical world-hypotheses are not. However, in conjuntion with a meta-model world-hypotheses constitute the overall, generic background for empirical research and descriptions (the data level), as well as theoretical explanations and interpretations of the world (the hypothetical level).

2. *Philosophy of science* includes metatheses about epistemological, metatheoretical, and methodological problems. These metatheses are often formulated in a prescriptive language as *rules, norms,* or *ideals* for scientific research and the construction of scientific theories. This aspect of the metalevel has a guiding or directing role, related to the hypothetical level and the data level.

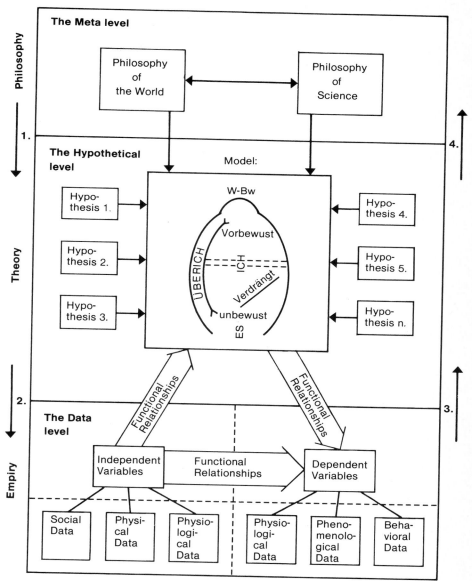

Figure 1. Our metatheory, called *systematology*, conceives of a scientific text as consisting of three levels of abstraction: the metalevel, containing metatheses (i.e., propositions about the philosophy of the world and the philosophy of science); the hypothetical level, containing hypotheses and explanatory models; and the data level, containing data theses (i.e., general functional relationships and specific descriptive propositions).

Definition of Science

We conclude this brief exposition of the development of the conception of science by a summarizing definition. Science can be defined as the social-cultural system of individuals who are engaged in empirical research, theoretical, and philosophical thinking. It produces scientific texts which, in their complete versions, include three levels of abstraction: the philosophical metalevel, the theoretical hypothetical level, and the empirical data level. We are now in a position to formulate our definition of *metascience*.

Definition of Metascience

We will start with a preliminary and very brief definition of metascience as the general term for all studies pertaining to science. In accordance with our previous definition of science, we can also classify the metascientific disciplines on three levels of abstraction: the philosophical level, the theoretical level, and the empirical level. Each level contains one or more metascientific disciplines.

The Philosophy of Science

On the most abstract, philosophical metalevel of metascience we have the philosophy of science. This metascientific discipline derives from the philosophy of knowledge in general, that is, from epistemology. Philosophy of science therefore developed *after* the emergence of modern science in the Renaissance. It was especially Immanuel Kant, August Comte, and John Stuart Mill who founded this branch of philosophy. However, the philosophy of science was not organized as an independent discipline with its own journals and professional societies until this century. Modern philosophy of science often deals with epistemological problems (of knowledge and truth in general) as well as with more specific problems concerning scientific theories and methods. Philosophical thinking about these problems often results in the formulation of prescriptions (rules, norms, or ideals) for how to construct scientific theories and use scientific methods in such a way that the theories and methods are accepted as genuinely scientific. It is by this prescriptive thinking that the philosophy of science can be distinguished from the next level, the hypothetical level of metascience, which also deals with scientific theories and methods, but in a more hypothetical or explanatory manner.

Metatheory (*Wissenschaftstheorie*)

In the years after the Second World War different kinds of theories about science developed. These theories were not exclusively based on the philosophy of science, but more on the empirical studies of science (such as the history of science and other disciplines which we shall deal with in the next paragraph). As examples of these new kinds of theories about science, we may mention Kuhn's well-known theory (1962), but also the theories of Lakatos (1970) and Hanson (1957). What these and other modern theories about science have in common is that they are based more upon the history of science than upon the philosophy of science, although the authors are also well versed in the philosophy of science. But the principal difference between these kinds of theories about science and the philosophy of science is that these modern theories about science are formulated as testable (scientific) theories, whereas the philosophy of science is often prescriptive in nature.

Thus, these modern theories about science belong to the theoretical or hypothetical level of the general category of metascience. This level has relationships both to the philosophical level, which may have been the inspiration for their formulation, and to the empirical level, from which data for testing the theories are drawn (cf. Figure 2).

Before we turn our attention to the empirical studies of science, we must deal with another problem of terminology: What is a proper name for this modern *theory of science*? In Anglo-American literature the term *philosophy of science* is often used in such an encompassing manner that it includes both the philosophy of science in the narrow sense (belonging to the philosophical level) and theory about science (belonging to the theoretical or hypothetical level). In German the term *Wissenschaftstheorie* is often used as equivalent to this modern theory about science (there are similar words in the Scandinavian languages). The English term 'theory *about* science' may be confused with 'theory of science,' which may be understood as 'a scientific theory.' Therefore, the author suggests that the term *metatheory* be used in English and in such a broad sense that it will include methodology. This broad meaning is equivalent to *Wissenschaftstheorie*. We may therefore conclude this paragraph with a definition: *Metatheory* can be defined as theory about scientific theories and methods which may be inspired by philosophy of science, and which can be tested by empirical studies of science. We turn now to these empirical studies of science.

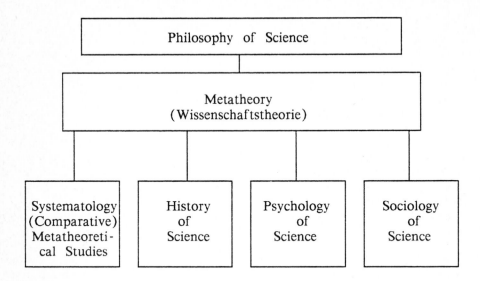

Figure 2. Three levels of metascience: the philosophical level (Philosophy of Science), the hypothetical level (Metatheory), and the empirical level (containing systematology, history of science, psychology of science, and sociology of science).

Empirical Sciences of Science

The empirical or data level of metascience includes several disciplines which are more or less well established as independent scientific disciplines (cf. Figure 2). The oldest and most well established discipline is the history of science, which has been in existence for many years and has its own journals and professional societies. Even a subdiscipline of this discipline, the history of psychology, flourishes in textbooks, journals, and societies. Many modern metatheories (in the sense defined above) are based especially upon historical studies of science. This is the case with the theories of Hanson, Kuhn, and Lakatos.

Another empirical metascientific discipline is the sociology of science, established between the two world wars. Often the name *science of science* is used exclusively to refer to this discipline. But this is, of course, too narrow a use of this term since the (empirical) science of science includes several disciplines. In addition to the two already mentioned - the history and sociology of science - we shall mention some less well established disciplines.

The psychology of science is a metascientific discipline not yet organized into its own journals and professional societies. However, several empirical studies exist in this area, both of the psychology of scientific knowledge (for example, Maslow, 1966; Royce, 1973) and the psychology of scientists' personalities (Roe, 1953; Coan, 1979).

In Figure 2 we placed the psychology of science between the history of science and the sociology of science because two additional disciplines exist on its borders. Thus, between sociology of science and psychology of science we have a discipline called the *social psychology of science*, which studies scientific teams. A well-known example is the work of Pelz (1958; 1964). Another metascientific discipline may be found between the history of science and the psychology of science, namely, the *psychobiography of science*. A representative example is Gruber's study of Charles Darwin (1974).

The last metascientific discipline to be mentioned here is the comparative study of scientific theories. As the classic work in this discipline we may refer to the six volumes edited by a pioneer in theoretical psychology, namely, Sigmund Koch, entitled *Psychology: A Study of a Science* (see Koch, 1959). This major endeavor in theoretical psychology analyzes about 80 psychological theories. The analyses are done either by the authors themselves or by another expert on the theory (in cases in which the original author died). These analyses follow a common metatheoretical outline established by the editor. Unfortunately, the planned comparative volume seven was never published.

Inspired by Koch and other theoretical psychologists and philosophers of science, I made a comparative study of about 50 psychological theories (Madsen, 1959; 1974; 1975). I suggested the term *systematology* for these comparative studies of theories, the purpose of which was to contribute to a general metatheory. Since the term *theory* is used with very different meanings, I have suggested instead the use of the term *scientific text* in accordance with the following definition: A scientific text is a text which contains one, two, or three of the following levels of abstraction: the descriptive level, the hypothetical level, and the philosophical level. With this definition of a scientific text, we can define systematology as the comparative, metatheoretical study of scientific texts.

This new metascientific discipline is closely related to the history of science, because scientific texts are also important materials for historical studies. The major difference between the history of science and systematology is that in historical studies other empirical materials are used in addition to scientific texts with the purpose of describing (and perhaps explaining) historical development or evolution, whereas the purpose of systematology is to contribute to a general metatheory. I am at present working on a combined historical and systematological study of psychological theories in which the main texts in psychology are studied with systematological methods and the results are then organized into a historical frame of reference (inspired by Kuhn; see Madsen, in press).

Concluding Definitions

We presented a preliminary definition of metascience in the introduction and may now conclude with a more extensive definition which summarizes the presentation of the various metascientific disciplines. Metascience can be defined as a common term for all those studies that have science as their object and which are organized on one or more of the following three levels of abstraction:

1. the philosophical (often prescriptive) level, containing the philosophy of science,

2. the theoretical (hypothetical) level, containing metatheory (in a broad sense, including methodology),

3. the empirical level, containing the history of science, the psychology of science, the sociology of science, and systematology.

A note about the term systematology: The author introduced the term *psychological systematology* in *Theories of Motivation* (Madsen, 1959), wherein the term was defined as *the study of psychological systems (theories)*. Later, the term *systematology* was used in Madsen (1974) and as the title of a book (in Danish, subtitled *A Comparative Metatheory for Psychologists*, Madsen, 1975). Still later, the author discovered that the term had been used by other authors. The Austrian philosopher Franz Körner used it in *Die Anarchie der philosophischen Systeme* in 1929. According to a symposium on systematology published in *Metaphilosophy*, Vol. 13, No. 3 and 4, July/October 1982, Körner used *systematology* as a name for the comparative metaphilosophical studies of philosophical systems.

This is parallel to our use of systematology as a name for the comparative metatheoretical studies of scientific theories. However, the term was used even earlier by the German philosopher, J. Heinrich Lambert, in his posthumously published *Philosophische Schriften* (Band I, 1782,

Band II, 1787). Volume II contains a *Fragment einer Systematologie* (pp. 385-413). This is a rough outline of what today would be called general systems theory because it deals with both physical systems, political systems, and intellectual systems (including scientific theories). Thus the term *systematology* has been used for at least two hundred years with different but overlapping meanings: essentially, the comparative metatheoretical study of scientific texts (theories).

We defined theoretical psychology in the introduction as the metascientific study of psychological theories and theory-problems. This definition does not need extensive reformulation; rather, we may present a shorter version. Thus, the *metascientific study of psychological theories and theory-problems* could be referred to by the phrase *psychological metatheory*. On this account, the definition of theoretical psychology is the same as psychological metatheory. According to this definition the history of psychology and other empirical studies of psychology (except systematology) do not belong to theoretical psychology unless their purpose is (as is that of systematology) to contribute to psychological metatheory.

Classification of the Conference Papers

Using the definitions presented in the above sections we shall try to make a rough classification of the various papers presented at the first conference for theoretical psychology. The classification is made on the basis of the abstracts provided at the conference. We present the results of our classification in a classification scheme with the names of the authors in the different levels of theoretical psychology. Some papers belong to two or three of the levels and therefore the authors' names are placed on the relevant levels. Doubtful cases are indicated with a question-mark. In this listing, the Empirical level should be seen as including historical, sociological, and psychological studies of science. The distribution is as follows:

Philosophical	Dalenoort, De Wit, Eysenck, Hammersley, Rychlak, Scheerer, Shotter, Tolman.
Metatheoretical	Corcoran & Mehmet?, Davies?, Elbers, Eysenck, van Gert, Gosling, Hammersley?, Hezewijk, Jorna, Maiers, Maze, McGuire, Noble, Parker, Shames, Staats, van Strien, Rychlak.
Empirical	Elbers?, Hezewijk?, Lovie, Maiers, McGuire, Noble, Scheerer, van Strien, Tolman.

174 Theoretical Psychology

References

Coan, R. W. (1979). *Psychologists: Personal and theoretical pathways.* New York: Irvington.

Gruber, H. E. (1974). *Darwin on man: A psychological study of scientific creativity.* New York: Dutton.

Hanson, N. R. (1957). *Patterns of discovery.* Cambridge: Cambridge University Press.

Koch, S. (Ed.). (1959-1963). *Psychology: A study of a science* (Vols. 1-6). New York: McGraw-Hill.

Kuhn, T. S. (1962). *The structure of scientific revolutions.* Chicago: University of Chicago Press.

Lakatos, I. (1970). Falsification and the methodology of scientific research-programs. In I. Lakatos & A. Musgrave (Eds.), *Criticism and the growth of knowledge* (pp. 91-96). Cambridge: Cambridge University Press.

Lambert, J. H. (1967, 1969). *Philosophische Schriften.* Berlin: Vol. 1, 1782, Vol. 2, 1787. Photographic Reprint. Hildesheim: Georg Olms Verlagsbuch-handel.

Madsen, K. B. (1959). *Theories of motivation.* Copenhagen: Munksgaard. (4th ed., 1968).

Madsen, K. B. (1974). *Modern theories of motivation.* Copenhagen: Munksgaard and New York: Wiley.

Madsen, K. B. (1975). *Systematology: Sammenlignende Videnskabteori.* Copenhagen: Munksgaard.

Madsen, K. B. (in press). *A history of psychology in metascientific perspective.* Copenhagen: The National Research Foundation.

Maslow, A. H. (1966). *The psychology of science.* New York: Harper & Row.

Pelz, D. (1958). Social factors in the motivation of engineers and scientists. *School, Science, and Mathematics, 58,* 417-429.

Pelz, D. (1964). Freedom in research. *International Science and Technique, 31,* 54-66.

Roe, A. (1953). *The making of a scientist.* New York: Dodd, Mead.

Royce, J. R. (1973). The present situation in theoretical psychology. In B. B. Wolman (Ed.), *Handbook of general psychology* (pp. 8-21). Englewood Cliffs: Prentice Hall.

Current Issues in Theoretical Psychology
Wm J. Baker, M.E. Hyland, H. Van Rappard, A.W. Staats (Editors)
© Elsevier Science Publishers B.V. (North-Holland), 1987

THE HISTORICAL APPROACH OF CRITICAL PSYCHOLOGY:

ANOTHER CASE OF 'PARADIGM PROMOTION'?

Wolfgang Maiers

Free University of Berlin
West Berlin

SUMMARY: This paper addresses some contemporary critiques of main-stream psychology, namely, the inappropriate emulation of the exact sciences, the consequent distortion of subject matter, and its prevention of relevant unified theorization. The trap of a subjectivist reversal, caught in the very same basic fiction of an 'abstract-isolated human individual' as the 'immediate' unit of psychological analysis, is also described. The approach of Critical Psychology is outlined as it systematically generates the basis for scientific theorizations about the concrete laws of subject development by means of a dialectical-materialistic reconstruction of the historical man-world context that determines empirical individual-environment relationships. Finally, reference is made to the meta-theoretical issue of the necessity and feasibility of scientific unity.

Our founding conference falls within a significant trend towards metatheoretical reflections: Increasingly philosophical prerequisites and conceptual/methodological tools are being discussed that will make possible adequate cognizance of characteristic psychological problems, and hence a resolution of traditional antinomies. These developments are urged in the context of the perennial debates concerning our discipline's crisis (e.g., Arnold, 1976).

Critique of Mainstream Psychology

In brief, current criticism asserts that mainstream psychology has been subject to the scientistic preconception of physics as the model for strictly objective inquiry. This emulation ignores the widely admitted failure of the neopositivistic doctrine of 'unitary science.' The due relation between matter and method has been inverted. Placing method in the dominant position has brought about a restrictive problem selection and treatment that distorts the genuine properties of the subject matter. Central in this has been the research maxim of 'nomological psychology' - to systematically theorize and empirically operationalize regularities of behaviour and experience in 'independent-intervening-dependent variable' form, and to establish their functions by means of (preferably) experimental analysis and statistical data evaluation. In this 'variable-schema' (cf. Blumer, 1969, passim), despite deviations from S-R conceptualization, the (neo-) behaviourist axiom is reified that antecedent and consequent observables alone are intersubjectively accessible. Processes of consciousness inside the 'black box' are accepted as a legitimate object of theoretical constructions so long as they can be inferred from variables controlled by the investigator. If, however, (experimental) subjects relate 'consciously' to the instruction and the proceeding of the trial, the supposed objective independent conditions move into the black box, so to speak, and one can never know for certain whether the responses actually indicate the predicted 'if-then' function. To sum up the traps of methodological objectivism, the fact is that the central root of 'interfering' factors which must be eliminated or neutralized in pursuit of experimental hypothesis testing is the 'subjective subject matter' itself. Add to this that inferential statistics refers to characteristic values in which empirical data are calculated as abstract elements of some distribution of random variables, whereby the concreteness of different individuals or individual features thematically disappears as deviations from a 'central tendency.' (Non-parametric statistics does not alter this problem of data reduction.) What exactly is 'variable-psychology' all about?

This approach implies an 'external view' of other people as 'individuals responding to conditions.' The result is the loss of opportunities of understanding human action on the basis of its objective and subjective premises, as is ubiquitous within common interpersonal communication. Reducing grounded action to conditioned behaviour and regarding subjective experience as unfit for 'objectified' and 'generalized' scientific knowledge presents a methodological artifact. It runs counter to the very goal of objectivity and generality of psychological assumptions as it undermines their unambiguous empirical reference and, as a consequence, necessitates unlimited speculation *ex post facto*. Examples of interpreting findings of uncertain significance 'as if' they matched the psychic phenomena of real human beings, tacitly attaching to them 'surplus meaning' in the light of common sense, are legion. Science adopted by 'variable-psychology' turns out science fiction; or, at best, a dubious representative of science proper. Considering its deficient relevance to the individual subject in his life-world and its failure to establish an accepted non-reductionist approach for integrating the disparate facets of the subject matter, it is not surprising that there is little unity in psychological theorizing. This becomes evident from long-lived rivalries between conceptually incompatible theories of the same domain, all claiming 'empirical confirmation.' Lacking the prospect of a crucial test of their respective validities, there are, accordingly, successions of theory fads without a definite progress in knowledge. Diverse proposals for correction (e.g., Giorgi, 1976) attempt to achieve unity by re-evaluation of the criteria of scientific objectivity, giving priority to 'relevance.' This is understood as a conceptual respect for the phenomenal attributes of human activity/subjectivity (such as intentionality, reflexivity, spontaneity) which should not be invalidated by exposing them to the methods of variable-analysis.

The Illusion of 'Immediacy'

The above variable-schema frames in physicalist particularity a universal insufficiency of traditional psychology, aptly labeled the "postulate of immediacy" (Uznadze, cited in Leont'ev, 1978, p. 47, English transl. corrected, W.M.). Objective life conditions are defined in terms of their immediate empirical relation to the individual ('environment'). The search for psychological laws is almost exclusively restricted to dimensions of human life-worlds or events which do not exceed - cross-sectionally - the limits of (inter-)individual situations or - longitudinally - the individual's biography. Their 'extra-psychological' reality is thus ignored. Although admitting some 'individuo-centered' contextualism and historicity (delegated to 'developmental' and 'social psychology' or adopted as their particular viewpoints), the individuals are accounted for as representatives of ahistorical-invariant ('general psychological') laws. (In this regard, current 'life-span' developmental and ecological approaches and their devices of time-series analyses and multivariate designs demand a critical inspection.)

The phantasm of an 'abstract-isolated human individual' (Marx) acts as the conceptual foil of any psychology trapped in the ideological forms of bourgeois society. In this respect it is of minor importance whether individuals as ultimate units are preferentially predicted from surrounding effects ('environmentalism') or, countering this objectivistic model of 'conditionality,' are comprehended from themselves. The latter approach, in emphasizing man's active ('conditioning') effect on the environment, usually views the actors as spontaneously constituting their own cosmos of 'meanings' - in contrast to causative stimuli - as an action frame of reference. Where, as in Symbolic Interactionism, this is conceptualized as a 'social product' of permanent inter-individual interpretative and constructive processes (Blumer, 1969), the consciousness of the individual subjects is still given priority. In eliminating the external reality as an independent determinant of action, meanings become psychologized. Deprived of its reference to objectively based meanings (see below), the psychic is converted into a 'private inwardness' - in silent agreement with the objectivistic antipode's bias.

The categorial and methodological effects of the 'postulate of immediacy' recur and are sanctioned on the level of an ahistorical logic of scientific rationality with its understanding of an 'anything goes' conceptualization. Consistent with a programmatic disregard of ideative processes in both logical empiricism and critical rationalism, psychology disposes at best of logical means to derive and subsequently prove empirical assumptions from an existing theory. No rigorous criteria for a nonarbitrary theory formation are offered; nor does the empirical confirmation of hypotheses provide an independent test for the validity of the pertinent theory. With regard to the (conceptually represented) reality dimensions there is a circular interrelationship between the systematic propositions, experimental variables, and data. This includes the eventuality that theoretical conceptions whose hypotheses have been sufficiently supported refer to totally peripheral or artificial effects. If psychology is to avoid proliferating propositions about empirical events based on concepts with an indeterminate reality anchoring, scientific tools seem imperative in order to generate empirically substantiated basic categories which define the subject matter under investigation. These categories, that is, would locate it within the total structure of processes and phenomena in the material world, and elucidate its 'internal architecture' of relevant dimensions. These dimensions are the more essential, the more fundamental they are, relative to others. By way of a categorial reconstruction of this hierarchical dimensional system a growing variety of surface phenomena on increasingly subordinate dimensions can be integrated and explained by theoretical concepts. Scientific approaches become relevant themselves to the extent that they accomplish this. Accordingly, everyday life subjective states and ways of acting do not unveil *prima facie* their essential features. Moreover, they are bound to remain a largely ruleless congeries if the laws governing them are held to be explicable from isolated individual-environment relationships. Contrary to this ahistorical decontextualization, the latter connections are to be accounted for as dependent segments ('micro-aspects') of an encompassing order of determinative and mediate dimensions - here: of the 'man-world context' which emerged natural- and social-historically (cf. Holzkamp, 1977). The expectation of a unifying effect of relevant conceptualization (see above) is therefore illusory if this be simply fulfilled in a closer contact to phenomenal life-worlds.

Now, dialectical materialism would be reverted to a metaphysical variant, if the concrete historical reality were reduced to a medium of external agents impinging upon the individuals. It is men who through their labour are the conscious agents of the production, control, and alteration of their life circumstances - however dependent on the objectivity of nature and the objectifications of preceding collective praxis. How can we escape the Scylla of objectivism and the Charybdis of subjectivism? One requirement of concepts which allow for the subject-object-dialectic of the determination of human action is that human beings are not so conceived as to make their societally mediated existence, although indisputable, appear impossible. Basic psychological terms, that is, must recognize the connection between the individual maintenance of life and the super-individual relations of production. This involves a material system of intersubjectively generalized action-directing objective meanings, which is practically sustained by their individual acquisition and realization. For a full understanding of that basis of psychic ontogenesis the historical-materialistic analysis must unravel the contrariety of the individual's naturalness and his sociality as a myth. We have to account for the 'triviality' of man's unique potentiality for socialization in a scientific concept of 'human nature' (cf. Maiers, 1985).

Aspects of a Psychological 'Subject Science'

The Historical Approach of Critical Psychology. A concept of human nature can neither be directly derived from ontogenesis (as that will never reveal potentiality other than in some state of social realization - hence the futile nature-nurture debate within a non-historical approach) nor by way of an abstract man-animal comparison. In order to distinguish its specific and determinative, secondary, and unspecific qualities, it has to be elaborated how, in the process of human evolution, beginnings of an 'economic' mode of reproduction emerged which, by bringing forth immense selection advantages, reacted on the genomic information of the hominids. Their psychic possibilities became thus transformed into the disposition of participating in the new cooperative-social process of existence. The analysis of this development, implying the answer to the seeming paradox of a 'societal nature,' has to be pursued up to the transition from a purely phylogenetic evolution to the dominance of societal development as a particular historical process. On the other hand it must be based on the study of natural history in its entirety. The aim is to parsimoniously explain differentiations in psychic capacities as vital adjustments - 'functional reflections' - to momentous changes in the ecology of species. Because traditional psychology fails to apply this 'functional-historical' explanatory principle of 'developmental necessity,' the common *homo psychologicus* resembles in many respects a *homunculus* who is neither socially nor even biologically viable.

I cannot present here the 'logical-historical' methodology of dialectical-materialistic developmental analysis, let alone their results (but see Holzkamp, 1973; Holzkamp-Osterkamp, 1975, 1976; Schurig, 1976; Holzkamp, 1983). The point is to construct a conceptual taxonomy which is equivalent to the 'logic' of psychic development up to its complex result of human consciousness. In this sense, the category of 'the psychic' denotes the initial form of a life activity distinguished from previous processes of a direct 'irritability' by its mediation through a 'sensibility' to signals for vital factors. This elementary definition of psychic reflection also supplies the most general and abstract characterization of all further differentiations into 'cognitive' and 'emotional evaluation' processes or 'social-communicative' regulations. These interlocked 'functional aspects' take on a new quality with the phylogenetic emergence of the 'individual-adaptive modifiability' of the psychically mediated organism-environment relations. Its species-specific evolution specializes in the course of 'anthropogenesis,' producing 'human nature.' Ever since Cromagnon man this has remained relatively stationary - not as a collection of hereditary invariants fixing the phenotypes of individual development, but rather as a distinctive learning and developmental capacity which is to be realized as a conscious life process under the circumstances of historically concrete action demands and opportunities. In this regard there is a notable change with the transition from the cooperative prototype of social life with its plain reciprocity between the individual's and the community's survival to a provision for the individuals in self-regulating societal systems of reproduction: 'objective meanings' as indications of activities which are, on average, indispensible contributions of community members to the reproductive mechanism, present themselves to the individuals as 'possibilities of action.' These may be utilized or not, depending on how the individuals expect their engagement to influence their personal 'action potence' and, consequently, their quality of living. Human subjectivity with its unique reflexivity, i.e., a conscious relationship of the individual to the external world and himself, is founded on such freedom from sheer necessity.

The analysis of the human psyche has to be carried out in the concreteness of formation-specific circumstances. Fundamental in capitalist society is a contradiction between ample material resources of individual development and enjoyment of life and their unavailability due to restrictions such as the class-specific separation from control over individually relevant societal living conditions. This basic situation of alienation, which is mystified in the surface experiences of a private-form existence, penetrates everyday life praxis. It appears in the basic conflict of the individual to search after action potence by removing limitations or else, because of the possible risk of endangering his given level of acting, to put up with present dependencies. The latter attempt is in principle problematic. Although possibly advantageous in the short term, it helps to stabilize the restrictive frame of acting, thus obstructing long-term developmental interests. Consider as an example of that kind of 'self-enmity' the interdependency between 'childishness' and parental 'overprotectiveness.' We have categorized the above polarity as 'generalized vs. restrictive action potence' and investigated its respective consequences for the various aspects of psychic functioning. We have thus derived a system of relational concepts for cognitive modes ('comprehensive vs. interpretative thinking'), states of emotionality ('intersubjectively generalized emotional engagement vs. emotional introversion'), and of conation ('productive motivation vs. inner compulsion'). With the latter pair, for example, we distinguish between the willingness to make efforts and take risks in order to improve life circumstances in the interest of an emancipated development and a motivation-form internalization of an alien direction of action, unaware of the underlying external compulsions (cf. Holzkamp, 1983, Ch. 6 and 7). Under the assumption that nobody deliberately harms himself, the moments of 'self-enmity' as concomitants of restrictive acting have been demonstrated to be constitutive for the genesis of the unconscious (cf. Holzkamp-Osterkamp, 1976).

Our categories do not provide concrete descriptions but general determinations of possible directions of subject development. On their basis, individual manifestations may be empirically studied and theoretically comprehended. Since we are all permanently faced with the alternative of 'generalized' or 'restrictive' activity, the categories are also not to be understood as typological concepts 'about people' from the external standpoint of an aloof observer. Instead, they are concepts for 'myself and everyone' (*je mich*). They have to prove themselves by enabling those 'concerned' to discover opportunities of individual development that counteract tendencies of self-enmity. To this effect they must reveal interindividually generalizable characteristics of individual psychic states and point out necessities as well as possibilities of joint actions with other subjects. The aim is to plan, initiate, and check, in a 'controlled exemplary practice,' the steps to be taken in everyday life. This involves a new mode of intersubjective communication between the psychologist contributing his experience as an integral part of the matter under investigation and the client qualifying as co-investigator. Here I cannot present details about the 'actual-empirical research' of a psychological 'subject science' as opposed to the 'control-scientific' viewpoint of variable-psychology (cf. Holzkamp, 1983, Ch. 9.3). Let me return to the problem of securing scientific objectivity and generalization in a field where experiential data do not exist other than in the mode of first person singular.

Structural Generalization of Subjective Data. We must avoid two traps: firstly, to nullify concretenes as sheer exception by subsuming the individual under the abstract generality of a statistical average; secondly, to assume that idiographic case studies, which abandon all claims to generalized explanations exclusively do justice to individuality. We therefore propose the methodological alternative of 'structural generalization.' Its principle is by no means unknown to other disciplines. Physicists will scarcely test the validity of the law of falling bodies statistically; and biologists are well familiar with inferences from one specimen to any of a species (as, statistically speaking, a homogeneous population). As for psychology, let me remind you of Lewin's generalization concept (1931). Clearly, absolutizing the way of frequency thinking beyond the range of stochastic processes remained the reserve of variable-psychology. How, then, can 'objectifying the subjective' and 'generalizing the individuality' be accomplished? We start from the statement that individuals are experiencing while acting in societal meaning constellations. The task, then, is to demonstrate an individual case of subjectivity as a personal manifestation of a general pattern of psychic states related to typical coping activities vis-à-vis contradictory action demands and prospects (cf. above). The argument that under analogous premises individuals possess common possibilities of acting and experiencing is to be empirically scrutinized by specifying the *ceteris paribus* clause. This involves, as a first step, distinguishing that section of the generalized possibilities of action pertinent to an individual's class-specific position in society which are actually disposable or accessible to him according to his biographical experience. Through a comparative inspection of such empirical 'subjective possibility spaces' we attempt to find out their common structure. With a sufficient number of tentative (self-)applications to further individuals, this suppositional 'typical possibility space' will gain in contentual concreteness owing to all the additional particulars. The increase in new information will diminish as there is no infinitude of alternative action directions appropriate to certain life circumstances and interests. Eventually the 'type' construct may be taken to be an asymptotical approximation to a circumscribed basic situation of individual-environment relations. Thus, individual cases ('each case' of a 'subjective possibility space' of acting/experiencing) are objectified and generalized without neglecting their unique features by explaining them (via successful self-subsumptions under a 'type of possibilities') as specifications of 'such a case' (cf. Holzkamp, 1983, Ch. 9.4).

Provisional Result. Our approach is intended as a procedure to derive categories as foundations of specific theories. Its logical-historical method yields empirically testable results without moderating standards of scientific rigour - even though they differ from traditional empirical tests. To the extent of its demonstrated (irrefuted) substantiality, our reconstruction of relevance-graded dimensions of the man-world context supplies criteria for appraising the soundness - the range of validity and generality, hence the differential explanatory value - of competing theories. Besides detecting omissions of essential aspects, this approach enables us to classify the relative position and level of specifity of their concepts. The possible incorporation of critically reinterpreted results of theories that, so far, have stood in indeterminate opposition or juxtaposition, into an integrative progression of psychological knowledge would mean another crucial instance of verifying our conception. By the same token, the methodological necessity would be demonstrated to step outside the customary discipline boundaries and to lean on related branches of knowledge if a truly psychological inquiry is ever to be achieved.

In order to give at least a fragmentary sketch of Critical Psychology, I had to refrain from a meta-comment on current controversies about the necessity of scientific unification and, pertinent to this issue, about the feasibility of a unity-conferring paradigm. Let me finish, however, with a few notes.

Psychology in a Crisis?

The Quest for a New Foundation. As is well known, the attrition of the 'standard view of science' involved a trend to base critical historiography and metatheoretical inspections of psychology on Kuhn's theory of scientific development (1962). One typical opinion is that the contemporary disconcertion indicates the fall of a predominant paradigm and the rise of some brand new victorious successor. As Koch sarcastically remarked: "Paradigm promotion became the new form of psychological commerce" (1976, p. 480). I cannot explain here why I consider theses of conceptual 'revolutions' from 'behavioural' towards 'reflexive,' 'telic' models of man implying a radical revision of the obsolete methodology of mainstream psychology a fallacy. Neither can I point out in what respect Kuhn's approach is basically restricted by a deficient social theory and epistemology. However, the anti-thesis that psychology is 'preparadigmatic,' and that the assertion of a 'paradigm shift' has therefore to be refuted (e.g., Giorgi, 1976), seems to me more appropriate. It conforms with both Kuhn's initial idea that the 'puzzle-solving' of 'normal science' is monoparadigmatically regulated, that is, unified by one disciplinary world view at a time, and the fact of ubiquitous fractionation. What conclusion can be drawn from this? Consider Koch's exemplary dictum that 'psychology cannot be a coherent science' (Koch, 1969), irrespective of whether coherence be defined in terms of a contentual model of subject matter or of methodico-strategic commitments. He has been urging that it is illusory to search for a single paradigm and that therefore scientific psychology be reconceived as 'psychological studies' representing a multitude of epistemic perspectives. Koch's verdict appears delicate just because it coincides with the reasoning of the defenders of the hegemony of 'variable-psychology' which Koch has been so eager to attack! Making a virtue of necessity, they substitute disunion for 'plurality of views': As a network of heterogeneous research programmes, psychology is sufficiently defined by its nomological methodology. Conceptual unification tends to undermine critical rationality by essentialism and to dogmatically restrict scientific pluralism. Koch, for his part, blindly resting on the misconception of mainstream psychology, conceives of science exclusively in its analytical-experimental, mathematized form. Since the traditional logic of science has been unveiled (not least by Koch) as a misrepresentation of but one sort of science, this identification becomes untenable however. The criticism of scientism and objectivism, then, does not at all discredit the project of a psychology as a science *sui generis*. On the contrary, it gives it top priority, all the more so if a subjectivistic version of 'pseudo-knowledge' (Koch), e.g., that following from the humanist 'third force' credo that psychology has 'exaggerated the scientific character,' is to be rejected as a possible alternative.

We agree with those critics who hold any relativistic renunciation of a unitary conception of psychology a perpetuation of its prescientific state. They consequently urge the elaboration of a comprehensive research framework so that particular theorization and data bases can be related and, possibly, synthesized (i.e., Staats, 1981, and his present contribution). Indeed, the problems of a foundation of modern psychology can only be resolved through a discussion about a categorial-methodological definition of subject matter that obviates two critical trends: firstly, to level the respective specifity of multifarious aspects in the uniformity of a reductionist simplification of problems; secondly, to eternalize the actual diversity of meaningful research perspectives as distinct ways of viewing, one as good as another. This latter prejudice practically suggests eclectic combinations or separatistic adherence to one of the supposedly incommensurable positions. Returning to popular Kuhnian terms, that is, we need a consistent 'paradigm' able to do - in historical relativity - justice to the totality of psychic phenomena. (With the proviso mentioned above, to be sure, it is questionable whether under a metatheoretical aspect this project can be suitably couched in terms of Kuhn's paradigm analysis, or whether some different rationale should be chosen.)

Limits and Chance of Unification. Admittedly, contemporary psychology outside the mainstream exhibits a number of fundamental orientations. Although not yet sufficiently analyzed, their interrelation is obviously determined by opposing viewpoints as to the nature of the world, of the human being, and the foundations of knowledge, thus opening divergent scientific perspectives. Even if they partially overlap, the attempt to fuse different epistemic approaches to reality is bound to lead to conceptual and empirical confusion. There is ample evidence against (programmatic) eclecticism, so I need not detail my objections. Pluralism of competitive conceptions (including the level of ontology or epistemology) marks a transitory difficulty which will eventually be settled by human praxis and must not be hypostatized. This epistemological optimism is not contradicted by the insight that we have to be prepared for unresolved schisms perpetuating the divisiveness of psychology for a tidy stretch of time - so much the more as this difficulty has come to a head in the epochal antagonism between bourgeois and marxist ideology. Considering psychological cognizance on its inherent partiality with respect to the dialectic of human history, it is illusory to expect essential issues to be arbitrated, evading ideological dispute. It becomes evident that achieving paradigmaticity throughout the discipline (bearing comparison with the basic scientific agreement in the community of, say, physicists) is beyond the scope of an intra-scientific revolution of the prevailing disciplinary world view. It is contingent upon which of the conflicting contemporary ideological main forces wins the hegemony in society. If, by implication, the emergence of a common candidate against the 'variable-psychology' cannot be anticipated, how shall we ever escape the impasse of a dysfunctional mainstream?

Counterbalancing the foregoing emphasis upon epistemological discontinuity by recalling the moment of continuity in the history of knowledge, I can well imagine traditional problem-antinomies and obsolete incommensurabilities which may be overcome by concerted endeavours. There is no need for suspending decisive steps towards the unification of realms of psychologically relevant phenomena and of theorizing. Provided my preceding considerations are correct, we have no option but to elaborate the several proposed avenues out of crisis according to their specific research-strategic directives, and simultaneously to intensify critical dialogues between the approaches. Can they mutually support their scientific developments because their views partly concur? A second possibility would be that even apparently divergent positions appeal to each other as 'somehow significant' complementary selections and views of problems. The challenge then is to translate these conceptualizations into one's own system. The criterion of such a 'retheorization' lies in whether or not an even more profound, cogent, and parsimonious interpretation of the matters in question is reached, avoiding and accounting for the flaws ('anomalies') of the rivals. On the condition that a possible inter-positional consensus concerning the establishment of 'facts' is not a priori ruled out, which would be tantamount to an agnosticistic obstruction of scientific labour - what matters in avoiding isolationism is to become so explicit in one's own scientific basis and in the standards of critique and reinterpretation that fruitful comparison of conceptual-methodological systems and decisions on their respective fidelity and explicative scope and power become possible.

Conclusion

Proceeding from the dialectical-materialistic principle of 'reflection,' a logical-historical analysis of the origins, functions, and structural connections of discriminable psychic phenomena leads to a comprehensive fundamental psychological system to be filled in by concrete theoretical and empirical studies in an internally consistent manner. We are convinced that this foundation helps to overcome the *pars-pro-toto* logic of reductionism as well as the blind alley of the seemingly more concrete conceptual pluralism. It is in this perspective that Critical Psychology is indeed striving for the propagation of the Marxist historical approach as a, if you like, 'potential paradigm' for psychology.

References

Arnold, W. J. (Ed.) (1976). Conceptual foundations of psychology. *Nebraska Symposium on Motivation, 1975.* Lincoln/London: University of Nebraska Press.

Blumer, H. (1969). *Symbolic interactionism - perspective and method.* Englewood Cliffs, NJ: Prentice-Hall.

Giorgi, A. (1976). Phenomenology and the foundations of psychology. In W. J. Arnold (Ed.), *Nebraska Symposium on Motivation, 1975.* (pp. 281-348). Lincoln/London: University of Nebraska Press.

Holzkamp, K. (1973). *Sinnliche Erkenntnis - Historischer Ursprung und gesellschaftliche Funktion der Wahrnehmung* (Sensual cognition - historical origin and societal function of perception). Frankfurt/M.: Fischer-Athenäum.

Holzkamp, K. (1977). Die Überwindung der wissenschaftlichen Beliebigkeit psychologischer Theorien durch die Kritische Psychologie (Critical Psychology surmounts the scientific indeterminacy of psychological theories). *Zeitschrift für Sozialpsychologie, 8,* 1-22, 78-97.

Holzkamp, K. (1983). *Grundlegung der Psychologie.* (Foundation of psychology). Frankfurt/M.: Campus.

Holzkamp-Osterkamp, U. (1975). *Grundlagen der psychologischen Motivationsforschung 1.* (Fundamentals of psychological motivation research). Frankfurt/M.: Campus.

Holzkamp-Osterkamp, U. (1976). *Motivationsforschung 2. Die Besonderheit menschlicher Bedürfnisse - Problematik und Erkenntnisgehalt der Psychoanalyse.* (Motivation Research 2. The peculiarity of human needs - problematic nature and informative value of psychoanalysis). Frankfurt/M.: Campus.

Koch, S. (1969). Psychology cannot be a coherent science. *Psychology Today, 3,* 14, 64-68.

Koch, S. (1976). Language communities, search cells, and the psychological studies. In W. J. Arnold (Ed.), *Nebraska Symposium on Motivation, 1975* (pp. 477-559). Lincoln/London: University of Nebraska Press.

Kuhn, T. S. (1962). *The structure of scientific revolutions.* Chicago: University of Chicago Press.

Leont'ev, A. N. (1978). *Activity, consciousness, and personality.* (M. J. Hall, Trans.). Englewood Cliffs, NJ: Prentice Hall. (Original work published 1975).

Lewin, K. (1931). The conflict between Aristotelian and Galilean modes of thought in contemporary psychology. *Journal of General Psychology, 5,* 141-177.

Maiers, W. (1985). Menschliche Subjektivität und Natur. Zum Wissenschaftlichen Humanismus in den Ansätzen A. N. Leontjews und der Kritischen Psychologie. (Human subjectivity and nature. On the Scientific Humanism in the approaches of A. N. Leont'ev and of Critical Psychology). *Forum Kritische Psychologie 15*, 110-163.

Schurig, V. (1976). *Die Entstehung des Bewußtseins* (The genesis of consciousness). Frankfurt/M.: Campus.

Staats, A. W. (1981). Paradigmatic behaviorism, unified theory, unified theory construction methods, and the zeitgeist of separatism. *American Psychologist, 36,* (3), 239-256.

Current Issues in Theoretical Psychology
Wm J. Baker, M.E. Hyland, H. Van Rappard, A.W. Staats (Editors)
© Elsevier Science Publishers B.V. (North-Holland), 1987

THE COMPOSITION OF THE EGO IN A DETERMINIST

PSYCHOLOGY

J. R. Maze

University of Sydney
Sydney, Australia

SUMMARY: Psychoanalytic ego psychology has discarded the concept of ego-instincts and treats the ego as a group of control functions autonomous of the instinctual drives and in fact opposed to them. The reality principle is supposed to give rise to the ego's policies, but the matters of fact yielded by reality-testing are policy-neutral and can only generate a policy through interaction with already existing drives. The ego's motivation is best accounted for in terms of ego-instincts. Those instinctual drives which are acceptable to the child's social environment become the ego while the unacceptable are repressed to form the id. To account for behaviour by reference to 'personal agency' allows no basis for either explanation or prediction.

Modern ego psychology regards it as one of its major achievements to have discarded Freud's early concept of ego-instincts, and to have substituted for it (following in the main the lines laid down by Hartmann shortly after Freud's death) the concept of an autonomous, 'conflict free' ego. Despite terminological preferences one can find this general trend of thought in, for example, Feffer (1982), Gedo (1979), Kohut (1978) and Schafer (1976). One noteworthy difference is that some of these authors specifically include the concept of personal agency as an unanalyzable primitive, a view foreign to the biological mode of thought that Hartmann was trying to maintain; however, this difference is more apparent than real, because, as I shall try to show, Hartmann's account of the ego's motivation leads inevitably to a similar conception. I base my discussion on Hartmann's work because the concepts I want to criticize find there a classical and fairly unambiguous exposition.

According to Hartmann, the ego develops independently of, and side by side with, the instincts of the id, and functions autonomously of the instincts or any biological motivational basis. It is in fact nothing but a set of functions, essentially those of perception (or reality-testing), memory, anticipation, rational planning, and control of motility. These disembodied functions are called apparatuses by Hartmann (Hartmann,

1958, 1964), a misleading usage, since 'apparatus' ordinarily means a piece of machinery whose functions we may or may not know, but Hartmann's apparatuses appear to be functions of no machinery or substantive entities whatever. The overall and indeed only goal of the ego is said to be adaptation; that is, the other two systems, id and superego, are to be adjusted to each other and to the demands of the life situation in such a way as to promote the individual's survival (e.g., Hartmann, 1964, pp. 43-44).

Two Strains in Freud's Thinking

This line of thought had actually been partially foreshadowed by Freud in the 1920's, and the two strains in his thinking about the ego appear strikingly within a single paragraph of *The ego and the id* (Freud, 1923). The remnants of the ego-instincts view can be found when he says that the ego is "that part of the id which has been modified by the direct influence of the external world." (Freud, 1923, p. 25). Since the mind at the beginning of life is described as "all id," which is to say, the complete set of instinctual drives and nothing else, then to say that the ego was originally a part of it suggests that the ego is a selection of the instinctual drives which have somehow separated from the remainder. But almost immediately we find Freud talking of the ego as if it were just a set of control functions, and saying that in the ego, perception "plays the part which in the id falls to instinct." (Freud, 1923, p. 25). That role would be to impel the organism to some specific course of action, which is easy to understand as far as the instinctual drives are concerned. Basically Freud thought of these as physiological mechanisms that were thrown into action by some combination of biochemical factors on the one hand and the perception of certain environmental facts on the other. To paraphrase his early views (Freud, 1905, 1915), each instinctual drive has a small number of wired-in action patterns, the "specific actions," incorporated into it; these are consummatory actions in that one or other of them must be performed if the accumulated tension of the instinctual drive is to be discharged, or, as one may reformulate this, if the biochemical input to the neurophysiological drive mechanism is to be terminated (Maze, 1983).

Perception Alone Cannot Initiate Action

The role of initiating directed behaviour cannot plausibly be attributed just to perception independent of the instinctual drives. Perception merely yields beliefs about matters of fact, and such factual beliefs cannot of themselves imply that any programme of action should be carried out, however the word *should* is meant. Any piece of information which can be put into the form *X leads to Y* can be used either in promoting Y or in avoiding it (Maze, 1973). The belief, for example, that a certain diet will increase body weight may lead one either to adopt that diet or to avoid it, depending on one's already existing motives or drive state; it may produce opposing behaviours in the same person at different times. Thus, as it is identically the same belief operating in each case, it cannot be said to imply either policy. Factual information in itself is policy-neutral; it can initiate behaviour only if it is perceived as relevant to one of the person's existing policies - that is, as relevant to the success of some action pattern specific to a currently active drive state. Perception, then, cannot play the same role as the instinctual drives whether in the ego or anywhere else. Both drive and perception acting together are necessary for the production of any coherent action pattern.

None of this should be taken as in any sense decrying the value or validity of reality-testing. If the concept of rational behaviour has any content apart from a moralistic one, then it means behaviour that is guided by a realistic apprehension of the conditions necessary for it to be effective, and of what its effects are likely to be, whether those conditions and consequences are altogether as one wishes, or not. But the *selection* of the effects aimed for is not itself the work of the reality-principle, but of its interaction with the primary drives.

The Implicit Moralism of "Adaptation"

The notion that the facts of the situation imply that any *right-thinking* person will act in a specific way can always be shown to conceal some moralism or other. It is simply another attempt to derive *ought* from *is*. Hartmann, correctly in my opinion, criticizes the concept of *reasonable behaviour* as being a relativistic moral one pretending to an objectivity it does not possess, yet in embracing the concept of adaptation as if it were objectively definable he allows the same kind of thinking to creep in (Hartmann, 1964, pp. 45-46). Adaptation is a relativistic concept. A condition of life which to one person seems a successful adaptation may be regarded as a fate worse than death by another. If, for example, an analyst should advocate one solution to a patient's problem of adaptation as being better than another in terms of some absolute standard rather than in relation to the analysand's special needs, that would be to impose a moralistic view of life upon the analysand. What such thinking appears to lead to in the practice of some psychoanalytic ego-psychologists is that they align themselves with the patient's superego and treat superego demands as part of the reality situation the patient

must adapt to. In effect this means that the analyst is helping to re-es-
tablish the patient's repressions, presenting him or her with a new set of
rationalizations. However, a radical critique of moral thought, a critique
for which Freud provided the material, would present moralism as lacking
any objective validity, arguing that there are no objective moral properties to be discovered. If so, a belief in their existence, leading to the acceptance of inscrutable moral imperatives, entails an abandonment of
reality-testing (Maze, 1973). From this viewpoint, the most mentally
healthy adjustment to the superego would be to dissipate it altogether -
i.e., for the analysand to see through and be disburdened of a set of moral fictions.

The Need for an Account of Ego-Motivation

If reality-testing alone cannot account for the ego's motivation,
what theoretical adjustments are necessary to do so? It is plain that the
ego does have motives. Even the ego psychologists agree that it throws its
weight sometimes on the side of the id and sometimes on that of the superego, or again that it pursues what they call its own *interests*. The impasse resulting from their discarding ego-instincts is epitomized by a
phrase of Anna Freud's, quoted with approval several times by Hartmann, referring to the "basic hostility of the ego toward the instincts."
(Freud, A., 1946). The ego could only be hostile toward the instincts if
their expression threatened its own interests - to be hostile is in itself to
be motivated - but how to explain the basis of such ego interests if the
ego is divorced from any physiological motivational basis (i.e., from the
instinctual drives) is difficult to imagine.

Hartmann himself (1964, pp. 123, 152) inclines toward the Allport
conception of the functional autonomy of motives (Allport, 1937) - the
conception that although a mode of action may have been taken up originally in the service of a primary drive, in the course of time it can develop its own intrinsic motivation. That is, it can become, like virtue, its
own reward, no longer being dependent on any primary drive gratification
to maintain it. Apart from such difficulties as explaining why one action
becomes functionally autonomous and another not - why a factory worker may perform the same action countless times and give it up the moment it is no longer necessary to earn a living - Allport's conception is
rather like saying that the spinning of a record player turntable can become functionally autonomous of the electric motor which originally
drove it, and of every other motor. Of course, in the case of human beings, the underlying notion is that they *choose* to continue certain occupa-
tions and cause themselves to do so - but such self-caused activities

would be beyond the scope of scientific explanation, as argued below.

Incoherence of Freud's "Ego-Libido"

Freud did realize, even after his shift of thought about the ego, that some motive force was required for it to perform certain acts, but the function of this force or energy was limited to the act of repression. He asked where the ego obtained the force necessary to oppose and repress the powerful instinctual impulses of the id (Freud, 1923). If he had retained the concept of ego-instincts, that question would have been unnecessary because, as we have seen, an instinctual drive is a mechanism that performs work. Having let them drop from sight, Freud was led into that sequence of theoretical constructions which even the most sympathetic of Freudians must find difficult to justify. The ego was said to offer itself as a love-object for the id, thus gaining control of a quantity of libido, just as a person gains control over any one who loves him or her. This captured libido, now called ego-libido, was turned away from its sexual aims and used by the ego to combat the unregenerate object-libido of the id (Freud, 1923, p. 31 ff.). Here one sees a tendency that was later to become pronounced, the tendency to think of energy not as a machine doing work but as a kind of fluid or stuff which can be moved about and channelled in various directions.

Instead of saying that one part of the mind, the id, came to love another, the ego, Freud spoke of the ego itself as becoming filled with desexualized libidinal fluid, leading to the irresolvable puzzle about whether the id or the ego was the "great reservoir of libido" (Bibring, 1941). That puzzle is irresolvable because of the ambiguity that developed in the concept of libidinal cathexis; it cannot really mean both that the id cathects the ego (that is, finds it a lovable object) and that the ego itself is charged with libidinal energy. This latter notion, not really understandable, is a remnant of the neurological theory embodied in the *Project* (Freud, 1895), when Freud thought of the ego as a specific set of neurons which could become charged with (*cathected with*) nervous energy. But even if we ignore the incoherence in the concept of ego-libido, Freud was not really addressing the central problem of the ego's motivation. He was asking merely how it obtained the power to carry out its policies, but the real question is, from what do its policies originate in the first place?

The Explanatory Value of Ego-Instincts

The solution lies ready to hand. It is to revive Freud's earlier concept of ego-instincts. There was never any good reason to abandon it. The behavioural observations which Freud appealed to did not require its abandonment. They were mainly concerned with narcissism; he saw that actions which at first glance seemed motivated by non-sexual needs sometimes turned out to be driven by narcissistic sexual motives (Freud, 1920). But that does not mean that hunger, for example, and its derivatives such as the impulse to accumulate material goods, is not a real motive force nor that it never functions independently of narcissistic libido.

Again, the supposed theoretical reason for becoming sceptical of ego-instincts, that they seemed able to be defined only by their aim and not by their source (Bibring, 1941), was not a sufficient one. It would indeed have been a substantial difficulty if it had been true, since it would have contravened Freud's sound deterministic principle that an instinct *must* be defined by its bodily source (Freud, 1915). That is, an instinct is defined or conceived *as* a functioning physiological entity of a specific kind, one that transforms chemical energy into mechanical action of a recognizable form. The only problem for psychology is that such entities cannot be inferred from behaviour alone, but must be identified by the methods of physiology. It is only the discovery of the structures whose functioning constitutes behaviour that makes behaviour explicable; to neglect this fundamental requirement is to begin to slide into teleology - that is, allegedly to explain behaviour by reference to its adaptive effects rather than to its causes.

Ironically enough, however, it is food-hunger, whose physiological bases are well known, which is the leading contender for inclusion as an ego-instinct - better known even than sexuality, which is traditionally consigned to the id, its status as an instinct not being in dispute. If one includes, with hunger, thirst, respiration, and pain-avoidance, all of which have good physiological credentials (elimination perhaps being better treated as a set of reflexes), one is well on the way to a workable list of ego-instincts. None of these is to be thought of as defined by its aim, and certainly not by the aim of adaptation to the environment, or of simple survival. Temporarily to retain, for brevity, the language of *aim*, the aim of hunger is just *to eat*, of thirst to drink, and so on.

Ego psychologists, rejecting ego-instincts, talk of the ego's motivation as its *interests*, specifying these as various goal-directed strivings. Hartmann, for example, gives *egoism* and *striving for what is useful* as the central ego interests, and adds ethical values, religious values, and interest in intellectual activities as possible others (Hartmann, 1964, pp. 136-138). But that is to define motivational constructs *solely* by their aims, to base their diagnosis solely on observations of behaviour, and the difficulty with that procedure is that one can postulate as many of such motivational forces as one wishes; they can never be falsified because the behaviour which is supposed to originate from them is always observable. It is precisely that way of postulating instincts that has brought the entire concept of instinct into disrepute in academic psychology. The only useful way of conceiving instincts is as identifiable physiological mechanisms, as Freud was insisting in saying that they must be defined by their somatic sources.

Conflict of Instincts

By tidying up some of Freud's hints (Freud, 1905), the following picture of the developed mental structure emerges. In the course of socialization, the instinctual drives are set in opposition to one another through the application of rewards and punishments. One cannot decide arbitrarily what will function as a reward and what as a punishment; that is determined by the nature of the creature one is dealing with. A reward can only be the gratification of a primary drive (or some associated token that it will be gratified, a *secondary reinforcer*) and a punishment can only be the frustration of one (similarly qualified) - e.g., corporal punishment directly frustrates the pain-avoidance drive. In every culture, socialization is directed to the suppression of particular instinctual impulses - in most case, of pregenital and incestuous sexual impulses and of aggressive impulses against authority figures. The suppression of a forbidden impulse is brought about by threats that its expression will be punished - that is, that some other instinctual impulse will be frustrated. In this way the drives, or some of them, are set in competition with one another. To give an over-simplified example, if a child is made to believe that giving vent to certain sexual impulses means that it will no longer be fed, then hunger is being set in opposition to sexuality. Each instinctual drive must be thought of as an information-registering entity, retaining, predominantly, information relevant to its own gratification. Thus hunger, in this example, is learning that one instrumental act necessary for its own gratification is the prevention of sexuality's gratification, which is what is meant by a conflict between drives. The conventional notion, of course, is that it is the *person* who learns, and who uses the information in order to gratify hunger. But that raises the same problems about the *person's* motivation as I have raised about the *ego's*.

Separation of Ego from Id

The conflict situation is further complicated by the fact that not only are children not allowed to *do* certain things, they are not even *supposed to wish to do* them. The consequence is repression rather than suppression; the child comes to deny the reality of some of its own impulses, a serious distortion of its development. Those impulses or drives whose expressions are socially acceptable remain unrepressed and come to constitute the child's ego. They declare themselves and speak up as if they were the whole person - *I*. The unacceptable ones now constitute the id. However, relationships are actually more complex than that. Although according to the classical canon sexuality and aggression are id instincts (in the theory which accepts aggression as an independent drive), nevertheless certain alignments of the sexual instinct are admitted to the ego as socially acceptable; in our society, sexual interest in a human being of the opposite sex and of a suitable age, provided there are no barriers of marriage or blood, is defined as legitimate. Again, aggression is not only permitted but demanded in certain situations against certain objects. Thus, the repressing instincts do not forbid all recognition or expression of the repressed; under special circumstances some sexual and aggressive impulses are allowed temporary membership of the ego. In the other direction, although hunger is ordinarily legitimate, in most societies hunger for human flesh is not, so that in situations which tempt to cannibalism, no other food being available, hunger might temporarily be forced into the id by other threatened drives. The basic point remains that at any particular time, depending on the prevailing conditions, certain instinctual tendencies would be dominant, and, functioning as ego, would claim to constitute the entire person, the remainder being disowned as foreign, i.e., as id.

The Superego as a Modification of the Ego

It is not necessary and would not express the facts to think of the superego as a third set of instinctual drives. Rather, the superego consists of the set of moral prohibitions that have been imposed on the ego. As Freud says, it is a modification of the ego. These prohibitions become introjected, that is, become accepted as moral truths by the ego, and are made binding by the fears of punishment if they are contravened. These fears become unconscious for a number of reasons; for one, that if their origin were remembered then the forbidden wishes would also be remembered; for another, if the fears of punishment remained conscious then the person would suffer the pain of knowing that the parents' love had been only conditional, and that he or she had been defeated in the struggle for self-expression. To avoid that humiliating memory, the growing person comes to believe that superego-derived behaviour is done in the name of virtue, and that fears of punishment have nothing to do with it. The introjected moral beliefs stand as internal barriers constraining the ego-instincts in their efforts to achieve their own gratification. It is their fears of being frustrated which determine their policies and provide the motive force for repression.

Of course, it sounds strange to talk of a person as consisting of a small community of instinctual drives each of which is a knower and a doer; however, some pluralistic conception is required for any serious attempt at a deterministic account of mental life. To anticipate a common criticism, it is *not* the case that the instinctual drives are homunculi; unlike the whole person, each has, in effect, only one motive, never restrains itself from seeking satisfaction, knows only a portion of the aggregate body of information, and suffers no internal conflict. An instinctual drive can no more restrain itself from working than any motor can, once the switches are thrown. If its operation is to be arrested, then that must be through some influence external to itself - in the case of repression, from other instinctual drives. It is through their interaction that the phenomena of inhibition and repression come about, and it is from their own inbuilt action programmes, not from some indivisible source of agency, that the person's behaviour comes.

Incompatibility of Agency and Determinism

To say that in the long run it is *I* that originates my acts (rather than that it is the causal interaction of my parts) is either an uninformative tautology - *my acts are mine* - or it is the postulation of a self-changing being, and that is just as uniformative, because if such an entity can change itself in any of its possible ways at any time, then it is in principle impossible to explain or predict its doing any specific thing at any specific time. The only conception of causality that is of any use in the natural sciences is one which assumes that any change in an entity is produced by the impact on it of some stimulus external to it. Both the intrinsic properties of the entity and those of whatever arrives at it are relevant to the change (Anderson, 1962). In psychology, the main relevant intrinsic properties of the organism will be its motivational or drive state, and its acquired beliefs about the nature of the stimulating object and what the outcome of various actions in the prevailing circumstances may be. (It hardly need be said that there are also general conditions such as its physical and sensory capabilities, and so on.) Given all these conditions, the organism is caused to behave, which is to say that its parts are caused to move in a characteristic way, such that more or less predict-able effects are produced in the environment (this likelihood being in-creased by sensory and perceptual feedback). The behaviour will be a learned modification of one of the wired-in action patterns specific to the instinctual drive which is regnant at the time. In that way, once we have a complete specification of the instinctual drives and their specific ac-tions, then the explanation of any action becomes possible in principle, if we can gain sufficient information about the organism's learning exper-iences.

But if an organism could initiate its own behaviour, could change itself, then no explanation of the causal kind (or indeed of any other) would be possible for such behaviour. There would be no necessary and sufficient set of antecedent conditions, the observation of which would enable us to predict or explain the behaviour. An organism so conceived would carry the potency for self-change with it all the time, and it would then be impossible to explain why it exercised this power at one time rather than another. One could only say that it *chose* to do so. Examples of this kind of thinking may be found in Harré (1983) and Rychlak (1979, 1981). Rather than accept such mysteries, it seems scien-tifically much more fruitful to elaborate and capitalize upon Freud's dic-tum that we are lived by our instincts.

References

Allport, G. (1937). *Personality.* New York: Henry Holt.

Anderson, J. (1962). The problem of causality. In J. Anderson (Ed.), *Studies in empirical philosophy.* Sydney: Angus & Robertson.

Bibring, E. (1941). The development and problems of the theory of instincts. *International Journal of Psychoanalysis, 22,* 102-131.

Feffer, M. (1982). *The structure of Freudian thought.* New York: International Universities Press.

Freud, A. (1946). *The ego and the mechanisms of defence.* New York: International Universities Press.

Freud, S. (1895). A project for a scientific psychology. *Standard edition of the complete psychological works of Sigmund Freud,* Vol. 1. London: Hogarth.

Freud, S. (1905). Three essays on the theory of sexuality. *Standard edition,* Vol. 7. London: Hogarth.

Freud, S. (1915). Instincts and their vicissitudes. *Standard edition,* Vol. 14. London: Hogarth.

Freud, S. (1920). Beyond the pleasure principle. *Standard edition,* Vol. 18. London: Hogarth.

Freud, S. (1923). The ego and the id. *Standard edition,* Vol. 19. London: Hogarth.

Gedo, J. E. (1978). *Beyond interpretation: Toward a revised theory for psychoanalysis.* New York: International Universities Press.

Harré, R. (1983). *Personal being: A theory for individual psychology.* Oxford: Blackwell.

Hartmann, H. (1958). *Ego psychology and the problem of adaptation.* New York: International Universities Press.

Hartmann, H. (1964). *Essays on ego psychology: Selected problems in psychoanalytic theory.* London: Hogarth.

Kohut, H. (1978). *The search for the self.* P.H. Ornstein (Ed.). New York: International Universities Press.

Maze, J. R. (1973). The concept of attitude. *Inquiry, 16,* 168-205.

Maze, J. R. (1983). *The meaning of behaviour.* London: George Allen & Unwin.

Rychlak, J. E. (1981). *A philosophy of science for personality theory.* (2nd ed.). Malabar, Fla.: Krieger.

Schafer, R. (1976). *A new language for psychoanalysis.* New Haven and London: Yale University Press.

Current Issues in Theoretical Psychology
Wm J. Baker, M.E. Hyland, H. Van Rappard, A.W. Staats (Editors)
© Elsevier Science Publishers B.V. (North-Holland), 1987

PATHOLOGICAL SUBCONSCIOUS AND IRRATIONAL

DETERMINISM IN THE SOCIAL PSYCHOLOGY OF THE CROWD:

THE LEGACY OF GUSTAVE LeBON[1]

Gregory R. McGuire

York University
Toronto, Ontario, Canada

SUMMARY: The following paper examines the primacy of irrational, pathological determinism as an explanatory reference in the social psychology of the crowd. Towards this goal, a detailed analysis is performed of the emergence and evolution of crowd psychology as an accepted social theory. Principal emphasis is placed upon the 1895 formulation of Gustave LeBon. It is suggested that the enduring influence of LeBon's crowd psychology has been fostered by the degree to which this work has been ahistorically isolated from both sociohistorical context and from LeBon's overall system of social psychology. A detailed historical analysis explores this model within the context of French social and political developments at the end of the last century, and suggests that this work owed a great deal of its initial ascendancy to the adoption of contemporary research in the psychopathology of the subconscious. A brief analysis of subsequent social theories of the crowd reveals that this irrational determinism has evolved into a largely unquestioned foundation for most theoretical approaches which have followed. The conclusion calls for a reconsideration of the automatic association of irrational determinism in the psychology of the crowd, and proposes a more objective approach to the theory of crowd psychology which would allow for both individual responsibility and collective aspirations in social interaction.

Decadence, Social Dissolution, and Conservative Ideology

.... LeBon is a neo-machiavellian, an elitist and an ademocratic thinker (since he refutes the notion of equality between individuals, the fundamental principle of modern democracy). His thought has its foundation in a liberal-conservative ideology more-or-less obsolete at the end of the nineteenth

[1]Research included in this paper has been performed in order to satisfy the doctoral requirements at York University, under the helpful guidance of Ray Fancher, Richard Goranson, and David Bakan. Gratitude is also expressed to Ian Lubek and Erika Apfelbaum for their help in all stages of the research.

century. (Thiec, 1983, p. 120)

The crowd psychology of Gustave LeBon stands as the basic model against which all ensuing social psychological theories of crowd behavior are inevitably compared. Yet the degree and the extent to which this original theory has been misinterpreted is striking. Miscomprehension and selective interpretation are principally due to the isolation of the theory from its social and historical context. Such evaluations largely overlook the necessary interdependence of social history and social theory and research (Gergen, 1977; Morawski, 1984). The crowd psychology proposed by LeBon is responsive to the juxtaposition of an influential tradition of social philosophy with social events of a well-defined historical and cultural context. A more historically responsive analysis of this theory would share the belief of Sampson that "our ideas and comprehension of human social theory are better understood as historically located principles rather than as psychological universals describing fundamental aspects of human behavior." (Sampson, 1977, p. 768).

LeBon's analysis of the psychology of the crowd directly addressed contemporary preoccupations with both the emergence of the urban masses and the image of the revolutionary crowd. His contention that man had entered the era of the crowd (l'ère des foules) has found substantive echo in many recent descriptions of the history of post-1850 Europe (e.g., Biddis, 1980; Hobsbawm, 1964; Moscovici, 1981).

The French Revolution of 1789 dominated French social and political development throughout the whole of the following century; most notably in the 1830 overthrow of the Bourbons, the revolution of the July monarchy in 1848, and the Commune uprising of 1870-1871 (Hobsbawm, 1964; Apfelbaum & McGuire, 1985). Although less directly motivated by open class revolution, such essentially crowd-dominated events during this period as Boulangisme (1886-1889), the Panamal scandal (1892), and the May Day rallies of 1889-1893 imparted a timely relevance to the 1895 publication of LeBon's *La psychologie des foules*. Within the same decade, the arrest of Dreyfus in 1894 would polarize the nation, engendering the appearance of large social movements and mass demonstrations, and leading to changes in the government, the military, and the educational system (Lubek, 1981; Apfelbaum, 1981). Each subsequent social upheaval demonstrated once again the emergence of the urban masses, and each was widely viewed by both ends of the political spectrum as a dress rehearsal for the second coming of the revolution of 1789.

The combination of constant social unrest and the perceived decline of France as an international power saw the emergence of the generalized belief among liberal and conservative circles that France was a nation in both moral and material decline. Scientific treatments of such topics as alcoholism, moral degeneration, social health, and 'women's illnesses' became legion (cf. Barrows, 1981). On a more global level, racial and evolutionary factors were brought forth as evidence that France had entered a period of extreme *decadence* and regression (extensively documented by Swart, 1964). This sense of a once-powerful nation in eclipse was, of course, not limited to France at this time, but the continuing social upheavals mentioned above served to lend a particularly parochial nature to French preoccupations. For proponents of a conservative liberalism such as LeBon, the nineteenth century in its closing moments seemed to herald the demise of historic France: "[the nineteenth century] goes forth, this poor type of human before it, thickening the gloom around its feet, at the same time both staggering and rash. It resembles a stumbling marcher, but a boastful one, who whistles with each step to conceal from himself the terrors which engulf him." (Hello, 1920). The portrayal of a nation in dissolution was a particularly selective interpretation; the moral degeneration decried by the liberal conservatives was greeted as profound social *regeneration* by many contemporary socialist writers (Apfelbaum, 1985).

The elitist, conservative ideology so present in the writings of LeBon was foreshadowed by a group of social theorists whose writings became collectively known as the decadent movement (cf. Bourget, 1883). The most influential of these theorists and social historians was Hyppolite Taine, whose *Les origines de la France contemporaine* (1872-1875) clearly foreshadows the crowd psychology of LeBon in both the portrayal of the irrational revolutionary masses and the implicit justification of an aristocratic elite. Taine, along with other liberal individualists such as Renan, recalled the perceived glories of l'Ancien Régime in order to highlight the moral degeneration of the present and to glorify the *triumph of the individual* in the past. From a scientific and theoretical perspective, the decline of the French nation was chiefly accomplished by recourse to hereditary evolution and the repudiation of rationalist theories of human behavior. These writings were marked by a profound admiration for the progress of the English *race*. It was argued that the French revolution of 1789 had served to deprive France of its superior members, and thus had embarked the nation upon a path of inevitable evolutionary regression. This was contrasted to the experiences of the English, who had preserved the enlightened elite and thus assured themselves of progressive social and racial evolution.

On the psychological level, the writings of Taine came to lead a mid-nineteenth century revolt against the spiritualist eclecticism of the followers of Maine de Biran and Victor Cousin. Along with the early writings of pioneering psychologist Théodule Ribot (1870, 1879), Taine helped foster an empirical approach to the study of the psychological process. Above all, Taine led the philosophical rebellion against the rationalist bias of his predecessors, which fostered a view of human nature that appeared untenable when compared to the reality of contemporary social events. Basing his analysis primarily on the events of the 1789 revolution, Taine came to believe in a vague irrational determinism, unconscious in nature, as the primary motivating force in the history of social man. The regression of the race, which Taine believed was a product of the revolution, reinforced the importance of considering irrational influences. The violent social crowds were unrefutable evidence of the triumph of the baser classes of France: ".... as is usually the case, it [the revolutionary crowd] is a purulent concentration of the most poisonous passions and foulest motives. The vilest of men and women were engaged in it." (Taine, 1878, p. 97).

LeBon and the Evolutionary Regression of Socialism

A major reason for the manner in which the LeBon theory continues to resonate through many succeeding social theories lies in the constant isolation of this work from the historical context in which it was written. More specifically, evaluations of *La psychologie des foules* have consistently disregarded the corpus of LeBon's writings in various fields of social theory. The crowd psychlogy of LeBon is the cornerstone of an evolving and extensive system of social theory which both reinforced and propagated his own particular vision of a racist, ademocratic elitism. These views are hinted at quite openly in *La psychologie des foules,* but it is only in the ensuing application of the psychology of the crowd to such areas as socialism, racial evolution, and political psychology that the nature of his crowd psychology becomes readily apparent. Most important among these works: *Les lois psychologiques de l'évolution des peuples* (1894-1978); *La psychologie du socialisme* (1896); *La psychologie politique* (1910); *Les opinions et les croyances* (1911); and *La psychologie de la révolution francaise et la psychologie des révolutions* (1912).

Reminiscent of the decadent writings, LeBon the social theorist depends heavily on a somewhat simplistic and questionable appeal to evolutionary theory. In the hands of LeBon, race was the underlying determinant in most instances of human interaction, effectively precluding mutual comprehension between "different races, different classes, and different sexes," with the exception of technical concepts (LeBon, 1896, pp. 74-75). "The chasm between diverse races" served to assure that the inferior races could never fully comprehend the civilization of the superior races (LeBon, 1894/1978, p. 33). One finds the Anglophilism of the earlier decadent writings combined with an open acknowledgement of the *racial inferiority* of Latin Europe (LeBon, 1896, pp. 135-136), which paradoxically led to a recurring concern over the purity of the French race. Warnings about the dilution of the French race evoke echoes of contemporary debate in France: "the preponderant influence of foreigners is an infallible dissolvant of the existence of States ... if these invasions are not halted, in little time a third of the French population will be German and a third Italian" (LeBon, 1910, pp. 87-88). Recently, some of LeBon's more racially oriented writings (e.g., LeBon 1894/1978) have been re-edited and published.

Within this conception, this simplified social Darwinist philosophy reinforces the previously established tendency to conceive of human interaction solely in terms of conflict and struggle. Within national boundaries, the conflict model served to justify the elite and the economic domination of the lower class, since: "If [the economy] does not always result in the triumph of the most capable, it generally eliminates the least capable. This formula is practically the expression of the law of selection ..." (LeBon, 1896, pp. 249-250). On the international and interracial levels, inherent interracial conflict justified "the necessity of war to social progress." Since "natural instinct" can be seen to "lead the strong to destroy the weak," it is only "the great warrior civilizations" which have made their mark on world progress (LeBon, 1910, p. 84). According to LeBon, 'statisticians' have all too often listed the losses to society brought about by war, but have forgotten to list the advantages.

Above all, it is socialism which provides the ultimate target for LeBon's conflict model of racial evolution and class differentiation. The inevitable appearance of socialism within this framework is, according to LeBon, readily apparent. The new economic conditions which led to the triumph of the elite also give rise to multitudes of the 'inadapted,' those who are brought together through "a hate for this civilization in which they cannot find a place." (LeBon, 1896, p. 345). Those who are left on the outside due to economic, racial, or class distinctions are joined by a "crowd of degenerates of all sorts." It is, of course, not when they are alone that the inadapted pose such a grave problem: "What renders all these degenerates, ricketeds, alcoholics, epileptics, alienated individuals, etc. dangerous is that they multiply the crowd of inferior beings ... these are, of course, the sure adepts of socialism." (LeBon, 1896, pp.

355-356).

These preceding quotations, although fragmentary in nature, emphasize the underlying ideology motivating LeBon's psychology of the social crowd. Concurrently, these examples serve to establish his position as a more radical continuateur of a specific French liberalist conservative tradition. Political ideology as social theory was certainly not limited to the conservative wing of the political spectrum. In France at the turn of the century, social theory, methodology, and political developments became inextricably interdependent (cf. Geiger, 1975), and opposition to the irrationalism of the collective psychologists was chiefly provided by Durkheim and his followers, who "sought in their work to elaborate a theory of social cohesion which could unite French society in support of the democratic institutions of the Third Republic." (Nye, 1973, p. 429).

Irrational Determinism and the Pathological Subconscious

The crowd psychology of LeBon differs from such predecessors as Taine (1872-1875), Mignet, or Michelet in one significant aspect: LeBon had recourse to the 'scientific' validation of man's irrational nature as provided by French psychopathology research of the day. In opposition to the Cartesian rationalism and eclecticism which had dominated the first half of the century, Taine (1870) and Ribot (1870, 1879) effectively switched the dominant emphasis in French psychology from the rational to the irrational. Ribot, heavily influenced by Hughlings Jackson and Claude Bernard, advocated the identification and description of normative psychological functioning through the study of the diseased and the pathological (McGuire, 1985). Through the study of psychic and mental 'dissolution,' and the examination of the inferior subconscious process, one could extrapolate a description of the more complex conscious processes. The distinction between conscious and subconscious processes was formulated as a question of levels of accessibility and degree of complexity, such that the study of mental pathology and abnormality permitted the investigation of complex psychic phenomena in a simplified, degraded state. Following Bernard, disease was considered the most efficient experiment possible, spontaneously provided by nature, and therefore not artificially induced.

The example of psychic dissolution would come to dominate experimental psychology in France until well into the present century, chiefly through the legitimization of an enduring French interest in animal magnetism in the guise of hypnosis and suggestion. Most importantly, hypnosis and suggestion were apparently essentially social phenomena, providing a plausible model for mechanisms of influence in all social interaction. When the generalization of hypnotic suggestion was extended to social life, the contention that psychic dissolution provided access to a more simplified, and therefore pathological, level of consciousness was largely untouched. Thus the statement by LeBon's contemporary, Gabriel Tarde: "The social state, as the hypnotic, is only a form of dream, a dream of command and a dream of action. Having only suggested ideas and thinking them to be spontaneous: this is the illusion of the somnambulist, and, as well, the social man." (Tarde, 1891, p. 1).

The importance of the hypnosis model is crucial to an adequate understanding of the LeBon conception of the irrational crowd, providing experimental (and therefore scientific) validation of LeBon's negative depiction of the crowd on two levels. On the one hand, hypnosis and suggestion research provided a widely accepted and apparently scientific demonstration of the existence of the irrational subconscious thought process. In serving as a more general model, this theory implied an automatic undercurrent of pathology applicable to all social interaction, since "We have said that one of the general characteristics of crowds is an excessive suggestibility, and shown how, in all human agglomerations, a suggestion is contagious." (LeBon, 1895, p. 25).

Although LeBon couches his descriptions in the terminology of the suggestion model of Bernheim and his followers, it is the organic hypnosis model of the Charcot school which provides the principal points of reference (Apfelbaum & McGuire, 1985). Applied to the social collectivity, this organic model of hypnosis is most clearly reflected in the reliance upon the medical metaphor of mental contagion, adapting the terminology of bacteriology (Dumas, 1911; Vigouroux & Juquelier, 1905). LeBon acknowledged the appropriateness of the medical metaphor in stating that "ideas, sentiments, emotions, and beliefs possess in crowds a contagious power as intense as that of microbes." (LeBon, 1895, p. 100). The medical model of social interaction would eventually be extended to differentiate between social contagion - nervous and mental troubles - and social epidemic - meteoric variations, war, etc. (Dumas, 1911). Most importantly, the extension of the organic contagion model to the social crowd fostered the depiction of the crowd participants as passive targets of undetectable (microbian) infection.

Within the Charcot conception of organic hypnosis, hypnotizability was considered to be automatically indicative of a hysterical imbalance (Apfelbaum & McGuire, 1985). This assumption, contested by Bernheim, Liébault, and Beaunis, among others, clearly came to the forefront in a late nineteenth century debate over the possibility of hypnotizing an individual into the commission of a crime (McGuire, 1986). While the followers of Charcot argued that only the predisposed could be hypnotized into committing a crime (Delboeuf, 1895), the Nancy school tended more towards the belief that suggestion affected all individuals to a varying degree (Liégeois, 1899). They did however allow that the *moral temperament* of an individual could determine their particular receptivity to unpleasant and/or criminal suggestions. This debate illustrates the degree to which the hypnosis/suggestion model became an important consideration in the many public debates which centered around questions of free will and control of the individual in social interaction.

Consider, therefore, the depiction of mass behavior which results from the application of the hypnosis/suggestion model to the activities of the social crowd. Crowd psychology addressed the crowd as an entity in itself, yet the dependency of this analysis upon the hypnotic metaphor essentially restricts analysis to mechanisms of intra-individual processes (McGuire, 1984). The association of hypnotic suggestion and subconscious process also automatically negates any question of individual cognition of agency and motivation for behavior. Thus, the motivation of the social collectivity is subsumed by the behavior of the individuals, which is in turn irrational in nature and therefore to be discounted. Within the LeBon portrayal of the social crowd, there is clearly no place for conscious motivation, neither upon the individual nor the collective levels. This association was clearly not ideologically inert, for the psychology of the crowd "put the accent on the irrational and pathological character of the crowd; in so doing, they condemned all together popular movements, democratic institutions, and collective aspirations." (Margot-Duclos, 1961, p. 857).

More importantly, the introduction of the hypnosis model, with the accompanying assocation between subconscious process and mental pathology, lent valuable support to the depiction of the emergent socialist and trade unionist movements and mass gatherings as irrational and dangerous threats to society. The question of whether the crowd was a negative or positive social phenomenon was effectively relegated to the simple question of social control. Given that the crowd was ultimately passive (to hypnotic/suggestive commands), LeBon contended that conservative politicians should accept the existence of the crowd and learn to effectively manipulate it, as he considered the socialists to be already doing. "The docility of the crowd is extreme, in effect, when one knows how to guide them ... The most necessary knowledge of the Statesman in a democracy is that of the psychology of the crowd." (LeBon, 1910, pp. 124-125).

LeBon was disconcerted that conservative leaders did not immediately seize upon his advice, although he constantly congratulated himself that the military was teaching the basic principles set forth in *La psychologie des foules.*

Irrational Determinism in Subsequent Theories of Crowd Psychology

If the irrational determinism of LeBon's crowd psychology is unavoidably associated with a particular context-bound conception of the collective gathering, how, one might ask, have subsequent psychological theories of crowd behavior evolved in alternative socio-historical contexts? To a large extent, the irrationalist motivation of the LeBon crowd has continued to be considered as an intrinsic component of crowd behavior in many succeeding social theories. Only a brief overview of selected theoretical formulations is possible here, and the following analysis will be confined to examining the mechanisms of influence in crowd behavior and the continued accpetance of modified forms of irrational determinism as explanation, despite a dramaticallly changing socio-political backdrop since the time of LeBon's writings.

As an early example, examine Freud's mass psychology (massenpsychologie), the first third of which specifically addresses the advantages and limitations of the LeBon theory (Freud, 1921). In terms of motivation in crowd behavior, Freud's mass psychology replaces the hypnosis/suggestion model with a determinism based upon libidinal drive and identification (cf. van Ginneken, 1984; Rey, 1985). One might even argue that the sections of *Group psychology and the analysis of the ego,* which discuss LeBon's use of the hypnosis model, are strikingly informative about Freud's well-known discomfort with hypnosis as a means of access to the subconscious. The transfer from hypnotic suggestion to libidinal drive does very little, however, to change the conception of the irrational subconscious as the primary source of motivation in crowd behavior.

In contrast, Trotter's (1916) *Instincts of the herd in peace and war* rejects the 'unfortunate' association of suggestibility with the abnormal (p. 33). Within the Trotter conception, suggestibility is an important component of social gregariousness, which is in turn a vital element of the herd instinct. However, as the recurrent use of the term instinct would indicate, gregarious suggestions are still primarily carried out at a subconscious level, effectively precluding a rational understanding of their influence by those who are affected by these instincts. Moreover, Trotter's employment of the metaphor of the herd is chiefly based upon racial differentiation, a perspective quite evidently swayed by an attempt to explain the outbreak of World War I. Trotter seems to accept the herd instinct as a progressive influence in human evolution, but the emphasis on submission to herd suggestion continues to imply a lack of conscious awareness and response on the part of the individual. To a certain extent, individual awareness (experience) is viewed as an impediment to successful integration into the herd; the mentally ill are precisely those who cannot balance individual experience and herd suggestion.

Another innovative approach to the psychology of collective behavior was proposed in McDougall's (1920) *The group mind.* Although the majority of the text is concerned with the collective and national will, based once again on instinct, it is the initial chapter in *The mental life of the crowd* which most closely touches upon the present discussion. Like Trotter, McDougall was writing at a time when the hypnosis/suggestion debate had been decisively resolved in favor of the suggestion theory. His greatest criticism of LeBon was therefore directed towards the belief that suggestibility automatically implies hypnosis. To replace the hypnosis model, McDougall tentatively proposes two alternative mechanisms of influence in the suggestibility of the social crowd; telepathy and a collective conscious. The former lacked critical scientific verification, although it seemed plausible enough if one assumed that the proximity of others in the crowd intensified "telepathic influence" (McDougall, 1920, p. 41). The possibility of a collective consciousness was supported by a wide range of research into animal societies and personality disassociation (p. 43).

Note that both influences, according to McDougall, are still carried out at the subconscious level, and McDougall's theoretical approach to the psychology of the crowd retains many of the associations implied by the subconscious process: "it [the crowd] is excessively emotional, impulsive, violent, fickle, inconsistent, irresolute, and extreme in action, displaying only the coarser emotions and the less refined sentiments ..." (p. 63). The McDougall conception of the crowd clearly upholds the abdication of individual cognition and control of action. This is most evidently demonstrated in his criticism of Edmund Burke for attributing the violence of the French revolution to the individual participants. According to McDougall, the actions of the crowd tell one nothing about the character of the individual participants, since the crowd reduces all members to a lower and more primitive level of social evolution.

These early theories are indicative of the degree to which irrational determinism very rapidly evolved into a basic a priori foundation in the social psychology of the crowd. Such a *tradition,* once established, appears difficult to contradict, as exemplified by a brief consideration of several more recent theories of the crowd.

The first is the brief exploration of collective behavior written by Herbert Blumer (1953), an important statement in that it provides a comprehensive synopsis of contemporary theoretical initiatives in both sociology and psychology. Significantly, it is crowd behavior which seems to represent the sole consistent instance of collective behavior in which an interpretation of social interaction does not enter into the picture. Whereas other social interactions are instructed and directed by an *interpretative* reaction, the behavior of the crowd is principally determined by a *circular* reaction, marked by the absence of any degree of effective interpretation (see also Turner & Killian, 1972). Note the similarity between Blumer's definition of circular reaction and LeBon's theory of contagious suggestion. Once again, it is an irrational process by which one is able to distinguish the social crowd from other social collectivities.

A decade later saw the emergence of Smelser's (1962) *Theory of collective behavior.* From the initial chapter, Smelser makes it quite clear that his model is based upon the sociological conception of structural strain, quantified by means of a value-added model adopted from economic science. Smelser takes great pains to distance his sociological model from the psychological theories of LeBon, Ross, and Freud, (p. 20). Yet, irrational psychological factors clearly continue to play a major role in collective behavior, which is always motivated by "general beliefs." There are five varieties of general beliefs in a hierarchy in which each stage also comprises the preceding stages. The initial stage of all generalized belief is *hysteria:* "all other generalized beliefs have an implied hysteria as one component," (p. 86). Thus, all generalized beliefs which serve to motivate collective behavior (wish-fulfillment, hostility, norm-oriented beliefs, value-oriented beliefs) are fundamentally hysterical in origin. Even more importantly, later sections which explore the nature of the hysterical belief (i.e., Fear: The specific element of hysterical belief, pp. 150 & ff.) demonstrate the degree to which irrational determinism continues to serve as a foundation for collective theory. Despite the avowed distancing of his theory from the earlier psychological theories, one finds an acceptance of the appropriation of the mental contagion metaphor as an explanatory reference for hostile outbursts (p. 257), and a citation to the original writings of LeBon in order to demonstrate the irrationality of the hostile crowd.

Finally, the publication of Moscovici (1981) *L'age des foules* returns the social psychology of the crowd to its intital roots. Moscovici argues that the turn-of-the-century crowd psychologies of LeBon and Freud represent one of the most significant and prophetic social theories of the present century. While admitting that there are certain antedated ideas which may cause difficulties for modern readers, he claims that "all the psychological and political evolutions of our century are anticipated [in LeBon's theory]" (p. 86). Moscovici suggests that events of the present century have validated the arguments of both LeBon and Freud, that the social crowd leads to the psychic degeneration of the individual: "in social life ... the less noble psychic layers replace the nobler layers, heated instincts supplant cold reason just as, in nature, the noble energies (gravity, energy) degrade into less noble energy, that is, heat." (pp. 32-33).

The Possibility of a Pro-Social Psychology of the Crowd

There are two distinct trends which have served to nurture the continuing influence of the pathological approach to the study of crowd behavior. One source of bias is the restriction of theoretical considerations and analysis first demonstrated by LeBon. A second restriction is found in the manner in which the emphasis of contemporary methodological and research practice limits the theoretical operationalization of the social collectivity. This reflects a dominant trend in modern social psychology in general, what Pepitone (1981) has elsewhere called the individuocentric bias. The LeBon analysis focused exclusively on the intra-individual, and totally excluded the interindividual process from the field of inquiry (Apfelbaum & McGuire, 1985). Later revisions of the crowd psychology have largely preserved this bias. This is, in and of itself, a necessary outcome of the elitist social philosophy to which LeBon adhered, and the continuing impact this theory has manifested is partly a result of the congruence of this perspective with the overall emphasis on the isolated individual in modern social psychology.

Methodological bias has significantly contributed to the static nature of this particular area of theory and research through the emphasis modern social psychology places on laboratory experimentation. The ascendancy of experimental methodology, particularly in North America, evolved in part as a response to the perceived quasi-scientific nature of preceding 'group mind' theories (i.e., Allport, 1924). The crowd psychology of LeBon was often proposed as a prominent example of the group mind theory. More accurately, in relying upon the hypnotic/suggestive process as the principal explanation for motivation, the LeBon crowd is subject to an interior reaction wherein actions are transmitted from one individual to the next. Far from positing a theory in which the whole is greater than the sum, as Allport contended, LeBon postulated a process whereby the whole became significantly *less* than the sum of the parts (McGuire, 1984).

With the rise of experimentalism in post-World War I social psychological research, social psychology has been methodologically ill-prepared to address the question of the crowd as an acting entity with definitive behavioral characteristics. The very problems which have caused many social psychologists to call attention to the 'crisis' in the discipline (i.e., Nederhof & Zwier, 1983; Silverman, 1977), particularly the relevancy of experimental research to social theory (i.e., Chapanis, 1967; Homans, 1970), have also helped to keep the social crowd at the margins of contemporary theory and research. In place of an examination of the mechanisms by which external influences (including, in some instances, the actions of the leader, an individual) determine the collective actions of the social group, more recent efforts have restricted consideration to the manner in which the group determines the actions of the individual. Thus one finds in many recent social psychology textbooks an assumption of logical continuity between the crowd psychology of LeBon and the small group research of the 1950's (cf. Mills, 1969).

There are several major impediments which must be addressed before modern social psychology can effect appreciable progress towards a more objective, less restricted theory of crowd behavior. First, it is necessary to reevaluate the strictures and narrowing of focus imposed by experimental methodology and theoretical preconceptions which focus upon the individual, yet ignore the collective. Only when it is realized that the social collectivity presents its own specific psychology, that the whole can be, if not necessarily greater, then at least qualitatively different from the sum of the parts, can this subject be broached in an innovative fashion.

This reconsideration would of necessity involve a refocusing of the ultimate object of analysis within the social crowd. Such a fundamental reevaluation is not easily accomplished, for it would demand an intrinsic reorientation of the way in which both the social individual and the crowd are conceptualized and addressed. The individuocentric bias of modern social psychology is not ideologically inert. Emphasis on the individual has always conveyed an implicit denial of the collective. At best, the two are seen as being somehow mutually exclusive. Thus, as both Sampson (1977) and Pepitone (1976) have argued, an alternative conceptualization of social interaction interdependent on both individual and collective factors goes against not only the force of tradition in social psychology, but must also address the dominance of established social norms.

The most important component of a nonsubjective theory of the crowd would entail a more balanced treatment of the question of individual responsibility and agency in the social crowd. The dominant conception of crowd behavior as irrationally determined is one which entirely negates the possibility of individual agency and cognition of action and, in so doing renders the responsibility of the individual for his or her actions beyond the accepted field of enquiry. More generally, the lack of individual responsibility and cognition of action implies that rational motivation in the social crowd is not only inexistent, it is essentially inconceivable. Applied to the social crowd, the simplified conception of irrationalism is too easily employed as justification for control of the individual as a social agent. Control of the individual members of the crowd was, in the final analysis, the stated goal of LeBon's original theory.

The question must therefore be raised: need the mechanism of influence in the social crowd *necessarily* be restricted to the subconscious? The priority of the subconscious process in crowd behavior is one which has never been significantly questioned in social psychology, forming instead the point of departure for most subsequent theories. The reliance on subconscious process as the sole mechanism of influence and motivation in the social crowd has limited theoretical treatments of crowd behavior to a very narrow range of possible outcomes. Situations of crowd behavior where participants are cognizant of their own actions, are aware of their surroundings, and make a deliberate decision as to the desirability of participating in the crowd's actions are certainly conceivable instances of collective behavior.

In order to foster the possibility of a less ideological conception of the psychology of crowd behavior, it is imperative that the social theorist first objectively assesses the validity of the afore-mentioned assumptions. In other words, does mass behavior necessarily involve the subconscious? If participation in a crowd does involve subconscious determinism, need one automatically invoke a pathological source? In opposition to the dominant conception, crowd behavior must be evaluated within the full spectrum of possible interpretations, from the antisocial to the prosocial. The violent and instinctive forces portrayed by LeBon are only one among many possible motivating factors in crowd behavior: awareness of the limitations imposed by this bias will hopefully lead to a more objective analysis of crowd psychology in the future.

References

Allport, F. H. (1924). The group fallacy in relation to social psychology. *American Journal of Sociology, 29,* 688-706.

Apfelbaum, E. (1985). Prolegomena for a history of social psychology: Some hypotheses concerning its emergence in the 20th Century and its raison d'être. In K. Larsen (Ed.), *Dialectics and ideology in psychology* (pp. 3-15). Norwood, NJ: Ablex.

Apefelbaum, E., & McGuire, G. R. (1985). Models of suggestive influence and the disqualification of the social crowd. In S. Moscovici & C. P. Graumann (Eds.), *Changing conceptions of crowd mind and behavior* (pp. 27-50). New York: Springer-Verlag.

Barrows, S. (1981). *Distorting mirrors: Visions of the crowd in late 19th century France.* New Haven: Yale University Press.

Biddis, M. D. (1980). *L'ère des masses.* Paris: Editions du Seuil.

Blumer, H. (1953). Collective behavior. In A. M. Lee (Ed.), *Principles of sociology.* New York: Barnes & Noble.

Bourget, P. (1883). *Essais de psychologie contemporaine.* Paris: Librairie Plon.

Chapanis, A. (1967). The relevance of laboratory studies to practical situations. *Ergonomics, 10,* 553-557.

Delboeuf, J. (1895). L'hypnose et les suggestions criminelles. *Revue de l'Hypnotisme Expérimental et Thérapeutique, 9,* 225-240, 260-266.

Dumas, G. (1911). Contagion mentale: Epidémies mentales - folies collectives - folies grégaires. *Revue Philosophique, 71,* 225-244.

Freud, S. (1921). *Group psychology and the analysis of the ego.* London: Hogarth Press.

Geiger, R. L. (1975). The institutionalization of sociological paradigms: Three examples from early French sociology. *Journal of the History of the Behavioral Sciences, 11,* 235-245.

Gergen, K. J. (1973). Social psychology as history. *Journal of Personality and Social Psychology, 26,* 309-320.

Ginneken, J. van, (1984). The killing of the father: The background of Freud's 'Group Psychology.' *Political Psychology, 5,* 391-414.

Hello, E. (1920). *Le siècle: Les hommes et les idées.* Paris: Perrin. (original work, 1895).

Hobsbawm, E. J. (1964). *The age of revolution: 1789-1848.* New York: Mentor Books.

Homans, G. C. (1970). The relevance of psychology to the explanation of social phenomena. In R. Borger & F. Cioffi (Eds.), *Explanation in the behavior sciences* (pp. 313-328). Cambridge, MA: Cambridge University Press.

LeBon, G. (1894). *Les lois psychologiques de l'évolution des peuples.*

Paris: Flammarion. (Reedited, 1978, by Les Amis de Gustave LeBon, Paris).

LeBon, G. (1895). *La psychologie des foules.* Paris: F. Alcan.

LeBon, G. (1896). *La psychologie du socialisme.* Paris: F. Alcan.

LeBon, G. (1910). *La psychologie politique.* Paris: Flammarion.

LeBon, G. (1911). *Les opinions et les croyances.* Paris: Flammarion.

LeBon, G. (1912). *La psychologie de la révolution francaise et la psychologie des révolutions.* Paris: Flammarion.

Liégeois, J. (1889). *De la suggestion et du somnambulisme dans leurs rapports avec ·le jurisprudence et la médicine légale.* Paris: Octave Doin.

Margot-Duclos, J. (1961). Les phénomènes de foules. *Bulletin de Psychologie, 14,* 856-862.

McDougall, W. (1920). *The group mind.* Cambridge: Cambridge University Press.

McGuire, G. R. (1984). *Floyd Allport and the rejection of the social conscious: Possible fallacies of the group fallacy.* Presented at the annual meeting of Cheiron: International Society for the History of the Behavioural and Social Sciences, June 13-16, Poughkeepsie, NY.

McGuire, G. R. (1985). *Gustave LeBon and the irrationalism of the social crowd.* Unpublished manuscript, York University.

McGuire, G. R. (1986). Hypnotic suggestion and criminal responsibility: Free will and individual agency in late nineteenth century French psychopathology. In S. Bem, H. Rappard & W. van Hoorn (Eds.), *Studies in the history of psychology and the social sciences 4.* Leiden, The Netherlands: Rijksuniversiteit Leiden.

Merton, R. K. (1960). The ambivalence of LeBon's 'The crowd', Introduction to G. LeBon, *The crowd: A study of the popular mind.* New York: Viking Press, pp. v-xxxix.

Morawski, J. G. (1984). Historiography as a metatheoretical text for social psychology. In K. J. Gergen & M. Gergen (Eds.), *Historical social psychology.* Hillsdale, NJ: Lawrence Erlbaum (pp. 37-60).

Moscovici, S. (1981). *L'âge des foules.* Paris: Fayard.

Nederhof, A. J., & Zwier, A. G. (1983). The "crisis" in social psychology: An empirical approach. *European Journal of Social Psychology, 13,* 255-280.

Pepitone, A. (1976). Toward a normative and comparative biocultural social psychology. *Journal of Personality and Social Psychology, 34,* 641-653.

Pepitone, A. (1981). Lessons from the history of social psychology. *American Psychologist, 36,* 972-985.

Rey, J-M. (1985). Freud and massenpsychologie. In S. Moscovici & C. P. Graumann (Eds.), *Changing conceptions of crowd mind and behavior* (pp. 51-67). New York: Springer-Verlag.

Ribot, T. (1870). *La psychologie anglaise contemporaine.* Paris: F. Alcan.

Ribot, T. (1879). *La psychologie allemande contemporaine.* Paris: F. Alcan.

Sampson, E. E. (1977). Psychology and the American deal. *Journal of Personality and Social Psychology, 35,* 765-782.

Silverman, I. (1977). Why social psychology fails. *Canadian Psychological Review, 18,* 353-358.

Smelser, N. J. (1962). *Theory of collective behavior.* London: Routledge & Kegan Paul.

Swart, K. W. (1964). *The sense of decadence in nineteenth century France.* The Hague: Martinus Nijhoff.

Taine, H. (1870). *De l'intelligence.* Paris: Hachette.

Taine, H. (1872-1875). *Les origines de la France contemporaine.* (6 Vols.) Paris: Hachette.

Taine, H. (1878). *The revolution.* London: Sampson Low, Marston, Searle, & Rivington.

Tarde, G. (1890). *La philosophie pénale.* Paris: Maloine.

Tarde, G. (1891) Les lois de l'imitation (1): Le somnambulisme social. *Revue de l'Hypnotisme Expérimental et Thérapeutique, 5,* 1-17.

Thiec, Y. J. (1981). Gustave LeBon, prophète de l'irrationalisme de masse. *Revue Française de Sociologie, 22,* 409-428.

Thiec, Y. J. (1983). La foule comme objet de "science." *Revue Française de Sociologie, 24,* 119-123.

Trotter, W. (1916). *Instincts of the herd in war and peace.* London: E. Bean.

Turner, R. H., & Killian, L. M. (1972). *Collective behavior.* (2nd ed.) Englewood Cliffs, NJ: Prentice Hall.

Vigouroux, A., & Juquelier, P. (1905). *La contagion mentale.* Paris: O. Doin.

Current Issues in Theoretical Psychology
Wm J. Baker, M.E. Hyland, H. Van Rappard, A.W. Staats (Editors)
© Elsevier Science Publishers B.V. (North-Holland), 1987

TOWARD A THEORY OF LIFE-SPAN DEVELOPMENT

Rodney S. Noble

Bolton Institute of Higher Education
Bolton, England

SUMMARY: Most existing theories of development are theories of the development of a particular aspect of the child - for example, Piaget's (1968, 1970) theory of cognitive development. This paper outlines a theory of development which attempts to describe development throughout the lifespan and to integrate cognitive, individual, and social aspects of development. Such an integration has been occurring piecemeal in both adult and child psychology. The present theory seeks to pull the various strands together to provide an account of personal development - of the development of an entire person. It is closely based on the work of G. A. Kelly and T. G. R. Bower. The nature of the theory is outlined and related to recent theoretical and empirical work in developmental and adult psychology. The application of the theory to social development in the first months of life is used by way of example. Various advantages of the theoretical position are outlined and new areas of potential interest in adult psychology are explored.

The problem with most of the classical theories of development is that they are theories of parts of the person developing into adulthood - that is, post-adolescence. For example, Piaget describes how the cognitive part of a person develops into 'formal operational' thought in adolescence while Freud (1940) relates the vicissitudes of emotional and motivational development up to the formation of adult personality structure at the end of adolescence.

The few theories which transcend this limitation have their problems. Erikson's (1950) theory of the eight ages of man is one such exception which examines psychological, social, and biological processes in development and attempts to integrate, to some extent, the cognitive and emotional/motivational aspects of development. The most crucial weakness of Erikson's theory is its failure to take into account the concepts and results of mainstream psychological research. It is essentially a psychoanalytic theory which has not generated much useful or important empirical research.

A further problem of Erikson's theory is that it fails to account convincingly for inter-individual differences since the cognitive resolutions which he suggests for each of his crises are universal. Also, each of the stages he describes, beyond the adolescent period, is more vague than the preceding one and the relationships between the various adult stages are poorly defined.

Modern psychology demands a new theory of development. This demand arises from the emergence of new integrations between different aspects of the person both in developmental psychology (which is, in the main, child psychology) and in main-stream or adult psychology. At present we have a developmental perspective upon each of the main areas of psychological investigation, namely: perception, cognition, emotion, motivation, personality, and social interaction. Each of these perspectives has grown in relative isolation from the others. There are local theories of perceptual development, cognitive development, and so on but there is no theory of personal development - of the person developing as an individual in each of these aspects.

Let us begin consideration of the integrations mentioned above with adult psychology and a movement which was very important in shaping the thinking of this paper - the integration of personality, cognition, and social perception outlined in Magnusson and Endler's volume, *Personality at the Crossroads* (1977). While real differences of emphasis are apparent among the different contributors to this collection, it was also clear that a basis of agreement had emerged. Studying personality would in future require simultaneous assessment of three 'factors' - the person, the situation, and the person's understanding of the situation, i.e., the interaction between person and situation. Theories of personality would have to account for both consistency and change in individual behaviour.

These considerations raise the question of whether or not a theory exists which already meets these requirements. I believe the answer is George Kelly's 'theory of personal constructs.' Kelly's work is only beginning to make a major impact on the heartlands of academic psychology in any sense other than as an investigative technology. Recent publications, however, especially a book entitled *Self-Organized Learning* (Thomas & Harri-Augustine, 1985), published this year by members of the Brunel University Centre for Studies in Human Learning, suggest that the situation is changing. The very title of the book suggests how Kelly's theory meets many of our needs in trying to conceptualize life-span development, as we will see below.

Embracing 'Personal Construct' theory (PC theory) for this purpose immediately raises a problem, bringing us back to the emerging integrations within developmental psychology referred to above. Kelly's is not an adequate developmental theory in its original form. Its range of convenience is the nature and structure of the adult psyche and the patterns of change which can occur in relatively mature construct systems as a result of experience or psychotherapy. This limitation is partly due to the focus of Kelly's own interests but is mainly the result of his corollary on the origins of constructs in which he maintains that they are in some way abstracted from successive replications of events.

This process, like that of reflective abstraction as used by Piaget to explain transitions between stages in cognitive development, falls foul of the problem of induction. The way in which this is a problem for such a theoretical process is illustrated by the following series of questions:

a) How many instances of a particular event are required to formulate a construct?

b) What procedure or process could be validly used to abstract a construct?

c) How, in the absence of an appropriate construct, could a construer determine which events in a sequence are similar or different from others, thus providing the basis for a construct to be abstracted?

There are new theories, like those of Werner (1948) and, especially of T. G. R. Bower, which avoid this problem completely. Bower (1979) shows that an approach which views development as proceeding from abstract to specific rather than by abstraction from the specific is logically defensible and suggests a process of mental development which is analogous to the concepts of the geneticist C. H. Waddington (1957) on gene expression in general.

By combining Bower's developmental process with the concepts of 'mental structure' derived from PC theory we emerge with an outline of a theory which is 'interactional' at many levels. It is interactional in the sense of the interactional psychology sought by Magnusson and Endler in 1977 in that we can use it to understand stability and change in individuals' constructions of themselves, the other people around them, and their expectancies and evaluations of the situations they find themselves participating in. It is interactional in an ontogenetic sense in that the pathway of development is seen as the interaction of the genetically shaped epigenetic landscape with various environmental inputs. Neither is predominant and any outcome can only be understood as an interaction. This new sort of theory also offers the possibility of conceptualizing, in interesting and meaningful ways, the interaction between the individual and social influences and forces which are known to affect his/her life and life possibilities, for example, the effects of social class or group membership.

Although Bower's direction of development is the opposite of that suggested by Kelly, the outcome of the developmental process he describes is remarkably similar in that each person develops a hierarchically organized set of discriminations and "rules" at different levels of specificity. The abstractness of early discriminations, or 'constructs' to use Kelly's term, is logical rather than semantic. This distinction is fundamental to understanding how Bower's account of development works.

In a semantic sense, good and evil are more abstract terms than tall and short; this is not the sense in which the young infant's constructs are abstract. The concept of logical abstractness is drawn from the work of Russell on logical types (Copi, 1971), and was first used in a psychological context by Gregory Bateson (1973). Abstract constructs apply to large areas of an individual's experience. They define similarities and differences between elements that subsequent development will show to be various sets of elements which can in turn be differentiated by other subordinate and more specific constructs. An example of this, which will be given in detail later, is the changing pattern of response shown by the infant to other human beings in the first few months of life. Recognition of the abstract nature of early construing is one of the integrations emerging from current work in child psychology.

Another equally vital theme, which relates to the interaction of the individual and society, is that of the importance of the social context for understanding development in human beings. The number of papers relevant to this area is increasing daily so only a few examplars can be considered here. One of the pioneering studies was the work of Margaret Donaldson (1978) and her co-workers who showed that the way children perform on the cognitive tasks devised by Piaget can be influenced by altering the social context and personal relevance of the task. Another striking example is the studies by E. J. and W. P. Robinson (1977, 1980, 1981, 1982, 1983) of communication failure. The speaker-blamer/listener-blamer dichotomy has a wide range of cognitive and linguistic consequences for children, but their performance on these tasks is crucially influenced by the ways in which communication failures are dealt with in the home, or by the kind of feedback on their performance provided by an adult interactant in the test situation. Further examples of this integration between cognition and social development are provided by Butterwork and Light (1982), and Elbers (1984).

Looking at the very earliest periods of the lifespan, preparedness for communication and the importance of social communication in the life of infants has now been demonstrated in a wide range of studies. The most outstanding are those of Condon and Sander (1974), Trevarthen (1975), Murray (1981), Carpenter (1975), and Meltzoff and Moore (1977). This predisposition towards communication Trevarthen terms intersubjectivity. Bower concludes that interactional synchrony and neonatal imitation (Condon & Sander, 1974; Melzoff & Moore, 1977), the latter also demonstrated by Dunkeld-Turnbull (1972), show that the neonate can make an *I-thou* versus *I-it* distinction and respond to fellow human beings as people rather than objects.

We can now begin to exemplify and fill in our outline theory of lifespan development. An individual's knowledge can be represented as a construct system. The very earliest constructs are non-verbal and highly abstract in the sense described above. The nature of these early constructs can be guessed at from the behaviour shown by infants. Thus, if Bower is correct and neonates indeed show *I-thou* behaviours to people which they do not address to objects, then the child is probably operating with a single, highly abstract construct which can be approximated verbally as *animate, human, like-me,* as opposed to *inanimate, non-human, not like me.* The abstractness of this construct is such that any living creature encountered at this stage would probably be classified as *like me* assuming that the child happened to come in contact with it - for example, a dog or cat. Normally, such encounters do not occur.

By the time the infant is a few weeks old this 'primordial construct' has differentiated into a number of other constructs which operate within the domains originally defined. Thus, inanimate objects will be differentiated into *things which are affected predictably by my actions - giving me pleasure* as opposed to *things which are not influenced by my actions.* This construct can be inferred from J. S. Watson's (1966, 1973) experiments with contingent and non-contingent mobiles, for example, and from various operant conditioning experiments in young infants. Carpenter's work suggests the division (by two weeks of age) of the realm of 'people' into *person I know (Mother)* versus *person I do not know* and *known person refusing to communicate (bad)* versus *known per-*

son communicating with me (good). Lewis and Brooks (1974) demonstrate further differentiation of the *person I do not know* set into *person I
do not know but like me, person like mother, person not like either*, and so
the process proceeds.

The driving force for the formation of new constructs or new ways
of acting is the experience of conflict among different ways of construing
a particular series of events. This was recognized by Piaget and has been
shown in the context of the theory suggested here by the series of experimental investigations into 'object identity' theory carried out by Bower
and Wishart (Bower & Paterson 1972, 1973; Bower & Wishart, 1973; Wishart, 1979; Wishart & Bower, 1984, 1985). Object identity is the same
set of behaviours termed the 'object concept' by Piaget. The need for
conflict, or experience of disconfirmation of predictions, to produce construing change was also recognized by G. A. Kelly (1955).

The content of communication between child and adult will be
based on their different construct systems. Some of the child's discriminations or constructs will be understood by the adults whom he or she
comes in contact with and will be elaborated and given verbal labels by
them. Others will be incomprehensible and ignored. By this process the
child's understanding of the world will be shaped by the significant adults
in her/his life and by the cultural and linguistic community which she/he
is part of.

As the person grows older his/her construct system will become increasingly well-specified; the number of levels of abstraction increases and
becomes more clearly defined. This process automatically reduces the opportunities for change in the system, and limits the likely extent of impact
for new learning. Fresh experience will tend to be assimilated into the existing system with minimal disturbance. Despite these constraints, development has not ceased, and if situations generating sufficient conflict are
encountered with appropriate social support available, then profound
changes (or learning experiences) can occur in adult life, as Bateson
(1973) points out.

Examples of such circumstances would be the development of a
neurotic disorder of such severity that the sufferer feels obliged to seek
therapy, or the experience of a first pregnancy in women - a less dramatic
but much more common situation. Another equally frequent example
would be coping with the changes in life occasioned by redundancy or re-
tirement - all of these events can create conflict in a person's construct
system and produce the conditions for change and further development.

The theory outlined here has several points in its favour. Firstly, it proposes a form of mental representation and a developmental process which exist and operate throughout an individual life. Secondly, it follows the spirit of current trends in psychology by integrating the social, cognitive, and personality aspects of development. Kelly's theory also covers certain aspects of emotion and motivation but this is an area for further work. Thirdly, it accounts for some of the most robust findings of life-span development psychology - namely, the apparent decrease with age in an individual's ability to adapt to change and learn new skills.

Fourthly, Kelly's concepts of guilt, threat, fear, anxiety, hostility, and aggression have proved very useful in a variety of clinical situations - not only in clinical psychology practise, but in the 'caring professions' in general. As Thomas and Harri-Agustines' book (1985) demonstrates, it has considerable potential as a theory for guiding educational practice in both older and younger age groups. *Self-Organized Learning* speaks for itself with regard to dealing with adult learning situations, but consider one implication of research described by Bower (1974) for teaching children. In the tracking studies using the Mundy-Castle apparatus, interpolation of trajectory which transferred to other cognitive performance was obtained after a moderate period of exposure. Prolonged practice on the apparatus produced very effective strategies for following the pattern of lights, but interpolation dropped out of the infant's repertoire and less transfer to other situations was shown. This is analogous to the effects of rote-learning of tables in school mathematics which produced very good arithmetic performance but little comprehension, if not active fear, of mathematical principles.

Finally, looking at life-span development in this way raises a number of interesting new issues, both theoretical and empirical. As the examples given above suggest, and as Bower (1979) explains in much greater detail, the theory can be used to account for a wide body of findings in developmental research. The new empirical issues which it suggests arise from its application to life-span development. These issues include the following possibilities:

1. There are different ways of representing human knowledge whose links are not clear. A construct system is one form of mental representation; 'Mental Models' are another (Johnson-Laird, 1983). Are these representations compatible? Is one reducible to the other or are they essentially different ways of representing disparate information for different purposes? This set of questions primarily requires rigorous conceptual and theoretical analysis.

2. Although development is regarded as continuing throughout life,
   the theory suggests that the possibilities for learning become more
   restricted as one grows older. The empirical questions this suggests are:

   a) How do adults recognize the need, or experience the desire to
      change?

   b) How do they cope with situations in which active learning is
      expected or required - for example, taking a college course or
      professional training?

   c) How much change can a life-event, which brings the person's
      construct system into conflict, be expected to make?

   d) How can we (as psychologists, counselors, or therapists, or
      just people) act to ensure as far as possible that experienced
      conflicts lead to positive growth and development rather than
      experiences of anxiety or threat?

   e) Can the 'limits of growth,' or those parts of a construct sys-
      tem which have a capacity for growth, be determined?

These questions have considerable practical as well as theoretical
importance. Bower (1979) takes a fairly pessimistic view of life-span development and the examples he takes of high level learning - gender identity, psychopathic lack of affection, etc., do seem to be established in
early childhood and remain stable thereafter. On the other hand, gender
identity is not something most people wish to change as adults, and those
who do so wish sometimes succeed admirably. Further, the Clarkes
(1976), for example, do not see the failure to leave an institution until
after the age of three as being as irreversibly debilitating as perhaps
Rutter's (1972) book suggested. Perhaps the reason why we see so little
adult learning is that, through lack of an appropriate theory, we have not
been looking at the right things at the right time nor in the right place.
Some workers have already started this search, as Whitbourne and Weinstock (1979) suggest. The work of these authors is in many ways very
close to the theoretical position being developed here, especially their
'Transactional Model of Aging.' The conceptual framework which they
use is unfortunately narrow and inappropriate, being based almost entirely on the outcomes found by Marcia in his attempted operationalization
of Erikson's concept of 'identity crisis' (e.g., Marcia, 1976), or more
directly (if more loosely) upon Erikson's theory itself. While Whit-

bourne and Weinstock's book is an extremely valuable addition to the literature on adult development, it still does not address the whole of life-span development nor systematically integrate the various aspects of the person.

References

Bateson, G. (1973). *Steps to an ecology of mind.* St. Albans: Granada.

Bower, T. G. R. (1974). *Development in infancy.* San Francisco: Free-man.

Bower, T. G. R. (1979). *Human development.* San Francisco: Freeman.

Bower, T. G. R., & Paterson, T. G. (1972). Stages in the development of the object concept. *Cognition, 1(1),* 47-55.

Bower, T. G. R., & Paterson, T. G. (1973). The separation of place, movement and objects in the world of the infant. *Journal of Experimental Child Psychology, 1(15),* 161-168.

Bower, T. G. R., & Wishart, J. G. (1973). The effects of motor skill on object permanence. *Cognition, 1,* 165-171.

Butterworth, G., & Light, P. (Ed.) (1982). *Social Cognition.* Brighton: Harvester Press.

Carpenter, G. (1975). Mother's face and the newborn. In R. Lewin (Ed.), *Child Alive.* (pp. 126-136). London: Temple Smith.

Clarke, A. M., & Clarke, A. B. (1976). *Early experience: Myth and evidence.* London: Open Books.

Condon, W. S., & Sander, L. (1974). Neonate movement is synchronized with adult speech: Interactional participation and language acquisition. *Science, 183,* 99-101.

Copi, I. (1971). *The theory of logical types.* (Monographs in Modern Logic). London: Routledge & Kegan Paul.

Donaldson, M. (1978). *Children's minds.* Glasgow: Fontana.

Dunkeld-Turnbull, J. (1972). *The development of imitation in infancy.* Ph.D. Thesis (Unpub.), University of Edinburgh.

Elbers, E. (1974). *The social psychology of the conservation task.* Paper presented at B.P.S. (Developmental Psychology Section) Conference, September, 1984.

Erikson, E. H. (1950). *Childhood and society.* New York: Norton.

Freud, S. (1940). *An outline of psychoanalysis.* (Trans. & Ed. by J. Strachey, 1973). London: Hogarth.

Johnson-Laird, P. N. (1983). *Mental models.* Cambridge: Cambridge University Press.

Kelly, G. A. (1955). *The psychology of personal constructs.* (Vols. 1 & 2). New York: Norton.

Lewis, M., & Brooks, J. (1974). Infants' social perception: a constructivist view. In L. B. Cohen & P. Salapatek (Eds.), *Infant perception: From sensation to cognition.* (Vol. 2, pp. 101-148). New York: Academic Press.

Magnusson, D., & Endler, N. S. (Eds.) (1977). *Personality at the crossroads: Current issues in interactional psychology.* Hillsdale, N.J.:

Lawrence Erlbaum.

Marcia, J. E. (1976). Identity six years after: a follow-up study. *Journal of Youth and Adolescence, 5(2)*, 145-160.

Meltzoff, A. N., & Moore, M. H. (1977). Imitation of facial and manual gestures by human neonates. *Science, 198*, 75-78.

Murray, L. (1980). *The sensitivities and expressive capacities of young infants in communication with their mothers*. Ph.D. Thesis (Unpub), University of Edinburgh.

Piaget, J. (1968). *Structuralism*. London: Routledge & Kegan Paul.

Piaget, J. (1970). *The principles of genetic epistemology*. London: Routledge & Kegan Paul.

Robinson, E. J. (1980). Mother-child interaction and the child's understanding about communication. *International Journal of Psycholinguistics, 7*, 85-101.

Robinson, E. J., & Robinson, W. P. (1977). Development in the understanding of causes of success and failure in verbal communication. *Cognition, 5*, 363-378.

Robinson, E. J., & Robinson, W. P. (1981). Ways of reacting to communication failure in relation to the development of the child's understanding about verbal communication. *European Journal of Social Psychology, 11*, 189-208.

Robinson, E. J., & Robinson, W. P. (1982). The advancement of children's verbal referential communication skills: The role of metacognitive guidance. *International Journal of Behavioural Development, 5*, 329-355.

Robinson, E. J., & Robinson, W. P. (1983). Communication and metacommunication: Quality of children's instructions in relation to judgements about the adequacy of instructions and the locus of responsibility for communication failure. *Journal of Experimental Child Psychology, 36*, 305-320.

Rutter, M. (1972). *Maternal deprivation reassessed*. Middlesex: Penguin Books.

Thomas, L. F., & Harri-Augustine, E. S. (1985). *Self-organized learning*. London: Routledge & Kegan Paul.

Trevarthen, C. (1975). Early attempts at speech. In R. Lewin (Ed.), *Child alive*. (pp. 62-80). London: Temple Smith.

Waddington, C. H. (1957). *The strategy of the genes*. London: Allen & Unwin.

Watson, J. S. (1966). The development and generalization of 'contingency awareness' in early infancy: some hypotheses. *Merrill-Palmer Quarterly, 12(1)*, 123-135.

Watson, J. S. (1973). Smiling, cooing and the game. *Merrill-Palmer Quarterly, 18(4)*, 323-339.

Werner, H. (1948). *Comparative psychology of mental development.*
Chicago: Follett.

Whitbourne, S. K., & Weinstock, C. S. (1979). *Adult development: The differentiation of experience.* New York: Holt, Rinehart & Winston.

Wishart, J. G. (1979). *The development of the object concept in infancy.* Ph.D. Thesis (Unpub), University of Edinburgh.

Wishart, J. G., & Bower, T. G. R. (1984). Spatial relations and the object concept: A normative study. In L. P. Lipsitt & C. K. Rovee-Collier (Eds.), *Advances in infancy research.* (Vol. 3). Norwood, N.J.: Abler.

Wishart, J. G., & Bower, T. G. R. (1985). A longitudinal study of the development of the object concept. *British Journal of Developmental Psychology, 3,* 243-258.

Current Issues in Theoretical Psychology
Wm J. Baker, M.E. Hyland, H. Van Rappard, A.W. Staats (Editors)
© Elsevier Science Publishers B.V. (North-Holland), 1987

THE SOCIAL STATUS OF MENTALISTIC CONSTRUCTS

Ian Parker

Manchester Polytechnic
Manchester, England

SUMMARY: This paper examines traditional descriptions of 'intervening variables' and the various subsets of 'hypothetical constructs' and finds them wanting. I propose a thoroughly non-individualist approach to theory in psychology, and outline some conditions which support the social status of 'mentalistic constructs.' In this view, persons demand, through the medium of discourse, that interpretations of their own, and others', psychologies be recognized. I argue that if we accept that there is a crucial *discursive* aspect of mental phenomena we may thereby facilitate an enrichment of psychology (so permitting contact with developments in sociology, psychoanalysis, and early psychological research). The account of mentalistic constructs I offer here deliberately and systematically frustrates the unifying project of theoretical psychology and promotes, instead, a critical 'theoretical social psychology' allied to the ethogenic 'new paradigm.'

Conceptual Phenomenology and Discourse

This paper draws on the traditions of 'ordinary language' philosophy and ethomethodology, traditions which have been synthesized into what has been termed 'conceptual phenomenology' (Coulter, 1981, 1983). The approach will be used to contest a series of distinctions which appear to underlie Michael Hyland's account of theoretical psychology, as described in his '*An Introduction to Theoretical Psychology*' (Hyland, 1981). The Hyland volume is distinctive in being, as the author writes, "... the first textbook to be written solely on theory construction and theory testing in psychology" (Hyland, 1981, p. viii).

The crucial message of Coulter's (1981, 1983) work in 'conceptual phenomenology' is that notions of 'cognition,' 'representation,' and 'information processing' can and should be re-described as fully social intersubjective processes. These are to be understood as processes which are inscribed within language. In Coulter's view: "Human behaviour is made up of activities (including stating things) *whose ascription conditions are logically irreducible to those for organic occurrences and emissions*" (Coulter, 1983, p. 13).

I want to go on from this starting point, however, to argue that we should include within the scope of any description of those processes the recognition that language is organized in wider structures or systems of discourse, and that discourses are culturally circumscribed. This view is consistent with the tradition of writing in the recent 'post-structuralist' tradition of French thought, and allows us to carry through a programme of research and theoretical analysis into the historically produced conceptual foundations of the language we use. The earlier work of Foucault is particularly pertinent, though the writings of Derrida and Lacan offer valuable support to the position to be advanced here (Derrida, 1981; Foucault, 1970, 1972; Lacan, 1977). Foucault provided an historical account of the emergence of what will be termed in this paper 'mentalistic discourse.' The discipline of psychology subsists on 'mentalistic discourse.'

Social Effects and Social Psychology

It is possible to throw this 'mentalistic discourse' into relief by showing that the phenomenon of mentalism has an important part to play in social psychology. Social psychology would then become a study of the 'discursive mentalism' which survives in our present day conversational practices (and written texts) by way of the 'real effects' it has on explanations of social behaviour.

The eventual focus of the paper will be on the notion of mentalistic constructs - a subset of 'hypothetical constructs' - with the aim of rescuing social psychology from the implicit though pervasive individualism which marks theoretical psychology. As will become clear during the course of the paper, the variety of social psychology that would be supported by Coulter's and Foucault's arguments could not be that promoted by the dominant laboratory-experimental tradition, but would be closer to the so-called 'new paradigm,' or 'new social psychology,' which was outlined by Rom Harré and Paul Secord (Harré & Secord, 1972) in their powerful critique of positivism and individualism in social psychology, and which was developed later to encompass an alternative project for psychology as a whole (Harré, 1979, 1983; Shotter, 1984).

The discussion runs through the following steps: I will explain why the distinction between 'intervening variables' and 'hypothetical constructs' is mistaken; an alternative account of the status and role of 'hypothetical constructs' will be given; and then an outline of the conditions which support the existential quality of mentalistic constructs will be offered; finally, some of the consequences for a theoretical social psychology will be drawn out.

Constructs and Variables

An Introduction to Theoretical Psychology (Hyland, 1981) is grounded on an earlier hitherto neglected but key distinction between 'intervening variables' and 'hypothetical constructs' (MacCorquodale & Meehl, 1948). The distinction, and the supporting argument, which have far reaching consequences for the whole project of theoretical psychology, runs as follows. Some approaches, most notably those advocated by a variety of neobehaviourists, choose to offer empirical generalizations of 'observable' behaviour leavened by convenient abstractions as explanation. Radical behaviourism, of course, abjures even the use of these analytic additions as 'explanatory fictions.' When neobehaviourist psychologists transcend mere description they enter this 'theoretical' realm and are dealing in 'intervening variables' - 'intervening variables' are "... absolutely precise concepts with precise boundaries" (Hyland, 1981, p. 34). Those who trade in them know that they are not calling into being new 'real' entities.

Theoretical psychology proper and its friends within the discipline, on the other hand, go beyond accounts in which all the measures are operationally defined, and prefer to employ 'hypothetical constructs' - hypothetical constructs are "... theoretical terms of an existential or hypothetical nature" (Hyland, 1981, p. 33). They contain (in MacCorquodale & Meehl's, 1948, terminology) "surplus meaning" by virtue of the fact that they are assumed to be actually there. As Hyland (1985) notes, many psychologists do prefer to speak of 'person variables'; they tacitly recognize the existential quality of the entities they describe whilst allowing MacCorquodale and Meehl's original wording to fall by the wayside. In the present paper, then, 'hypothetical constructs' could just as well be written as 'person variables.' 'Hypothetical constructs' do, in some sense, exist. But in what sense?

The distinction between 'intervening variables' and 'hypothetical constructs' is further elaborated by Hyland when he goes on to distinguish between different types of 'hypothetical construct.' He describes the operational and nature components of Physiological, Mechanistic, and Mentalistic constructs. This classification will be returned to below.

Problems with the Variable/Construct Distinction

The first point that should immediately be made is that the distinction pre-empts a number of the questions which have been raised by critics of psychology's 'old paradigm' (e.g., Harré & Secord, 1972). Not

least, the distinction sustains unexamined assumptions of cognitivism, individualism, and ahistoricism in the mainstream of the discipline. These
three assumptions lie at the core of traditional psychology, and an adequate account of the role they play is essential to any attempt to construct an alternative social psychology.

Observation and Depth. The distinction between 'intervening variables' and 'hypothetical constructs' privileges the notion of 'observability.' Whilst it rejects the use of 'intervening variables' precisely because
they are 'observable' (they have no reality beyond the terms, which we all
can see), it then embraces 'hypothetical constructs' only insofar as they
can be *counterposed* to what is 'observable.' It is crucial that 'hypothetical constructs' should be hidden; they obtain their 'surplus meaning' by
virtue of this fact. There is a metaphor of depth at work here which ensures that the psychologist must assume that behind or underneath every
item of behaviour there lies some essentially different series of cognitive
processes. The 'hypothetical constructs' have an 'existential quality'
which is necessarily separate from observation or explanation.

Individuality. The metaphor of depth operates around and within
individual heads. There could be no other location for such entities.
Here, Hyland is quite right to say that theoretical psychology can only be
concerned   with   individuals   and   their   mental   paraphenalia:
"inter-individual variation is explained by postulating unobservable individual characteristics" (Hyland, 1981, p. 8). Hence the rationale for accepting, in later accounts, the formulation 'person variables' in place of
'hypothetical constructs' (Hyland, 1985).

Historical Specificity. Theoretical psychology's variety of individualism, predicated on the search for hidden cognitive functions, is rooted
firmly in present-day cultural concerns and patterns of thought. In fact,
there are, in psychology, not only changes over time in the operation of
the 'hypothetical constructs,' but the particular historical location of the
whole enterprise of modern psychology upon which theoretical psychology
rides must always be stressed. The claim that further, more 'real' reasons
for behaviour should be found inside individuals behind the veneer of responsible, accountable, action is unexamined. In this sense, theoretical
psychology stands as an historically conditioned intellectual form - an intellectualist form of life which was identified by Ryle (1963) in his discussion of the 'intellectualist fallacy,' and which Foucault (1970) argued

was an important part of our peculiarly modern discourse.

Mentation and Mechanism

The problems which emerge from the categorization that theoretical psychology makes are compounded by the division of 'hypothetical constructs' into types which are supposed to have "different kinds of ontological status" (Hyland, 1981, p. 46). The differentiation flows from the application of correspondence rules, and it is significant that these correspondence rules are used as "sentences which link the theoretical terms to statements in an observation vocabulary" (p. 42). We have smuggled in once again the notion of 'observability' noted above. The three types of 'hypothetical construct' which Hyland distinguishes are Physiological (such entities as neurones and hormones), Mechanistic (such as filters), and Mentalistic (such as constructs).

If the aim of theoretical psychology is to account for the operation of these three types of constructs, it will remain trapped in an ahistorical cognitivist variety of individualism. I would argue that the middle Mechanistic construct (proposed by Craik, 1943, and championed by Fodor, 1968) is the pivot upon which the project of theoretical psychology is hinged, and is the flaw through which it should fall. Hyland (1985) does admit, in anticipation of just such criticisms of theoretical psychology, that a weakness may lie in this key item of his meta-psychological taxonomy:

> The ontological status of mechanistic person variables [i.e., 'Hypothetical Constructs'] seems less certain than the other two, and, after all, mechanism could be incorporated as an aspect of either physiological or mentalistic person variables. The reason for proposing mechanistic person variables as an independent form of person variables is simply a reflection of use. (p. 1007)

This is a clearly formulated instance of the kind of post hoc theoretical juggling which an intellectual enterprise betwitched with the purity of psychological terms is led into. I will return to this point below, but first I will offer an alternative account of 'hypothetical constructs,' and of their different natures or 'powers' (with the word 'powers' carrying the meanings conveyed in Harré & Secord, 1972) which may skirt these problems.

Social Demands and Social Objects

'Hypothetical constructs' can be differentiated from 'intervening variables' by means of a criterion of 'real effects.' There could not, of course, be a sense in which the 'effects' were not 'real,' and there could be an argument levelled against the terms of the criterion on that basis. However, there is a point that should be made in defence of the notion of 'real effects': the effects referred to in this context are social, and it is crucial to the argument of the paper that the social world(s) we inhabit should be taken as 'realities.'

Interpretation and Explanation

There is an important respect here in which an alternative psychology focussing on 'real effects' of terms in the social world shares ground with theoretical psychology. I retain the idea that there are objects to which a theoretically informed research project could attend, objects which are not immediately visible (and much social life is, after all, not transparent but disturbingly enigmatic). Here, though, 'hypothetical constructs' should not be thought to possess an existential quality because they may be captured by empirical studies (supposedly) uncontaminated by social context. Rather, 'hypothetical constructs' exist insofar as they serve a purpose for persons. They inveigle their way into everyday discourse; they demand of other explanations that they be admitted into the terms of accounts.

Demand. What are the nature of these demands? The reference to demands deliberately implies the willed activity of human beings. This is because it is often the case that these 'hypothetical constructs' are retained, either habitually or obstinately, within the repertoire of interpretations which people employ. Whilst the place of those constructs is *between* people rather than within them (the occasions for their use inhere in the social relations which bind persons together), they are re-invoked from the community concept pool in separate encounters. It is through the demands of persons that their accounts be heard that the constructs circulate, and the constructs repeatedly intrude into conversations and texts.

Discourse. One way of capturing the spoken (conversational) nature of the constructs and the written (textual) character of the life of constructs is to say that they possess a discursive character. 'Discourse' in linguistics simply refers to the units of language larger than a sentence, but in the present case, 'discourse' refers to the series of statements that are made about a social object (cf. Foucault, 1972). The point is that the 'social object' is only delineated within discourse itself. It has an intrinsically self-referential character. The self-referentiality, however, is not susceptible of elaboration within a single theoretical frame and its social form is therefore not transparent. It is persistently masked.

Using the criterion of 'real effects' as the basis for the distinction between 'hypothetical constructs' and 'intervening variables' cuts across the definitions employed by theoretical psychology. It also breaks the ('correspondence') rules which differentiate 'hypothetical constructs' into the Physiological, the Mechanistic, and the Mentalistic varieties. There are at least three consequences.

The Social Reality of Linguistic Variables.

'Intervening variables' always have the potential to become 'hypothetical constructs' by way of the continual 'contamination' of the precise language of behavioural description, but also, socially, through 'reification.' (However, this process is not susceptible to the controlled process of 'metatheoretic reification' optimistically described by Royce, 1978.) 'Reification' is prevalent in psychology, as can be seen in the continual slippage of one use to the other in both theoretical and empirical accounts.

Moscovici's (1981) work on the dissemination of 'social representations' throughout a culture, and the studies conducted under the umbrella of 'social representations' (cf. Farr & Moscovici, 1984), demonstrate the force of collective conceptual systems on the construction of individual selves. The work on 'social representations' connects with the idea that the psychologies which are constructed within the language of a culture are quite 'real': they are, in Heelas and Lock's (1981) phrase 'indigenous psychologies' built on a transient skeleton of 'hypothetical constructs.'

The Dissolution of Mental Mechanisms.

The Mechanistic category should be abandoned. Some of what are taken to be Mechanistic constructs could be rescued from the mysterious 'as if' realm and absorbed by one of the two other constructs.

Physiological Mechanisms. Mechanistic and Physiological constructs could simply be merged. The resulting 'Mechanistic/Physiological' construct would then be taken to be 'real' by virtue of its installation in biological matter. One way of understanding the character of this construct could be by way of the formulation of a "psycho-physical mix" (Harré & Secord, 1972, pp. 264-292). Here the notion of 'function' is retained in the possible elaborations of a systems approach informed by developments in cybernetics.

It is important here that the 'matter' should not be thought of as confined to the cortex or the central nervous system in dualist fashion, but should be thought of as an aspect of psychological phenomena. It should certainly include at least what J. J. Gibson called the 'perceptual system,' if not the body as a whole. In other words, the ecology of the organism would be viewed as at one with the social ecology of the person (Gibson, 1966, 1979).

Social Mechanisms. Alternatively, the Mechanistic constructs could in some cases be reinterpreted socially and used to augment our under- standing of Mentalistic constructs. An illustration can be given which pertains to the way psychologists understand the import of psychoanaly- sis. Freud is taken by theoretical psychologists (cf. Hyland, 1981, p. 51) to have pioneered the use of Mechanistic constructs. A counter to this view is to be found in Sulloway's (1980) portrayal of a Freud firmly committted to the idea that mental phenomena should be reduced to biol- ogy, to Physiology.

Recently, though, and of more potential interest to psychologists, there have been re-interpretaions which privilege the phenomenological and linguisitic aspects of psychoanalysis. One example is Bettleheim's (1985) study which re-translates, in the service of humanism, key ele- ments of the Freudian vocabulary. Another more radical case is that of Lacan (1977) where the Mental is seen as *social*. (Lacan is often taken to have adopted, along with Foucault and Derrida, a 'post-structuralist' me- taphysics.)

Discursive Constructs.

Mentalistic constructs should not end up as the poor cousins of the Physiological and the Mechanistic constructs, but should be attributed the 'reality' of social facts. This is particularly important to social psychol- ogy, and this is why Mentalistic constructs should be understood as Social constructs. They should be understood as part of the apparatus of 'dis- cursive mentalism' which allows us to elaborate to others the reasons for our actions.

Just as Mechanistic/Physiological constructs need to be understood as materially sustained by biological matter, so Social/Mentalistic constructs are materially sustained by communication media. Some examples are inscriptions in the case of writing, patterns of vibration in the medium of air in the case of speech, magnetic disruptions on the surface of tape in the case of recorded speech. To insist that something is Social/Mentalistic is not to infer that it is floating around in an as yet unlocated ether. Without a conception of the 'real' as being inclusive of effective linguistic constructions, a social psychology would not be possible - what would count as social psychology would be in fact a mere adumbration of individual psychology (so-called 'social' behaviour) and the debates over the merits or otherwise of methodological individualism would be pre-empted.

The Existential Status of Mental Phenomena in Social Life

To summarize the argument so far: (a) the terms which become 'hypothetical constructs' are created in concert with others, they have 'real effects,' and it is therefore to the social relations, and the symbolic content of those relations, that we should look; (b) mental phenomena, crystallized into Mentalistic constructs, exist within the symbolic matrix which can be conceived as a variety of 'discursive mentalism.' These are the reasons why a particular 'hypothetical construct' is not made anew at each social encounter at the bidding of creative individuals; instead the 'hypothetical construct' possesses a reality - a social reality - all of its own.

Mental predicates suffuse not only academic accounts but also the 'ordinary language' of the lay community. This point can be taken further, and the privileged relationship that orthodox psychology's discourse hopes to hold over everyday speech can be turned upside down. (The relationship can be thought of as being susceptible to what the 'post-structuralist' Derrida, 1981, calls a 'deconstruction.') When we pursue this line of argument we see that it is surely the case that 'ordinary language' is the main conceptual resource for 'hypothetical constructs.' The fluidity of 'ordinary language' - its metaphorical, contradictory, 'fuzzy' character - is the basis of the "surplus meaning" that 'hypothetical constructs' possess. Any scientific description of behaviour (whether it is behaviour elicited by the processes of experimentation or through controlled observation) relies on the ambiguous devices of 'ordinary language,' and any 'new' findings must be communicated by way of 'ordinary language' to other members of the psychological community.

Social Contexts of Mental Phenomena

The alternative to theoretical psychology proposed here stresses the facticity of the social realm. Such a view of mentation has an additional advantage; we are thereby able to reforge links with a number of research traditions which have been excluded from psychology in the service of cognitivism. There are three such cases.

Sociology. Moscovici's (1981) outline of a theory of 'social representations' draws on the sociology of Emile Durkheim. Durkheim (1938) treated of 'social facts' as if they were things. This sociology effectively examines the creation and dissemination of Mentalistic 'hypothetical constructs.' Whilst it is true that, in Durkheim's (1953) view, the mind of the person contained simulacra of social phenomena ('individual representations') which were to be examined by psychology, sociological research was to be predicated on the existence of a thoroughly social level of thought consisting of Social/ Mentalistic elements ('collective representations').

Psychoanalysis. The psychoanalytic approach is often distorted by psychology. Psychology seeks to understand psychoanalysis within its own frame of reference and makes great play of its unscientific descriptions and speculations. Despite the rituals of exorcism, re-interpretations of Freud still abound inside and outside the discipline, and one of those interpretations is of particular interest. Lacan's (1977) writings (which are often bracketed under the 'post-structuralist' rubric with Foucault's & Derrida's) present an account of the 'ego' as a linguistic construct, and the 'unconscious' as a social 'other' to the individual. Lacan, then, goes beyond humanistic revisions of Freud (e.g., Bettelheim, 1985), to implicate Mentalistic constructs in the social arena.

Psychology. Finally, when we re-interpret mental phenomena as social constructions, we are in a better position to recover some of the lost history of our own discipline, to recognize the original 'social' psychology advocated by Wundt in the second half of his career. Wundt saw the higher mental processes as being present in the *'Völkseele'* or collective mind, but his later work, which was discussed by Durkheim and by Freud, was excised by American positivist psychologists (cf. Danziger, 1979; Farr, 1980).

Consequences for Social Research

The logic of the preceding pages has been towards social psychology. In my view, the only way to rescue social psycholgy from the grip of positivism is to replace the distinctions between 'intervening variables' and 'hypothetical constructs' and those between different types of constructs with a notion of Social/Mentalistic constructs embedded in discourse and of Mechanistic/Physiological constructs understood through that discourse as part of the ecology of human action. A 'hypothetical construct,' then, operates as a fictitious entity which is endowed with the potential to manifest itself empirically within language. The maintenance of this state is accomplished within the field of Social/Mentalistic 'hypothetical constructs.'

A social psychology sensitive to these issues would attend to the 'ordinary language' which enables us to appreciate them. In 'ordinary language,' 'hypothetical constructs' unselfconsciously leaven descriptions of behaviour, attributions of responsibility, and explanations of puzzling social events. In psychology, however, these constructs become problems or clues in their own right. The discourse of psychology wrenches these Social/Mentalistic constructs out of their everyday context, and then, when they are positively senseless, tries to discover what they really mean.

Clusters of discussions and papers within the psychological community generate the parameters of the Social/Mentalistic constructs. Practices within the laboratory and in the field provide material for further elaboration. Such material is not raw 'data' but is itself merely the crux of interpretations based in the presuppositions of the experimenter and the joint interactive mediation of those interpretations by the subject and researcher in the experimental setting.

At the same time, psychology guards its status as a 'science' by continually tightening the forms of its descriptions. The ultimate end point of this process of purification and unification is, paradoxically, operationalism, and a consequence is that 'hypothetical constructs' no longer exist in the account - there only remain the 'precise' intervening variables. This is, of course, what Hempel (1958) calls the 'Paradox of Theorizing' (cf. Hyland, 1981, p. 6). Now, though, it is clear that it is not a logical problem but a social/institutional process in which psychology is locked.

The outcome of the argument is, I think, to pose a stark choice between a theoretical psychology parasitic on the positivist, individualist, non-historical, 'old paradigm' and a theoretical social psychology which has a place in its account for the set of discourses which comprise modern psychology.

Theoretical Psychology

If we accept the terms of theoretical psychology, we have to accept the systematic reduction of social phenomena to an individual level. It is clear that theoretical psychology would not suffer the existence of a fully *social* psychology (in the sense conveyed in the present paper) alongside other approaches, for the explicit aim of this meta-psychology is to unify the discipline: "different approaches should be integrated within a general theoretical structure" (Hyland, 1981, p. 12). The insistence that Mental phenomena must be located within the individual, for example, informs the interpretation offered of 'new social psychology' (Harré & Secord's, 1972). It is asserted that were this 'new paradigm' approach to be adopted, behaviour should be explained "by reference to the thoughts of the person engaged in that behaviour" (Hyland, 1981, p. 48).

This is to misunderstand the logic of the ethogenic 'new paradigm' which actually runs *against* attempts at introspection, and draws instead on the resources of ethomethodology and linguistic analysis to show that 'thoughts' are largely warrants for action and selfhood to other persons (for an elaboration of this point, see Shotter, 1984).

Theoretical Social Psychology

So, we come to the alternative, and a theoretical social psychology which would entail an account of psychology itself as an irremediably 'mentalistic discourse.' An appropriate historical conceptual category which recognizes this is that of 'discursive mentalism.' An important resource for such a theoretical social psychology would be the corpus of 'post-structuralist' writing which gives an urgent conceptual and historical cutting edge to the ethogenic alternatives to positivist psychology. Central to the activity of such theoretical social psychology would be the academic and institutional deconstruction of the language used to describe people and their mental accomplishments (cf. Derrida, 1981). It is also possible to recover the tradition of analysis which formed the conceptual grounds for the 'new paradigm' - the attempt, exemplified by Ryle's (1963) 'ordinary language' philosophy - to bridge the frameworks of phenomenology and behaviourism.

Conclusion

Opposition to a rigorous behaviourism is, of course, where theoretical psychology comes in. In the writings of neobehaviourists, there are attempts to employ only 'intervening variables.' Radical behaviourism does not even go that far, and this necessitates a choice between radical behaviourism and theoretical psychology (Hyland, 1981, p. 4). Theoretical social psychology, on the other hand, would appreciate one key insight from radical behaviourism. That is, that we should dispute the claim that "the contents of consciousness are not publicly observable" (Hyland, 1981, p. 48). Such contents may not be directly 'observable' in the sense in which empiricists would like, but they are *public*. They are, however, also re-worked by social actors in their interpretations of behaviour in such a way as to defy the logic of any behaviourist research programme (that is, methodological behaviourism). Social actors make demands, within discourse, that their voices be heard. New 'hypothetical constructs' - the Social/Mentalistic constructs described in this paper - suffuse descriptions of behaviour in 'ordinary language' and give a phenomenological richness to descriptions of the social world. They do exist, but theoretical psychology is looking in the wrong place.

References

Bettelheim, B. (1985). *Freud and man's soul.* London: Flamingo/Fontana.

Coulter, J. (1979). *The social construction of mind.* London: Macmillan.

Coulter, J. (1983). *Rethinking cognitive theory.* London: Macmillan.

Craik, K. J. W. (1943). *The nature of explanation.* Cambridge, England: Cambridge University Press.

Danziger, K. (1979). The positivist repudiation of Wundt. *Journal of the History of the Behavioural Sciences, 15,* 205-230.

Derrida, J. (1981). *Positions.* London: Athlone Press.

Durkheim, E. (1983). *The rules of sociological method.* Chicago: University of Chicago Press.

Durkheim, E. (1953). Individual and collective representations. In E. Durkheim, *Sociology and philosophy* (pp. 1-34). London: Cohen & West.

Farr, R. M. (1980). Homo socio-psychologicus. In A. J. Chapman & D. M. Jones (Eds.), *Models of man* (pp. 183-199). Leicester, England: British Psychological Society.

Farr, R. M., & Moscovici, S. (Eds.).(1984). *Social representations.* Cambridge, England: Cambridge University Press.

Fodor, J. (1968). *Psychological explanation: An introduction to the philosophy of psychology.* New York: Random House.

Foucault, M. (1970). *The order of things.* London: Tavistock Press.

Foucault, M. (1972). *The archaeology of knowledge.* London: Tavistock Press.

Gibson, J. J. (1966). *The senses considered as perceptual systems.* Boston: Houghton-Mifflin.

Gibson, J. J. (1979). *The ecological approach to visual perception.* Boston: Houghton-Mifflin.

Harré, R. (1979). *Social being.* Oxford, England: Basil Blackwell.

Harré, R. (1983). *Personal being.* Oxford, England: Basil Blackwell.

Harré, R., & Secord, P. F. (1972). *The explanation of social behaviour.* Oxford, England: Basil Blackwell.

Heelas, P., & Lock, A. (Eds.).(1981). *Indigenous psychologies: The anthropology of the self.* London: Academic Press.

Hempel, C. G. (1958). The theoretician's dilemma. A study in the logic of theory construction. In H. Feigl, M. Scriven, & G. Maxwell (Eds.), *Minnesota Studies in the Philosophy of Science. Vol. 2.* Minnesota: University of Minnesota Press.

Hyland, M. (1981). *Introduction to theoretical psychology.* London: Macmillan.

Hyland, M. (1985). Do person variables exist in different ways? *Ameri-

can Psychologist, 40, 1003-1010.

Lacan, J. (1977). *Ecrits: A selection.* London: Tavistock Press.

MacCorquodale, K., & Meehl, P. E. (1948). On a distinction between hypothetical constructs and intervening variables. *Psychological Review, 55,* 95-107.

Moscovici, S. (1981). On social representations. In J. Forgas (Ed.), *Social cognition: Perspectives on everyday understanding* (pp. 181-209). London: Academic Press.

Royce, J. R. (1978). How we can best advance the construction of theory in psychology. *Canadian Psychological Review, 19,* 259-276.

Ryle, G. (1963). *The concept of mind.* Harmondsworth, England: Peregrine/Penguin.

Shotter, J. (1984). *Social accountability and selfhood.* Oxford, England: Basil Blackwell.

Sulloway, F. J. (1980). *Freud, biologist of the mind: Beyond the psychoanalytic legend.* London: Fontana.

Current Issues in Theoretical Psychology
Wm J. Baker, M.E. Hyland, H. Van Rappard, A.W. Staats (Editors)
© Elsevier Science Publishers B.V. (North-Holland), 1987

THE CONCEPT OF TELOSPONSIVITY:

ANSWERING AN UNMET NEED IN PSYCHOLOGY

Joseph F. Rychlak

Loyola University of Chicago
Chicago, Illinois, U.S.A.

SUMMARY: Psychologists have eschewed the description of behavior in terms of purpose, intention, or free will. The reason for this anti-teleological bias is traced to psychology's adoption of the *natural science* theoretical model, which dictates that no formal or final causation is to be employed in the description of events. The upshot is that a continuing theoretical bias has been institutionalized in psychology, one which distorts agential conceptions as used by people in everyday circumstances as well as by clinicians in psychodynamic contexts. To remedy this situation, the author proposes the adoption of a formal-final cause conception termed the *telosponse*. This construct defines behavior as enacted through the affirmation of a premised meaning, which is carried forward in precedent-sequacious fashion. Important foundation conceptions enabling a theorist to speak of telosponsivity include dialectical reasoning and tautological meaning extension.

The popular view of the psychologist is of someone who tries to find out how people function *as people*, as organisms that are more than simply a collection of chemicals, tissues, and physical energies. Even professionally educated colleagues in various specialties tend to think of psychologists as students of the *dynamics* of behavior. It takes considerable contact with psychologists to learn that not all of them are *head shrinkers* or investigators of the quirks, secrets, and wishes that so typify human behavior. Of course, many psychologists *do* endeavor to capture the grandeur of being human, the victories and foibles of a behavioral pattern that seems at times above and even beyond the *natural* course of events. We can think of Sigmund Freud as probably the major psychiatrist/psychologist to make this effort. Freud broke the bounds of medical theorizing, assigning intentionality, compromise, and self-delusion to the normal and abnormal person alike.

Freud found it difficult to bring this language of description into line with the reigning biological explanations of his time (see his grumblings to Jung concerning this matter as cited in McGuire, 1974, pp.

115-116). Even more significant for present purposes, when experimental psychologists later attempted to bring Freudian explanations into line with accepted *rigorous* learning theories, the heart of Freud's meaning dropped out of the theoretical description. Thus, Dollard and Miller's (1950) subsumption of Freudian by Hullian theory resulted in some obvious distortions. For example, in accounting for unconscious behavior, Dollard and Miller suggested that it was a form of *unverbalized* behavior (p. 136), that is, an instrumental rather than a cue-mediated line of behavior. Actually, Freud (1953) makes it quite clear that from his point of view "the most complicated achievements of thought are possible without the assistance of consciousness" (p. 593). The upshot is that whereas, in Freudian theory, the unconscious knows *more* than the conscious realm of mind, in Dollard and Miller's (1950) rigorized account of Freudian theory, the unconscious is essentially *stupid* (p. 14).

According to the popular view, psychologists are not only supposed to figure out *what makes people tick,* but they are supposed to have a sense of the direction that a person's behavior is taking. The *prediction of behavior* has become a variant way of speaking about psychology. But whereas the average individual might be thinking of such predictions as *figuring out* what people are looking for in life or what they are strategizing to obtain in life, the profession of psychology has framed this task in terms of a kind of engineering problem, the accurate measurement of *variables* that direct human behavior much as the atmospheric *variables* direct the course of our weather each day. In other words, whereas the popular imagination assumes that psychologists look for the grounds on the basis of which people behave - grounds that are freely chosen, opted for, or even uniquely created - the profession of psychology actually seeks to find forces in the environment or the biology of a person which *really* determine these lines of behavior. The problem of behavioral prediction therefore becomes a matter of statistical prediction, of sampling from a parameter and predicting to a criterion. The challenge of psychology is thus to find the *right* parameters, do the *correct* sampling, and frequently *update* such measurements in a continuing effort to describe what behavior is like.

Sometimes this prediction of variables is done using personality or attitudinal scales of various types (Pervin, 1985), and sometimes it is done in actual experiments that are designed on the assumption that they are mapping the variables which direct behavior. The determinism here is construed as extra-individual. A beautiful example of the image of behavior implied in such approaches to the description of behavior is provided in a paper by Donald O. Hebb (1974) entitled "What psychology is all about." The following self-characterization nicely sums up what a professional psychologist thinks human behavior is all about:

> I am a determinist. I assume that what I am and how I think are entirely the products of my heredity and my environmental history. I have no freedom about what I *am*. But that is not what free will is all about. The question is whether my behavior is entirely controlled by present circumstances. Heredity and environment shaped me, largely while I was growing up. That shaping, including how I think about things, may incline me to act in opposition to the shaping that the *present* environment would be likely to induce: And so I may decide to be polite to others, or sit down to write this article when I'd rather not, or, on the other hand, decide to goof off when I should be working. If my past has shaped me to goof off, and I do goof off despite my secretary's urging, that's free will. (Hebb, 1974, p. 75)

Now, in the popular imagination, free will or human agency is definitely *not* understood as yesterday's shapings counteracting today's shapings totally without self-influence by the person qua chooser or selector of what will eventuate. Hebb's reference to a *decision* here is completely off the mark when we realize that he is saying his past shapings do the deciding for him. This is not what people *on the street* think of when they speak of their free wills. They are assuming that the psychologist is capable of guessing at what their personally derived choices or decisions *will be like*, and not that there is a force from out of the past doing the deciding for them. There is clearly an impasse here between what the public expects of psychology on the matter of personal behavior and what the profession of psychology has to offer on this question.

The response of many psychologists to this disparity between how their science explains behavior and how people understand their behavior is frequently something like this: "All sciences redefine the person's naive understanding of the subject matter under study. Medicine introduced new terminology to account for biological processes which common sense did not have an inkling of to begin with." Though this is true, we should remind ourselves that medicine and other sciences rarely *explain away* the item under consideration in framing their reconceptualizations of common sense experience. The process of digestion may have had many quaint common sense theories concerning it that scientific investigation negated or clarified, but the process of digestion per se was not explained *out of existence* as is continually occurring in psychology's treatment of the human being as non-agential *by definition*.

Human Agency and Causal Predication

Psychologists have been highly unsuccessful in circumscribing a theory of human agency. Aside from notable exceptions like William McDougall, Gordon Allport, or Gardner Murphy, they have seemed to avoid the issue entirely in the name of scientific rigor. And yet, there would seem to be a scholarly role and responsibility going begging here. On what basis have we psychologists dismissed all serious theoretical consideration of the person as an agent of his or her behavior, turning the Freudian unconscious intention into the stupidity of not knowing what is taking place, or the decision to act one way rather than another in the present as the manifestation of yesterday's push acting as today's shove?

This writer believes that such theorizing is due to psychology's early identification with a Newtonian brand of science in which final causation was *properly* drummed out of usage for inanimate events, but is now being sustained erroneously in the descriptions of human behavior (see Rychlak, 1984a, 1984b, for more extensive analyses of this issue). For the first 1500 years or so in the A.D. world it was customary to describe anything in the natural order in terms of *four* causal terms. The names for these causes were coined by Aristotle, but all four meanings were employed in explanations of things in the B.C. world even before he came on the historical scene. We can think of these causal meanings as four ways in which to predicate anything, that is, to lend meaningful understanding to anything in our experience we can use one or more of these four principles of explanation.

Aristotle (1952a, p. 128) held that to account for anything in nature we can use one or more of the following predicates: (1) We can use a *material cause*, in which case we are trying to account for something based upon what kind of substance 'makes it up'; for example, making a chair out of wood results in an item of furniture with different properties and a shorter 'life' expectancy than one made of marble. (2) We can use an *efficient cause*, in which case we would try to capture the impetus, push, or thrust in events that go to assemble them, or to cue them along as they unfold; billiard balls bumping each other about on a cushioned table or the flashing red light of an emergency vehicle in traffic exemplify such causation. (3) We could also bring a *formal cause* meaning to bear, in which case we would be using the pattern, shape, or order of events or objects as a basis for descriptive understanding; thus, the patterned sequence of a mathematical proof or the outlined shape of a friend's physiognomy enables us to know something about what is taking place as we sit in the mathematics class or spy a friendly face in the crowd. (4) We can also use the *final cause* or, as Aristotle named it, "that for the sake of which" an action takes place or anything is said to *be* in existence; final causes subsume the meaning of reason, purpose, or intention. The reason a person has a yearly physical is *for the sake of* maintaining a satisfactory level of health.

Final causes deal with ends, and as the Greek word for *end* is *telos,* we refer to explanations embracing final-cause meanings as teleologies or telic accounts. Teleological explanation was common in science up to the 16th century, when a combination of historical occurrences was to 'do in' such theorizing. Galileo's notorious clash with the churchmen of the Inquisition was one source of the decline in teleological description among scientists. The churchmen, relying upon Biblical accounts stemming from a deity teleology had the solar system *geocentric* whereas Galileo was proposing a *heliocentric* explanation of the solar system and offered empirical evidence in support of his views. His house arrest and recantation heralded the beginning of the demise of final-cause description in science.

But there were even more telling reasons for questioning telic description in science. Aristotle had favored using *all four* of the causal meanings in scientific description, believing that this could only enrich the account. He therefore attributed purposivity to everything in nature, suggesting in his *Physics* (1952c, pp. 276-277) that leaves exist for the sake of providing shade for the fruit on trees. It was Sir Francis Bacon who led the assault on such final-cause description in science. Pointing his guns at Aristotle, Bacon (1952) said that it is bad scientific explanation to suggest that leaves on trees are *for the sake of* shading fruit, or that bones on the body are *for the sake of* holding up the fleshy parts of the body (p. 45). Indeed, Bacon also derided the use of formal-cause description, noting that it was pointless to ask the *form* of water, gold, or even that of a lion in the wild (p. 44). What the proper *natural* scientist must do is find the underlying material and efficient causes that move events along, bring about formal-cause patterns, and thereby carry out the flow of events *in* nature. Bacon did not reject formal and final causation altogether, feeling that such conceptions were proper in the realm of metaphysics and ethics.

Bacon and other founding fathers of the *natural science* tradition were not actually thinking of themselves as the objects of such sicentific description. They were thinking of the flow of physical events, not the

dynamics of psychological events. However, with the rise of psychology
in the closing decades of the 19th century we find a remarkable development occurring. The Newtonian brand of science which was fostered by
thinkers like Bacon, Hobbes, Locke, and others in the British Associa-
tionistic tradition had become the accepted style of explanation. Formal
and especially final causation were not held to be acceptable (*basic*) principles of explanation in science. Scientific accounts were to be *reductive*
in the sense that the four causal meanings were to be limited to (reduced
to) just two - material and efficient causation! And as psychology now
made its way onto the historical scene this Newtonian/ LaPlacian aspira-
tion was maintained. From its inception, psychology has been framed
primarily as a *natural* (i.e., non-telic) science. Constructs such as the reflex arc, the stimulus-response connection and, more recently, the
input-output flow (with or without feedback), reflect an essentially
non-teleological effort to account for behavior without purpose, intention, or self-direction.

It is the contention of the writer that there has never been a proper
effort made in basic, experimental psychology to describe behavior teleologically. We have *no* extant learning theories which encompass telic description as a basic tenet. All of our traditional learning theories begin
from an efficient-cause presumption, enhanced by the material-cause assumptions of drives, neural mechanisms of various types, and so forth.
Tolman's (1932/1967) purposive behaviorism is no more a genuine teleology than is Hebb's (refer above). Indeed, Tolman specifically contrasts
his view of purpose as an "objectively defined variable" (p. 16) to that of
William McDougall's, with the latter conception reflecting the common
sense meaning of purpose and the former conception reflecting an
efficiently-caused manipulation. The custom in psychology of referring
to intervening variables coming between the stimulus (input) and the response (output) can be seen originating in Tolmanian theorizing. This
unfortunate custom erroneously confounds the context of proof (or
method) with the context of theory. The independent variable (method)
is equated with the response (theory). Intervening variables are thought
to be fluctuating between these two sides of the efficient-cause tandem
known as a behavioral *law*.

The confounding of method with theory served to strengthen the
grip that efficient causality had - and continues to have - on psychological theorizing. The tendency to refer to *S-R lawfulness* reflects this confounding. In truth, there can be no such thing as an S-R law, because
the concept of lawful regularity refers to the relationship between an independent (I) and dependent (D) variable (V) in the methodological con-

text. There *are* IV-DV laws, open to theoretical interpretation. Once interpreted, *a* point of view might hold that these lawfully observed regularities meet the requirements of an efficient-cause, S-R theory. But on the other side of the coin, it must be possible in principle to put to test, within the IV-DV format, a theory of behavior which is construed teleologically (indeed, the writer has been doing precisely this for some time; see Rychlak, 1977, 1981a). A teleological theory cannot accept the view of S-R laws, that is, of *nothing but* S-R laws issuing from the methodological context, because this would take away any possibility of a final cause meaning entering into the description of an experimental outcome by default. If lawful regularities in behavior are construed as *solely* efficiently causal they cannot be said to be finally causal. At least, it is difficult to see how these two formulations can be combined without doing great harm to the telic position. This is precisely what happened in the Hullian translation of Freudian constructs mentioned above.

If the scientific method of validation forecloses on the kind of theory put to it, if every study done using the IV-DV strategy results in *only* S-R findings, then the scientific method is not objective (Rychlak, 1980). The method would dictate the theoretical interpretation of the findings, and this situation could not be tolerated in a true science. It would then be quite impossible to falsify S-R theory. The problem in psychology has always been and continues to be the fact that: (1) a clear and distinct separation of theory and method has been disregarded, leading to murky theorizing, method madness, and little respect for an innovative idea departing from what is immediately observed; and (2) there is a consequent absence of a conception based upon the meaning of final causation to parallel the efficient-cause meaning encompassed in the stimulus-response or input-output conceptions. We cannot put a telic theory to test unless we first recognize what a telic conception is, and then make it possible for suitable tests of this style of theorizing to be carried out in the rigorous context of empirical validation.

It is the writer's contention that psychology can be a viable science only if it accepts the responsibility to study the person in the way that people who are not psychologists expect to be studied. People have defined themselves in telic terms since the beginnings of recorded history. All legal systems in advanced societies begin from the assumption that human beings have a free will, and this assumption is not going to change in the future no matter what sort of mechanical or cybernetic theoretical formulation psychologists are likely to come up with as a substitute for agential action. Final-causation is the essential ingredient left out of the human image to date. At least some of us in psychology must find a way of describing behavior in terms of *that (reason, purpose, goal, wish, etc.) for the sake of which* it is intentionally enacted. Let mechanistic formulations continue, but let teleological formulations now begin, and let us see which point of view will prove the most instructive in the long run.

Telosponsivity

In an effort to fill the void that now exists in psychological theorizing at the most basic levels of description, the writer proposes that we view human behavior as *telosponsive* in addition to being responsive. Responses to stimuli in the traditional efficient-cause manner undoubtedly occur, but they can be thought of as instrumental actions, employed in the carrying out of pre-selected patterns of behavior that have been taken on as premises by human organisms. The complete definition of a telosponse is as follows:

> A *telosponse* is the person's affirming or taking on (premising) of a meaningful item (image[s], word[s], judgmental comparison[s], etc.) relating to a referent acting as a purpose for the sake of which behavior is then intended.

The purpose of the meaningful item can be assumed without question, as in observing factually that *the door out of room is over there* or it can be difficult to ascertain as in the subtlety of a dream content. When the individual behaves *for the sake of* this purpose he/she is telosponding or acting intentionally, although this may be exclusively at the level of understanding and not be seen in his or her overt actions. In this sense, concepts (meaningful items) have purpose, and human beings intend.

A telosponse is a final cause of behavior (Rychlak, 1977. p. 283). To avoid the kind of theoretical trap that Hebb's concept of free will (refer above) falls into we must have a way of describing how it is that the person as an agent can actually set the *that* (formal-cause patterned meaning encompassed by a premise) *for the sake of which* he or she will intend a line of reasoning/behavior. Hebb's problem is due to his placing himself *in between* an efficient cause (S) and its ultimate effect (R) - and no more! Such mediation-model thinking is currently predominant in psychology. Many psychologists believe that there are several non-mediational theories of behavior currently in the literature, including those which routinely refer to goal directedness (e.g., Schank & Abelson, 1977), reflective thought (e.g., Bandura, 1977), and even morality (e.g., Harré, 1984). However, when we look carefully at such theories, they all fall back on an acquisition, social learning type of explanation which leads inevitably to yesterday's shapings efficiently causing today's shapings in the style of Hebb, as an environmentally acquired schema, a discriminative stimulus, or as a linguistic convention shaped by common verbal usage.

The point is: Such theories *cannot do otherwise* but fall back on mediation explanations. They lack a basic learning theory in which the final-cause, teleological alternative is taken seriously. But if we accept telosponsivity we begin to think of behavior as *predicated* rather than mediated in this fashion. Mediation models presume that humans reason *only* in what Aristotle (1952b) termed a demonstrative fashion (p. 143). When we reason demonstratively we take it as given that *this* and only *this* stimulus quality or meaning now entering our cognizance is involved in what is transpiring. When Hebb's early shaping supposedly prompted him to goof off this day, it was because *in theory* he had been sent in this direction thanks to a demonstratively unipolar prompting from out of his past.

But now, Aristotle also suggests that human beings reason *dialectically*. That is, humans see immediate opposites to the stimulus qualities or meanings being input *at the instant of input!* The human being who is looking *up* the sides of a canyon implicitly understands that he/she is *down* in the valley. This is so because human mentation is dialectical, it is continually on the lookout for a premising *that for the sake of which* it will intend to behave. And opposites provide an instant source of alternative formulations, enabling the person to influence what will eventuate in his or her behavior, e.g., decide where to locate: *in* the valley or *out* of the valley. According to this formulation, Hebb was not unidirectionally shaped by his early environment to goof off or not to goof off. He lived through a life circumstance in which he *opted* to begin behaving one way or the other based upon personally construed advantages or preferences. At some point he could be said to have taken on a unidirectional and unquestioned premise (in demonstrative fashion) to the effect "I like to goof off" or "I never goof off when there is work to be done."

But the point of importance is that if we human beings can see what is *not there* by way of what *is there* in our experience, and opt thereby to behave in *either* of two directions based upon the *same* set of input circumstances, then we are not the mediated mechanisms that psychology has been making us out to be. If we learn through so-called observational learning (Bandura, 1977) that "Doing *X* leads to *Y*" then we *also* learn that "Not doing *X* leads to *non-Y*" without additional observational input! Whether we eventually do *X* depends on many things, including the meanings of *X* and *Y*, not to mention our personal preferences (generated, incidentally, by dialectical judgments of likes and dislikes; see Rychlak, 1977, Chps. 9 and 10). If *X* is *taking drugs* and *Y* is *happiness* we will enact something quite in contrast to what will occur if our conception of *Y* is *misery* (i.e., non-happiness).

Behavior from this theoretical view is more akin to *taking a position on* alternatives than *responding to* input influences from a uniformly *given* environment. To understand how it is possible to affirm or not affirm a premise, affirm one meaning or another meaning of the same premise, we must accept the fact that people *do* reason in a dialectical as well as a demonstrative manner.[1] Indeed, this is where we find the real source of what the popular imagination holds as the capacity for free will. Every person senses a personal choice or a personal contribution to what will be enacted in the fact that he or she always sees to the opposite of what *is* and can thereby generate alternatives in the direction of what *is not*. This enables one to transcend the Hebbian present and generate alternatives *not* based upon previous unidirectional (i.e., non-oppositional) shapings, but based upon the fact that there are always implicit alternatives in any experienced *fact* pattern. Hebb had the same options when he was first shaped as he had at the moment, to do or not to do what the environment was impelling him to do.

We cannot always reject an environmental prompt, of course. A parent who whips a child into one pattern of behavior leaves no alternative for the child but to submit. However, this child is necessarily learning what the parent is whipping out of his or her *overt* behavioral pattern. And one day, when the parental pressure is off, what was *not* intended by the parent becomes the intention of the child. Physical *shapings* are also difficult to alter or ignore. The pangs of hunger seem to propel us demonstratively, in one direction and only one direction. However, as is well known, people have intentionally starved themselves to death in order to make a *higher* point under the premise that certain principles are more important than life itself. If we begin with the assumption that human

---

[1]For a thorough review of the concept of dialectic, see Rychlak (1976, 1977, 1981b). Many modern readers seem to believe that the concept of dialectic originates with Hegel. Actually, dialectical meaning and dialectical reasoning is reflected in the ancient writings of the Vedic literature in India (about 1500 B. C.), and we can find historico-cultural evidence for dialectic in each age and in all cultures - primitive and civilized! - ever since. Hegel formalized this oppositional/ contradictory style of reasoning as an evolution of a world principle, a deity coming to consciousness over the ages. Marx and Engels set the march of dialectic in material reality. Thus, theoretical applications of dialectic abound but the important point for present purposes is that human beings *do* reason in this unique manner of seeing through oppositionality and contradiction more sides to an issue than is originally *there* for the knowing.

beings can reason dialectically then we open up alternatives to the individual which our present psychological theories simply do not make possible due to their exclusive reliance on demonstrative assumptions. Agency may be defined as "behavior that is carried out in opposition to, in addition to, or without regard for stimulation issuing from environmental and biological sources."

It should be appreciated that in speaking about premises we are referring to formal-cause patterns which frame meanings. Such meanings encompass predications in the sense of certain terms lending meanings to other terms (e.g., "Man is mortal" has the latter meaning being extended to the former). In addition, the *flow* of meaning is based on logic, on the relations of patterns, rather than on the efficient-cause thrust of a literal motion. Indeed, time's passage is irrelevant to the *flow* of a logical course of behavior. Syllogisms *move* logically from major to minor premises and thence to a conclusion without any literal motion taking place. We now suggest that this is true for mentation in general. This course of meaning-extension occurs in a precedent-sequacious fashion.

A *precedent* meaning is one that goes before others in order or arrangement and thereby sets the tone, frame of reference, or ambience of the meaning-extension to follow. Major premises serve as precedents to minor premises and the conclusions which flow thereby. To capture this extension of meaningful patterning we employ the term *sequacious* which is defined in the sense of a *slavish compliance* and gets at what we mean by the thrust of logical necessity. Thus, given that the scientist has telosponded through affirming the precedent *paradigm X* (Kuhn, 1970), he or she will view all research data as *X-like*. If *paradigm Y* had been taken on as a precedent, the sequacious extension of this grand premise would have resulted in *Y-like* empirical findings.

This course of precedent-sequacious meaning-extension in telosponsivity occurs through a tautological process of the sort *If A then A* (i.e., If *A-like precedents* then *A-like sequacious extensions*). To tautologize in mentation is not simply to offer meaningless repetitions of what is known already; to tautologize is to extend what is known to what is unknown but knowable (Rychlak, 1977, p. 278). It is often overlooked that analogizing or using metaphors to frame what is under conceptualization relies upon tautological extension *in part*. A tautology is a meaningful relation of identity between items, e.g., the subject and predicate of a logical proposition; but an analogy or metaphor is a relation of *partial* identity between such items. There is a dialectical aspect to analogical reasoning, in which we have the demonstrative equivalence between two items (e.g., beer is a liquid identical in this quality to root beer) but also the non-equivalence in the dis-analogy (i.e., beer has intoxicating properties whereas root beer does not).

In order to understand telosponsive behavior we must always view the premises under affirmation introspectively, that is, from the point of view of the human reasoner (the *affirmer*). We appreciate that what the person construes predicationally is as important to the ongoing course of behavior as what sort of environmental and biological *variables* are at play. Indeed, as the vast empirical findings on awareness in human conditioning suggest (Brewer, 1974), such *variables* are frequently only capable of influencing behavior because the person concerned has premised them appropriately and opted to conform to what they signify. The more we give credence to telosponsivity in human behavior, the more evidence we find in its support (for extensive literature reviews along this theoretical line see Rychlak, 1977; 1981a; 1981b).

In closing, it is our hope that, in the future, psychologists will begin conceptualizing human beings in terms of telosponsivity rather than simply responsivity. It is the writer's view that if we psychologists fail to advance our thinking concerning human behavior we will fall ever more out of step with the basic assumptions of our very civilization. The innovation here is not great, but the apparent break with the natural science tradition has seemed to hold us up. Through continuing study and dialogue as well as appropriate researches we might yet effect a teleological revolution in psychology for the twenty-first century.

References

Aristotle. (1952a). Posterior analytics. In R. M. Hutchins (Ed.),*Great books of the western world* (Vol. 8, pp. 37-137). Chicago: Encyclopedia Britannica.

Aristotle. (1952b). Topics. In R. M. Hutchins (Ed.), *Great books of the western world* (Vol. 8, pp. 143-223). Chicago: Encyclopedia Britannica.

Aristotle. (1952c). Physics. In R. M. Hutchins (Ed.), *Great books of the western world* (Vol. 8, pp. 257-355). Chicago: Encylopedia Britannica.

Bacon, F. (1952). Advancement of learning. In R. M. Hutchins (Ed.), *Great books of the western world* (Vol. 30, pp. 1-101). Chicago: Encylopedia Britannica.

Bandura, A. (1977). *Social learning theory.* Englewood Cliffs, NJ: Prentice-Hall, Inc.

Brewer, W. F. (1974). There is no convincing evidence for operant or classical conditioning in adult humans. In W. B. Weimer & D. S. Palermo (Eds.), *Cognition and the symbolic processes.* Hillsdale, NJ: Lawrence Erlbaum Associates.

Dollard, J. , & Miller, N. E. (1950). *Personality and psychotherapy: An analysis in terms of learning, thinking, and culture.* McGraw-Hill Book Co., Inc.

Freud, S. (1953). The interpretation of dreams (second part). In J. Strachey (Ed.), *The standard edition of the complete psychological works of Sigmund Freud* (Vol. V). London: The Hogarth Press.

Harré, R. (1984). *Personal being: A theory for individual psychology.* Cambridge, MA: Harvard University Press.

Hebb, D. O. (1974). What psychology is all about. *American Psychologist, 29,* 71-79.

Kuhn, T. S. (1970). *The structure of scientific revolutions* (2nd ed.). Chicago: University of Chicago Press.

McGuire, W. (1974). *The Freud/Jung letters.* Bollingen Series XCIV. Princeton, NJ: Princeton University Press.

Pervin, L. A. (1985). Personality: Current controversies, issues, and directions. In M. R. Rosenzweig & L. W. Porter (Eds.), *Annual Review of Psychology, 36,* 83-114.

Rychlak, J. F. (Ed.), (1976). *Dialectic: Humanistic rationale for behavior and development.* Basel, Switzerland: S. Karger AG.

Rychlak, J. F. (1977). *The psychology of rigorous humanism.* New York: Wiley-Interscience.

Rychlak, J. F. (1980). The false promise of falsification. *The Journal of*

Mind and Behavior, 1, 183-195.

Rychlak, J. F. (1981a). Logical learning theory: Propositions, corollaries, and research evidence. *Journal of Personality and Social Psychology, 40,* 731-749.

Rychlak, J. F. (1981b). *A philosophy of science for personality theory* (2nd ed.). Malabar, FL: Krieger Publishing Co.

Rychlak, J. F. (1984a). The nature and challenge of teleological psychological theory. In J. R. Royce & L. P. Mos (Eds.), *Annals of Theoretical Psychology, 2,* 115-150.

Rychlak, J. F. (1984b). Newtonianism and the professional responsibility of psychologists: Who speaks for humanity? *Professional Psychology: Research and Practice, 15,* 82-95.

Schank, R. C., & Abelson, R. P. (1977). *Scripts, plans, goals, and understanding.* Hillsdale, NJ: Lawrence Erlbaum Associates.

Tolman, E. C. (1967). *Purposive behavior in animals and men.* New York: Appleton-Century-Crofts.

Current Issues in Theoretical Psychology
Wm J. Baker, M.E. Hyland, H. Van Rappard, A.W. Staats (Editors)
© Elsevier Science Publishers B.V. (North-Holland), 1987

METHODOCENTRICITY, THEORETICAL STERILITY,

AND THE SOCIO-BEHAVIOURAL SCIENCES

Morris L. Shames

Concordia University
Montreal, Quebec, Canada

SUMMARY: Notwithstanding Bacon's clearly articulated mistrust of induction and Hume's postulation of the seemingly insuperable problem
with induction, much of modern science - in particular, the socio-behavioural sciences - have seen fit to anchor themselves fastidiously to a uni-
form methodology despite its logical invalidity and faulty premises. The
null hypothesis testing procedure, for instance, affirms the consequent
and, moreover, does not jibe with the diachronic character of the socio-
behavioural sciences, given its synchronic thrust; yet, despite this lack of
appositeness, it continues to be the dominant epistemology in the methodological armamentary of psychology in general, and social psychology in
particular. This scientistic approach entirely neglects the creative side of
science, that is, the proveniently creative act of discovery whose cognitive
substratum can be better understood in terms of metaphor theory rather
than an obdurately practiced hypothetico-deductive method. It is from
an approach such as this that the theoretical sterility of the socio-behavioural sciences can begin to be remedied and the task of generative theory
can begin in earnest.

Introduction

It is an irony indeed that one of science's most famous epistemolo-
gists - who, if anyone, could be pardoned for excessive zeal in respect of
'scientific method,' as it were - was most cautious in this respect, indicating that:

> the induction which proceeds by simple enumeration is
> puerile, leads to uncertain conclusions, and is exposed to
> danger from one contradictory instance, deciding generally
> from too small a number of facts, and those only the most
> obvious. (Bacon, 1620/1900, p. 353)

He sounded the tocsin against the methodocentrism of the time in favour
of his *interpretatio naturae*, the view which recognized and accepted the
fallibility of human cognitive capacity and which, at core, embodied the

method of falsification in arriving at certain and demonstrable knowledge, a true interpretation of nature.

On psychological grounds alone Bacon (1620/1900) found scientific methodocentrism to be untenable owing to the fact that "anticipations are far more powerful than interpretations" (IV, p. 51) and, in keeping with the idols of the tribe, he proffered the view that:

> the human understanding when it has once adopted an opinion draws all things to support and agree with it. And though there be a greater number and weight of instances to be found on the other side, yet these either it neglects and despises, or else by some distinction sets aside and rejects; in order that by this great and pernicious predetermination the authority of its former conclusions may remain inviolate. (IV, p. 56)

Thus Bacon's formulation of method had as one of its principal aims the overthrow of the then extant seventeenth century methodocentricity which was grounded on the notion of the autonomy and infallibility of the human mind in its formulation of hypotheses and speculations and the accumulation of evidentiary support - where such rare activity *did* occur - only in the service of the scientist's 'anticipations.'

This most portentous view was further adumbrated by Hume (1748/1965) when he expatiated upon the logical problem with induction. In an insightfully reasoned argument, which turned on the conclusion that inductive inference patently lacks the 'necessity' characteristic of deductive inference, he averred that:

> in all reasonings from experience, there is a step taken by the mind which is not supported by any argument or process of the understanding; there is no danger that these reasonings, on which almost all knowledge depends, will ever be affected by such a discovery. If the mind be not engaged by argument to make this step, it must be induced by some other principle of equal weight and authority; and that principle will preserve its influence as long as human nature remains the same. (p. 40)

The attainment to effect from cause, he suggested, was not by dint of demonstratively grounded reasoning since, as he phrased it, "the particular powers, by which all natural operations are performed, never appear to the senses" (pp. 40-41). Instead, the principle he fixes on is 'custom' or 'habit' and all inferences from experience, that is, inductive inferences are thus effects of custom, not of logically defensible reasoning. To Hume, as to Bacon, the limitations of scientific method were clear.

In point of fact, these limitations were sufficiently clear as to spur Mill (1843/1919) to a remediation of the problem, to ground inductive logic on the same kind of demonstrative necessity characteristic of deductive inference. His effort, culminating in his major canons, was not as successful as Aristotle's treatment of deductive inference owing to the implicit principle of the uniformity of nature and the infinite regress through which one is led in justifying induction itself by means of such an inductively derived principle. The problem appeared sufficiently knotty as to defy solution of any kind.

The modern era, too, has produced its share of impugnment in respect of the traditionally conceived scientific method. Among the leading critics, Popper (1965) has pointed out that:

> an attempt to justify the practice of induction by an appeal to experience must lead to an *infinite regress*. As a result we can say that theories can never be inferred by observation statements, or rationally justified by them. (p. 42)

To no one's amazement now, he adds that "the belief that science proceeds from observation to theory is still so widely and so firmly held that my denial of it is often met with incredulity" (p. 46). From this he concludes that induction is indeed mythical in that it is not a psychological fact, it is not a fact of ordinary life, nor is it one of scientific procedure. Rather, the *modus operandi* of science is to pass and repass between conjectures and refutations in that "only the falsity of the theory can be inferred from empirical evidence, and this inference is a purely deductive one" (p. 55). By this means he is presumed to have settled the long-standing problem of induction - by shearing away its inductive content. Again, this argument speaks to the issue of traditionally conceived scientific method, the hypothetico-deductive method more particularly, and the methodocentricity of much of the scientific community.

Notwithstanding these nontrivial lessons of history and contemporary philosophy of science, psychology has seen fit to anchor itself, for the greatest part of the twentieth century, to a classical methodocentrism which permeates all of its parts. It is to the issues which flow therefrom, the methodocentricity of science in general, and psychology in particular, that this discussion now turns. It considers the flawed methodology to which psychology fastidiously clings, and the appositeness of the hypothetico-deductive method for the socio-behavioural sciences, and the theoretical sterility which is the primary consequent of this approach. It then considers the role of metaphor theory in underwriting the creative side of science, the proveniently creative, cognitive act of discovery.

The Methodocentrism of Psychology

Methodocentrism is the rule in science, as Kuhn's (1962/1970) epistemological relativism has made clear by pointing out that science is essentially "a paradigm-governed social activity whose essence is to periodically undergo *revolutionary* transformations in its own *normative self-definition*" (Doppelt, 1983, p. 109). However, psychology appears to be the most fastidiously committed, among the scientific disciplines (Doyle, 1965), to a socially dominated disciplinary matrix which is almost exclusively centred on method. Perhaps no one has put it as eloquently as has Bakan (1967/1974) in dubbing psychology "methodolatrous" where there is a seeming inexorable tendency toward the worship of the methods of science themselves rather than the object toward which these methods are directed. This, most conspicuously in the case of psychology, has yielded "a scientism which stands in the way of psychology becoming scientific" (p. XV).

Among the most trenchant abjurements is Sigmund Koch's (1981) repudiation of methodocentricity in psychology based on his perspicuous insight that:

> a syndrome of 'ameaningful thinking' is seen to underlie much of modern scholarship, especially the inquiring practices of the psychological sciences. Ameaningful thought regards knowledge as an almost automatic result of a self-corrective rule structure, a fail-proof heuristic, a methodology - rather than of discovery. In consequence, much of psychological history can be seen as a form of scientific role playing which, however sophisticated, entails the trivialization, and even evasion, of significant problems. (p. 257)

Koch, in short, is making the case for epistemopathy in the service of scientism. This methodocentrism, he argues, fails to recognize that:

psychologists must finally accept the circumstance that extensive and important sectors of psychological study require modes of inquiry rather more like those of the humanities than the sciences. ....a moral analysis of the past, by inviting a change of heart, is a surer bridge to a tolerable future than any confident methodological manifesto. (p. 269)

To his disappointment and considerable chagrin, Koch concludes with the following sentiment:

It is incredible to contemplate that during a century dominated by the tidy imagery of prediction and control of human and social events, the perverse cognitive pathology housed in such imagery has not been rooted out. In fact, such notions have rarely been seen as problematic and still more rarely subjected even to perfunctory modes of analysis. (p. 266)

One might be inclined to share Koch's amazement over this state of affairs but not all of his conclusions. In fact, over the past quarter century there has been a sustained body of criticism apropos of methodocentrism and the flawed methodology to which psychology tenaciously clings but this corpus of critical literature has not yet served to revolutionize psychology in any significant Kuhnian sense. For instance, Sanford, in 1965, wrote that:

psychology is really in the doldrums right now. It is fragmented, overspecialized, method centered and dull. I can rarely find anything in the journals that I am tempted to read. And when I do read psychological papers, as I must as an editorial consultant, I become very unhappy; I am annoyed by the fact that they have all been forced into the same mold, in research design and style of reporting, and I am apalled by the degree to which an inflation of jargon and professional baggage has been substituted for psychological insight and sensitivity. (p. 192)

Writing on the same topic seventeen years later, Sanford (1982) found no melioration of affairs in that psychology still appeared characterized by "too-far advanced overspecialization and fragmentation" (p. 896).

This litany of condemnation has not abated in recent times although psychology has remained almost obdurate in its heedlessness to which a diachronic assay of its journals, curricula and policy statements attest. For instance, Wachtel (1980), in no less august a journal than the *American Psychologist,* has continued the clarion call condemning:

> ....the emphasis on productivity and its encouragement of quickly doing, at the expense of reflecting on what one does and determining the resources to do the job well; ...and the often exclusive reliance on experiments as the sole means of experimental inquiry - all interact to produce a pattern of research activity that has limited progress in our field. (p. 408)

Moreover, this insalubrious state of affairs becomes especially exacerbated in the case of social psychology where its social nature is most often abandoned owing to its individuocentric bias which stems from "methodological doctrines associated with the concept of psychology as a natural empirical science" (Pepitone, 1981, p. 972).

The Flawed Methodology of Psychology

There is a particular irony which grows out of an obdurately method-centred psychology when that methodocentrism is wedded to an almost fully flawed methodology. This is not an idle charge brought against psychology but an elegantly reasoned argument, of twenty-five years standing, that the very linchpin of empirical, experimental psychology - the null hypothesis testing procedure - is a logically flawed experimental procedure with no theoretical payoff whatever (Bakan, 1966, 1967/1974; Bolles, 1962; Lykken, 1968; Meehl, 1967, 1978; Rozeboom, 1960). Bakan (1966), for instance, has argued that:

> the test of significance does not provide the information concerning psychological phenomena characteristically attributed to it; and a great deal of mischief has been associated with its use. ...The null hypothesis is characteristically false under any circumstances. Publication practices foster the reporting of small effects in populations. Psychologists have 'adjusted' by misinterpretation, taking the *p* value as a 'measure', assuming the test of significance provides automaticity of inference, and confusing the aggregate with the general. (p. 423)

This argument is predicated upon the asseveration that the null hypothesis is never strictly true, "such predictions having about a 50-50 chance of being confirmed by experiment when the theory in question is false, since the statistical significance of the result is a function of sample size" (Lykken, 1968, p. 150). Moreover, it is properly contended that statistical significance is almost inconsequential in the grand design of experimental verification and the effect of any single experimental verification is not to confirm a scientific hypothesis but only to make its *a posteriori* probability a little higher than its *a priori* probability" (Bolles, 1962, p. 645). To grant more significance to the null hypothesis testing procedure is to conflate statistical and scientific hypotheses and, in this respect, it should be noted that "tests of statistical significance and rules of experimental sophistication must be supplemented with some concept of theoretical significance" (Lachenmeyer, 1969, p. 621). The psychological enterprise, it is argued, falls far short of the mark for its piecemeal nomological experimentation - a tack which is not conducive to the development of theories of human behavior - and for the zeal with which it commits the fallacy of the *modus ponens,* the fallacy which, despite avowals to the contrary, is the lifeblood of science itself (Kaplan, 1964; Lachenmeyer, 1969).

Perhaps no one has delineated the procedural and logical invalidity of the hypothetico-deductive method, as it is employed in psychology in general, and its 'soft' areas in particular, than Paul Meehl (1967). Firstly, he has adumbrated a methodological paradox which should have proved fatal to psychological experimental practice. He has, for instance, pointed out that:

> in the physical sciences, the usual result of an improvement in experimental design, instrumentation, or numerical mass of data, is to increase the difficulty of the 'observational hurdle' which the physical theory of interest must successfully surmount; whereas, in psychology and some of the allied behavior sciences, the usual effect of such improvement in experimental precision is to provide an easier hurdle for the theory to surmount. (p. 103)

An improvement in the power of a statistical design, in consequence of this reasoning, yields a scientifically unrespectable result in psychology while the reverse obtains in the physical sciences. However, the portrait of logical invalidity which he paints is even more - perhaps fatally - damaging to psychology's methodological cause. He reasons that an:

inadequate appreciation of the extreme weakness of the test to which a substantive theory T is subjected by merely predicting a directional statistical difference $\bar{d} > 0$ is then compounded by a truly remarkable failure to recognize the logical asymmetry between, on the one hand (formally invalid) 'confirmation' of a theory via affirming the consequent in an argument of the form (T $\supset$ H$_1$, H$_1$, infer T), and on the other hand the deductively tight *refutation* of the theory *modus tollens* by a falsified prediction, the logical form being (T $\supset$ H$_1$, ~H$_1$, infer ~T). (p. 112)

This application of the Popperian project is not only seductive, owing to its persuasiveness, it is - most importantly - *logically* compelling. Nonetheless, more than a decade later, Meehl (1978) found himself sounding the same alarm as before:

I believe that the almost universal reliance on merely refuting the null hypothesis as the standard method for corroborating substantive theories in the soft areas is a terrible mistake, is basically unsound, poor scientific strategy, and one of the worst things that ever happened in the history of psychology. (p. 817)

This attestation to the invalidity of methodological practice in much of psychology is a clear, consistent, and resounding impugnment yet the discipline, for the most part, seems not to have noticed.

This methodological indisposition diagnosed in terms of ideological and logical symptomatology, although serious in itself, is further aggravated by procedural infirmity - the corpus of impugnment being as ably documented and as long-standing as the above-cited assault on methodology in the socio-behavioural sciences which has turned essentially on questions of internal validity. The laboratory experiment, for instance, has suffered serious oppugnance at the hands of critics for its lack of external validity (Adair, 1982; Berkowitz & Donnerstein, 1982; Harré & Secord, 1972; Mitchell & McKillip, 1982) resulting from the artifact which stems from experimenter and subject effects both (Adair, 1973; Barber, 1976; Rosenthal, 1976; Rosnow, 1981) although the claim has been made that "the expectancy effect is neither inexorable nor unquestionably general in psychological research" (Shames, 1979, p. 387) and, as such, does "not - as is claimed - sound the tocsin for the limitations on scientific method" (Shames, 1983, p. 106). Add to this taxonomy of contaminants such contextual variables as demand characteristics, viz., the experimental subject's inclination to divine and validate the experimental hypothesis (Orne, 1962, 1973) or, for that matter, the experimental subject's disinclination to participate cooperatively (Masling, 1966), and the threat to both internal and external validity becomes more than merely worrisome.

The Hypothetico-Deductive Approach and the Socio-Behavioural Sciences

The socio-behavioural sciences, in general, and social psychology, in particular, have, by most self-reflective estimates, become marginalized in both the worlds of science and social theory. This case was first made by Moscovici (1972) when he wrote that:

> despite its technical achievements, social psychology has become an isolated and secondary science... the gap that has been created between our discipline and other social sciences... has led into a situation of ignorant expertise. The questions we ask are most often very restricted; and if it happens that important problems are taken up, we manage to transform them again into minor questions. (p. 63)

and later, by Wexler (1983), when he argued that "social psychology's historical role has been the methodological occlusion of deeper problems in society in the name of science" (p. XV). The resultant has been psychology's chaotic status as a theoretical science (Peele, 1981; Royce, 1982), a condition which Gergen (1973) - continuing in a metamethodological vein - attributes to social psychology's subject matter, owing to the observation that:

> social psychology is primarily an historical inquiry. Unlike the natural sciences, it deals with facts that are largely nonrepeatable and which fluctuate markedly over time. Principles of human interaction cannot readily be developed over time because the facts on which they are based do not generally remain stable. Knowledge cannot accumulate in the usual scientific sense because such knowledge does not generally transcend its historical boundaries. (p. 310)

It is thus argued that the events of social life are *diachronic,* that is to say, authentic only in respect of their cultural and historical imbeddedness, while the controlled experiment is *synchronic* in character slicing, as it were, through the very fibre of social life. To put it baldly, then, there is a clear mismatch between the epistemology and the ontology of social psychology. More particularly, the hypothetico-deductive method is predicated on the principle of control whereas social events are culturally imbedded, sequentially imbedded, openly competitive with other simultaneously occurring stimuli, complexly determined - to state the case simply - and, in addition, they represent a "final common pathway" for a number of interacting psychological states (Gergen, 1978). It is this line of argument which has served as a fillip for the call to a reorientation to a diachronic, genetic social psychology (Rosnow, 1978, 1981).

On a less metamethodological and, perhaps, more fundamental note it has been argued that the socio-behavioural sciences are simply characterologically different from the disciplines of natural science. For instance, Jurgen Habermas' (1971) critical theory - grounded as it is in the moral-political thought running from Kant to Marx and whose aim it is to transmogrify social systems which prove themselves inimical to the masses of people - is first and formemost a general theory of knowledge which "views social theory so broadly as to include virtually the entire range of systematic knowledge about man" (McCarthy, 1978, p. X). It is, furthermore, profoundly committed to opposition to the 'objectivist illusion' and calls for a clearly self-critical epistemology, one which is rarely, if ever, recognized in dogmatic scientific practice. In this matter, it should be noted, the hermeneutic tradition finds itself on common ground with critical theory, eschewing the methodocentricity born out of the objectivist claim and asserting instead that science "does not see nature as an intelligible whole but as a process that has nothing to do with human beings, a process on which scientific research throws a limited but reliable light, thus making it possible to control it" (Gadamer, 1975, p. 2ll). The net effect of such a revitalized epistemology is the promise of generative theory (Gergen, 1978) in lieu of the extant, wizened social theory in psychology.

Habermas (1971) conceives his principal task as the explanation of how the dissolution of epistemology has led to the ascendancy of philosophy of science. As a result, critical consciousness has been lost and his major undertaking, therefore, his radical epistemology, is to revivify these abandoned stages of reflection. His central thesis suggests that "'the specific viewpoints from which we apprehend reality', the 'general cognitive strategies' that guide systematic inquiry, have their 'basis in the natural history of the human species'" (McCarthy, 1978, p. 55). Moreover, they are inextricably rooted in the "imperatives of the socio-cultural form of life" (p. 55) and, thus, inquiry takes the form of: (1) the empirical-analytic sciences, (2) the historical-hermeneutical sciences, and

(3) the critically-oriented sciences.

The socio-behavioural sciences have staked out the high 'empirical-analytical' ground for themselves which is generally under-pinned by "an 'anthropologically deep-seated interest' in predicting and controlling events in the natural environment" (McCarthy, 1978, p. 55), and is linked to the 'technical interest.' However, the subject of the so-cio-behavioural sciences, in general, and social psychology, in particular, jibes more with the "historical-hermeneutic" sciences and the "critically-oriented" sciences (Shames, 1984a, 1985a), the former underpinned by the "anthropologically deep-seated interest in securing and expanding possi-blities of mutual and self-understanding in the conduct of life" (McCarthy, 1978, p. 56) and guided by the 'practical interest,' while the latter is moved by the aim of "emancipation from pseudonatural con-straints whose power resides in their non-transparency" (McCarthy, 1978, p. 56) and is guided by "emancipatory cognitive interests." Moreover, this is not a loosely conceived thematization since Habermas (1973) adds that:

> these cognitive interests are of significance neither for the psychology nor for the sociology of knowledge, nor for the critique of ideology in any narrower sense; for they are in-variant... [They are not] influences on cognition that have to be eliminated for the sake of the objectivity of know-ledge; rather they themselves determine the aspect under which reality can be objectified and thus made accessible to experience in the first place. (pp. 8-9)

In a more recent emendatory shift from consciousness to language, Ha-bermas (1973) has formulated a theory of social evolution and communi-cative competence, a universal pragmatics, as he calls it, but his aim, nonetheless, still remains emancipatory, that is, he wishes to free modern, scientized epistemology from its rigid methodocentrism and to radicalize the enterprise by opening up the possibility of critical choice based upon reflection.

Scientific Method and Metaphor Theory

Although the volume, by practice, of "yeoman science" (Shames, 1985a, 1985b), that is to say, methodocentric science, has outstripped its more creative counterpart, the science of discovery has played a dispro-portionately important role in the historical record of science. It is ar-gued that the science of discovery is grounded less in method and more in

insight and intuition guided by, among other factors, analogy and metaphor. This speaks to the issue of the proveniently cognitive, creative moment, one of whose fundaments is analogy, which has long been recognized as "one of the first steps in all knowledge and accompanies its progress throughout" (Wolf, 1930/1962, p. 129). In fact the physicist,
N. R. Campbell (1920) was so wedded to this idea that he proffered the
following suggestions:

> Analogies are not "aids" to the establishment of theories;
> they are an utterly essential part of theories, without which
> theories would be completely valueless and unworthy of the
> name. It is often suggested that the analogy leads to the
> formulation of the theory, but once the theory is formu-
> lated the analogy has served its purpose and may be re-
> moved or forgotten. Such a suggestion is absolutely false
> and perniciously misleading. (p. 129)

As important as analogy is (Weitzenfeld, 1984), the creative imagination in science turns on more than mere tropes and similes and, for
that matter, the *formal* and *material* analogies employed explicitly in scientific models (Hesse, 1963). The cognitive process that bespeaks the
eureka moment in scientific discovery is very frequently an intuitionistic,
nonlogically scripted psychological process (Bunge, 1962; Medawar, 1969)
mediated, more likely, by metaphor than analogy. The role of metaphor
was made clear at a symposium, devoted in its entirety to the subject,
where it was argued by Cassirer, among others, that:

> if this is indeed the case - if metaphor taken in this general
> sense, is not just a certain development of speech, but
> must be regarded as one of its essential conditions - then
> any effort to understand its function leads us back, once
> more, to the fundamental form of *conceiving*. [Moreover,
> metaphor] has achieved an unprecedented importance in
> modern thought, moving from a place on the ornamental
> fringes of discourse to a central position in the under-
> standing of human understanding itself. (Sacks, 1979,
> Foreword)

The logician, Quine (1979), has argued for the epistemological universali-
ty of metaphor, suggesting, for instance, that "it flourishes in playful
prose and high poetic art, but it is vital also at the growing edges of
science and philosophy" (p. 159). He was not intimating that metaphor,
in science, is mere sweetmeat - as many have been wont to believe is the

case - as in literature. Rather, he made the case that:

> along the philosophical fringes of science we may find rea-
> sons to question basic conceptual structures and to grope
> for ways to refashion them. Old idioms are bound to fail
> us here, and only metaphor can begin to limn the new or-
> der. (p. 159)

That science is profoundly rooted in metaphor, that its importance is broad and generic, appear to be arguments beyond exception. It has been suggested, for instance, that the metaphorical language of both science and theology are strikingly similar (MacCormac, 1976). This does, however, tend to wreak a fair bit of violence apropos of the conventionally cherished beliefs governing science in that "scientists must use metaphors to postulate new hypotheses and... this necessity does lead in the direction of conceptual relativism where objectivity becomes difficult to discern and defend" (MacCormac, 1983, p. 61).

It seems, therefore, that metaphor lies at the very heart of language itself governing, in some measure, both its acquisition and growth and, since conceptualization is largely language-mediated, it lies at the very core of cognition. In respect of this very issue Ricoeur (1979) has noted that:

> there is a *structural analogy* between the cognitive, the
> imaginative, and the emotional components of the com-
> plete metaphorical act and that the metaphorical process
> draws its concreteness and its completeness from this
> structural analogy and this complementary functioning.
> (p. 157)

Thus an assay of metaphor and the metaphorical process itself is in order, especially in light of the supporting postulation of "an epistemic drive present in man [which] provides the basis for the development of symbolizing activity" (Royce, Coward, Egan, Kessel, & Mos, 1978, p. 340).

Apropos of the former, there is perhaps no theory of metaphor better delineated than Frye's (1957) 'systematics.' This theory, it should be noted, *obliquely* implies the *creative*, cognitive act, a provenient process common, in the most fundatory way, to all intellectual endeavour and, especially, to science which depends at least as much upon creativity as methodology. From a metatheoretical perspective, finally, the construction of this theory was patently a scientific undertaking although the product does not itself address the issues of science in any conventional sense.

Frye's theory of symbols - his theory of metaphor - is the centre-piece of this paper owing to the view taken that metaphor is the medium for the creative process whose compass embraces not only literature and religion - the breeding-ground of exegesis - but science as well. This model, furthermore, turns on an exhaustive trans-historical assay of Western literature and, as such, is not apodeictically grounded but, rather, is heuristically proffered based on a confluence of *analytical psychology,* that is to say, an understanding of the collectivce unconscious (Jung 1959/1969), and literary theory, the integration of which impinge meaningfully on understanding the creative imagination.

This schema treats of symbolism in terms of a hierarchy of phases in the classic sense of that term and based on the commonplace but none-theless compelling observation that nature - the advertation here is to the 'higher' products of nature - loves hierarchies (Simon, 1973). From the perspective of symbols as isolated units, Frye constructs a schema with fundamental *literal* and *descriptive* phases of symbolism where the symbol is understood as inextricably both *sign* and *motif.* On a higher level of organization, the *formal* phase of symbolism, the symbol is apprehended in terms of the *imagery* it evokes. Ascending this hierarchy even further there is the *mythical* phase of symbolism where the symbol is *archetypal,* "usually an image, which recurs often enough in literature to be recogniz-able as an element of one's literary experience as a whole" (Frye, 1957, p. 365). At the very apogeal point, the *anagogic* phase of symbolism, the symbol assumes a virtually apocalyptic, *monadic* nature where the symbol is at the very heart of one's total literary experience yielding - given the entire taxonomy of this symbology - the *dianoia,* or meaning of literature which Frye's *logos* of literature intended.

Thus far, the analysis has turned only on symbols as isolated units. The creative imagination, however, is more clearly bespoken by the rela-tionships between and among symbols, the unit of relationship being the metaphor. Thus, Frye's theory of metaphor flows directly from his theory of symbols. This theory is grounded on the *literal* level of mean-ing where metaphor assumes no form other than straightforward *juxtapo-sition.* The exegetical possibilities are widened somewhat on the *descrip-tive* level where there is "the double perspective of the verbal structure and the phenomena to which it is related" (Frye, 1957, p. 123), that is to say, where there is the postulation of *likeness* or *similarity.* Still drawing on the wealth of Western literature, Frye (1957) formulates a yet higher level, the *formal* level of metaphor, "where symbols are images or natural phenomena conceived as matter or content" (p. 124) and where metaphor is thus conceived as an *analogy* of natural proportion which, according to the author, requires four terms of which two share a common factor. There is, therefore, a *syllogistic* dimension underpinning this level of metaphor. The level of organization becomes considerably more complex when dealing with the concrete universal or *archetypal* metaphor. Here the symbol is *associative*, that is to say, archetypal in that metaphor, in this instance, "unites two individual images, each of which is a specific representative of a class or genus" (Frye, 1957, p. 124). The *anagogic* dimension of meaning enjoys apical status in this hierarchy involving, as it indeed does, the radical form of metaphor. It is at this point that he posits hypothetical *identity* where "identity is the opposite of similarity or likeness, and total identity is not uniformity, still less monotony, but a unity of various things" (Frye, 1957, p. 125).

It is at the apical point of Frye's hierarchy of metaphorical meaning that analytical psychology becomes especially germane to the analysis in that it widens the reach of Frye's work beyond the compass of simple literary theory. Once this interface is effected, it is at once appreciated that anagogic metaphor is not a mere literary device but, rather, it implies a profound psychological process invoking, as it does, the collective unconscious, that ancestral repository of *inherited* symbolism. The symbol in Jung's psychiatric superstructure is, in fact, the focal point of his entire research project (de Laszlo, 1958). It is a living symbol that expresses an *essential unconscious* factor. As Jung put it himself:

> Inasmuch as every scientific theory contains a hypothesis, and therefore an anticipatory designation of a fact still essentially unknown, it is a symbol. Furthermore, every psychological phenomenon is a symbol when we are willing to assume that it purports or signifies something different and still greater, something therefore which is withheld from present knowledge. (de Laszlo, 1959, p. 275)

The archetypes are such symbols of the unconscious and these "are not disseminated only by tradition, language and migration, but these can rearise spontaneously, at any time, at any place, and without any outside influence" (Jung, 1959/1969, p. 13). They are, in short, the anagogic material out of which *dianoia* is forged.

It thus seems that metaphor, especially *anagogic* metaphor bespeaks a significant, cognitive process especially germane for scientific epistemology (Shames, 1984b). Moreover, the creativity reflected by such a trope, it is suggested, has a profound psychological underpinning with analytical psychology at its base. There is ample 'empirical' evidence for this heuristic project, the most prototypical being Kekule's 'reasoned' discovery that the molecular structure of benzene was a closed carbon ring. This by now banal example is nonetheless extremely instructive in virtue of the fact that it was by dint of *anagogia*-mediated creativity, not by strict adherence to the tenets of methodology, that this discovery issued. More particularly, it was a dream of the the archetypal symbol of the snake with its own tail in its mouth that is held responsible for this great discovery in chemistry.

Methodocentricity, in fact, has rarely proved as invaluable as intuition and the creative imagination, given an accurate reading of the historical record in science. Thus, it has been persuasively argued that Darwin's work was largely predicated upon a number of key metaphors, chief among these being the branching tree of nature, artificial selection, war, wedges, the tangled bank and contrivances (Gruber, 1981). Notwithstanding the root nature of some of these metaphors (MacCormac, 1976) there is perhaps nothing quite as telling in respect of the general thesis herein delineated as Darwin's intuition vis-a-vis the *principle of divergence* and the apparent abandonment, in this particular instance, of his usual methodological punctilio. Testament to the latter point can be found in Darwin's recognition - anachronistically speaking - of experimenter effects, affirming that:

> I had, also, during many years, followed a golden rule, namely, that whenever a published fact, a new observation or thought came across me, which was opposed to my general results, to make a memorandum of it without fail and at once; for I had found by experience that such facts and thoughts were far more apt to escape from memory than favourable ones. (Darwin, 1929, p. 60)

However, despite this recognition of methodological contamination and his self-conscious attunement to his own methodological practices, especially in respect of his work on the variation of animals and plants under domestication and nature where he clearly pleaded his inductive case, affirming that he "worked on true Baconian principles and without any theory collected facts on a wholesale scale" (Darwin, 1929, p. 56), he was seemingly occaecated nonetheless by his *deductively*-engineered bias when it came to his consideration of the *principle of divergence* (Browne, 1980; Parshall, 1982; Shames, 1985b). This principle, after all, weighed heavily on Darwin and, furthermore, the superstructure of evolution through natural selection would founder seriously without it. Thus, in view of Darwin's intuition of this principle in light of his theory, his 'botanical arithmetic' (Browne, 1980) apparently overrode meticulous scientific methodology in favour of theoretical necessity and cogency both (Shames, 1985b).

That is, perhaps, the way it should be with scientific genius where creativity, grounded as it frequently is on expectation and intuition - as in most epistemological undertakings - holds sway over formalistic methodocentrism. After all, in the extreme, the latter yields a poor payoff in that there appears to exist an inverse relationship between method-centredness and the degree of theoretical sterility characterizing any discipline. Much of socio-behavioural science, for a large part of the twentieth century, has defined itself almost solely in terms of method - and a unidimensional conception of method, at that - yielding a *scientism* which effectively denies the possibility of *discovery* and *generative* theory (Gergen, 1978). The other sciences - as the evidence adduced in this paper clearly shows - have chosen another way in virtue of which they have thrived while socio-behavioural science has wizened.

References

Adair, J. G. (1973). *The human subject: The social psychology of the psychological experiment.* Boston: Little, Brown & Co.

Adair, J. G. (1982). Meaning of the situation to subjects. *American Psychologist, 37(12),* 1406-1408.

Bacon, R. (1900). *Advancement of learning and Novum Organum.* New York: P. F. Collier & Son (Originally published, 1620).

Bakan, D. (1966). The test of significance in psychological research. *Psychological Bulletin, 66,* 423-427.

Bakan, D. (1974). *On method: Toward a reconstruction of psychological investigation.* San Francisco: Jossey-Bass Publishers (Originally published, 1967).

Barber, T. X. (1976). *Pitfalls in human research: Ten pivotal points.* New York: Pergamon Press.

Berkowitz, L., & Donnerstein, E. (1982). External validity is more than skin deep: Some answers to criticisms of laboratory experiments. *American Psychologist, 37(3),* 245-257.

Bolles, R. C. (1962) The difference between statistical hypotheses and scientific hypotheses. *Psychological Reports, 11,* 639-645.

Browne, J. (1980). Darwin's botanical arithmetic and the "principle of divergence," 1854-1858. *Journal of the History of Biology, 13(11),* 53-89.

Bunge, M. (1962). *Intuition and science.* Englewood Cliffs, New Jersey: Prentice-Hall.

Campbell, N. R. (1920). *Physics, the elements.* Cambridge: Cambridge University Press.

Darwin, Sir Frances (1929). *Autobiography of Charles Darwin.* London: Watson & Co. (The Thinkers Library).

de Lazlo, V. S. (1958). (Ed.). *Psyche and symbol: A selection from the writings of C. G. Jung.* Garden City, N.J.: Doubleday & Company.

de Lazlo, V. S. (1959). *The basic writings of C. G. Jung.* New York: Modern Library.

Doppelt, G. (1983). Relativism and recent pragmatic conceptions of scientific rationality. In N. Rescher (Ed.), *Scientific explanation and understanding.* Lanham, Maryland: University Press of America.

Doyle, C. L. (1965). *Psychology, science, and the western democratic tradition.* Unpublished doctoral dissertation, University of Michigan.

Frye, N. (1957). *Anatomy of criticism.* Princeton, N.J.: Princeton University Press.

Gadamer, H-G. (1975). *Truth and method.* New York: Continuum Publishing.

Gergen, K. J. (1973). Social psychology as history. *Journal of Personality and Social Psychology, 26,* 309-320.

Gergen, K. J. (1978). Toward generative theory. *Journal of Personality and Social Psychology, 36(11),* 1344-1360.

Gruber, H. E. (1981). *Darwin on man: A psychological study of scientific creativity.* Chicago, Ill.: University of Chicago Press.

Habermas, J. (1971). *Knowledge and human interests.* Boston: Beacon Press.

Habermas, J. (1973). *Theory and practice.* Boston: Beacon Press.

Harré, R., & Secord, P. F. (1972). *The explanation of social behavior.* Totowa, N.J.: Rowman & Littlefield.

Hesse, M. B. (1963). *Models and analogies in science.* London: Sheed and Ward.

Hume, D. (1965). *An enquiry concerning human understanding.* Chicago: Gateway Editions (Originally published, 1748).

Jung, C. G. (1969). *Four archetypes: Mother/rebirth/spirit/trickster.* Princeton, N.J.: Princeton University Press (Originally published, 1959).

Kaplan, A. (1964). *Conduct of inquiry.* San Francisco: Chandler.

Koch, S. (1981). The nature and limits of psychological knowledge: Lessons of a century qua "science." *American Psychologist, 36,* 257-269.

Kuhn, T. S. (1970). *The structure of scientific revolutions.* Chicago: University of Chicago Press (Originally published, 1962).

Lachenmeyer, C. W. (1969). Experimentation: A misunderstood methodology in psychological and socio-psychological research. *American Psychologist, 24(12),* 617-624.

Lykken, D. T. (1968). Statistical significance in psychological research. *Psychological Bulletin, 70,* 151-159.

MacCormac, E. R. (1976). *Metaphor and myth in science and religion.* Durham, N.C.: Duke University Press.

MacCormac, E. R. (1983). Scientific metaphors as necessary conceptual limitations of science. In N. Rescher (Ed.), *The limits of lawfulness.* Lanham, Maryland: University Press of America.

Masling, J. (1966). Role-related behavior of the subject and the psychologist and its effects upon psychological data. In D. Levin (Ed.), *Nebraska Symposium on Motivation* (pp. 67-103). Lincoln, Nebraska.: University of Nebraska Press.

McCarthy, T. (1978). *The critical theory of Jurgen Habermas.* Cambridge, Mass.: MIT Press.

Medawar, P. B. (1969). *Induction and intuition in scientific thought.* Philadelphia: American Philosophical Society.

Meehl, P. E. (1967). Theory-testing in psychology and physics: A methodological paradox. *Philosophy of Science,* June, 103-115.

Meehl, P. E. (1978). Theoretical risks and tabular asterisks: Sir Karl, Sir Ronald, and the slow process of soft psychology. *Journal of Consulting and Clinical Psychology, 46(4),* 806-834.

Mill, J. S. (1919). *A system of logic: Ratiocinative and inductive.* London: Longmans, Green and Company (Originally published, 1843).

Mitchell, T. O., & McKillip, J. (1982). The defense that fails. *American Psychologist, 37(12),* 1408-1409.

Moscovici, S. (1972). Society and theory in social psychology. In J. Israel and H. Tajfel (Eds.), *The context of social psychology: A critical assessment.* London: Academic Press.

Orne, M. J. (1962). On the social psychology of the psychological experiment: with particular reference to demand characteristics and their implications. *American Psychologist, 17,* 776-783.

Orne, M. J. (1973). Communication by the total experimental situation. In P. Pliner, L. Krames, & T. Alloway (Eds.), *Communication and affect.* New York: Academic Press.

Parshall, K. H. (1982). Varieties as incipient species: Darwin's numerical analysis. *Journal of the History of Biology, 15(2),* 191-214.

Peele, S. (1981). Reductionism in the psychology of the eighties: Can biochemistry eliminate addiction, mental illness, and pain? *American Psychologist, 36(8),* 807-818.

Pepitone, A. (1981). Lessons from the history of social psychology. *American Psychologist, 36(9),* 972-985.

Popper, K. R. (1965). *Conjectures and refutations: The growth of scientific knowledge.* New York: Harper & Row.

Quine, W. V. (1979). A postscript on metaphor. In S. Sacks (Ed.), *On metaphor.* Chicago, Ill.: University of Chicago Press.

Ricoeur, P. (1979). The metaphorical process as cognition, imagination and feeling. In S. Sacks (Ed.), *On metaphor.* Chicago: Chicago University Press.

Rosenthal, R. (1976). *Experimenter effects in behavioural research: Enlarged edition.* New York: Irvington Publisher, Inc.

Rosnow, R. L. (1978). The prophetic vision of Giambattista Vico: Implications for the state of social psychological theory. *Journal of Personality and Social Psychology, 36(11),* 1322-1331.

Rosnow, R. L. (1981). *Paradigms in transition: The methodology of social inquiry.* New York: Oxford University Press.

Royce, J. R. (1982). Philosophic issues, Division 24, and the future. *American Psychologist, 37(3),* 258-266.

Royce, J. R., Coward, H., Egan, E., Kessel, F., & Mos, L. (1978). Psychological epistemology: A critical review of the empirical literature and the theoretical issues. *Genetic Psychology*

Monographs, 97, 265-353.

Rozeboom, W. W. (1960). The fallacy of the null-hypothesis significance test. *Psychological Bulletin, 57,* 416-428.

Sacks, S. (Ed.) (1979). *On metaphor.* Chicago, Ill.: University of Chicago Press.

Sanford, N. (1965). Will psychologists study human problems. *American Psychologist, 20,* 192-202.

Sanford, N. (1982). Social psychology: Its place in personology. *American Psychologist, 37,* 896-903.

Shames, M. L. (1979). On the metamethodological dimension of the "expectancy paradox". *Philosophy of Science, 46(3),* 382-388.

Shames, M. L. (1983). Experimenter bias and the biased experimental paradigm. In N. Rescher (Ed.), *The limits of lawfulness: Studies on the scope and nature of scientific knowledge* (pp. 101-107). Lanham, Maryland: University Press of America.

Shames, M. L. (1984a, April). *Lagging behind the papacy: Whither psychology's aggiornamento?* Invited speaker at the conference on Metapsychology: Problems and prospects; Calgary, Canada.

Shames, M. L. (1984b, August). *A systems model of analogical thought and transcendence: On the importance of Northrop Frye in scientific thinking.* Paper presented at the Conference on Systems Research, Informatics and Systematics, Baden-Baden.

Shames, M. L. (1985a, February). *On demarcation and the primacy of scientific epistemology.* Invited address given to the McGill chapter of Sigma XI, the Scientific Research Society at Redpath Museum, Montréal.

Shames, M. L. (1985b, June). *Creative bias and the formulation of Darwin's "Principle of Divergence."* Paper delivered at the Summer Conference of the History, Philosophy and Sociology of Biology, Notre Dame, Indiana.

Shames, M. L. (1985c, August). *Literary theory, analytical psychology and the scientific imagination.* Paper delivered at the XVII International Congress of History of Science, University of California, Berkeley.

Simon, H. A. (1973). The organization of complex systems. In H. H. Pattee (Ed.), *Hierarch theory: The challenge of complex systems.* New York: George Braziller, Inc.

Wachtel, P. (1980). Investigation and its discontents: Some constraints on progress in psychological research. *American Psychologist, 35(5),* 399-408.

Weitzenfeld, F. S. (1984). Valid reasoning by analogy. *Philosophy of Science, 51(1),* 137-149.

Wexler, P. (1983). *Critical social psychology.* Boston: Routledge & Kegan Paul.

Wolf, A. (1962). *Textbook of logic.* New York: Collier Books (originally published, 1930).

Current Issues in Theoretical Psychology
Wm J. Baker, M.E. Hyland, H. Van Rappard, A.W. Staats (Editors)
© Elsevier Science Publishers B.V. (North-Holland), 1987

THE RHETORIC OF THEORY IN PSYCHOLOGY

John Shotter

University of Nottingham
Nottingham, England

SUMMARY: If the function of language is *not* to represent reality, but to give form to, or to help coordinate, our diverse social activities, then theories cannot be taken simply as possible representations of reality either. The *formative* nature of theoretical language is such that the very stating of a theory works rhetorically to influence our perceptions selec- tively: to render aspects of our own activities 'rationally invisible' to us, as well as to induce in us 'illusions of discourse,' i.e., to lead us to treat fictions as realities.

Currently, there is a great deal of interest in what might be called a "common sense psychology of everyday life" (e.g., Antaki, 1981; Furn- ham, 1983; Heider, 1958). Implied in such an interest is the restoration of *rhetoric* (as in classical times) to its original place as a discipline more basic than that of logic (Booth, 1974; Burke, 1969; Perelman & Olbrechts-Tyteca, 1969). For originally, rhetoric was concerned with matters about which people were not decided and for which no science presents adequate answers - the usual state of affairs in everyday life.

The point in returning to an interest in rhetoric is put by Kenneth Burke (1969, p. xiv): it is, he says, to do with "the ways in which members of a social group promote social cohesion by acting rhetorically upon one another" - and rather than "persuasion," Burke takes "identifi- cation" (the establishment of a commonality) as the basis of his ap- proach. For the study of rhetoric was not only to do with techniques of argumentation, with persuasive forms of speech; a shared understanding is necessary if argumentation is to proceed. Hence rhetoric is also con- cerned with procedures for establishing *topics*, with the formation of *commonplaces* ($\tau o \pi o s$ = place), with the production within a group of a shared significance for one's shared circumstances. This suggests a whol- ly new starting point for a corporate enterprise than that which takes the doing of a science as a model for all properly founded social activities. Rather than doubt and the detection of error being the major step in the acquisition of knowledge, rhetoricians take it, as Wayne Booth (1974) says, that:

... the primary mental act of man is ...'to take in' and even
'to be taken in,' rather than 'to resist being taken in'... Notions of 'in-spiration' have been found in every historical
period, and regardless of who or what provides the breath,
they have always entailed the mysterious process of two becoming one." (p. xvi)

The Establishment of an identity

Thus, central to the new approach I want to adopt is the repudiation of the attempt always to produce enlightenment by the process of
first formulating a *theory* and of then attempting to prove it true - the
goal in modern life which belongs to what might be called 'the age of
theory' and which Michel Foucault (1972; Sheridan, 1980) has called "the
will to truth." Instead, I want to outline a more *practical* approach, one
which, as I have said, elevates the study of *rhetoric* to a position of primacy over that of *logic* - where by rhetoric, I mean the study of those
aspects of language usage aimed simply at 'giving shape or form' to the
thought and activity of the human world. For central to the study of
rhetoric is 'the art of topics': the study of those processes of communication and interaction between people within which they 'specify' or 'construct' the common *objects* or *topics* of their discourse - what people are
pleased to call the 'realities' they think of themselves as dealing with and
as talking about in their practical everyday activities (and also, of course,
in their scientific investigations).

Elsewhere, I have discussed the power of rhetorical operations positively in the establishment of social realities and identities (Shotter, in
press). My purpose here, however, is to be entirely negative and critical
of psychology as a theory formulating and theory testing discipline. For I
want first to emphasize that we cannot take our ways of talking for
granted as neutral forms of expression which simply reflect in their structure the structure of what, seemingly, we are talking about. The different
structures of our topics of discourse are lent or given to them in a number of different ways by the different ways in which we discourse about
them. Secondly, I want to show that, so great is the power of rhetoric,
that it can produce an illusory 'reality': the feeling that our experiences
are such that they can only be properly described in one certain kind of
way; they 'must' have a nature of a certain kind - how else could they
be?

Thus, in discussing rhetoric, I first want to discuss what might be
called a 'formative' view of language and the 'self-specifying' nature of

everyday practical activities, i.e., embedded within our sayings and doings are *methods or procedures* which work to render the point of our sayings and doings intelligible, both to others and ourselves. I then want to turn to a discussion of how a way of talking can be used to create the impression that certain topics exist and are worthy of investigation, when in fact the reality is that they do not, and we waste our time investigating chimeras, mythic monsters of our own making.

The Self-specifying Nature of Practical Activity

How might the *practical* nature of our practical social activities be best described? How is it that something so apparently immaterial as talk can have such powerful material effects upon those involved in such communicative activities? As many workers have suggested (e.g., Dewey, 1896; Bartlett, 1932; and Mead, 1934; and now many of the Gibsonians, e.g., Bransford, Franks & McCarrell, 1977), our past activity can be thought of working *formatively* to create an 'organized setting' (as Bartlett put it) which can then function as an already partially structured context into which to direct our present activities. That is, rather than acting 'out of' an inner schema, one may act 'into' one's own current situation, taking up some of the opportunities and invitations one perceives it as offering, while avoiding what appear to be its obstacles and barriers. It is in this formative sense that practical activities can be called 'self-specifying.'

Mead (1934, p. 140) provides the following common example:

...being aware of what one is saying to determine what one is going to say thereafter - that is a process with which we are all familiar.

Garfinkel (1967, p. vii) also, suggests that the nature of the flow of our everyday social activity is such that it is reflexively self-specifying; such activities contain within themselves, he says:

methods for making those same activities visibly-rational-and -reportable-for-all-practical-purposes, i.e., "accountable," as organizations of commonplace everyday activities.

What would otherwise be an undifferentiated flow of activity is perceived as a sequence of recognizable events, Garfinkel suggests, because actors act so as *to make* their actions perceivable by others *as* 'accountable.' Perceivers also, confronting the otherwise indeterminate activities of others, act so as to 'make it out' *as* 'sensible' or 'accountable.' We always see at least aspects of people's behaviour as behaviour for which they *themselves* are responsible (Heritage, 1984).

From a formal point of view, the structure, the 'logical' structure of our actions, although sufficiently specifiable in different ways for different purposes, is *always vague* and open to other, equally true descriptions (Goodman, 1972). Thus what we mean, practically, in our actions depends upon us. This conception of knowledge is sometimes called *finitism.* "Its core assertion," says Barnes (1982, p. 30):

> is that proper usage is developed step-by-step, in processes involving successions of on-the-spot judgements. Every instance of use, or of proper use, of a concept must in the last analysis be accounted for separately, by reference to specific, local, contingent determinants.

'Rational invisibility' and Illusions of Discourse

Above, I have not represented our ways of speaking as working to reflect, or to picture, or to depict, or otherwise to 'mirror' states of affairs which are taken as existing in an already fixed and finished form. I have presented them as working *procedurally* to invoke or provoke in us, as listeners or readers, a creative process in which we determine what it is which is 'rationally visible' to us. In other words, what I have called our 'accounting practices,' work to 'lend' to our perception of an otherwise indeterminate flow of activity, a form *which otherwise it would not have.*

But we can now see that the very same processes which work to render certain aspects of the flow of activity around us 'rationally visible,' *will also* work to render other aspects of what occurs 'rationally *in*visible' to us. And, given the *formative* nature of the language, they will also render us in fact the victims of certain kinds of illusion - what might be called, 'illusions of discourse.'

To discuss 'rational invisibility' first: In our everyday lives we are embedded within a social order which, morally, we must continually reproduce in all the mundane activities we perform from our 'place,' 'position,' or status within it. Thus we must account for all our experiences in terms both intelligible and legitimate within it, otherwise we will be sanctioned in some way or ignored or laughed at. And currently, we live in an order which, officially, is both individualistic and scientistic, oriented, as Rorty has pointed out, around the idea of knowledge as accura-

cy of representation. These are the terms in which everything which occurs must be made sense of and justified.

It is because of this, I think, that we have concentrated far too
much attention upon the isolated individual studied from the point of
view of the 3rd-person, uninvolved observer. But ironically, what has
been rendered 'rationally invisible' to us in such practices, are the very
sense-making procedures, going on between 1st and 2nd-persons, made
available to us diffusely in the social orders into which we have been so-
cialized - the very resources which I am now attempting to describe. Such
procedures have their provenance in the history of our culture, in the 'organized settings' constructed in our (and our predecessor's) past activites,
and in terms of which, as Garfinkel and the ethnomethodologists have
shown, we perceive the flow of activity around us as 'visibly rational.'

Currently, however, we do not 'see' them as *social* procedures,
operating primarily between people; we talk of them in other terms: as
the operation of cognitive mechanisms 'in' individuals; as structures with
their own dynamic which determine people's observed behaviour - see this
process at work in the Jones and Nisbett example cited below. It is in
these terms also, that language appears, not as a formative activity, but
as a kind of 'logical calculus' within individuals. In this view, communication *is* simply a matter of transferring information from point A to
point B, and the special function of an audience as such - in providing a
set of enabling constraints for a speaker to speak *into* - disappears.

An even more important phenomenon, perhaps, than 'rational invisibility,' and certainly more bewildering, is the imaginary entities our
ways of speaking convince us exist. These are illusions which arise from
projecting back into the phenomena of our concern, our methods of representing it - so that it appears to us as if we *were* simply 'mirroring' in
the structure of our representations the structure of reality. They lead us,
as Goodman (1972, p. 24) says, to "mistake features of discourse for
features of the subject of discourse." We speak of understanding as a
mental process and wonder what goes on in our heads which enables us to
do it, and we set out to attempt to discover its nature. "But," says Wittgenstein (1981, no. 446):

> don't think of understanding as a 'mental process' at all. -
> For *that* is the way of speaking that is confusing you.
> Rather ask yourself: in what kind of case, under what cir-
> cumstances do we say "Now I can go on".... [A] way of
> speaking is what prevents us from seeing the facts without

> prejudice .... *That* is how it can come about that the
> means of representation produces something *imaginary*. So
> let us not think we *must* find a specific mental process, be-
> cause the verb "to understand" is there and because one
> says: Understanding is an activity of the mind.

And this is my point here: that the main influence exerted by our language is a *practical* influence: it provides a way of going on. Unless we
become sensitive to the ways in which our ways of speaking form and
shape the topics of our discourse, we shall often be seeking after *fictions*
of our own devising without recognizing them as such (Baker & Hacker,
1984). Psychologists, in adopting a 'theory-relevant' approach, often attempt to discover how people *would* perceive the world if it was as they
depict it to be. But is it?

The Rhetoric of Theory

To turn now to my main concern in this paper with the rhetoric of
theory, i.e., to an examination of the informal 'wrap-round' accounts
theorists provide in introducing their theories to potential users of them.
By rhetoric here I do not mean the 'hype' indulged in by some theorists
who, as part of an imperialistic attempt to colonize the whole of the psychological endeavour for themselves, make grandiose claims of an unwarranted kind. I mean the serious but informal talk theorists use in introducing the topics of their concern and the problems they wish to investigate, which the theories they formulate can then be seen as solving.

Such informal talk, such wrap-round accounts *are* necessary for,
unlike ordinary talk, theoretical statements are not self-specifying. Their
meaning and application is not immediately intelligible, and a good deal
of further talk is necessary to specify their use (and the particular form
of doubt they should engender in us). It is in such talk that we can find
the procedures by which the 'topics,' which the theories take as their subject matter, are constituted.

The Rhetoric of Reality

As naive realists, we are prone to see the world 'out there' as obviously full of recognizable objects. From a rhetorical point of view, however, exactly the opposite seems to be the case: 1) 'Events' do not speak
for themselves as to their own nature; 2) nor are 'objects' self-descrip-
tive; 3) furthermore, what we understand as 'our experiences' are no
more intrinsically subjective that what we recognizes as 'objects' are in-

trinsically objective. All are rendered recognizable and accountable as such by the use of the appropriate figurative or rhetorical practices or procedures embedded in our modes of everyday communication. What we distinguish as objective and subjective is *projected* by us either into the 'outer reality' of our 'world' or the 'inner reality' of our mind. In either case the result, although perceived as 'reality,' is a construction; it is an "enabling fiction" (Norris, 1983). Perceiving things in terms of such fictions can produce at least the following consequences: 1) The reversal of causation; 2) the invention of wholly fictitious entities; 3) the perception of processes as a sequence of such fictitious products; 4) the unwarranted localization of diffuse influences; and 5) the mislocation of influences - such that what infuses a whole field of (social) activity is seen, incorrectly, as due to the capacities of individuals. I shall examine these consequences in turn.

The Reversal of Causality

Following Culler (1982, pp. 86-88), consider, for instance, talk of 'causality' as being a basic principle of our world. We could not think or live in it as we do without taking it for granted that certain events are caused by other events, that causes produce effects. But, as Nietzsche argues in *The will to power*, this concept is not something *given* in the very nature of the world or in the objects around us; it is the product of a certain topological or rhetorical operation - an enabling fiction. And Nietzsche, so to speak, 'deconstructs' it by showing that our way of talking about causes hides from us the true nature of the mental operations involved in us 'seeing' a cause at work. For often, he claims, we introduce a chronological reversal into our perception of what occurs. Take the following example: Suppose one feels a pain. This *causes* one to look for 'a cause' and spying, perhaps, a pin, one posits a link, and reverses the perceptual or phenomenal order, *pain...pin,* to produce a causal sequence, *pin...pain.*

> In the phenomalism of the 'inner world' we invert the chronology of cause and effect. The basic fact of 'inner experience' is that the cause gets imagined after the effect has occurred.

The causal scheme is produced by a metonymy, or to be precise, a metalepsis, that is, the identification of something by substituting for its name the name of something else to which it is closely related (the substitution of 'cause' by 'effect'); thus causality is not an indubitable foundation for our perceptions in the world. but a *construction,* a product of our ways of making sense of things.

In other words, we cannot in psychology, for the purposes of psychological theorizing, simply take our 'taken for granted' experiences as the basic givens (data); even before we begin to theorize, we must accept the possibility that our experiences are shaped and formed by a *rhetoric* intrinsic in our social practices - in those of our practices to do with the reproduction of our particular version of what we take social reality to be.

'Deconstructing' Freud

To turn now to my first example in psychological theory: Freud's construction of psychoanalysis. In a way similar to Nietzsche's deconstruction of causality, recent commentators have 'deconstructed' psychoanalysis (Steele & Jacobsen, 1978). They point out that Freud, in building his causal science of the psyche, had in mind the same simple causal schema as above - that what comes *before* is a cause of what occurs *later*. Thus infantile development, at least in part, causes adult personality.

This is the developmental path he constructs in his theory, and it is the path he means us to follow in interpreting the meanings of psychoanalytic 'observations' (I use the term ironically, because what is 'observed' is of course determined by the theory, not vice-versa). But this is not the path which Freud himself followed in formulating his explanatory accounts of his observations. His path was from observed adult functioning, via interpretations, to infantile events (and via interpretations again), to our species history - in, for instance, *Totem and taboo,* and other such works. In constructing 'causes' out of his interpretations, Freud is concerned to put us on 'the true path of science.' We end up, however, mystified, for he obscures from us the interpretative processes in terms of which psychoanalysis has its only existence. Psychoanalysis is presented in such a way as to obscure the fact that it really works, not as a causal/explanatory science of 'finding,' but as a rhetorical/interpretative process of 'making.' For, not only does it hide from us the processes which make us see inverted causal processes at work, but *what* we see as being caused is constructed for us by the theory also: we 'see,' Freud claims, for instance, 'castration anxieties' and 'Oedipus complexes.'

But, just as children, says Freud, actually construct for themselves what he claims are, for them, *real* 'castration anxieties,' "out of the slightest hints," so might psychoanalytic patients also "out of the slightest hints" from analysts, construct their upsets as being an expression of, say, an 'unresolved oedipus conflict,' or whatever. Thus, just as one may question the 'psychological reality' of 'castration anxieties,' so by the same token, one can also question the reality of the 'Oedipus complex.' Do people *really* want to possess the parent of the opposite sex and eliminate that of the same sex? Or is the 'Oedipus complex' itself a rhetorical construction, a synecdoche - in which merely a particular exemplar of a state of affairs represents the whole, i.e., the mastery and possession present in the 'possessive individualism' of the whole of western culture? Perhaps what Freud really hides from us in suggesting the centrality of sex, is the *will to power* intrinsic in much of our current social activity (Gellner, 1985).

Here, then, far from Freud's theory providing the answer to an independent problem worthy of investigation, the 'problem' is parasitic on the 'solution;' hence, if the theory were to be put aside, the 'problem' would disappear (Baker & Hacker, 1984, p. 372). At least, it would disappear in the form in which it is presented - as, say, having to do with one's *past* relations to one's parents - and reappear in a new form, a form perhaps more amenable to solution - as perhaps an aspect of one's *present* political relations to others.

Remembering Bartlett's "Remembering"

Freud's construction of psychoanalysis as a causal science was influenced by what he thought *must* be the nature of reality: it must be made up of certain 'objects' affecting one another causally - what else could it be? And he invented all kinds of objects to furnish such a world. Somewhat similar influences are at work, for instance, in the study of remembering: we seek the 'things' necessary to make memory possible; it *must,* we feel, involve objective things in a causal relation to one another which 'store' or 'record' past events in some way. Yet, nearly 100 years ago, Ebbinghaus (1885, p. 5) said:

> To express our ideas concerning [the physical basis of memory processes] we use different mataphors - stored up ideas, engraved images, well-beaten paths. There is only one thing certain about these figures of speech and that is they are not suitable.

Indeed, Bartlett (1932) in, as he says, attempting "to develop a theory of memory," also considered the storehouse notion, but rejected it.

> The schemata are, we are told, living, constantly developing,
> affected by every bit of incoming sensational experience of a
> given kind. The storehouse notion is as far removed from
> this as it well could be. (p. 200)

Bartlett's whole approach to memory was, in fact, *social,* to do with processes going on *between* people:

> Social organization gives a persistent framework into which
> all detailed recall must fit, and it very powerfully influences
> both the manner and matter of recall. (p. 296)

Yet so strong were the requirements of the rhetoric of reality implicit in
the practices to do with us reproducing our version of what we take reality to be, that he continued to talk, not of diffuse social processes, but of
localizable things.

> I strongly dislike the term 'schema' ... it does not indicate
> what is very essential to the whole notion, that the organized
> mass results of past changes of position and posture are
> actively *doing* something all the time ... I think probably the
> term 'organized setting' approximates most closely and clearly
> to the notion required. I shall, however, continue to use the
> term 'schema' when it seems best to do so ... (p. 201)

And that was the term which gained currency, while the much more useful phrase 'organized setting' was ignored.

Indeed, if we look into Claxton's (1980) well reviewed survey of
cognitive psychology we find him saying, notwithstanding Bartlett's and
Ebbinghaus's strictures: "Still the most prevalent metaphor for memory
...is that of storage: we could call it the 'warehouse'... metaphor."
Gleitman (1984) too, in his acclaimed introductory text, also assimilates
Bartlett's work to a view of memory as storage. This is how he estab-
lishes the context for a discussion of Bartlett's experiments on serial reproduction:

> The term *retrieval* imples the recovery of the same material
> that was originally stored. But memorial retrieval is some-
> times different, for we may *reconstruct* the past from partial
> knowledge in the process of trying to remember it. (p. 294)

There *must* be a memory trace of some kind, we say, what else could there be? How else would remembering be possible?

Dewey, Bartlett, and Mead have provided us with alternatives. But - because, I would say, of their 'rational invisibility' within our current individualistic, scientistic social order - we are incapable of recognizing the practical worth of their proposals, concerning the sociohistorical nature of *all* human activities. We simply insist again and again that memory is a present record 'in the head' of our past activities, and that its nature can only be understood by describing the 'inner' processes of *storage* and *retrieval* involved. The nature and importance of sociohistorical processes still remains unrecognized (Shotter, 1983, and in press).

The Invisibility of the 'Social' in Social Psychology

Nowhere is the invisibility of genuine 'social' processes more prevalent than in social psychology itself. To show the nature of its neglect consider, for instance, how Jones and Nisbett (1972) introduce their information processing, or cognitive theory, of the so-called "fundamental attribution error": the "pervasive tendency for actors to attribute their actions to situational requirements, whereas observers tend to attribute the same actions to stable personal dispositions." They begin by considering two possible explanations of this phenomenon. But one - to do with the ordinary everyday activity of people having socially to *justify* their actions to one another - is ruled out for their scientific purposes. How? Well, this is what they say:

> Th[e] tendency often stems in part from the actor's need to justify blameworthy action, but may also reflect a variety of other factors *having nothing to do with the maintenance of self-esteem.* We shall emphasize these other more cognitive factors .... (p. 80, my emphasis)

In other words, in order to dismiss a more straightforward, common sense account, they construct "justification" as being mainly to do with an *individual's* self-esteem. They can say that it is a matter of "individual motivation," which, they say, "could go either way;" thus, as something unsystematic, it is "best pursued empirically" (p. 93). This, ironically, works *to justify* their introduction of their non-social, *cognitive* account; one which now 'justifiably' (I speak ironically) ignores completely the actual social context and the fact that in everyday life, the ability to justify one's conduct is central to one's performance of it. The "fundamental attribution error" has, since its introduction, given rise to a great deal of research, much of it recently, however, aimed at showing that it is not an 'error' at all, that it is in fact a psuedo-problem (see, for instance, Semin, 1980). What a waste of time!

Concluding Comments

As to my own rhetoric: well, I have purposely been using the current 'procedural' rhetoric of artificial intelligence (AI) researchers who claim to be breaking new ground in their forms of theory. For they have, they say: "... not just a formal language but a procedural one." (Boden, 1982, p. 216). That is, they are not so much concerned with a language which 'pictures,' but with one which 'in-structs,' or 'in-forms' a computer in its operations.

Rather than an effective procedure for a computer, however, I am concerned with what might constitute an effective procedure for use by people in the recognition of the nature of their own practical knowing. As it cannot be described theoretically, I have not attempted to present a set of statements which can be proved to be true by reference to evidence; but to communicate a set of 'instructions,' a set of hints, indications, images, ways of talking, etc. And I have attempted to 'warrant' or to justify them as adequate characterizations by reference, not to their established usages, but to the nature of our intuitive grasp of the nature of our social practices. In other words, I have not attempted to warrant them theoretically but practically, in terms of their fittedness to our practices (see Wittgenstein, 1980, Vol. 1, no. 548); to show that no matter what we might theoretically convince ourselves is the case, the fact is that we can no more jump out of our everyday common sense practices of sense making than we can jump out of our skins. Even in our disagreements, if we are to find them intelligible disagreements, we must agree in our practices. Thus ultimately, all any of us can do in our attempts to convince one another of something, is to offer one another good reasons for accepting what we say. For certainties in social affairs ... there are none.

References

Antaki, C. (1981). *The psychology of ordinary explanations of behaviour.* London & New York: Academic Press.

Baker, G. P., & Hacker, P. M. S. (1984). *Language, sense and nonsense.* Oxford: Blackwell.

Barnes, B. (1982). *T. S. Kuhn and social science.* London: Macmillan.

Bartlett, Sir F. C. (1932). *Remembering: a study in experimental psychology.* London: Cambridge University Press.

Boden, M. (1982). Formalism and fancy. *New Universities Quarterly, 36,* 217-224.

Booth, W. C. (1974). *Modern dogma and the rhetoric of assent.* Chicago: University of Chicago Press.

Bransford, J. D. , Franks, J. J., & McCarrell, N. S. (1977). Toward un-explaining memory. In R. Shaw & J. Bransford (Eds.), *Perceiving, acting, and knowing: Toward an ecological psychology.* Hillsdale, NY: Erlbaum.

Burke, K. (1969). *A rhetoric of motives.* Berkeley, CA: University of California Press.

Claxton, G. (1980). *Cognitive psychology: New directions.* London: Routledge & Kegan Paul.

Culler, J. (1982). *On deconstruction: Theory and criticism after structuralism.* Ithaca, NY: Cornell University Press.

Dewey, J. (1896). The concept of the reflex arc in psychology. *Psychological Review, 3,* 13-32. Reprinted in W. Dennis (Ed.), *Readings in the history of psychology.* New York: Appleton-Century-Crofts.

Ebbinghaus, H. (1913). *Memory: a contribution to experimental psychology,* 1885 (trans. by H. A. Roger & C. E. Bussenius) New York: Columbia University Press.

Foucault, M. (1972). *The archaeology of knowledge.* (trans. by A. M. Sheridan) London: Tavistock.

Furnham, A. (1983). Social psychology as common sense. *Bulletin of British Psychological Society, 36,* 105-109.

Garfinkel, H. (1967). *Studies in ethnomethodology.* Englewood Cliffs: Prentice-Hall.

Gellner, E. (1985). *The psychoanalytic movement: or The coming of unreason.* London: Paladin.

Gleitman, H. (1984). *Psychology.* New York: Holt.

Goodman, N. (1972). *Problems and Projects.* New York: Bobbs-Merrill, Chap. 2.

Heider, F. (1958). *The psychology of interpersonal relations.* New York: John Wiley & Sons.

Heritage, J. (1984). *Garfinkel and ethnomethodology.* Oxford: Polity

Press.

Jones, E. E., & Nisbett, R. E. (1972). The actor and observer: divergent perceptions of the causes of behaviour. In E. E. Jones, D. E. Kanouse, H. H. Kelley, R. E. Nisbett, S. Valins, & B. Weiner (Eds.), *Attribution: Perceiving the causes of behaviour.* Morristown: General Learning Press.

Mead, G. H. (1934). *Mind, self and society.* Chicago: University of Chicago Press.

Norris, C. (1983). *The deconstructive turn: essays in the rhetoric of philosophy.* London: Methuen.

Perelman, C. , & Olbrechts-Tyteca, L. (1969). *The new rhetoric: a treatise on argumentation.* Notre Dame: University of Notre Dame Press.

Semin, G. (1980). A gloss on attribution theory. *British Journal of Sociology and Clinical Psychology, 19,* 291-300.

Sheridan, A. (1980). *Michel Foucault: the will to truth.* London: Tavistock.

Shotter, J. (1983). 'Duality of structure' and 'intentionality' in an ecological psychology. *Journal of Theory and Social Behavior, 13,* 19-43.

Shotter, J. (in press). Vico and the social production of social identities. *British Journal of Social Psychology, 25.*

Steele, R. S., & Jacobsen, P. B. (1978). From present to past: the development of Freudian theory. *International Review of Psychological Analysis, 5,* 393-412.

Wittgenstein, L. (1980). *Remarks on the philosophy of psychology.* Vol. 1. Oxford: Blackwell.

Wittgenstein, L. (1981). *Zettel.* (2nd ed.) (G. E. M. Anscombe & G. H. v. Wright, Eds. & Trans.) Oxford: Blackwell.

Current Issues in Theoretical Psychology
Wm J. Baker, M.E. Hyland, H. Van Rappard, A.W. Staats (Editors)
© Elsevier Science Publishers B.V. (North-Holland), 1987

UNIFIED POSITIVISM:

PHILOSOPHY FOR UNINOMIC PSYCHOLOGY

Arthur W. Staats

University of Hawaii
Honolulu, Hawaii, U.S.A.

SUMMARY: Logical positivism has been employed as a fundamental philosophy to guide psychology's work. The position taken is that logical positivism was based on the natural sciences and thus could not contribute to the solution of psychology's special problems, particularly those from being a 'modern disunified science.' Without a philosophical framework to indicate some of its fundamental tasks, psychology has developed a crisis of empirically-centered aimlessness. As a consequence, new subjective philosophies have emerged. Unified positivism, however, recognizes the fundamental empirical nature of science, including psychology, although observations are not considered the ultimate, nonsubjective truth. The new subjective philosophies will not provide the answer. The crisis of psychology is seen to stem from its disunity, the characteristics of which stamp the science with insuperable obstacles to achieving the general meaning, cohesiveness, consensual purposiveness, and so on, of the unified sciences. Unified positivism is a philosophy for the disunified science. A framework is provided showing paths of development for advancing psychology from its present chaos of knowledge to the powerful characteristics of the unified science. The philosophy and methodology create the basis for a new field of study - to be called uninomic (unification) psychology. Various areas of theoretical work are outlined in describing this new field.

A new philosophy of science has been proposed, one that especially aims at dealing with the problems of the "disunified sciences" (Staats, 1983). This philosophy states, among other things, that there is a central dimension of progress in science that can be abstracted from some descriptions of early science, but that has been largely ignored. Moreover, the significance of this dimension of progress in science has not been seen. The dimension refers to progress in the unification of the elements of science, of the findings, the theories, the problems, the methods, the organizations, as well as to progress in developing a philosophy of unification, with its goal of achieving unification.

In the beginning, according to this view, when the science is still disunified, the works of its members are all different. The scientists all select different phenomena to study, they use different methods and apparatus, they have different theories, and their work stems from different world views. As individuals and groups, these differences provide the basis for separations from and contests with each other. Scientists in such a disunified science spend much time in discrediting the approaches, methods, philosophy, and findings of other scientists. This is accepted as a major activity of the science. What is produced by the multiple antagonists is a chaos of knowledge.

In the early history of the natural sciences this chaos was finite. There were few scientists. Their methods for gaining knowledge were not well developed. They had few sources of publication. This simplicity made it possible for some scientists to have a good grasp of a wide range of the existent knowledge such that finding relationships between the different parts constituted puzzles, but not puzzles of insuperable difficulty.

Nevertheless, great effort and ingenuity were required to bring the different elements of knowledge into unified conceptual structures, in making the formerly chaotic knowledge compact, coherent, meaningful and, because of this, important. This development changed the social activity of the science from one of mutual recrimination and incommensurability to that of competition for generally agreed goals, employing consensually accepted methods, within an agreed upon characterization (philosophy) of science (Staats, 1983a). In the history of science there are indications that unification took long years of time and much effort and originality (cf. Shapere, 1977, for some relevant descriptions), although no systematic account has been given of the process.

The Modern Disunified Science

The behavioral sciences, including psychology, exist in the present and they are thus modern sciences. Psychology, for example, has inherited the skills of the general scientific method and has developed sophisticated apparatus, statistics, experimental methods, and so on. It can create scientifically advanced knowledge at a prolific rate. Yet it is still a primitive science with respect to its ability to meaningfully interrelate what it produces. It has achieved very little in the way of a philosophy of unification, or in the way of methods and standards and goals by which to produce unification. And it has created little substantive knowledge that is unified and consensual.

What is paradoxical, in elaborating this concept, is the fact that psychology's characteristics of modernity exacerbate the problems that are created by its primitive state of development on the unity dimension. Several decades ago H. L. Mencken - the specialist in criticism - said "The so-called science of psychology is now in chaos, with no sign that order is soon to be restored. It is hard to find two of its professors who agree" (1927, p. 382). Today the problem of disunity in psychology is far more grave than it was in 1927. Psychology has expanded enormously since then, and each expansion has made its disunity worse. Today there must be more than a hundred thousand psychologists in the United States and Europe. They produce many psychology journals, innumerable articles and books, many research projects producing reports, and so on, each churning out knowledge in a torrent that drowns us with disconnected, inconsistent, mutually discrediting and, hence, meaningless knowledge elements. The sheer volume of knowledge makes the achievement of the parsimony, generality, unity, consensuality, and power of the natural science a task of huge proportions. And this is why the dimension of unification is a fundamental consideration for the philosophy of science. This is why it is necessary to systematically consider the nature of the modern disunified science and what must be done to confront the task of advancing such a science to the stage of unification. For at present psychology is impossible to comprehend. There is such a chaos of contentious, inconsistent, unrelated elements in the field that it is impossible to make sense of it, let alone consider it to be scientific.

Psychology's Crisis

The disunified and unified sciences have been characterized as different in some very essential features (Staats, 1983a). The unified natural sciences, in their arduous work that established unification of formerly separate and disparate knowledge elements, have gained an appreciation of efforts to unify knowledge. Unity is a goal, and natural scientists follow methods that yield unification, even though the goal and the methods are not made explicit. The disunified science does not have this experience, and does not recognize the importance of working toward such unification. In the disunified science, success as a scientist has come from introducing elements of knowledge that are considered to be new, and hence different. The standards of originality thus focus on the novel. And practitioners of the disunified science learn how to make their works as different as possible from the works of others. They have not developed a goal of unification, let alone a methodology of unification.

This feature gives central characteristics to the disunified science. For one thing, there is much less building activity, where each generation of scientists adds new elaborations of knowledge to that which has been developed before. Rather, in searching always for the new, the science has a faddish quality. Various psychologists have recognized this problem of jumping from one research fad to another (Elms, 1975; Evans, 1978; Moscovici, 1972). What results is aimlessness and lack of direction - a failure to build great edifices of integrated knowledge in successive generations of work, in a manner that can be seen to progress with ever greater clarity toward recognized goals - characterics of the unified science.

Discontent with psychology's aimlessness has been voiced by a number of psychologists (Berkowitz, 1970; Elms, 1975; Evans, 1978; Moscovici, 1972; Rappard 1984). There is a general opinion that psychology is in a state of crisis (for example, Elms, 1975), and that calls for further consideration.

Biting the Hand That Has Fed Psychology

When things go wrong in an endeavor there is a general discontent and the basic framework of the endeavor comes into question. Criticism has come from within the philosophy of science, where philosophers such as Toulmin (1972) have called psychology a "would be science," because of its chaotic state of disorganization and disagreement. Moreover, the philosophy of science - logical positivism (and operationism) - that provided the underpinnings for psychology for so long have been pretty well rejected. Thus, for example, the manner in which logical positivism made observations the ultimate truth has been rejected. As Lakatos (1970, p. 98) has indicated, observations are not theory free, that is, purely objective.

In the face of the insoluble problems psychology evidences, and the criticism of the old *received truth* of logical positivism, voices have emerged in psychology that have questioned the foundation of the psychological edifice. Gergen (1973) has said that psychology should not be considered a science in the natural science mold, but should be considered to be a historical science. Earlier, van Hoorn (1972) also said that psychology was not a natural science, but should consider itself an interpretive, relativistic field of hermeneutic inquiry. And Koch (1981) has said that psychology is not a science at all, but rather is just a conglomeration of incommensurable studies.

These voices are important in giving support to the fact that some-thing is wrong with psychology - that a crisis exists that demands atten-tion. But these criticisms, in the present view, are nihilistic or atavistic. Simple criticism of logical positivism does not provide a positive philo-sophical position upon which to base the activities of science. Moreover, retreat to subjectivist doctrines, rejection of experimental science, and so on, is simply that, a return to philosophies that have already shown they cannot provide a productive foundation for our science and profession of psychology.

Unified Positivism

It is the present position that all sciences have their limitations, one of them being the contamination by subjective factors. There are also special limitations that each science has to work within - in physics, some of the central events are so miniscule that problems result; in astronomy, the central events are so distant that observation is difficult and manipu-lative experimentation impossible; in paleontology and archeology, the li-mitations are imposed by the great lapse between occurrence of the events and their study. A science can only maximize its methods of observing and treating the observations that are available. Sciences should be evalu-ated by their cleverness in maximizing their observations in the face of li-mitations, rather than in the absolute goodness of the observations that is achieved.

Logical positivism was in error in glorifying observations and in considering them the ultimate truth, uncontaminated by subjective fac-tors. But this error should not turn us away from observation as a basic aspect of science. What is needed is a new rationale concerning observa-tions, as will be summarized. Unified positivism considers observation to be a central pillar of science in general, and no less in psychology. And experimentation is a refined form of observation, the achievement of which is very valuable to the science. Observation is not, and cannot be, perfect or perfectly objective. *Truth* is an absolute. Thus, to consider observations as truth, as logical positivism did, makes for an absolutistic doctrine. Unified positivism considers observations as useful, which is not absolutistic. Observations are useful when one wishes to construct a theory that is concerned with knowing about and understanding some set of worldly phenomena, and in predicting and controlling those phenome-na. Unified positivism recognizes the importance of observation in science as well as the fact that observation can be improved. Actually, that improvement is one of the dimensions of progress of a science. Uni-fied positivism states that there is interaction of theory and fact; what is

observable fact is affected by what the scientist believes. But observations *may* improve these beliefs in individual scientists and over generations of scientists. Moreover, that improvement in beliefs (or theory)
will in turn provide a basis for better observations to be made, which can
then lead to better theory, and so on. Such a progression can be involved
in examples of continuing knowledge advancement as they occur in
science. It is the present view that this is an essential process (Staats,
1983a, pp. 40-45).

Unified positivism states that in science we have one of those progressive activities of humans. Science begins in a crude way with common
knowledge and then advances in a generational way that involves improvements in theory, method, observations, scientific organization, the
rules of the conduct of science (as in patent and copyright laws), and so
on (Staats, 1983a).

The Need for Plural Philosophies

A major point here is that there are features that are general to all
sciences. But there are also features that are idiosyncratic to particular
sciences only, determined by the special subject matter of the science. It
is important that these two types of characteristics not be confused. It is
for this reason that we can have a philosophy of science for all sciences -
but it can deal only with those general characteristics.

Logical positivism, in some of its positions, e.g., that theory must
be axiomatic (Suppe, 1977, p. 64), confused characteristics that were relevant for physics with those that are relevant for a science like psychology. Psychology's problems of theory construction do no centrally involve the process of constructing axiomatic theories (Staats, 1983a), and
various psychologists were mislead by logical positivism to concentrate on
the construction of axiomatic theory (cf. Hull, 1943).

The modern disunified sciences have problems not seen any longer
in the natural sciences. Philosophies of science that are drawn from the
current state of natural sciences will thus not provide ways of solving
those problems. The modern disunified sciences need a special philosophy
of science that treats their special problems, to indicate paths by which to
solve those problems. Logical positivism did not offer this to psychology,
nor do the newer *Weltanschauung* philosophies. The present philosophy
has been presented at greater length, at least in its beginning form
(Staats, 1983a). This philosophy has emphasized the special character
and problems of the disunified science, hence its name of unified positiv-

ism. Moreover, it has begun the systematic consideration of the methodological developments that are needed to begin working on the special
problems of the disunified science. The rest of this chapter will be devoted to treating some of these methodological topics.

What Psychology Needs for Its Revolution to Unity

It is now recognized in the philosophy of science and the sociology
of science that there are sociological, political, economic, and personal
factors involved in science (Hagstrom, 1965; Merton, 1973; Toulmin,
1972). We can expect in the present case, for example, that simply
pointing out that psychology is disunified will not have an easy or immediate affect upon the conduct of the science. There is a tradition and an
establishment in psychology which assumes that psychology is a full
science and wishes to advance that notion. There are economic benefits
(research support, for example) related to psychology's status as a
science. Clinical psychology also competes with the medical establishment, and profits similarly from the acceptance of their mother discipline
of psychology as a full science. I have already had opportunity to learn
that there are psychologists opposed to the present conception that psychology is a disunified science. For example, opposition to the philosophy of unification has already been set forth by a cognitive psychologist
(Baars, 1984; 1985) in a manner that harmonizes very much with a philo-
sohy of separatism that has been set forth by a Skinnerian behaviorist
(Epstein, 1984). Each says that his particular orientation will provide the
unifying foundation for psychology. And each rejects the other (and all
other approaches) as having anything to offer. That is the traditional
position of the disunified science, that the way to the achievement of a
science of psychology is through the victory of one's own theory. The
fact that this *methodology* simply produces a babel, and is hence a failure,
makes no difference. Such positions represent one example of the challenges that will be made to the philosophy of unity and the lines of work
this philosophy suggests.

What this means is that there is a need for a number of works
whose aim is to illucidate a full philosophy of unification, the history of
unification in science, and the sociology of the modern disunified science
(cf. Staats, 1983a). Needed also are studies that compare psychology to
unified sciences in a contemporary as well as a historical way. If the
disunity-unity of a science is indeed the fundamental characteristic that I
have said it is, then this is a topic that will require extensive study, for
various sciences, including psychology. Thus, one important direction of
development is in resolving the various philosophical, sociological, and

historical issues that unified positivism brings forth.

However, we cannot wait until this battle concerning philsophy is resolved before we engage ourselves in other battles in this revolution to unity. For those who already recognize, in one form or another, that psychology suffers from its lack of coherence and consensuality, the question is not if their science is disunified, but what to do about the problems that are involved. For them a framework is necessary within which they can put forth efforts in the solution of the problems of disunity. I cannot, in this paper, give the full nature of the thinking that has gone into this topic (cf. Fishman, 1986; Gosling, 1986; Minke, in press; Staats, 1983a; 1983b; 1984; 1985; in press a, b, c, d), but there is need of a large program of works, of different types, whose aim will be to make coherent, parsimonious, general, and unified large parts of the knowledge, methodology, and goals of psychology as well as to create new theory while doing so. Several types of work will be described that have the aim of establishing theoretical relationships between presently separated elements of knowledge in psychology. Some of these relationships are relatively apparent, once the goal of establishing those relationships has been set. There is thus a dimension of difficulty involved, since many of our presently disparate knowledge elements can only be seen to be related through the mechanism of constructing new theoretical analyses and principles that show underlying connections. We will see this dimension of difficulty involved in the following descriptions of the several types of work.

Unification of Citation

Most psychologists who have read very widely in their field, and who are concerned with finding general meaning, will have had the frequent experience of seeing materials that are actually very similar presented within conceptual positions that are considered to be quite separate and different. Sometimes this occurs so that one will say that many psychologists continue to rediscover the wheel, that is, continue to introduce things as new that have previously been set forth, usually in a somewhat different but closely related way. This characteristic of duplication in psychology is so widespread that it does not merit comment, and is generally accepted. Even when there are similarities, there will ordinarily be other differences between theories or positions, and the differences will define the total separation so that the similarities disappear. The standards of the science do not demand explicit citations of other related materials across differences in subjects, problems, theory languages and so on. The resulting practices are pretty much foreign to unified sciences.

They arise in psychology because there is so much disparity and disagreement that everyone has a free hand in treating his/her own work. Moreover, that same diversity, much of it produced because no one has to refer to anyone else, makes it difficult to cite all related materials. It has been said that the reward system of our science encourages psychologists to make their work, artificially, to appear to be different and new (Eifert, 1985; MacIntyre, 1985; Maher, 1985). This constitutes a vicious circle. Artificial differences make our field complicated so it is difficult to cite relevant works. As a result the standards of citation become loose. This encourages more artificial diversity, and so on. The extent to which this characteristic contributes to psychology's disunity and impedes its unification must be systematically studied. For one thing we must realize that a methodology is involved, the methodology of relating one's work to the work of others. We presently have methodological standards that allow the introduction of new names for principles, concepts, and findings in the generation of theories, regardless of the fact that there are pre-existing elements that are very similar in other theories (Staats, 1983a). What is necessary is that psychology must consider systematically what its standards are to be. We need studies to consider systematically the various methodological questions involved in eliminating the vast artificial diversity present in psychology, and in preventing the production of more artificial diversity.

As I will indicate, we also need a profusion of published works whose goal is to provide the citations that have been missing in such vast quantities in the literature. The fact is, the first line of work for unification, the one most ready to hand, is simply the organization of psychology's many diverse works by cross-reference. We have to change our science so that publication of this type of work is made possible. A study showing the close relationship in the concepts and principles of two theories, formerly considred to be quite different, would be more important to publish than would some new theory that is being set forth as different from all the rest - a simple addition to the deluge of diversity that already drowns us. This calls for a change in our criteria of value.

Unification by the Research Review

The research review is one of the few mechanisms for establishing unified knowledge in psychology. We might think, thusly, that this would be a highly developed form, since our science needs such mechanisms so desparately. This is not the case, however, as Jackson (1980) has so clearly shown. Almost no consideration has been given in psychology to the methodology of the research review. Without such a methodology there is rather complete license for doing the reviewing in a manner that suits the purposes of the writer. Since few people in the disunified science will be familiar with the area of research covered, there are few restraints on the expression of personal as well as theoretical motivations, as Jackson recognizes. "A person with a thorough knowledge of the research on the topic will be able to infer ... omissions by carefully examining the bibliography, but a person with less thorough knowledge of the topic will not be able to do so." (Jackson, 1980, p. 457). It is thus the present position that we need to study systematically the methodology of the research review, including how the reviewer can unify the knowledge domain involved across differences in fields of study, differences in subjects, in apparatus and methods, and so on. Moreover, review methodology should also consider not just research areas but also theory areas. Sets of theories with common elements should also be compared in reviews for the purpose of establishing what is consensual knowledge (Hishinuma, in press). This will take theoretical insight, in reviews, since the authors of the theories will have typically been motivated to enhance differences and uniqueness. More will be said of this in the next section.

In addition to establishing a systematic methodology for reviews of the literature, we need some active agency that insures that reviews are conducted when they are called for. After a sufficient number of works have been conducted in some area of concern there is a need for reviewing. There are too few research and, especially, theory reviews today, because of the emphasis upon innovation at the expense of integration. We thus need to study the means by which the science reaches out for integrative reviewing, by establishing the goals of articulation of the chaotic knowledge of the science, and enlisting the review process as one of the weapons in the revolution to unity. Reviews are customarily made of accepted subject areas. But psychology needs reviews that bridge works that are not as easily seen to be related. This demands a further step on the dimension of difficulty in seeing underlying relationships through the disguise of superficial differences, as the next section will indicate.

Unified Theory: Bridging Works

It has been said that seeing resemblances between things that appear to be different is the essence of science (cf. Kuhn, 1977, p. 471). Natural science has many examples of success in finding common underlying principles for phenomena that were once thought to be quite different. Students in the natural sciences learn about principles that apply to diverse phenomena and come to expect that the different events they study are actually connected.

Psychology has not yet established such bridges among the phenomena it studies. Psychology does not put forth an investment into establishing such bridges and students are not taught how to do so. Psychology does have a tradition of attempting to achieve some unity through the formulation of grand theories, as yet without success, as will be indicated. But psychology has not considered systematically what characteristics theories must have in order to be of a unifying nature. Nor has psychology considered if there are unifying theory works to be done, other than that of constructing grand theories. The following sections will outline some of the various theory-construction tasks that face psychology in pursuit of unification (in addition to those already mentioned).

Theory Unification. The disunity of psychology has resulted in the production of theories that are considered to be entirely different even though they have much commonality of principles, concepts, and analyses. The learning theories of Thorndike, Watson, Hull, and Skinner, for example, were all based upon the same, or similar, findings. Yet they were all considered to be independent, different, mutually exclusive theories. In fact, "a major part of the theoretical and experimental work performed by the proponents of each theory constituted an attempt ... to do in a rival, or to avoid being done in." (Mackenzie, 1977, p. 19). This era of the development of behaviorism was largely a waste, as a consequence, in the sense of being useful to other scientists (Hilgard, 1948, p. 457).

What should have been done in this era of theory conflict was to have a unified theorist make an analysis showing the commonality that these theories actually had in their philosophies of science, in the findings to which they addressed themselves, in their program of study that depended upon laboratory study of animals, and so on. Such a theoretical analysis - putting all of this knowledge within one language system versus the diverse systems employed by the different theorists - would have provided a body of agreed upon consensual knowledge. It would have been the preponderance of the knowledge in the basic field of behaviorism, since the disagreements between the theories actually constituted a much less proportion. Moreover, the disagreements and differences could have been set forth with explicit clarity that would have better enabled psychologists to realize what was and what was not important to dispute. As an example of a different kind, one recent analysis has shown the commonality that exists between psychoanalytic theory and cognitive dissonance theory (Hishinuma, in press) in underlying principles. Yet, these theories and their substantive works have never been systematically interrelated. A yet different example involves attempts to join psychoanalytic theory and behaviorism (Dollard & Miller, 1950), an effort that has some modern forms (Staats, 1963, pp. 386-394; 1975, Chapter 9; Wachtel, 1977).

Other examples could also be given. But the central point is that it has not been recognized that we need a large-scale, systematic area devoted to this type of theoretical work; that is, the analysis of theories that are presently considered to be different and separate in order to indicate commonalities. I suggest that this is one of the foremost tasks for a unified psychology. Through an area devoted to this type of work psychology will begin to realize its great untapped store of general, consensual knowledge.

An additional product of such theory unifications, which can only be mentioned here, is that novel principles, concepts, and analyses ordinarily result (cf. Staats, 1983a). This is a feature that has characterized classic theory in the natural sciences, and it can be expected from unified theory in psychology (cf. Staats, 1975; in press c; Staats & Heiby, 1985). Such products can normally expect to result in each of the unified theory endeavors to be discussed.

Unification of Schisms. In psychology there exist broad conceptual positions that are in opposition. They are not theories in the sense of organized symbolic bodies identified with a person or a school. They are informal frameworks that constitute part of one's world view. Since the positions are in polar opposition, they inspire works that are also in opposition. Even when there are common elements in the works these go unnoticed because of the opposition in the basic positions that are taken.

One example of such a schism is the nature-nurture issue. This divides psychologists and psychology in a never-ending way. Another schism revolves around the acceptance or rejection of consciousness as a legitimate object of study. As another example, there are those who accept atomistic analysis in the study of behavior while others consider that only holistic acts can be productively studied. There are a number of other equally important schisms (cf. Kimble, 1984; Staats, 1975, Chapter 13; 1983a).

The important thing is that these schisms have served as obstacles to the development of unification in psychology. Yet this source of disagreement and contradiction in each schism - hence weakness and disorganization - is never dealt with from the point of view of creating a position - a tightly reasoned theoretical position - that would resolve the differences and rationalize major works conducted on both sides and project new, unified works as well. At most a truce may be declared from time to time by taking an eclectic position that says both sides are valuable, e.g., that both heredity and environment affect behavior. These ulti- mately fail, however, for what is needed is a theoretical analysis that takes account of the knowledge on both sides of the schisms and relates them in a unified theory effort. There is a large number of theoretical tasks of this type demanding investment. Psychology needs to accept a philosophical framework that sets this type of theoretical effort as an im- portant goal.

Unification of Methods and Apparatuses. In the natural sciences, although there are areas where there are alternative methods of study and there is disagreement with respect to their relative merits, there is, by and large, great agreement on the major methods of the science. In contrast, psychology has separate and non-communicating approaches that are sharply divided by methodological schisms. For example, operant behav- iorists who follow Skinner do not accept various methodologies, such as the personality measurement methodology, the methodology of using groups of subjects and statistical averages, and so on. On the other hand, traditional child developmentalists, humanists, and others ignore the findings concerning learning theory in good part because they do not accept the fundamental methodology involved, that of gaining under- standing of human development through principles found in the study of animal learning. As a similar example, I remember one of my past col- leagues, a psychoanalyst, who used to scoff at and reject the value of the work of Pavlov and his "slobbering dogs." As a final example, one of the primary rifts of psychology - the division between applied and basic psychologists - is in good part methodological in nature. Many basic psy- chologists consider the methods of study of behavior in therapy and other naturalistic situations to be non-scientific and unacceptable. The applied psychologist in turn rejects the analytic approach of basic psychology that, in using laboratory analysis, reduces important things to trivia.

It is the present position that before each of these types of psychol- ogist can begin using knowledge obtained by methods other than their own, they must have a theoretical framework that shows them the legiti- macy and importance of the other knowledge and the methods by which it was obtained. For this reason resolving the schisms that exist in psychol- ogy because of methodology depends upon theory development. It is a theoretical task. I cannot go into what is involved here (cf. Staats, 1983a), but let me give one example. Skinnerians do not accept the me- thodology of psychological testing. Central in this is that Skinnerians do not have in their approach a theory of personality as source of causation in the determination of human behavior. The task of legitimizing personality testing methodology for Skinnerians, thus, depends upon first introducing a causal concept of personality into a behavioristic theory (cf. Leduc, 1984; Staats, 1971; 1975, Chapter 12; in press a). When behaviorists can accept such a theory of personality, they then have a basis for seeing the importance of the methods of personality measurement.

The general point that I am making is that a large number of theoretical achievements must be accomplished to provide a basis for establishing methodological unification in psychology. Psychology needs theoretical analyses that isolate psychology's methodological schisms, and unifying formulations that provide a basis for resolving the schisms (cf. Staats, 1983a).

Unifying Phenomena. It must be explicitly realized that psychology is a science with a great range of phenomena to study. Psychologists come to that study with a great diversity of theoretical languages, methodological beliefs, and so on. Different aspects of the same phenomena will in many cases be studied by different psychologists. And there will be differences in subjects used and apparatus employed. Different theory languages will be employed. Thus there will be manifold differences that result even when the same or closely related phenomena are involved.

What must be expected in such circumstances has resulted, that is, a chaos of studies and fields of study that seemingly are separate from one another and are frequently inconsistent and competitive. One can take the position that this is the natural state of psychology. Or, one can take the view that what psychology has is a huge task of relating the various phenomena through theoretical analysis. The amazing thing - one of the characteristics that best defines the disunified science - is that there is little or no effort devoted within psychology to theoretical analysis that would bridge its diverse phenomena. More often efforts are expended on developing competitive approaches within the same area of study, or different areas are simply left as separate and unrelated.

Psychology proliferates new studies at what is an alarming rate without any countering effort in providing linkages among the separated knowledge elements. It is not experimentation itself that is bad, as some subjectivist philosophies suggest, it is experimentation for its own sake, without regard to producing knowledge that links with other knowledge. One avenue of reversing that progression is through the creation of theorists whose objective is the provision of unified analyses of phenomena now considered to be different but that actually operate according to the same principles. Where are such theorists today? Where are they trained? Where are there journals to publish their works? We need all of these things.

Grand Unifying Theory. The major recognized way of establishing unification in psychology has been via the grand theory. The model has been that of the grand theories of the natural sciences. There has always been the implicit hope that a Newton would appear in psychology (Giddens, 1976, p. 13). And we have had a number of theorists who have seen their theories in that way, among whom we can mention Freud, Hull, Skinner, Piaget, and various others. There are those who wish now to claim that cognitive psychology is a grand, unified theory (Baars, 1984; 1985). The problem has been that none of these grand theories has produced a general acceptance in our science. Each of them has had an impact and has created numbers of adherents to his theory. But none has gained a consensus. And each has been opposed by many more psychologists than the number of those supporting the theory.

We thus have to conclude that all of the grand theories have failed to produce unification, to create a consensus, to provide general meaning, to make psychology more compact, cohesive, parsimonious, and unified. Perhaps this should tell us that this avenue is a dead end and should be discarded. Koch (1981) has advanced this philosophy, along with his general conclusion that we should accept as established that it is psychology's fate to remain divided and incommensurate across its many parts.

But the present view tells us to ask, "Have the grand theories ever tried to unify psychology?" Koch (1981) refers derisively to the failure in unification of the grand behavioristic theories as a ridiculous "age of theory." However, we have to examine that interpretation. For one thing, were the theories of Tolman, Hull, Skinner, and the others really unified theories? Did any of them try to unify even the field of animal learning? Did any of these theories have an announced program for establishing a coherent science? Did any of them stipulate the methodology by which this was to be done? Did any of them study how to establish unified knowledge in psychology? The answer is no to each question. Behaviorism has never been more advanced with respect to constructing unified theory than has the rest of the approaches of the science (cf. Baars, 1984; Staats, 1983b; 1985).

We cannot but agree that the various theories of Freud, Hull, Skinner, Piaget, and others, have not unified psychology. But we must ask whether these theories are to be considered representative of the total class of possible grand theories. Should we be content that this avenue has been fully tried, as Koch (1981) suggests, and that it should be abandoned? Or should we conclude that these specific attempts failed, but that this does not generally condemn the avenue of work? Perhaps a grand theory could be constructed that would have the unifying, consensus-producing characteristics we desire.

If the latter conclusion is made, as the present view suggests, then we can add other implications. One implication, for example, is that perhaps we need to study what it is about the traditional grand theories that made them failures as unifying formulations. Was it that they were actually special area theories? Were their principles formulated only within the confines of a small part of the study of psychology? Did the theories make an attempt to incorporate principles, concepts, and findings from the various areas of psychology? What was their methodology for doing so? We must also ask whether psychology has ever devoted systematic effort to studying what the nature of the task is in constructing a grand theory for psychology. What will such a theory need to do to be successful? What knowledge must it unify? What characteristics will such a theory have to exhibit?

We can see that psychology has never taken the task of constructing unified theories seriously. For there has been no real study of such things. There has not even been comparative study of the various grand theories with respect to their methodology for achieving unification or for the extent to which they were successful, and so on (cf. Minke, in press, for an example). As a consequence, psychology has little to say regarding what grand theory is or should be in our science, or even theory that is less than grand theory.

A beginning has been made in formulating a methodology for constructing grand theories in psychology that will have unification as a goal (Leduc, 1984; Staats, 1975; 1981; 1983b; 1985; in press a, b, c, d). The methodology is called multilevel theory. The methodology advances a concept of bridging theory and how bridging theory is at the heart of the theory-construction task (Staats, 1983a, Chapter 8). This analysis also indicates how developments in the philosophy of science, concerned with constructing theory in the biochemical sciences, support the theory-construction methodology (cf. Darden & Maull, 1977). The general point, however, is that we must begin to treat the construction of grand theories systematically - both by the theorists interested in constructing such theories and by methodologists who wish to deal with the area abstractly. Analytic studies must be made of the different grand theories with respect to how they were constructed to serve in the unifying role. This must be done to begin to understand the features of such theories, how they can be evaluated, how they can be improved, and so on, with respect to their potential for serving as unifying frameworks for the science.

Grand theories are not the only avenue to be followed in psychology's revolution to unity. This must be underscored. We need a multitude of smaller works that provide the elements for larger unifications. But we cannot neglect the contribution that grand theories can make to the huge task of unification. Furthermore, we need studies of the characteristics of unified theories, theories of all sizes. Within this framework there are many metatheoretical studies to be conducted.

Theory, Philosophy, Unity: How Do They Relate?

The analysis that I have outlined here has many implications for psychology. For example, since psychology has so many organizations devoted to special field and special theory interests, which contribute to the fragmentation of psychology, it needs an organization devoted to the creation of unification. This is part of making an investment in unification. Another part of the investment must be in establishing a journal for the publication of works that are devoted to works in unification. There are presently many journals devoted to specialized fragmentation of psychology, and we need journal media for publishing works that unify methodological, philosophical, and substantive knowledge. Some of these implications have already been indicated (cf. Staats, 1983a; 1984). There are more to derive in the conduct of the many works needed. The purpose of the present paper has been to describe the philosophy of unified positivism, a goal of which is to open to our science a new field of study, that of uninomic or unification psychlogy (see Fishman, 1986; Staats, 1986).

References

Baars, B. J. (1984). View from a road not taken. *Contemporary Psychology, 29,* 804-805.

Baars, B. J. (1985). The logic of unification. *Contemporary Psychology, 30,* 340.

Darden, L., & Maull, N. (1977). Interfield theories. *Philosophy of Science, 44,* 43-64.

Dollard, J., & Miller, N. (1950). *Personality and psychotherapy.* New York: McGraw-Hill.

Eifert, G. H. (1985). Rewards for fragmentation. *International Newsletter for Paradigmatic Psychology, 1,* 19.

Elms, A. C. (1975). The crisis of confidence in social psychology. *American Psychologist, 30,* 967-976.

Epstein, R. (1984). The case for praxics. *The Behavior Analyst, 7,* 101-119.

Evans, P. (1978). A visit with Michael Argyle. *APA Monitor, 9(8),* 6-7.

Fishman, D. B. (1986). Where the underlying boundaries are: Organizing psychology by paradigm analysis. *International Newsletter of Uninomic Psychology, 2,* 4-9.

Gergen, K. J. (1973). Social psychology as history. *Journal of Personality and Social Psychology, 26,* 309-320.

Giddens, A. (1976). *New rules of sociological method.* New York: Basic Books.

Gosling, J. (1986). Analysis and strategy in the search for unity: Epistemic principles for psychology. *International Newsletter for Uninomic Psychology, 2,* 13-19.

Hagstrom, W. O. (1965). *The scientific community.* New York: Basic Books.

Hilgard, E. R. (1948). *Theories of learning.* (2nd ed.). New York: Appleton-Century-Crofts.

Hishinuma, E. S. (in press). Psychoanalytic and cognitive dissonance theories: Producing unification through the unified theory review. In A. W. Staats & L. P. Mos (Eds.), *Annals of Theoretical Psychology,* (Vol. 5). New York: Plenum.

Hoorn, W. van (1972). *As images unwind.* Amsterdam: University Press.

Hull, C. L. (1943). *Principles of Behavior.* New York: Appleton-Century-Crofts.

Jackson, G. B. (1980). Methods for integrative reviews. *Review of Educational Research, 50,* 438-460.

Kimble, G. A. (1984). Psychology's two cultures. *American Psychologist, 39,* 833-839.

Koch, S. (1981). The nature and limits of psychological knowledge: Lessons of a century qua 'science.' *American Psychologist, 36,* 257-269.

Kuhn, T. S. (1977). Second thoughts on paradigms. In F. Suppe (Ed.), *The structure of scientific theories.* Urbana, Ill.: University of Illinois Press.

Lakatos, I. (1970). Falsification and the methodology of scientific research programmes. In I. Lakatos & A. Musgrave (Eds.), *Criticism and the growth of knowledge.* London: Cambridge University Press.

Leduc, A. (Ed.) (1984). *Recherches sur le behaviorisme paradigmatique ou social.* Brossard, Quebec: Editions Behaviora.

MacIntyre, R. B. (1985). Psychology's fragmentation and suggested remedies. *International Newsletter for Paradigmatic Psychology, 1,* 20-21.

Mackenzie, R. D. (1977). *Behaviourism and the limits of scientific method.* Atlantic Highlands, N.J.: Humanities Press.

Maher, B. A. (1985). Underpinnings of today's chaotic diversity. *International Newsletter for Paradigmatic Psychology, 1,* 17-19.

Mencken, H. L. (1927). Psychologists in a fog. *American Mercury, 11,* 382-383.

Merton, R. K. (Edited and with an introduction by Norman W. Storer) (1973). *The sociology of science.* Chicago, Ill.: University of Chicago Press.

Minke, K. A. (in press). A comparative analysis of modern general behaviorisms: Unification by generational adavance. In A. W. Staats & L. P. Mos (Eds.), *Annals of Theoretical Psychology,* (Vol. 5). New York: Plenum.

Moscovici, S. (1972). Society and theory in social psychology. In J. Israel & H. Tajfel (Eds.), *The context of social psychology.* New York: Academic Press.

Rappard, H. V. (1984, August). *Theoretical psychology and the essence of the Leibnizian tradition.* Paper presented at the convention of the American Psychological Association, Toronto, Canada.

Shapere, D. (1977). Scientific theories and their domains. In F. Suppe (Ed.), *The structure of scientific theories* (2nd ed.). Urbana, Ill.: University of Illinois Press.

Staats, A. W. (1971). *Child learning, intelligence and personality.* New York: Harper and Row.

Staats, A. W. (1975). *Social behaviorism.* Homewood, Ill.: Dorsey Press.

Staats, A. W. (1981). Paradigmatic behaviorism, unified theory, unified theory construction methods, and the zeitgeist of separatism. *American Psychologist, 36,* 240-256.

Staats, A. W. (1983a). *Psychology's crisis of disunity: Philosophy and method for a unified science.* New York: Praeger.

Staats, A. W. (1983b). Paradigmatic behaviorism: Unified theory for social-personality psychology. In L. Berkowitz (Ed.), *Advances in experimental social psychology. Vol. 16. Theorizing in social psychology: Theoretical perspectives.* New York: Academic Press.

Staats, A. W. (1984, August). Scientific chaos is not science: a proposal to solve psychology's disunity. Invited address, American Psychological Association Convention, Toronto, Canada.

Staats, A. W. (1985). Disunity's prisoner, blind to a new approach to unification. *Contemporary Psychology, 30,* 339-340.

Staats, A. W. (1986). Unified positivism. *International Newsletter of Uninomic Psychology, 2,* 10-12.

Staats, A. W. (in press a). Behaviorism with a personality: The paradigmatic behavioral assessment approach. In R. O. Nelson & S. C. Hayes (Eds.), *Conceptual foundations of behavioral assessment.* New York: Guilford Press.

Staats, A. W. (in press b). Paradigmatic behavior therapy: A unified framework for theory, research, and practice. In I. M. Evans (Ed.), *Paradigmatic behavior therapy.* New York: Springer.

Staats, A. W. (in press c). Paradigmatic behaviorism, unified positivism, and paradigmatic behavior therapy. In D. Fishman, R. Rotgers, and C. Franks (Eds.), *Paradigms in behavior therapy.* New York: Springer.

Staats, A. W. (in press d). Unified positivism: Philosophy for a unification psychology. In A. W. Staats & L. P. Mos (Eds.), *Annals of theoretical psychology: Vol. 5.* New York: Plenum.

Suppe, F. (1977). *The structure of scientific theories.* Urbana, Ill.: University of Illinois Press.

Toulmin, S. (1972). *Human understanding.* Princeton: Princeton University.

Wachtel, P. (1977). *Psychoanalysis and behavior therapy.* New York: Basic Books.

Current Issues in Theoretical Psychology
Wm J. Baker, M.E. Hyland, H. Van Rappard, A.W. Staats (Editors)
© Elsevier Science Publishers B.V. (North-Holland), 1987

DESYNCHRONY AMONG MEASURES OF FEAR AND EMOTIONAL

PROCESSING: TOWARD A CONSTRUCTIONIST PERSPECTIVE

Henderikus J. Stam and Kimberley L. McEwan

The University of Calgary
Calgary, Alberta, Canada

SUMMARY: The 'three-systems' model of fear is examined in the light
of recent theorizing about the concept of emotional processing. The latter is seen as a move that places fear research in the domain of cognitive
psychology. Neither the three-systems model nor the notion of emotional
processing, however, address fundamental problems in current fear
theories. Rather, they can be viewed as continuing the ideology of individualism in the psychology of emotions. A social - constructionist perspective argues instead that fear is an emotion ritual, the enactment of
which constitutes the fear experience. Implications of this position are
discussed.

For some time now, investigators of human fear have discontinued
defining fear as a unitary phenomenon (Agras & Jacob, 1981; Arena,
Blanchard, Andrasik, Cotch, & Myers, 1983; Borkovec, 1976; Gray, 1971;
Hodgson & Rachman, 1974; Lang, 1971; 1978; Rachman, 1978; Rachman
& Hodgson, 1974; Vermilyea, Boice, & Barlow, 1984). This argument
rests on the findings that behavioral, physiological, and verbal measures
of fear do not always covary but have, to some extent, been found to
vary independently (see Hugdahl, 1981; Thayer, 1970). Rachman (1978)
has thus defined fear as "comprising three main components: the subjective experience of apprehension, associated physiological changes, and attempts to avoid or escape from certain situations." (p. 4). This has
been called the 'three-systems' or 'three-components' model of fear and
has been accepted by various authors as a useful model. Whenever any
one component does not display elevations in the presence of a feared
stimulus and one or both of the remaining components are elevated, then
fear responding is said to be discordant. The discordance or desynchrony
observed among response systems appears to have been accepted as at
least a reasonable working hypothesis by most investigators in the area
(see overview by Vermilyea et al., 1984).

In this paper we begin with a discussion of the problems of the three-systems model for treatment and the *discovery* that concordance may be important for treatment success. We then outline several of the conceptual problems inherent in the three-systems model and the subsequent attempt to solve these with an *emotional processing* conception of fear. This brings fear into modern psychology via the information processing metaphor but it does not solve the strong individual/social dualism embedded in this notion. The final section of the paper is then devoted to a discussion of a social constructionist view of fear.

Treatment and the Problems of the Three-Systems Model of Individual Differences

One obvious implication of the three-systems model of fear is that there are multiple ways in which people can differ in the extent to which their systems are desynchronized. With the importance thus assigned to individual difference factors in fear and anxiety (e.g., Borkovec, 1976; Eysenck, 1975; Lazarus, 1980; Paul, 1969), the three-systems approach has incorporated individual differences to the extent that it has accepted Lacey and Lacey's (1958) individual response stereotype. This has led to two expectations: (a) that individual patterns of physiological responding could predict treatment outcome, and (b) that the matching of therapy techniques to response topography could facilitate treatment outcome (e.g., Barlow, Mavissakalian, & Schofield, 1980; Norton, Dinardo, & Barlow, 1983). Whether individual patterns of physiological responding predict treatment outcome is rarely tested and the available research is far from clear (e.g., Vermilyea et al., 1984). There have been several attempts, however, to predict treatment outcome from fear response patterns.

In an earlier paper, Rachman (1976) advanced the idea that response topography in anxiety might be differentially related to the success of various treatments. Norton, Dinardo, and Barlow (1983) concluded that the data available from a number of recent treatment studies support the position that fear reduction techniques should be matched to patients' pretreatment patterns of cognitive, physiological, and behavioral reactions. Even if we were to accept this claim on its own terms, however, the data only weakly support, and in some instances contradict, this approach. For example, a number of studies have found inconsistent results in attempting to tailor treatments to fear response patterns in patients with social skill deficits or in social phobics (Ost, Jerremalm, & Johansson, 1981; Shahar & Merbaum, 1981; Trower, Yardley, Bryant, & Shaw, 1978).

Treatments which target the most elevated of the three response components in fearful individuals are therefore not necessarily the most effective in eliminating fear. After response-congruent treatments, some fear is still manifest both in the channel targetted for change and in the untargetted channels. Difficulties arise even in defining individuals as *physiological reactors* given the low reliabilities observed in psychophysiological assessment (Arena et al., 1983). Similar problems of measurement occur in the assessment of the cognitive (Glass & Merluzzi, 1981) and behavioral components.

Concordance and Treatment Success

Some authors have argued that discordance or desynchrony among responses to fear stimuli is associated with the *return of fear*, that is, a relapse following treatment. Lang et al. (1970) first noted that synchrony was associated with a positive outcome in treatment. Similarily, Barlow et al. (1980) reported that, of three agoraphobics, a relapse was suffered by the one who evidenced marked desynchrony during treatment. Grey, Rachman, and Sartory (1981) also questioned whether the return of fear might be predicted by patterns of fear responses observed during treatment. Further support for the association between successful treatment and response patterning came from authors who argued that prolonged phobic exposure during flooding is reported to be more successful in eliminating fear (Stern & Marks, 1973; Marks, 1978) and results in significantly higher correlations between subjective anxiety and physiological measures than short exposures (Lande, 1982). These views eventually led to the emotional processing notion which we will discuss below.

From the perspective of the desynchrony position, it follows that efforts should be directed at promoting concordant response patterns during treatment. Naturally, while intense phobic stimulation may produce concordant fear responses (Hodgson & Rachman, 1974), procedures which produce intense levels of fear such as flooding are not always viable. Nevertheless, according to this view, the induction of correspondence among response systems should facilitate the effectiveness of less dramatic and more practical forms of treatment. This does not mean, of course, that fear theorists should now promote avoidance during therapy. Rather, the implication of the need for concordant responses is that fear be experienced in more sub-systems than the cognitive. While on the surface this appears straightforward, the notions of synchrony and desynchrony are themselves problematic.

Conceptual Difficulties of the Three-Systems Model

The three-systems model can be viewed as a descendant of classical and operant conditioning theories of fear acquisition. The objections to these theories were numerous (e.g., Rachman, 1984). For example, classical conditioning predicts that extinction should occur following repeated exposure to the CS. This does not occur reliably. Operant models, on the other hand, cannot account for the fact that avoidance is not always associated with fear or anxiety. The three-systems model appeared, in part, to solve some of these difficulties.

An important implication of the three-systems model is that the presence or absence of fear cannot be adequately defined in either stimulus or response terms (Hugdahl, 1981). The three-systems model is fettered in tautological subservience to stimulus situations. Since no single response pattern within the three-systems can be reliably said to represent fear, then fear-eliciting stimuli must index fearful behavior. However, two very different events may elicit the same fearful behavior. This circularity then precludes any adequate definition of fear (Hugdahl, 1981). Furthermore, it follows then that we refer not to agoraphobics per se, but to *physiological agoraphobics, behavioral agoraphobics*, or *cognitive agoraphobics*.

The assumed partial independence of the response system in the three-systems model has largely been responsible for these definitional problems. Fear is no longer viewed as a single emotion manifested behaviorally, physiologically, and cognitively. Rather, fear is now seen as having components, any one of which may be sufficient to constitute the presence of fear. Conceptually, however, what do we mean when we say a person is afraid *cognitively* but not *physiologically*? More confusing still, can a person be said to be afraid *physiologically* but not *behaviorally* or *cognitively*? Emotional attributes are usually only admissable as predicated of unified organisms, in this case, persons (e.g., Averill, 1982; 1983). While persons have physical as well as mental attributes ascribed to them, they are nonetheless functionally unified entities (Margolis, 1978; Robinson, 1982; Strawson, 1959). As a consequence, when we make statements about fear, we are ascribing an attribute to a person. The three-systems model as such is at most a descriptive model and not an explanatory model of fear (Wilson, 1982).

It is important to note here that the problems of definition are not unique to fear. They also occur with emotions generally. The question "what is an emotion?" has never been satisfactorily answered and is, for some, a pseudo-question (Mandler, 1984). That is, to explain what an emotion is requires an explication of what emotion refers to in ordinary language. But ordinary language uses of emotional concepts are *fuzzy* and prototypically organized (e.g., Fehr & Russell, 1984). They lack clear defining attributes, and instances in each case vary in their degree of family resemblance to the prototype. Instances shade gradually into non-prototypes and finally into nonmembers (cf. Rosch, 1978). That is not to say that attempts to define emotions precisely have not been made. To the contrary, various authors have argued the case that emotions can be defined in terms of fundamental states of the organism (e.g., Izard, 1977; Plutchik, 1980: Tomkins, 1980). Each of these theorists has attempted to place fundamental emotions within organisms. The implication of this position is that the individual is viewed as emotionally autonomous.

Despite difficulties in defining emotions, both fundamental-emotion theorists and ordinary language conceptions of emotions posit fear as a central and easily classifiable emotion. Thus, whatever difficulties may ensue in attempting to define emotion, there is no question of the status of fear in that class of events considered emotional.

In short, confusion between the descriptive and explanatory capacity of the three-systems model of fear has lead to an oversimplification of fear response phenomena. Rather than viewing discordant responses as suspect, the phenomena have been all too readily accommodated into current theorizing about fear disorders. Consequently, Lang's call for efforts to "define the variables which modulate system interaction" (1978, p. 386) has largely been ignored. Moreover, unfounded assumptions have been made regarding the causal or pathogenic role of the most elevated response system. As we noted above, it is apparent that categorizing fearful individuals as physiological, behavioral, or cognitive phobics and applying treatments which uniquely target these response systems is not an efficient practice. Emotional processing then is a concept that can be viewed as attempting to rescue theories of fear from hopeless confusion.

Emotional Processing

When an individual reports fear, the verbal report indicates that fear is publicly acknowledged. Since language is usually the medium of diagnosis and treatment, discordance in clinical contexts typically refers to situations wherein behavior and, most often, physiological reactivity are not in agreement with the verbal reports of fear. Lang (1978) noted that the successful therapy of fear and anxiety may depend on clients' abilities to react cardiovascularly and to be able to generate the physiological components of the fear response. He suggested that "the ability to self-generate arousal may also be a key to the central processing of emotion which is a goal of psychotherapy." (p. 382). In other words, concordant responding may lead to greater emotional processing and is then more likely to lead to successful outcomes in therapy.

It was Rachman, however, who fully developed the notion of emotional processing in his 1980 paper. He argued that many aspects of persistent fear (i.e., the return of fear, incubation of fear) may be the result of incomplete emotional processing. The latter is "a process whereby emotional disturbances are absorbed, and decline to the extent that other experiences and behavior can proceed without disruption." (1980, p. 51). If an emotional disturbance is not absorbed, however, there will be certain signs that, at intermittent intervals, intrude into emotional activity (e.g., obsessions, nightmares, phobias). Successful processing has occurred when a person has the "ability to talk about, see, listen to or be reminded of the emotional events without experiencing distress or disruptions." (p. 52). Rachman specified three criteria that must apply before emotional processing has been completed; (a) evidence of an emotional disturbance, (b) evidence of a decline in the disturbance, and (c) evidence of a return to undisrupted behavior. Test probes attempt to re-evoke the emotional reaction, to measure the degree to which emotional disturbances have been absorbed.

In support of his proposal, Rachman noted that systematic desensitization studies have reported the least success with those patients who show weak responses to fear stimuli. He argued that in phobic patients, any technique which enhances the physiological reaction will facilitate emotional processing. That is, a physiological response must accompany the subjective or verbal fear response. Thus, in keeping with Lang (1978), Rachman concluded that "fear must be experienced before it can be reduced or eliminated" (1980, p. 52).

At the outset, we need to address several problems. First, it is never clear how Rachman uses the term *absorption*. If emotional processing is a process whereby emotions are absorbed, the least we need to know to use this concept is: How it is that emotions can be absorbed and why do they need to be absorbed to be processed? As it is, this definition makes the concept of emotional processing appear circular and perhaps superfluous.

Second, the processing metaphor has obvious ties to information processing metaphors and cognitive psychology. This appears deliberate.

Rachman writes at length and raises numerous questions about the connections between emotional processing and information processing (e.g., "are people capable of simultaneously processing emotional and intellectual material, and what are the inter-relationships between these two processes?" (p. 58). He implies that he views information and emotional processing to be two complementary models, each of which require substantial research. Nevertheless, apart from the word *processing,* the connection is more implied than real.

In a recent paper, Lang has also proposed what is an even more explicit information processing model of emotions with special reference to anxiety disorders (Lang & Cuthbert, 1984). Emotions are conceived of "as affective programs within the brain, with information coded as propositions organized into associative networks." (p. 369). More important for the present purposes is the clear admonition that, for anxiety disorders, "individual differences in accessing and *processing emotional information* may bear significant implications for prognosis and treatment selection." (p. 369, italics ours). Emotional processing *is* information processing, according to Lang and Cuthbert, and not two separate processes to be explained.

Emotional Processing and the Three-Systems Model

As Rachman (1980, p. 57) noted, "the main goals of this theoretical framework [of emotional processing] are: to introduce some order, to unify some disparate findings, to identify new questions and invite new solutions." The idea that emotion must be fully expressed before it can be absorbed has obvious implications for the *three-systems model* of fear. Some correspondence among the three response components of fear is viewed as a necessary requisite for successful processing and elimination of fear. Furthermore, "the major influences on emotional processing will act generally, i.e., across systems, to at least some degree." (Rachman, 1980, p. 57). According to Rachman, factors which impede processing include a refusal to verbalize feelings toward disturbing stimuli, the lack of an autonomic reaction to such stimuli, and avoidance of the disturbing situation. By implication, inhibition of a response in one or more of the three systems may provide a serious obstacle to the diminution of excessive fear. In this light, the concept of emotional processing is closely linked to what may be termed emotional concordance. Grayson, Foa, and Steketee have suggested that "synchrony may be an indicant of the degree to which emotional processing has taken place." (1982, p. 328). Accordingly, attempts to account for *failures in emotional processing* can be seen as attempts to *explain discordance* in the various response channels. Hence, the re-unified person, in the guise of emotional processor, can be discordant in a way that is no longer problematic. Unlike the three-systems model, the emotional processing metaphor requires a person to process and absorb emotions.

Critique

The proposed rescue of fear research by emotional processing is, in our view, largely unsuccessful because it does not answer fundamental theoretical questions about the nature of fear. The three-systems model asserts behaviorism's irrational individual, buffeted on the seas of environmental stimuli (Buss, 1978; Morawski, in press). Even emotions cannot be reliably attributed to persons. Instead they are operational entities, appearing now as cognitions, now as behaviors, and now as physiological responses. Emotional processing brings fear research into line with the remainder of psychology - that is, the psychology of information processing. Emotional processing is a loose metaphor based on an information processing model of human functioning that attempts to overcome, in part, the circularity of the desynchrony problem. By adding the processing metaphor, fear has been taken out of its niche in neo-behaviorism and behavior therapies and placed within the cognitive tradition, since, by most definitions, cognitivism treats mind as an information processing system (e.g., Haugland, 1978).

Our argument with the three-systems perspective and the emotional processing perspective is that they share a reliance on an ideology of individualism (Sampson, 1981; 1983; Woolfolk & Richardson, 1984). Both views classify emotions as asocial entities and near mechanistic events. If we accept Sampson's (1981) characterization of ideology as both false consciousness (a systematic distortion of reality) and as a true description of a particular sociohistorical context, then it is possible to see the psychology of fear as ideological. By defining an emotional event in subjectivist and individualist terms, certain Western cultural traditions that strongly promote individualism are unreflexively reproduced.

The information processing metaphor (and its associated cognitive models) confuses content with process (Sampson, 1981; Henriques et al., 1984). In the case of emotional processing, emotions are items to be processed that come to the individual in a non-problematic manner and are divorced from the social domain. Thus, while the neurological, physiological, and chemical features of the central nervous system provide the boundaries of emotional processing, they will shed little light on the processes involved in the development of fear in the world of persons.

Although many cognitive models of emotions acknowledge the importance of the social world, they typically do so in an artificial, post-hoc and rigidly dualist fashion. For example, Mandler states that "when all has been said about mental processes, we can return to the importance of the social conditions under which they operate, to the recognition that life and society determine consciousness, not vice versa." (1984, p. 299). Despite this acknowledgement, discussions of the social realm are completely unnecessary to a cognitive model of emotions such as Mandler's, that is schema based. Social variables mechanically interact with the individual's cognitive-interpretive system.

There is a further illusion, however, behind the adoption of information processing models of fear. This is the belief that we are progressing beyond behavioral metapsychology. Neither behaviorist nor cognitivist disagrees on what constitutes the locus of study. Both work from a mechanical model of personhood wherein people are viewed as "high-grade automata" (Harré,1984), even though a more sophisticated version exists in cognitive psychology. Both adhere to an individualism in their descriptions of persons, behavior, cognitions, or emotions. Neither approach is contextual; the social milieu is separate from, and interacts mechanically with, the self-contained individuals that are paradigmatic of persons (Sampson, 1983). As has been made evident by a number of recent writers, the use of individualist conceptions in psychology results from particular metapsychological assumptions that are themselves embedded in the psychological works (Gergen, 1982; Harré, 1984; Stam, in press; Wexler, 1983). Nevertheless, in the positivist tradition, they are treated as universal, scientific constructs that are not laden with implicit values.

Re-Socializing Fear

One approach, recently brought to bear on the problems of emotions that may be usefully applied to fear, is the notion of constructionism (see Gergen, 1985). We will thus devote the remainder of the paper to this view. The basic premise of this approach is that emotions are socially constructed, that is, "emotions are explained as responses to happenings in the environment which are presented through specific modes of social organization, normative expectations, beliefs and values ... it is essential to contructionism that emotions be understood not as natural, passive states but as socially determined patterns of ritual action." (Armon-Jones, 1985). Indeed, Armon-Jones argues that emotion rituals (or syndromes in Averill's terminology) are not only culturally determined, but that the performance of emotion rituals leads to both the validating criteria and the experiential content of emotions. Thus, emotions are learned by the social validation of various emotion rituals. They are ontologically dependent on the performance and practise of the actions (whether physical or mental) that constitute the criteria for that particular emotion. Note here however that a child may display a wide range of actions of which only a few are validated as certain *emotions* that are appropriate to certain contexts. Other actions, by virtue of their lack of validation, fall into disuse as emotion rituals. Further performances of previously validated emotion rituals serve to identify these emotions as fundamental to a certain context for the actor.

Averill (and Lewin before him in 1935) also rejects what he calls the essentialist case for emotions in modern psychology in favor of a conception of emotions as socially constituted syndromes. He argued that "there is still a tendency to think of emotions in terms of essential characteristics - that is, intervening drive variables, certain kinds of physiological or expressive reactions, neurological 'affect programs,' particular modes of cognition, or particular subjective states." (Averill, 1983, p. 1156). Averill's (1982; 1983) social-constructivist view rests instead on four assumptions: Emotions are responses of persons, not subsystems of persons; emotions are polythetic syndromes that can only be viewed as wholes; emotions are organized through social processes; and emotions serve social functions.

Now, it could be argued that *fear* is such a basic, natural, and evolutionarily important emotion that it is possible to exclude it from a social-constructionist viewpoint. Instead, we might simply argue that fear is reinforced in appropriate contexts. As Armon-Jones (1985) indicates, however, fear must already be present before it can be reinforced. The origins of the emotion lie in the enacting of the emotion rituals that are culturally constituted as *fear* rituals, and their enactment generates *fear experiences*. This takes us away from a conception of fear as having internal (i.e., cognitive) components. Rather, fear is an action ritual (involving some things traditionally called behavioral, cognitive, and physiological) capable of generation and disgeneration. For example, "to cower, shudder and occupy one's thoughts with fearful images may not be to intensify a pre-existent fear feeling but to generate fear." (Armon-Jones, 1985, p. 7). In other words, the experience of fear is a direct function of the manifest emotion action. Such an analysis readily cuts through the strong dualism inherent in the three-systems model of fear. It also deprivileges the cognitive analysis and its individualist bias in the emotional processing view.

The notion of *anxiety* can likewise be rendered into a construction-ist view. As Sarbin (1982/1968) pointed out, anxiety did not make it into psychology textbooks until the 1930s, and by 1961 one could already iden-tify at least 120 different procedures for inferring its presence. The mental state corresponding to anxiety is, according to Sarbin, ontological-ly mythical. The term itself found its way into English as a metaphor that eventually replaced the medieval use of *anguish*, itself a dispositional term that was converted to a mental state term. This hardly means that anxiety is not somehow *real*. To the contrary, it is an emotion that, once learned, is performed in its appropriate context and reinforces both the cultural values embedded in the concept and the actor's commitment to those values (Armon-Jones, 1985).

The more difficult task now is to develop a model of phobias that is constructionist. One approach would be to view someone's *excessive* fear as somehow integral to his/her self conception. Thus, while fear may be unwarrranted from the perspective of social norms, it may at the same time preserve the basic premises that lead one to express that emo-tion in other circumstances. This is because the individual adopts an *in-tentional set* that may be highly idiosyncratic but that, once disclosed, makes the fear an appropriate response to a situation that resembles the conditions in which that person originally learned and normally applies the fear (Armon-Jones, 1985). Although resembling a learning theory interpretation, this resemblance is superficial. The constructionist posits an actor engaged in a pattern of ritual action that serves social functions, not a high-grade automaton to whom emotions occur.

This is, of necessity, only an outline of the implications of the con-structionist position for a psychology of fear. It requires a systematic analysis of fears and phobias in order to be useful. It is our belief, how-ever, that this effort is justified by the potential gains such a theory will make over the traditional behavioral and cognitive versions of fear. For example, if we view fear as a socially constituted syndrome that is pri-marily an appraisal of situations interpreted as passions rather than as ac-tions (Averill, 1985), certain implications immediately follow. The ap-praised object will have an aim (avoidance), an instigator (danger), and a target (which is flexible). Research programs such as those conducted by Averill on anger (1982) could usefully elucidate the nature of fear re-sponding and their construction as syndromes. Very little is currently known as to how such syndromes are constructed. Certainly, the three-systems model has done little to inform us on this score.

Constructionist perspectives do not constitute a unified theory but are more a collection of approaches that share some metapsychological assumptions about the primacy of social conventions. When applied to emotions they at least make explicit the notion that emotional expressions and experiences are not simply *natural* or passive events but are vehicles of cultural beliefs and values. As such, they are also very effective. An attitude, proposition, or intention does not necessarily entail an emotion, whereas the reverse is always true (Armon-Jones, 1985). Thus, a psychology of emotions based on a constructionist perspective could at least begin to grapple with the reflexive nature of psychological discourse.

Of course, a constructionist perspective could also become normative to the degree that it simply surveys and documents everyday experience. In Sampson's (in press) words "given its emphasis on the social construction of psychological and social reality, to what extent can the constructionist position adopt a critical rather than accepting stance towards any current societal constructions?" To evaluate constructionism and prevent its lapse into relativism, Sampson (in press) proposes a critical constructionist position. While not yet sufficiently developed, a critical constructionism maintains an attitude of suspicion about all constructions and attempts to uncover their societal roles and functions.

In order for a constructionist position of emotions to become reflexive, it needs to be explicit about the relationship between social constructions and social forms, institutions, and history. It could then move beyond normative models of emotionality and question their production and maintenance. It might also answer some questions about the role emotions play in the reproduction of ideology at the individual level (Wexler, 1983). At the least it would move us away from highly noncontextual and individualistic conceptions of emotions.

References

Agras, W. S., & Jacob, R. G. (1981). Phobia: Nature and measurement. In M. Mavissakalian & D. H. Barlow (Eds.), *Phobia: Psychological and pharmacological treatment*. New York: Guilford.

Arena, J. G., Blanchard, E. B., Andrasik, F., Cotch, P. A., & Myers, P. E. (1983). Reliability of psychophysiological assessment. *Behavior Research and Therapy, 21*, 447-460.

Armon-Jones, C. (1985). Prescription, explication and the social construction of emotion. *Journal for the Theory of Social Behavior, 15*, 1-22.

Averill, J. R. (1982). *Anger and aggression: An essay on emotion*. New York: Springer Verlag.

Averill, J. R. (1985). The social construction of emotion: With special reference to love. In K. J. Gergen & K. E. Davis (Eds.), *The social construction of the person*. New York: Springer-Verlag.

Averill, J. R. (1983). Studies on anger and aggression: Implications for theories of emotion. *American psychologist, 38*, 1145-1160.

Barlow, D. H., Mavissakalian, M., & Schofield, L. D. (1980). Patterns of desynchrony in agoraphobia: A preliminary report. *Behavior Research and Therapy, 18*, 441-448.

Borkovec, T. D. (1976). Physiologogical and cognitive processes in the regulation of anxiety. In G. E. Schwartz, & D. Schapiro (Eds.), *Consciousness and self-regulation: advances in research* (Vol. 1). New York: Plenum.

Buss, A. R. (1978). The structure of psychological revolutions. *Journal of the History of the Behavioral Sciences, 14*, 57-64.

Eysenck, H. J. (1975). The measurement of emotion: Psychological parameters and methods. In L. Levi (Ed.), *Emotions: Their parameters and measurement*. New York: Raven.

Fehr, B., & Russell, J. A. (1984). Concept of emotion viewed from a prototype perspective. *Journal of Experimental Psychology: General, 113*, 464-486.

Gergen, K. J. (1982). *Toward transformation in social knowledge*. New York: Springer-Verlag.

Gergen, K. J. (1985). The social constructionist movement in modern psychology. *American Psychologist, 40*, 266-275.

Glass, C., & Merluzzi, T. (1981). Cognitive assessment of social-evaluative anxiety. In T. Merluzzi, C. Glass, & M. Genest (Eds.), *Cognitive assessment*. New York: Guilford.

Gray, J. (1971). *The psychology of fear and stress*. London: Weidenfeld and Nicolson.

Grayson, J. B., Foa, E. B., & Steketee, G. (1982). Habituation during exposure treatment: Distraction vs attention-focusing. *Behavior Research and Therapy, 20,* 323-328.

Grey, S. J., Rachman, S., & Sartory, G. (1981). Return of fear: the role of inhibition. *Behavior Research and Therapy, 19,* 135-143.

Harré, R. (1984). *Personal being.* Cambridge, Mass.: Harvard University Press.

Haugeland, J. (1978). The nature and plausibility of cognitivism. *Behavioral and Brain Sciences, 1,* 135-143.

Henriques, J., et al. (1984). *Changing the subject.* London: Methuen.

Hodgson, R. O., & Rachman, S. J. (1974). Desynchrony in measures of fear. *Behavior Research and Therapy, 12,* 314-326.

Hugdahl, K. (1981). The three-systems model of fear and emotions - a critical examination. *Behavior Research and Therapy, 19,* 75-85.

Izard, C. E. (1977). *Human emotions.* New York: Plenum.

Lacey, J. I., & Lacey, B. C. (1958). Verification and extention of the principle of autonomic response-stereotypy. *American Journal of Psychology, 71,* 50-73.

Lande, S. D. (1982). Physiological and subjective measures of anxiety during flooding. *Behavior Research and Therapy, 20,* 81-88.

Lang, P. J. (1971). The application of psychological methods to the study of psychotherapy and behavior modification. In A. E. Bergin & S. L. Garfield (Eds.), *Handbook of psychotherapy and behavior change.* New York: Wiley.

Lang, P. J. (1978). Anxiety: Toward a psychobiological definition. In H. S. Akiskal & W. H. Webb (Eds.), *Psychiatric diagnosis: Exploration of biological criteria.* New York: Spectrum.

Lang, P. J., & Cuthbert, B. N. (1984). Affective information processing and the assessment of anxiety. *Journal of Behavioral Assessment, 6,* 369-395.

Lang, P. J., Melamed, B. G., & Hart, J. A. (1970). A psychophysiological analysis of fear modification using an automated desensitization procedure. *Journal of Abnormal Psychology, 76,* 229-234.

Lazarus, R. S. (1980). The stress and coping paradigm. In C. Eisdorfer, D. Cohen, A. Kleinman, & P. Maxim (Eds.), *Theoretical bases for psychopathology.* New York: Spectrum.

Mandler, G. (1984). *Mind and body: Psychology of emotion and stress.* New York: Norton.

Margolis, J. (1978). *Persons and minds: Prospects of nonreductive materialism.* Dordecht, Holland: D. Reidel.

Marks, I. M. (1978). Behavioral psychotherapy of adult neurosis. In S. L. Garfield & A. E. Bergin (Eds.), *Handbook of psychotherapy and behavior change: An empirical analysis.* New York: Wiley.

Morawski, J. G. (in press). After reflection: Psychologists' use of history. In H. J. Stam, T. B. Rogers, & K. J. Gergen (Eds.), *Metapsychology: The analysis of psychological theory.* New York: Hemisphere.

Norton, G. N., DiNardo, P. A., & Barlow, D. (1983). Predicting phobics' response to therapy: A consideration of subjective, physiological and behavioral measures. *Canadian Psychology, 24,* 50-58.

Ost, L., Jerremalm, A., & Johansson, J. (1981). Individual response patterns and the effects of different behavioral methods in the treatment of social phobia. *Behavior Research and Therapy, 19,* 1-16.

Paul, G. L. (1969). Behavior modification research: Design and tactics. In C. M. Franks (Ed.), *Behavior therapy: Appraisal and status.* New York: McGraw-Hill.

Plutchik, R. (1980). *Emotion: A psychoevolutionary synthesis.* New York: Harper & Row.

Rachman, S. J. (1976). The passing of the two-stage theory of fear and avoidance: Fresh possibilities. *Behavior Research and Therapy, 14,* 125-131.

Rachman, S. J. (1978). Human fears: A three-systems analysis. *Scandinavian Journal of Behavior Therapy, 7,* 23-245.

Rachman, S. J. (1980). Emotional Processing. *Behavior Research and Therapy, 18,* 51-60.

Rachman, S. J. (1984). Anxiety disorders: Some emerging theories. *Journal of Behavioral Assessment, 4,* 281-299.

Rachman, S. J., Hodgson, R. I. (1974). Synchrony and desynchrony in fear and avoidance. *Behavior Research and Therapy, 12,* 311-318.

Robinson, D. N. (1982). Cerebral plurality and the unity of self. *American Psychologist, 37,* 904-910.

Rosch, E. (1978). Principles of categorization. In E. Rosch & B. B. Lloyd (Eds.), *Cognition and categorization.* Hillsdale, NJ: Erlbaum.

Sampson, E. E. (1981). Cognitive psychology as ideology. *American Psychologist, 36,* 730-743.

Sampson, E. E. (1983). *Justice and the critique of pure psychology.* New York: Plenum.

Sampson, E. E. (in press). A critical constructionist view of psychology and personhood. In H. J. Stam, T. B. Rogers, & K. J. Gergen (Eds.), *Metapsychology: The analysis of psychological theory.* New York: Hemisphere.

Sarbin, T. (1982). Ontology recapitulates philology: The mythic nature of anxiety. In V. L. Allen & K. E. Scheibe (Eds.), *The social context of conduct.* New York: Praeger. (Originally published 1968).

Shahar, A., & Merbaum, M. (1981). The interaction between subject characteristics and self control procedures in the treatment of inter-

personal anxiety. *Cognitive Therapy and Research, 5,* 221-224.
Stam, H. J. (in press). The psychology of control: A textual critique. In
H. J. Stam, T. B. Rogers, & K. J. Gergen (Eds.), *Metapsychology:
The analysis of psychological theory.* New York: Hemisphere.
Stern, R. S., & Marks, I. M. (1973). A comparison of brief and pro-
longed flooding in agoraphobics. *Archives of General Psychiatry,
28,* 210.
Strawson, P. F. (1959). *Individuals: An essay in descriptive metaphysics.*
London: Methuen.
Thayer, R. E. (1970). Activation states as assessed by verbal report and
four psychophysiological variables. *Psychophysiology, 7,* 86-94.
Tomkins, S. S. (1980). Affect as amplification: Some modifications in
theory. In R. Plutchik & H. Kellerman (Eds.), *Emotion: Theory,
research, and experience.* New York: Academic Press.
Trower, P., Yardley, K., Bryant, B. M., & Shaw, P. (1978). The treat-
ment of social failure. *Behavior Modification, 2,* 41-60.
Vermilyea, J. A., Boice, R., & Barlow, D. H. (1984). Rachman and
Hodgson (1974) a decade later: How do desynchronous response
systems relate to the treatment of agoraphobics? *Behavior Research
and Therapy, 22,* 615-621.
Wexler, P. (1983). *Critical social psychology.* Boston: Routledge & Kegan Paul.
Wilson, G. T. (1982). Fear reduction methods and the treatment of
anxiety disorders. In C. M. Franks, G. T. Wilson, P. C. Kendall,
& K. D. Brownell (Eds.), *Annual review of behavior therapy* Vol.
8. New York: Guilford.
Woolfolk, R. L., & Richardson, F. C. (1984). Behavior therapy and the
ideology of modernity. *American Psychologist, 39,* 777-786.

Current Issues in Theoretical Psychology
Wm J. Baker, M.E. Hyland, H. Van Rappard, A.W. Staats (Editors)
© Elsevier Science Publishers B.V. (North-Holland), 1987

MODEL DISCIPLINES, RESEARCH TRADITIONS, AND THE
THEORETICAL UNIFICATION OF PSYCHOLOGY

P. J. van Strien

Groningen University
Groningen, The Netherlands

SUMMARY: Will psychology ever become a unified science? The history of the discipline shows a number of bold attempts to place the available knowledge in an encompassing system, or at least to trace out a route to greater unification (Staats, 1983). In the meantime the number of schools and persuasions is growing instead of diminishing. In America, cognitive psychology disputes with (neo-)behaviorism for its leading position. In Europe, the cultural-historical theory and theories of action enjoy an increasing popularity. When we also include psychological practice in our picture, the diversity becomes still more evident. Psychoanalytic and humanistic approaches compete with applied behaviorism with its background theories of behavior modification and therapy. The aim of this paper is to explore the feasibility and the limits of a theoretical unification of psychology. Understanding the dynamics of the way science and its practice develop appears to be a way to get a better insight into this matter. At the Foundations and History of Psychology Unit of the University of Groningen the dynamics of the history of psychology in the Netherlands are being studied in a way that might also shed light on the dynamics of the development of psychology in general. In the first paragraph I will give a brief exposition of the components of our 'multi-relational' approach to the dynamics of history that are relevant to our problem. In the next section this approach will be used to explain the origination of so many competing schools in the history of psychology. In the final section I will discuss the unity and disunity of the discipline in the light of our findings.

The Dynamics of the History of Social Science

To describe the diversity and confusion in scientific research and theory-building, Kuhn's paradigm concept is often used (Kuhn, 1962). In pleas for paradigmatic unification mono-paradigmatic science is seen as the ideal of a mature science. Psychologists disagree about the paradigmatic status of their discipline. In the early seventies Palermo (1971) stated that psychology is in the middle of a transitional crisis from its second paradigmatic period (behaviorism) to its third (structuralistic linguistics and cognitivism). Warren (1971) has objected that behaviorism reached the status of a generally accepted paradigm only in America. In his opinion psychology has, from an international perspective, never been a monoparadigmatic science. This view had been expressed before by Breger (1969) and Scriven (1969). Staats (1983) also analyzes the lack of paradigmatic unity in psychology. In his history of psychology Leahey (1980) uses the paradigm-concept in his description of the crises which characterized the succession of the most important schools in psychology.

The discussion is complicated by the lack of precision in the way Kuhn uses the paradigm concept. Masterman(1970) has shown that Kuhn uses the term in at least 22 ways. In our analysis, Laudan's (1977) concept (research-tradition) will be used to denote the set of common basic theoretical and methodological assumptions which guide the approach to problems in a discipline. This roughly corresponds to what Kuhn calls the 'disciplinary matrix' aspect of paradigms (Kuhn, 1970). The schools mentioned at the beginning of this paper can be viewed as research traditions in this sense.

The *paradigm* concept will be used here in the much more specific sense of a set of assumptions and shared exemplars that provide the framework within which a group of scientists work. This is the sense in which Lachman, Lachman, and Butterfield (1979) use the concept in their treatment of cognitive psychology and information processing. They view paradigms as no more than specific lines of research around a specific theme, e.g., animal maze learning, short-term memory, information processing, etc. In this perspective it makes no sense to speak of a preparadigmatic or monoparadigmatic science, or of the striving for paradigmatic unity. Specific paradigms can get into a crisis in this view, but this will seldom affect the discipline as a whole.

Just as in theory-directed science, the development of practice is also characterized by a succession, and partly also a coëxistence of paradigms. I will use the concept *practical paradigm* as a circumscribed way of dealing with a set of problems about which applied science is asked for advise. When we take organizational research and practice as an example, we find there a succession of paradigms from scientific management through human relations thinking and the resulting participation paradigm, the socio-technical paradigm, and so on, up to the present time (van Strien, 1978; see also van Strien, 1982). Other examples of practical paradigms are psychoanalytic treatment, behavior therapy of phobias, intelligence testing with paper-and-pencil tests, and so on. The reason for including also the development of practical paradigms in our analysis is that our historical investigations have shown that professional practice has had a substantial influence on the historical development of psychology in general (van Strien, 1984; Dehue & DeVries, in press).

In our multi-relational model, the emergence of, and the shift to new research and practical paradigms is explained by four factors:

(a) The questions that are posed to psychology.

(b) The models of thinking that are available in the general scientific culture in a given period to guide thinking.

(c) The establishment of educational cadres.

(d) The acceptance by the academic world and by the wider society of the legitimacy of the answers given by psychologists.

For the present purpose, the first two factors are the most important. I will begin with point (a). The *questions* that early experimental psychology tried to answer had their origin mainly in philosophical discussions within the broader 'academic public'; e.g., the relationship between experiences in the consciousness (mind), and physical stimuli (body). As the sociology of psychological knowledge (Buss, 1979) shows, the majority of the problems modern psychology has dealt with since the turn of the century have a social background. Practice and its paradigms, of course, are guided from the outset by the questions that engage specific clients and society at large. Topics like perception, memory, learning, and adjustment, however, have been studied not just out of intellectual curiosity, but just as well because of their relevance for the human problems a rapidly changing society faced. In this sense practical and laboratory paradigms are much more intertwined than most reviews of the history of psychology suggest. Of course the direct connection with practical problems may get lost in laboratory research. Pure research traditions have come about here, where new paradigms originated not from new external questions, but from the failure of an earlier paradigm to provide satisfactory answers (Kuhn's 'anomalies'). On the whole, however, pure research is regularly fed with extra-scientific questions which influence the direction of the investigations.

With respect to point (b), because the discipline itself could hardly provide the early psychologists with appropriate methods and theoretical conceptions, the 'tools' needed to attack the questions posed had, to a large extent, to be borrowed from other disciplines. Many psychologists used physics or physiology as the *model discipline* to which they looked for examples. Others took their inspiration from biology; yet others, from the humanities.

The inspiration by, and emulation of, model disciplines is not only characteristic of a young, beginning science; it can also be clearly recognized in present psychological thinking. Lachman et al. (1979) show that the analogies used in modern cognitive psychology, its concepts and language, its research methods, and its 'pretheoretical ideas' about man and the world, are often borrowed from other disciplines. The research traditions, defined above, can be seen as 'lines of research' or 'practice' which are inspired by a common model discipline. They serve as the intellectual background of broader 'families' of research and practical paradigms.

The intellectual appeal of specific disciplines as a model for other disciplines depends on the general intellectual climate in the culture of a given time. As the history of psychology shows, changes in the general climate had an influence on the rise and decline of research traditions that was greater than the influence of internal scientific progress and stagnation. As Vroon (this volume) shows, programs and paradigms are often abandoned without the occurrence of real anomalies, or without the availability of superior programs. Not infrequently, already abandoned theories are taken up at a later moment in a slightly modified form because the external general climate so dictates. There are similar dynamics in the other social sciences. That is, internal factors also are to a much lesser degree sufficient to explain the dynamics of history than in the natural sciences.

In Figure 1 I have visualized the concepts that are used in this approach to the dynamics of history. The intellectual and cultural climate in the discipline and in contemporary science in general are presented by the outer circle.

The dominance of a certain model discipline in this climate determines the character of the research tradition that prevails in psychology in a given period. The characters of the research paradigms and the practical paradigms that become current in the discipline and its professional practice depend in turn on the leading research tradition.

We call this approach multi-relational because the interplay of a variety of mutually dependent determinants rather than one single factor is used as an explanation of the course of history (e.g., the internal progression of scientific knowledge, or the external influence of technical-

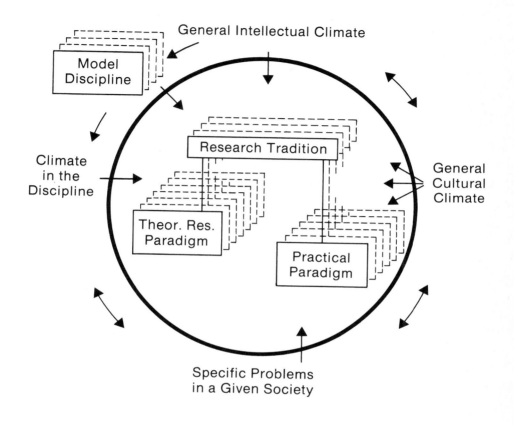

Fig. 1. Influence of model disciplines on historical development of psychological research and practice.

economical factors in society). This approach is discussed more fully in van Strien and Dehue (in press).

The Influence of External Problems and Model Disciplines in the History of Psychology

The importance of the factors specified in the preceding section first became apparent to us in our study of the history of psychology in the Netherlands. Just as in Germany, the first research tradition here, initiated by the empirist Heymans (1857-1930), was inspired by philosophical questions. The method of the natural sciences was seen as the

only way to get clear answers. In his later investigations on character ty-
pology Heymans (cited in Van der Werff, 1985) also tried to contribute
to the solution of the social problems of the time (van Strien, 1983).
When a client public presented itself after World War I, asking for professional advice about individual problems, the need for other, more holistic methods made itself felt. These methods were provided by the new
'Geisteswissenschaftliche' psychology which, in the cultural climate of
that time, was becoming the dominant research tradition. In the fifties,
when institutional decision making became predominant in practice,
empirical psychometric methods took the lead again in applied psychology. At the same time the international oriented research climate at the
universities fostered new lines of fundamental research that found their
theoretical and methodological inspiration again in the natural sciences
(see, for a brief historical sketch, van Strien, Takens, & De Wolff, in
press).

The influence of external problems and model disciplines is also apparent in school formation in psychology on an international scale. It is,
of course, in the context of this paper, only possible to illustrate this with
some examples. I will not dwell further on the research tradition in the
first nineteenth-century laboratories on which I have commented already.
Physics was, as we saw, the model discipline. For our purpose, however,
it is especially interesting to see what happened in the first decades of the
century when several competing programs were proclaimed in psychology.
This circumstance initiated a number of rivalling psychological traditions:
functionalism, behaviorism, psychoanalysis, Gestalt psychology, phenomenology, and so on.

Why did the old psychology of consciousness lose its appeal in this
period? Not primarily because of anomalies arising in paradigmatic research, but because of a change in the general cultural and intellectual
climate, and because of new problems posed to psychologists on the part
of an interested 'public' that gradually presented itself.

When we look at American *functionalism,* we see that the old
'structuralistic' thinking of the European intellectual culture was considered unsuitable as an approach to the problems of the dynamic melting
pot of the thriving, expansionistic culture in America in which problems
of learning and adaptation were the central problems (Danziger, 1979).
The *evolutionary biological inspiration* was more suited to fulfill the place
of model discipline. In this cultural climate there was a strong pressure
on psychology to contribute to the solution of the problems of education,
industry, and mental health. To cater to these problems, a new pragma-

tistic philosophy was developed that expressed the general intellectual climate of the New World. These new cultural and intellectual forces lead to a new research tradition, in which new research paradigms came to the fore: animal research (for example, the puzzle box of Thorndike), maze learning, and so on. By the same token also a number of practical paradigms arose, as in educational psychology (Dewey).

In the *programmatic behaviorism* of Watson this practical orientation was preserved. His emphasis on behavioral engineering was an expression of this orientation (Bakan, 1966, 1980; Bruder, 1982). On the other hand we find, with Watson and his followers, a strong concern to put psychology at last on the firm methodological basis of a rigorous natural science, and to gain scientific respectability in the eyes of the 'academic public' (Breger, 1969). The consequence of this striving was that the *natural sciences* regained their place as the model. In following the development of (neo-)behaviorism we see that this inspiration dominates in what Koch has named the 'age of theories.' The attempts to mould behavioristic thinking along the rigid prescriptions of logical empiricism also reflect this inspiration. This 'scientistic' climate has led to a growing distance between theory and practice.

Skinner and the other new applied behaviorists of the 1950's, 1960's, and 1970's, gave a new impetus to behaviorism and brought it again nearer to practice. New practical paradigms were developed: programmed instruction (teaching machines), behavior modification, behavior therapy, and behavioral assessment. In these new developments within behaviorism the physicalistic inspiration is superseded by the functionalistic biological inspiration.

Psychoanalysis also is characterized by a mixed inspiration. As a theoretical thinker and a pupil of Brücke, involved in the academic discussion on the explanation of mental phenomena and disturbances, Freud's ideas are moulded by the *materialistic climate* of 19th century medicine in Vienna. As a psychiatrist, however, working in a hypocritical culture, he presents himself as the hermeneutic interpreter of hidden meanings in the dreams and narrative accounts of his patients. Here the *historical and literary text-analysis* of the 'Geisteswissenschaften' serves as an example.

A similar analysis could be made of *Gestalt-psychology* and other holistic movements (see, for instance, Leichtman, 1979; Scheerer, 1985), and of *humanistic psychology* (see van Belle, 1980). The dynamic forces behind the divergence in psychological thinking and practice will, however, have become sufficiently clear in the preceding examples.

Implications for Theoretical Unification

What are the perspectives for theoretical unification in the light of our analysis of the dynamics of history? To get a clear picture, this question has to be analyzed on two levels: within the same tradition, and between different traditions.

Within the Same Research Tradition. Here there is a strong need for bridging concepts and theories that organize the results of paradigmatic research into a more coherent whole. This applies not only to theory-directed research, but also to the theory used in practical paradigms. As I have shown recently (van Strien, 1986) practical change-oriented thinking is guided by problem-directed theories. They are formulated on the specific level of categories of problems that are current in practice (e.g., work motivation, reading disabilities, minimal brain disfunctions, anorexia nervosa, phobias, and so on). Often these theories are nothing more than loosely formulated generalizations of practical experiences and rules of thumb in treatment. One could say that many of them have stayed too close to the direct questions posed to professional psychologists. In the course of practical experience answers are found, and routines of treatments that work are developed. Theoretically, however, they are formulated on an insufficiently reflected level. A science-based practice will only come into being when practical problem-oriented theories are linked with general 'nomological' theories, and with theories on the same level that are developed within the framework of related research-paradigms. The relation of the general and the problem-specific theories should, however, not be forced into the logical form of syllogistic deductions of the particular from the general. The general should be viewed primarily as a heuristic 'searchlight' in developing low-level theory, just as problem-oriented theory in its turn often has been a stimulus in the generation of general theory. When this mutual interaction materializes, the present gap between theory and practice will gradually be bridged.

The striving for unification within a research tradition does not mean that competing paradigms should be completely eliminated. A pluralistic approach, with elements of intellectual rivalry, can stimulate a more thorough search into all relevant aspects of the investigated problems, and save researchers from intellectual lazyness. A precondition, however, is that researchers who work along the lines of different paradigms should be aware of each other's work, and that a platform for theoretical discussion should exist. An example of this type of discussion is given by Staats (1985) in his endeavour to combine cognitive and behavioral approaches.

Unification Between Different Research Traditions. In this case there is much more difficulty. The divergence is not, as in experimental and in practical paradigms, the result of the diversity of problems which the psychologist tries to answer, but of fundamental differences in theoretical and methodological suppositions. Philosophers of science sometimes speak of different 'language games,' that make theories that are inspired by different model disciplines, and loaded with different cultural values, incommensurable.

An interesting attempt to bring perhaps not unity, but at least order into the approaches followed in the different traditions has been made by Sanders and van Rappard (1985). They call the mechanistic, the functional-biological and the humanistic-intentional mode of thinking different 'levels of structuring reality.' In the *mechanistic* approach physics is seen as the master-science. Just as in physics, qualitative complexity is reduced to quantifyable elementary variables between which lawful connections are sought. In the *functional-biological* approach, organic, molar patterns of behavior are studied in the light of their survival value in coping with the threats and challenges of the environment. In the *humanistic-intentional* approach man is seen as a being that is able to make symbolic representation of its environment, and to reflect on its own position in the world. In this approach, the hermeneutic mode of thinking that is typical of the humanities serves as the example. Of course, within different cultural climates each 'way of looking' has been developed in a different way (van Strien, 1985). Within the perspective of a given culture it should, however, become possible to develop a 'master model,' in which the approaches followed in the principal model disciplines are placed in an encompassing framework.

That the subject matter of psychology is studied from radically differing angles is not just a matter of historically and geographically diverging cultural climates. It is primarily a consequence of the special character of the subject matter itself: man as a material body, as a biological organism, and as an intentional cultural being. In different intellectual climates one side or the other side of man is stressed. Trying to bring unity in psychology, for instance by fanatically emulating the natural sciences, can occur only at the cost of neglecting essentials. Those who are looking for a 'Newton of the social sciences' who will bring this kind of unity, are reminded of the warning of Anthony Giddens (1976, p. 13) that they "are not only waiting for a train that won't arrive, they're in the wrong station altogether." I would like to conclude with paraphrasing a saying of Whitehead: "Seek simplicity - and distrust it!"

References

Bakan, D. (1966). Behaviorism and American urbanization. *Journal of the History of the Behavioral Sciences, 2*, 5-28.

Bakan, D. (1980). Politics and American psychology. In R. W. Rieber & K. Salzinger (Eds.), *The roots of American psychology: Historical influences and implications for the future.* New York: Academic Press.

Belle, H. A. van (1980). *Basic interest and therapeutic approach of Carl R. Rogers.* Burnaby, BC: Academic Press.

Breger, L. (1969). The ideology of behaviorism. In L. Breger (Ed.), *Clinical-cognitive psychology, models and integrations* (pp. 9-24). Englewood Cliffs, NJ: Prentice Hall.

Bruder, K. J. (1982). *Psychologie ohne Bewustsein. Die Geburt der behavioristischen Socialtechnologie.* Frankfurt: Suhrkamp.

Buss, A. R. (1975). The emerging field of the sociology of psychological knowledge. *American Psychologist, 30*, 988-1002.

Buss, A. R. (Ed.).(1979). *Psychology in social context.* New York: Irvington.

Danziger, K. (1979). The social origins of modern psychology. In A. R. Buss (Ed.), *Psychology in social context.* New York: Irvington.

Giddens, A. (1976). *New rules of sociological method.* London: Hutchinson.

Kuhn, T. S. (1962). *The structure of scientific revolutions.* Chicago: University of Chicago Press.

Kuhn, T. S. (1970). Reflections on my critics. In I. Lakatos & A. Musgrave (Eds.), *Criticism and the growth of knowledge.* London: Cambridge University Press.

Lachman, R., Lachman, J. L., & Butterfield, E. C. (1979). *Cognitive psychology and information processing.* New York: Halsted Press.

Laudan, L. (1977). *Progress and its problem.* Berkeley: University of California Press.

Leahey, T. H. (1980). *A history of psychology: Main currents of psychological thought.* Englewood Cliffs, NJ: Prentice Hall.

Leichtman, M. (1979). Gestalt theory and the revolt against positivism. In A. R. Buss (Ed.), *Psychology in social context.* New York: Irvington.

Masterman, M. (1970). The nature of a paradigm. In I. Lakatos & A. Musgrave (Eds.), *Criticism and the growth of knowledge.* London: Cambridge University Press.

Palermo, D. S. (1971). Is a scientific revolution taking place in psychology? *Science Studies, l*, 135-155.

Sanders, C., & Rappard, H. van (1985). Psychology and philosophy of science. In K. B. Madsen & L. P. Mos (Eds.), *Annals of Theoretical Psychology* (Vol. 3, pp. 219-278). New York: Plenum Press.

Scheerer, E. (1985). Organische Weltanschauung und Ganzheitspsychologie. In C. F. Graumann (Ed.), *Psychologie im Nationalsozialismus*. Berlin: Springer.

Scriven, M. (1969). Psychology without a paradigm. In L. Berger (Ed.), *Clinical-cognitive psychology*. Englewood Cliffs, NJ: Prentice-Hall.

Staats, A. W. (1983). *Psychology's crisis of disunity*. New York: Praeger.

Strien, P. J. van (1978). Paradigms in organizational research and practice. *Journal of Occupational Psychology, 51,* 291-300.

Strien, P. J. van (1982). In search of an emancipatory social psychology. In P. Stringer (Ed.), *Confronting Social Issues*. London: Academic Press.

Strien, P. J. van (1983). Heymans' objectieve heilsleer. In D. Draaisma, et al., *Gerard Heymans: objectiviteit in psychologie en filosofie*. Baarn: Het Wereldvenster.

Strien, P. J. van (1984). Psychology and its social legitimation. The case of the Netherlands. *Proceedings of the Second Meeting of Cheiron, Heidelberg 1983*. Leiden: Psychology Institute of Rijksuniversiteit.

Strien, P. J. van (1985). De mens is méér: niveaus van structurering en In L. K. A. Eisenga, et al., (Eds.) *Over de grenzen van de psychologie* (pp. 39-53). Lisse: Swets & Zeitlinger.

Strien, P. J. van (1986). *Praktijk als wetenschap. Methodologie van het sociaal-wetenschappelijk handelen*. Assen: Van Gorcum.

Strien, P. J. van, & Dehue, T. (in press). A multi-relational model of the historiography of psychology. *Proceedings of the Fourth Meeting of Cheiron, Paris*. Leiden: Psychology Institute of Rijksuniversiteit Leiden.

Strien, P. J. van, Takens, R. J., & De Wolff, C. J. (in press). Psychology in the Netherlands. In A. R. Gilgen & C. Gilgen (Eds.), *International handbook of psychology*. New York: Greenwood Press.

Warren, N. (1971). Is a scientific revolution taking place in psychology? Doubts and reservations. *Science Studies, 1,* 407-413.

Werff, J. J. van (1985). Heymans' temperamental dimensions in personality research. *Journal of Research in Personality, 19,* 279-287.

Current Issues in Theoretical Psychology
Wm J. Baker, M.E. Hyland, H. Van Rappard, A.W. Staats (Editors)
© Elsevier Science Publishers B.V. (North-Holland), 1987

ORDINAL PATTERN ANALYSIS: A METHOD FOR ASSESSING

THEORY-DATA FIT[1]

Warren Thorngate

Carleton University
Ottawa, Canada

SUMMARY: Statistical analyses can be classified into three general categories: descriptive analysis; inferential analysis; and analysis of fit. Almost all statistical procedures used by psychologists fall into the first two categories. Ironically, almost all statistical procedures useful for the assessment of psychological theories fall into the third. One such analysis of fit procedure, Ordinal Pattern Analysis, is outlined herein. Examples are provided to illustrate its use in assessing the predictive validity of theories addressed to changes in individuals over time.

The development of theory in psychology is often viewed as a complex interplay between conceptual, speculative activities and empirical, evaluative activities. This interplay is supposed to be governed by the rules and norms of science. One such rule or norm is that numbers should serve as the medium of exchange between theory and research. For most psychologists this implies that they must learn something about statistics, a task they generally view with fear, dread, or despair. The goal of most statistics courses in psychology is to develop skill in matching particular statisical procedures to idiosyncracies of measurements and research designs, and skills of interpreting the results of these procedures. The skills are somewhat unnatural, and are rarely learned without some degree of agony or intimidation. As a result, few psychologists are prepared or motivated to criticize the logic or rationality of their own statistical practice.

Yet criticism is long overdue. Statistical practice is not a neutral, unbiased or transparent means of evaluating the fit between theoretical predictions and empirical observations. On the contrary, as language can often influence perception and thought, statistical practice can strongly influence the development of theory by directing theoretical attention and

[1]Preparation of this manuscript was supported by a grant from the Faculty of Graduate Studies and Research, Carleton University, 1985.

constraining the forms of theoretical propositions. In this chapter I shall try to describe how the use of currently popular statistical procedures in psychology can retard the development of psychological theory. I shall then outline a new statistical procedure designed to overcome many of the constraints that current statistical practice imposes upon psychology's theoretical development.

The Evils of Statistical Practice

Let us begin with some fundamental considerations. There are at least three forms, modes, or flavours of statistical analysis. The first form may be termed *descriptive analysis*. It is designed to provide a caricature or summary of many numbers with fewer numbers. Descriptive analyses produce summary statistics such as the mean, median, standard deviation, range, or index of kurtosis. Several innovative methods of descriptive analysis have recently been developed (e.g., see Tukey, 1977). Yet, even though descriptive analyses are considered necessary and useful, psychologists rarely consider them sufficient for a proper account of data obtained. To complete the account, a second form of analysis is almost always employed.

This second form is usually called *inferential analysis.* It is designed to determine the chances that descriptive statistics from a sample of numbers are characteristic of a population of numbers from which the sample came. Inferential analyses produce statistics with such defining letters as *t, z, F, G,* or *H.* While these statistics may often be useful as descriptors, they are usually used to reference tables that convert their values to another statistic, *p,* which is then used to make inferences from sample to population.

Techniques of descriptive analysis and inferential analysis constitute the bulk of statistical procedures used by psychologists; indeed, most psychologists - save the few interested in mathematical modelling - know and use nothing else, and are unaware that a third form of analysis exists. This third form of statistical analysis may be termed *analysis of fit.* The purpose of an analysis of fit is to determine how well the predictions of theories or hypotheses are matched by relevant observations. Ideally, analyses of fit should provide readily interpretable, descriptive measures of the fit or distance between predictions and observations, and inferential statistics indicating the probability that values of the fit or distance measures would be obtained by chance. Alas, relatively little work has been done in statistics to develop cookbook, or off-the-shelf analysis of fit procedures (cf. Bush, 1963). As a result, most psychologists have been forced to employ adaptations of inferential analysis techniques for purposes of fitness analysis. In normal use, these adaptations lead psychologists to translate theoretical propositions into predictions of differences between means or proportions, and to test these predictions by gathering data in a manner compatible with the inferential statistical model employed, calculating values of $p(\alpha \mid H_0)$, and making decisions regarding the significance of the results.

Adaptations are rarely perfect, so it is not surprising that adaptations of sample-to-population inferential tests for the assessment of theory-data fit have necessitated several compromises in the manner by which psychologists develop and test their theories. Reactions to these compromises have resulted in debates over such issues as one-tailed vs. two-tailed tests, the logic of statistical inference, significance levels vs. variance explained, robustness and power-efficiency, the statistical appropriateness of repeated measure designs, and distortions of aggregation (e.g., see Bradley, 1968; Lieberman, 1971; Sidman, 1952; Thorngate, in press). These debates have been supplemented by discussions of some pernicious ways in which the statistical practices of psychologists influence and constrain their theoretical thinking (e.g., Blumer, 1956; Brunswik, 1956; Cronbach, 1975; London & Thorngate, 1981; Meehl, 1975; Newell, 1973; Thorngate, 1976). Behaviour, for example, is commonly assumed to be influenced by variables and residuals or by main effects, interactions and error in contrast to, say, meanings, habits, or content. Theories address themselves to differences in central tendency or location in contrast to differences in variability or dispersion. Theory-data fits are assessed by dichotomous statistical significance decisions, much like a game of '20-Questions.' Most importantly, because statistical rigour is not predicated upon theoretical rigour, elaborate and rigorous experiments are often undertaken to test very simple-minded and poorly developed *theories*. Statistical significance and experimental control thus become more important than theoretical development; "What?" questions drive out "Why?" questions; statistical tails wag theoretical dogs.

The statistical models psychologists have adapted to analyses of fit are themselves unimpeachable. It is only psychologists' misuse of them as fitness tests that creates the problems and constraints noted above. Many of these problems and constraints could be avoided by using statistical procedures developed specifically for the analysis of theory-data fit. The use of such procedures would, in principle, transform the statistical thinking and practice of psychologists. Hypothesis testing would become an extension of pattern recognition and analysis, rather than an exercise in mechanical induction and decision making (see Kanal, 1968; Kaufmann, 1975;

Thorngate, in press; Tukey, 1977). The central question of statistical analysis would no longer be concerned with the possibility of generalizing from sample to population, but with the possibility of generalizing from theory to data.

Within the last decade, a few statistically-inclined social scientists have attempted to develop methods of assessing theory-data fit that are suited to the nature of much theory and data generated in their disciplines. Baker and Derwing (1982), for example, have developed a means to assess the fit of theoretical classifications of subjects on the basis of similarities in response patterns. Hildebrand, Laing, and Rosenthal (1977) have shown how contingency tables can be analyzed for the relative frequency of predictive errors defined by various theories. The resulting descriptors of theory-data fit provide useful information about the capability of a theory to account for relevant data. Notably absent from these works are the kinds of significance tests that characterize most statistical practice in psychology. This is no oversight; such tests play only a small role in fitness analysis. However, their absence may account for the sad fact that these important techniques have not yet become popular in the psychology research literature.

The efforts of Baker and Derwing, Hildebrand, et al., are laudable, but they do not exhaust all possible procedures for the analysis of fit that may be useful to those who wish to test psychological conjectures. Most theories in psychology generate predictions about individuals, not about statistical aggregations of individuals. These predictions are almost always ordinal; they are stated as *greater than* or *less than* propositions, not point predictions of quantity or frequency. In addition, the measurements obtained to test these propositions can rarely be assumed to have more than an ordinal relation to the concept or quality assumed to be measured. As a result, there appears to be a need for analysis of fit procedures designed to assess the degree of correspondence to be found in the ordinal predictions of one or more theories or hypotheses, and the ordinal properties of relevant observations of single individuals. Ordinal Pattern Analysis has been developed to fill this need.

An Outline of Ordinal Pattern Analysis

Ordinal Pattern Analysis, or *OPA*, was inspired by a remarkable technique for coding the relations between the notes and names of musical tunes. As Denys Parsons (1975), the inventor of the technique, has shown, thousands of musical tunes can be distinguished by unique patterns of ordinal relations between the first few bars of their notes. These ordinal relations may be coded as a string of letters: 'H' appears in the string if one note is higher then the previous one; 'L' appears if one note is lower than the previous one; 'R' appears if one note is a repeat of the previous one. Consider, for example, *God Save the Queen* . The second note of this tune is a repeat of the first 'R'; the third note is higher than the second 'H'; the fourth note is lower than the third 'L'. If one continues such coding for the first 16 notes, the following string will result:

RHLHHHRHLLLHLLH = "God Save the Queen"

By way of comparison, consider another two codes:

HLLHLLLLHHLLRLH = "My Bonnie Lies Over the Ocean"

LHLLHHLLLHLHRLL = "Summertime"

Parsons collected over 10,000 of these codes for tunes and arranged them in alphabetical order. No two codes were the same. As a result, anyone who remembers one of the tunes and wishes to know its name can generate the appropriate code, then look it up in his directory.

The invention of Parsons does not itself provide a useful technique for assessing theory-data fit in psychology. However, it does demonstrate the discriminating capabilities of ordinal information, and points to a general strategy for measuring the distance between ordinal predictions and ordinal observations. This strategy is the foundation of OPA, and has been formally explicated elsewhere (Thorngate & Rodway, in press). Here I should like to outline OPA in a more didactic fashion, and shall thus present it by way of several examples.

Example 1: Index of Observed Fit

When people say they feel old, it does not mean they have ceased to be young, it means that nothing they do is new. The longer one lives, the more chances one has for life to become increasingly familiar. Cognition is replaced by recognition. Reminders fill the mind. Habits replace ideas. Repetition habituates emotion. We spend our lives attempting to adapt to our circumstances, or attempting to adapt these circumstances to ourselves. The more we succeed, the more predictable our lives become. To be well adjusted is to lead a life of no surprise. It is not surprising, therefore, that successful adjustment breeds boredom, and that in seeking an escape from boredom, we seek to become maladjusted.

Several interesting predictions may be derived from the above theoretical fragments. Some of these are relevant to my own work on the analysis of diaries. Consider, for example, the prediction that emotional reactions to experiences are attenuated as the experiences are repeated. People
who keep diaries often reveal their emotional reactions to events or experiences in several ways. One way is by the amount of information they record. Another is by the adjectives and adverbs they use to describe their
reactions. A 200 word diary entry describing in detail the writer's reactions
to viewing a play, and filled with such phrases as: absolutely wonderful,
utterly disgusting, temendously exciting, or a complete waste of time, is
likely to reflect a more extreme emotional reaction that a 20 word entry by
the same writer describing a play with terms such as: pleasant, interesting,
mildly amusing, or somewhat exciting. Thus, if the prediction about emotional attenuation and if this measurement assumption are correct, then we
should expect that diary entries made later in life should be shorter and
contain fewer emotional statements.

Between 1876 and 1882, Janet Hall (b. 1857) kept a diary of her life
in Ottawa, Canada. As an unmarried woman in her late teens and early
twenties, she often recorded her emotional reactions to daily events, as well
as the events themselves. Counts of the pages of a typed transcript of her
diary can serve as a simple index of the amount she wrote during each of
these years. Table 1 shows these page counts as well as the average number
of emotional expressions per page.

How well do our theoretical predictions match these observations?
To develop an index of fit, we begin by considering all possible pairs of
comparable observations. There are $(7 \times 6)/2 = 21$ such pairs for pages
$[(36, 30), (36, 26),..., (20, 14)]$, and $(7 \times 6)/2 = 21$ pairs for emotional
expressions $[(2.7, 2.0),..., (1.3, 1.8))]$. Because our theory makes predictions about strict inequalities, $(x > y)$ or $(x < y)$, we exclude all equal
data pairs, $(x = y)$, from tests of theory-data fit. The pairs that are left
comprise what is called the *Observed Ordinal Domain*, OOD, of a data set.
All 21 page-count pairs show a strict inequality, either $(x > y)$ or $(x <
y)$, so the OOD (pages) will include all of them. One of the
emotion-count pairs, $(1.3, 1.3)$, is equal, so only 20 of the 21
emotion-count pairs are included in the OOD (emotions). Our theory addresses itself to each of these $21 + 20$ pairs; in particular, it predicts that
for any two page counts, or any two emotion tallies, the earlier one will be
greater than the later one. Not all theories are this comprehensive. Later I
shall note how we may adjust fitness indices for the *scope* of predictions.

Table 1

Number of Pages and Emotional Expressions in
Janet Hall's Diaries

	Year						
	1876	1877	1878	1879	1880	1881	1882
Pages	36	30	26	24	18	20	14
Expressions/Page	2.7	2.0	2.2	1.3	1.0	1.3	1.8

Now we simply count the number of predicted orders that are matched by our observations. Each time we find a match, we add one to our count. Each time we find a mismatch, we subtract one from the count. We then divide the resulting total by the number of pairs we counted. The result is an *Index of Observed Fit* (IOF):

$$(1) \quad IOF = \frac{(\text{\# Matches - \# Mismatches})}{(\text{\# Matches + \# Mismatches})}$$

Like most indices of correlation, IOF ranges from +1.00 (a perfect fit) to -1.00 (a perfect misfit); tests for statistical *significance* of a fit/misfit are discussed below.

For page-counts, we find that 20 of the 21 pairs in OOD (pages) match our observations (e.g., (36 > 30), (36 > 26), ..., (20 > 14). One of the observed pairs does not: (18 < 20). Thus, using Equation 1, we calculate that:

IOF (page prediction) = (20 - 1)/(29 + 1) = +0.904.

For emotion-counts we find that 15 of the 20 pairs in OOD (emotions) match our observations (e.g., (2.7 > 2.0), (2.7 > 2.2),...., (1.3 > 1.0)). The remaining 5 pairs do not match: (2.0 < 2.2), (1.3 < 1.8), (1.0 < 1.3), (1.0 < 1.8), (1.3 < 1.8). Again using Equation 1, we calculate that:

IOF (emotion prediction) $= (15 - 5)/(15 + 5) = +0.500$.

How should these indices be interpreted? Both of them show that the observations of Janet Hall's diary display a moderate to strong corre-spondence with the predictions of our theory. One may thus feel at least moderately safe in concluding that the theory generalizes to some rough measures of Janet Hall's life between 1876 and 1892. Of course, other theories or hypotheses might also generate predictions about the same or-dinal domain that show equally good correspondences. Methods of com-paring the fits of competing hypotheses will be demonstrated in the next example.

To determine the chances that the obtained correspondences (IOFs) are coincidental, one may wish to deploy a test of statistical significance. Although I discourage this practice, experience informs me that psycholo-gists are most reluctant to break their significance test habits, so I shall demonstrate a randomization test procedure that may be applied to IOFs for habit maintenance. As with most randomization tests (e.g., see Brad-ley, 1968), our task is to determine what proportion of all possible data permutations will generate an IOF at least as large as the one obtained. In the case of the seven page-counts, one permutation will generate a perfect fit score: IOF $= +1.00$ when the seven counts in the first row of Table 1 are permuted as 36, 30, 26, 24, 20, 18, 14. Five more permutations will generate the next highest possible IOF $= +.904$. Two of these five per-mutations are (30, 36, 20, 26, 24, 20, 18, 14) and (36, 30, 26, 24, 18, 14, 20); a third is obviously the one shown in Table 1. All of the remaining permutations will yield lower IOFs. In total there are $7 \times 6 \times 5 \times \ldots \times 1 = 7!$ $= 5040$ possible permutations of the seven page-counts. Had all of them been equally likely to occur (the *null hypothesis*), then the chances of ob-taining an IOF of $+0.904$ or higher would be $(1+5)/5040 = 0.001$. Thus, in more popular parlance, the fit was significant at the 0.001 level.

One can generate the statistical significance level for IOF (emotions) in a similar manner, adjusting the relevant formulae for ties. At times, the adjustments and calculations will become quite tedious. To overcome the tedium, one may write very simple computer programmes to generate IOFs for all permutations (or a large subset of them), and check the IOF ob-tained with the resulting empirically derived IOF distribution. The ra-tionale and methods for doing this are discussed by Diaconis and Efron (1983).

Readers familiar with nonparametric statistics may recognize the IOF as a variant of Kendall's (1938) *Tau*. Indeed, in the example above,

IOF and Tau are virtually identical. They differ only because (1) IOF is used to test theory-data fit but Tau is used to test data-data fit, and (2) IOF excludes ties from its formula but Tau usually includes them as *half-fits*. The exclusion of ties in IOF calculations is somewhat arbitrary, and if they are relatively infrequent, a calculated IOF value should be close enough to Tau that significance tables for the latter may be used as 'quick and dirty' approximations to significance values for the former. However, the Tau statistic is calculated on complete sets of ordinal relations and, when a theory does not address itself to all possible pairs of observations (see the next example), the IOF of the theory will not be similar to Tau. At the risk of becoming too technical, one may view IOF as an extension of Tau for semi-orders.

Technicalities aside, a few general aspects of OPA should be noted from the first example. The OPA indices calculated for Janet Hall's data tell us only how well a few aspects of a few years of her life fit some theoretical predictions. If we wish to generalize the theory, as opposed to generalizing her data, it would obviously be desirable to do similar analyses on other years of her life, or to do similar analyses on diaries of the lives of others. No other diaries of Janet Hall exist, but thousands of other diaries do, and many of them should provide information necessary to test our theoretical propositions. If such analyses were performed, we could accumulate IOFs and look at the distribution of their values. It might happen that data from some diaries fit the theoretical predictions quite well; other diary data might show large misfits. It would then seem sagacious to determine what distinguished these two groups of diaries - the fits and the misfits - and limit or change the theory accordingly.

The results in Table 1 are aggregations of Janet Hall's within-year experiences. The aggregations were performed to simplify the example, and were not necessary for the analysis. Because the theory under assessment makes no explicit assumptions about the nature of measurements employed to test it, one should feel free to use any reasonable measure, and preferably several of them. For example, we could have employed the number of words per day for all $365 \times 7 = 2555$ days spanning her diary, and tested the theory against all $(2555 \times 2554)/2 = 3,262,735$ possible ordinal pairs. We also could have searched the diary for unfamiliar events (e.g., a trip to Maine, a trip to Niagra Falls) and familiar events (e.g., taking tea, going shopping, funerals) to count the emotional terms used to describe them. We would expect the outcomes of these measures to be related, hence their IOFs should be clustered more closely than chance would prescribe. But even visual inspection of the IOFs would provide some sense of the robustness of the predictions across measures, and perhaps direct us toward further theoretical refinement.

Example 2: Scope, Overlap, and Indices of Predictive Fit

It is usually dangerous to place much faith in a good fit between theoretical predictions and a small sample of observational or archival data. Though these sources of data are regularly used to test scientific propositions in astronomy, archeology, and geology, they tend to be a hotbed of counfounds in psychology, and a stimulant to those who enjoy watching correlational researchers squirm. The usual hedge against possible confounds is to test theories by subjecting them to increasingly complex experimental designs or statistical procedures in an attempt to control for everything imaginable. A less common, but arguably more effective, method of eliminating confounds is to search for special cases (observations or archives) that can clearly distinguish the predictions of alternative explanations. Such cases are usually hard to find. It is much easier to find cases for which alternate theories make some *common* predictions (e.g., theories T_1 & T_2 both predict that for observations x & y, x > y), some *opposite* predictions (e.g., T_1 predicts that x > y, T_2 predicts that x < y), and some *unique* predictions (T_1 predicts that w > x, T_2 predicts that y > z). To make use of these cases, it is desirable to develop indices of fit for the three classes of predictions, as well as indices of the proportion of data addressed by each theory. Ordinal Pattern Analysis can be easily extended to provide the indices.

To illustrate the extensions, consider the following statements:

T_1: Because certainty is the victim of experience, the older one becomes, the less extreme one's attitudes become;

T_2: Because old people become set in their ways, old people will show more extreme attitudes than young and middle aged people;

T_3: Because "The old forget, the young don't know", both old and young people will show more extreme attitudes than the middle aged.

These statements obviously are not derived from full-blown theories, but they can serve to direct our selection and analyses of relevant data, and serve as a basis of theoretical refinement. T_1 makes a prediction about attitude changes within individuals over time; it does not specify how much time, nor does it state which attitudes might become less extreme.

In the spirit of OPA we assume maximum generality until proven other-wise, and are thus free to assess the predictive validity of T_1 with any attitude data obtained from the same individuals on two or more occasions. If we do not find changes in extremity from one hour to the next, or changes in attitudes toward clothespins, we might add a minimum time or minimum relevance proviso to T_1. OPA indicators are useful for deciding when provisos should be added, and what the provisos should be. In this way one may develop a theory be successive instantiation. Of course, as provisos are added to a theory, both its elegance and domain of validity are reduced. An invalid theory may never be disproven, but it should eventually be crushed by its own provisional weight.

T_2 and T_3 make predictions about time-related attitude differences between individuals. Thus, tests of these theories should focus on people of different ages classified as young, old, and middle aged. These are fuzzy classifications, and neither T_2 nor T_3 as stated above serve to clarify their respective age ranges. We are therefore forced to make somewhat arbitrary decisions about these ranges just to test the theories, and to consider revising them for subsequent tests of theory-data fit. For the moment, I shall assume that young people are less than 30 years of age, middle aged people range in age from 30 to 59, and old people are those aged 60 and above (no offense intended).

Since people have a tendency to age, and thus could eventually be classified in all three age groups, one might argue that T_2 and T_3 should be tested on attitude data gathered from the same people over time, as well as people of different ages. It appears that acceptance of this argument is largely a matter of personal preference. To get on with the example, I shall accept it.

All three theories are addressed to extremities of attitudes, so we must find or invent a measure of attitude extremity in order to test them. One such measure might be obtained as follows: (1) ask people of different ages, or at different ages, to rate the extent of their agreement/disagreement with a standard set of statements about a variety of personal, social, economic, and political issues; (2) for each resulting set of ratings, caluculate its standard deviation as an index of extremity. The first prescription seems reasonable as a preliminary test of the theories, but the second does not. Someone who strongly agrees, or strongly disagrees, with every statement would show no rating variance - just as would someone who responds to every statement with "no opinion." Thus in order to give those with homogeneous extremities their due, we are better advised to use the absolute distance from some neutral point on our rating scale as the basis of our extremity measure. In principle, we could use the distance-from-neutral scores for each attitude item in our standard set as a separate OOD, and generate separate OPA tests for each item. Eventually, we may wish to do this in order to determine whether or not the three theories obtain differential support from specific kinds of attitude items. For now, however, I shall assume that only one overall extremity index is generated for each set of responses to chosen attitude items: the average extremity across responses.

Assume for the sake of illustration that we develop a standard set of 100 attitude items covering various topics, then ask several people to rate their agreement or disagreement to each item on the following scale:

Strongly Disagree -3 -2 -1   0 +1 +2 +3 Strongly Agree

where '0' indicates neutral or no opinion. Each time a repondent completes our 100-item questionnaire we calculate his/her average extremity score as noted above. Most respondents complete the questionnaire only once; a few, however, complete it several times during their lives. Finally, realizing that we too are aging and might perish before we publish, we sit down to examine the results. Some of these results (hypothetical, of course--I didn't have the time to do the study) appear in Table 2. Though the 'missing data' of Table 2 makes it look like a traditional research designer's nightmare, no user of OPA should fret. As long as at least one of our theories can be assessed by the data available, the data are quite acceptable for OPA.

We begin our data analysis with the results from Subject A. None of the six scores obtained from Subject A are tied, so the OOP_A contains all $(6 \times 5)/2 = 15$ pairs of scores. T_1 addresses itself to all of these pairs by predicting a monotonic decreasing relation between age and extremity. By contrast, T_2 and T_3 do not address themselves to all 15 pairs in OOP_A; T_2 only addresses itself to test pairs (5, 1), (5, 2), (5, 3), (5, 4), (6, 1), (6, 2), (6, 3), and (6, 4); T_3 only addresses itself to test pairs (1, 3), (1, 4), (2, 3), (2, 4), (5, 3), (5, 4), (6, 3), and (6, 4). In terms of OPA, we say that T_1 has greater *scope* than T_2 or T_3. More specifically, if we define POP_i as the predicted ordinal pattern of theory T_i and $\#POP_i$ as the number of elements (pairs) in POP_i, then the scope of T_i relative to the data collected from the jth subject is:

$$(2)\ \ Sc\ (T_i \mid OOP_j)\ =\ \frac{\#POP_i}{\#OOP_j}$$

Thus, we may calculate that:

Table 2

Mean Attitude Extremity Scores (and Ages at Testing)
for Ten Subjects

Subject	Test Number					
	1	2	3	4	5	6
A	1.57(22)	1.44(29)	1.16(40)	1.28(45)	1.35(65)	1.20(76)
B	0.82(18)	1.42(27)	1.31(41)	1.63(50)	1.75(54)	
C	1.26(38)	1.66(42)	1.37(53)	0.88(65)		
D	2.12(50)	1.98(60)	1.29(69)			
E	2.34(17)	1.67(23)				
F	2.21(19)					
G	1.83(28)					
H	1.60(42)					
I	1.78(45)					
J	0.52(87)					

$$Sc\ (T_1 | OOP_A) = 15/15 = 1.00;$$

$$Sc\ (T_2 | OOP_A) = 8/15 = 0.53;$$

$$Sc\ (T_3 | OOP_A) = 8/15 = 0.53.$$

The *Sc* value for any particular theory-data combination is an indicator of how much the theory 'sticks its neck out' in making predictions. This will become important when comparing the validities of, say, one theory that has a large scope and moderately good fit vs. a theory with small scope and very good fit.

Returning to Subject A, we may calculate the IOF values for each theory using subject A's data. $T_1 \rightarrow [(1 > 2), (1 > 3), (1 > 4), (1 > 5>, (1 > 6), (2 > 3), (2 > 4), (2 > 5), (2 > 6), (3 > 4), (3 > 5), (3 > 6), (4 > 5), (4 > 6), (5 > 6)]$. Of these predictions, 11 are matched by the results of Subject A, and 4 are not. Thus:

$$IOF\ (T_{1|A}) = (11-4)/(11+4) = +0.47.$$

T_2 makes the following 8 predictions: $T_2 \rightarrow [(5 > 1), (5 > 2), (5 > 3), (5 > 4), (6 > 1), (6 > 2), (6 > 3),(6 > 4)]$. Three of these predictions match A's data, so:

$$IOF\ (T_{2|A}) = (3-5)/(3+5) = -0.25$$

Finally, T_3 makes the following 8 predictions: $T_3 \rightarrow [(1 > 3), (1 > 4), (2 > 3), (2 > 4), (5 > 3), (5 > 4), (6 > 3), (6 > 4)]$. Seven of these predictions match A's data, so:

$$IOF\ (T_{3|A}) = (7-1)/(7+1) = +0.88.$$

Judging from the three IOFs, T_3 gives the best ordinal fit for Subject A. We might be tempted to conclude that T_3 is the most valid of the three theories. But the scope of T_3 is not especially large; it may give a good fit in its own domain, but it still fails to address almost half of the available data. To compensate for reduced scope in assessments of fit, we create a second fitness index, the *Index of Predictive Fit* (IPF), for each theory data-set pair by multiplying each IOF by its corresponding scope:

$$IPF\ (T_{i|j})\ x\ Sc\ (T_{i|j})$$

Thus:

$$IPF\ (T_{1|A}) = +0.47\ x\ 1.00 = +0.47$$

$$IPF\ (T_{2|A}) = -0.25\ x\ 0.53 = -0.13$$

$$IPF\ (T_{3|A}) = +0.88\ x\ 0.53 = +0.47$$

Comparisons of the IOF and the IPF values indicate that, while A's data match a greater proportion of predictions of T_3 than of T_1 or T_2 (cf. IOFs), both T_1 and T_3 are equally good at predicting A's data (cf. IPFs). T_2 seems to be out of contention; it does a somewhat worse job of predicting for A's data than does guessing (where the expected IOF and IPF would be 0.00). In order to further compare T_1 and T_3, it is useful to examine the fits of their common, opposing, and unique predictions. Both theories predict the following: T_1 and $T_3 \rightarrow [(1 > 3), (1 > 4), (2 > 3), (2 > 4)]$. All of these four predictions are matched in A's data, so:

$$IOF\ (T_{1|A}\ \&\ T_{3|A}) = (4-0)/(4+0) = +1.00$$

$$\text{IPF } (T_{1|A} \& T_{3|A}) = (4/15) \times +1.00 = +0.27$$

The opposing predictions of T_1 and T_3 are as follows: $T_1 \rightarrow [(3 > 5), (3 > 6), (4 > 5), (4 > 6)]$, $T_3 \rightarrow [(5 > 3), (6 > 3), (5 > 4), (6 > 4)]$. One of the T_1 predictions is matched by A's data; three of the T_3 predictions are so matched. Thus:

$$\text{IOF } (T_1 \& T'_3) = (1–3)/(1+3) = –0.50$$

$$\text{IPF } (T_1 \& T'_3) = (4/15) \times –0.50 = –0.13$$

$$\text{IOF } (T_3 \& T'_1) = (3–1)/(3+1) = +0.50$$

$$\text{IPF } (T_3 \& T'_1) = (4/15) \times +0.50 = +0.13$$

Finally, T_1 addresses itself to seven pairs of A's data that are not addressed by T_3. T_3 does not address itself to pairs that are unaddressed by T_1. The seven unique predictions of T_1 are: $T_1 \& {\sim}T_3 \rightarrow [(1 > 2), (1 > 5), (1 > 6), (2 > 5), (2 > 6), (3 > 4), (5 > 6)]$. Of these, six are matched by A's data, so:

$$\text{IOF } (T_1 \& {\sim}T_3) = (6–1)/(6+1) = +0.71$$

$$\text{IPF } (T_1 \& {\sim}T_3) = 7/15 \times +0.71 = +0.33$$

What are we to make of these comparative fitness statistics? The common predictions of T_1 and T_3 are well matched by A's data. When the predictions of T_1 and T_3 conflict, T_3 makes a few more correct predictions, but the theories do not often conflict so T_3's advantage here should probably not be given great weight. T_1 makes several predictions not addressed by T_3, and these predictions are rather well matched by A's data. In sum, I would judge that T_1 gives the best account of Subject A, followed by T_3. I would also judge T_2 as unsupported, if not invalidated, by A's data.

One subject down, nine to go. Space limitations prevent me from nine more detailed accounts of OPA in use, so I shall note a few additional aspects of OPA from the data in Table 2, then return to a more general discussion. Note that the scope of a theory can often be 0. T_2, for example, simply does not address itself to the data obtained by Subject B because B did not rate the attitude items when old. T_1 likewise does not address itself to Subjects F-J because they did not complete the attitude scale at least twice. These failings are not the fault of the theories, but of the data set obtained. Thus, limited scope cannot always be viewed as a theoretical limitation (of course, sometimes it can). A theory predicting only that 'a short male between 29 and 31 years of age, with less than two years of university education, and asked to respond to questionnaire items within 24 hours of a personally traumatic experience' will have more extreme attitudes than 'a tall female between 17 and 20 years old, with more than 5 years of university, and no recent traumatic experiences' cannot be considered to have great scope regardless of the data set used to test it. There will probably always be some trade-off between generality and accuracy (Thorngate, 1976). The scope and fitness indices of OPA can be used to measure generality and accuracy, but they cannot dictate a scientific tradition for determining which is more important.

Recall that T_2 and T_3 can generate predictions about extremity scores between subjects as well as within, so we are free to test their predictions between the rows of Table 2 as well as within them. To illustrate, the entire set of predictions that can be made by T_2 between and within subjects would appear as: Predicted $T_{2|A-J} \rightarrow$ [(A5, A6, C4, D2, D3, and J1) > (A1, A2, A3, A4, B1, B2, B3, B4, B5, C1, C2, C3, D1, E1, E2, F1, G1, H1, and I1)]. T_2 thus addresses itself to (6 x9) = 114 of the (25 x 24)/2 = 300 possible pairs of extremity scores in Table 2, so:

$$Sc\ (T_{2|A-J}) = 114/300 = 0.38$$

Only 27 of the 114 predictions of T_2 are matched by the data in Table 2. As a result:

$$IOF\ (T_{2|A-J}) = (27-87)/(27+87) = -0.53$$

$$IPF\ (T_{2|A-J}) = 0.38 \times -0.53 = -0.20$$

So far we have not resorted to tests of significance in assessing the relative merits of T_1 vs. T_3. Those who desire mental prosthetics to help with such assessements will be pleased to know that it is usually possible to devise or adapt some significance test for the job. For example, a randomization test may be devised to determine the chances that IOF $(T_{2|A-J}) = -0.53$ is significantly less than zero. With more *regular* data (e.g., six scores from each of the 10 subjects in Table 2 - two in each of the three age categories - one can generate a column of fitness scores for each theory, then perform an ANOVA on these columns to see if their averages are significantly different. Alternatively, one can collect another

set of data and try the theories again. I highly recommend this alternative.

Finally, note that T_1, T_2, and T_3 are by no means exhaustive of all
possible explanations of the data obtained. There are, for example, several different explanations of an attenuation in attitude extremity that
make the same predictions as T_1. Included are test-fatigue or
test-boredom, changes in subject-experimenter relationships, growing dis-
interest in attitude items, and other uninspiring methodological flaws.
Again, judicious selection of cases may help to eliminate many of these
alternative explanations, or eliminate T_1. Remember that OPA cannot
turn lead into gold. It can only indicate how ordered the patterns are that
one views through various theoretical glasses.

Conclusions

The two examples above demonstrate some of the ways in which
OPA can be employed to examine theory-data fit. Extensions of OPA allow for analyses of ordered differences (e.g., changes in attitude extremity will be greater when young than when old), analyses of stimulus or response contingent predictions (e.g., arguments will temporarily increase
attitude extremity, but eventually reduce it below its original value), and
analyses of predictions about frequency tables (e.g., most young men will
show greater than average attitude extremity, and most young women will
show less than average attitude extremity; the reverse will be true for old
men and women). In addition, it is possible to employ OPA indices as
distance measures for use in classifying subjects according to their degree
of correspondence with predictions from various theories. Used in this
manner, OPA may be viewed as a special case of Response Coincidence
Analysis (Baker & Derwing, 1982). Discussions of these OPA extensions
can be found in Thorngate and Rodway (in press).

Ordinal Pattern Analysis is not yet fully developed; its possible
uses, extensions, and limitations have not yet been fully explored. Further developments of OPA are in part predicated on its use, and there is
some reason to suspect that its use will never be common. Hundreds of
statistical procedures now exist, and all must compete for the limited attention of those who could make use of them. Proper use of OPA requires a radical reorientation in thinking about the role of statistics in research. OPA places heavy demands on theoretical explication and deriva-
tion. It does not provide formal rules for mechanical (objective?) assessments of theory-data fit. OPA has little to offer researchers who wish to
develop empirical generalizations from empirical samples, uncover empir-

ical regularities, or discover explanations in observations; these researchers are best advised to pay attention to more traditional statistical techniques. But for psychologists of more rationalist persuasion, for those who wish to employ statistics in the service of theories rather than methods or designs, Ordinal Pattern Analysis is worthy of serious consideration.

References

Baker, W., & Derwing, B. (1982). Response coincidence analysis as evidence for language acquisition strategies. *Applied Psycholinguistics, 3,* 193-221.

Blumer, H. ( ). Sociological analysis and the "variable." *American Sociological Review, 21,* 683-690.

Bradley, J. (1968). *Distribution free statistical tests.* Englewood Cliffs, NJ: Prentice Hall.

Brunswik, E. (1956). *Perception and the representative design of psychological experiments.* Berkeley: University of California Press.

Bush, R. (1963). Estimation and evaluation. In R. Luce, R. Bush, & E. Galanter (Eds.), *Handbook of mathematical psychology* (Vol. 1, pp. 429-469). New York: Wiley.

Cronbach, L. (1975). Beyond the two disciplines of scientific psychology. *American Psychologist, 30,* 116-127.

Diaconis, P., & Efron, B. (1983, May). Computer intensive methods in statistics. *Scientific American,* 116-130.

Hildebrand, D., Laing, J., & Rosenthal, H. (1977). *Prediction analysis of cross classifications.* New York: Wiley.

Kanal, L. (Ed.). (1968). *Pattern recognition.* Washington, DC: Thompson.

Kaufmann, A. (1975). *Introduction to the theory of fuzzy subsets.* New York: Academic Press.

Kendall, M. (1938). A new measure of rank correlation. *Biometrika, 30,* 81-93.

Lieberman, B. (Ed.). (1971). *Contemporary problems in statistics.* Oxford: Oxford University Press.

London, I., & Thorngate, W. (1981). Divergent amplification and social behavior: Some methodological considerations. *Psychological Reports, 48,* 203-228.

Meehl, P. (1978). Theoretical risks and tabular asterisks: Sir Karl, Sir Ronald, and the slow progress of soft psychology. *Journal of Consulting and Clinical Psychology, 46,* 806-834.

Newell, A. (1973). You can't play 20-Questions with nature and win. In W. Chase (Ed.), *Visual information processing* (pp. 283-308). New York: Academic Press.

Parsons, D. (1975). *Directory of tunes and musical themes.* Cambridge: S. Brown.

Sidman, M. (1952). A note on functional relations obtained from group data. *Psychological Bulletin, 49,* 263-269.

Thorngate, W. (1976). Possible limits on a science of social behaviour. In L. Strickland, F. Aboud, & K. Gergen (Eds.), *Social psychology in transition* (pp. 121-139). New York: Plenum.

Thorngate, W. (in press). The production, detection and explanation of behavioural patterns. In J. Valsiner (Ed.), *The individual subject in scientific psychology.* New York: Plenum.

Thorngate, W., & Rodway, B. (in press). Ordinal pattern analysis: A strategy for assessing hypotheses about individuals. In J. Valsiner (Ed.), *The individual subject in scientific psychology.* New York: Plenum.

Tukey, J. (1977). *Exploratory data analysis.* Reading, MA: Addison-Wesley.

Current Issues in Theoretical Psychology
Wm J. Baker, M.E. Hyland, H. Van Rappard, A.W. Staats (Editors)
© Elsevier Science Publishers B.V. (North-Holland), 1987

INTENTIONALITY, MEANING, AND EVOLUTION

Charles W. Tolman

University of Victoria
Victoria, British Columbia, Canada

SUMMARY: According to materialist philosophy, the mental is an attribute of an ultimately physical system. It is not a necessary consequence
of materialism, however, that the mental be reducible to, i.e., exhaustively explained by, the physics of that system. Nonreductive materialism
recognizes that systems evolve and, in so doing, produce new levels of attributes which require new principles for their understanding and explanation. The mental, or psychosocial, is undoubtedly such a level. In
dealing with attributional levels, the theorist is confronted with a dual
task. First, the distinguishing features of the level must be identified;
second, an account must be sought of the evolution of those features.
The present paper is to be understood in this context. Following Brentano it identifies intentionality as a distinguishing feature of the mental
and then, with the aid of a materialist theory of mental evolution, seeks
to clarify its nature through an account of its probable evolution.

Brentano on the Physical and the Mental

"All the data of our consciousness," wrote Franz Brentano (1973,
p. 77), "are divided into two great classes - the class of physical and the
class of mental phenomena." His meaning is illustrated by the following
examples:

> Every idea or presentation which we acquire either through
> sense perception or imagination is an example of a mental
> phenomenon. By presentation I do not mean that which is
> presented, but rather the act of presentation. Thus, hear-
> ing a sound, seeing a colored object, feeling warmth or
> cold, as well as similar states of imagination are examples
> of what I mean by this term. I also mean by it the think-
> ing of a general concept....Furthermore, every judgement,
> every recollection, every expectation, every inference, every
> conviction or opinion, every doubt, is a mental
> phenomenon....
>
> Examples of physical phenomena, on the other

hand, are of a color, a figure, a landscape which I sense;
as well as similar images which appear in the imagination.
(Brentano, 1973, pp. 78-80)

Brentano identified three characteristics of the mental which distinguished it from the physical. Of these, intentionality was the most important.

Intentionality of the Mental

In a well-known passage, Brentano described intentionality as follows:

Every mental phenomenon is characterized by what the
Scholastics of the Middle Ages called the intentional (or
mental) inexistence of an object, and what we might call,
though not wholly unambiguously, reference to a content,
direction toward an object (which is not to be understood
here as meaning a thing), or immanent objectivity. Every
mental phenomenon includes something as object within
itself, although they do not all do so in the same way. In
presentation something is presented, in judgement something is affirmed or denied, in love loved, in hate hated, in
desire desired and so on. (Brentano, 1973, p. 88)

Intentionality can be viewed as the property of "aboutness." Owen
Flanagan(1984, p. 29) has put it like this: "...We have beliefs about what
it's like on the top of Mt. Everest, but the top of Mt. Everest isn't about
anything. We have hopes about the quality of our dinner wine, but our
dinner wine isn't about anything... ."

The Ontological Thesis

Roderick Chisholm has pointed out that Brentano's doctrine of intentionality or "intentional inexistence" contains two distinct theses. The
first is the one obviously implied by Brentano's consideration of it in the
first place, namely that reference to an object distinguishes mental from
physical phenomena. This Chisholm calls the "psychological" thesis.
(Chisholm, 1967)

The second thesis is more problematic and deals with the status of
the intentional object. This Chisholm (1967) calls the "ontological" thesis. If someone thinks, say, of a unicorn, what, precisely, is the nature

of the object? According to Chisholm:

> It cannot be an actual unicorn, since there are no unicorns. According to the doctrine of intentional inexistence, the object of the thought about a unicorn *is* a unicorn, but a unicorn with a mode of being (intentional inexistence, immanent objectivity, or existence in the understanding) that is short of actuality but more than nothingness and that, according to most versions of the doctrine, lasts for just the length of time that the unicorn is thought about. (Chisholm, 1967, p. 201)

Three moments appear to be distinguishable in Brentano's ontology: the mental act itself, the intentional or mental object, and the actual thing. The object appears to have been understood as having reference to the thing. This means that when one thinks of a horse, we are not speaking of the actual horse, but of a contemplated horse. This would also be true of perception.

The implied Kantian dualism of thing-as-known and thing-in-itself is one that Brentano explicitly opposed, so it is not surprising that in later writings he rejected the ontological thesis. This he did by rejecting the referential character of the intentional object and by claiming that the distinction between the object and the thing is linguistic rather than ontological. In 1905, he had the following to say:

> ...I allowed myself the term "immanent object," in order to say, not that the object exists, but that it *is* an object whether or not there is anything that corresponds to it. Its *being* an object, however, is merely the linguistic correlate of the person experiencing *having* it as object, i.e., his thinking of it in his experience. (Brentano, 1966, p.78)

Mohanty summarizes this later view as follows:

> ...the word 'immanent' (or 'intentional') is used in order to say that there is an *object,* without implying any further that the object exists whether within or without the mind. Mental existence of the object has been rejected, extra-mental existence is irrelevant and is not entailed by the fact of being an object. (Mohanty, 1972, p. 7)

This maneuver of Brentano's, as well as more recent linguistic accounts of intentionality (e.g., Chisholm, 1967), while useful and informative, must surely be seen less as a solution than as an evasion of the ontological problem. That problem remains. The mountain exists and that existence cannot be ignored if the climber is to plan a successful ascent. The act of thinking out the best route exists and it has an object which both is, and is not, the mountain. The status of the intentional object is not clarified or solved by appeal to linguistic usage alone (though it will undoubtedly be part of the solution). Thus my intent here is to revive the ontological thesis as a real problem to be confronted by other forms of analysis than the purely linguistic. Before proceeding to an alternative account of the ontological status of the intentional object, however, it will be useful to examine the particular reasons why it represented such a difficult problem for Brentano.

Epistemological Problems

Brentano frequently wrote in a manner such as to suggest that he was a phenomenalist. As just one example, he advised the reader that: "... we will nevertheless make no mistake if in general we deny to physical phenomena any existence other than intentional existence." (Brentano, 1973, p. 94). We have already noted that the mind-independent thing does not figure into his analysis, indeed it is explicitly regarded as irrelevant (Rappard, 1979, p. 183, note 156). Elsewhere he argued that "apart from ourselves, there is no immediately evident knowledge of anything at all, 'nur Selbstwahrnehmungen sind evident'" (quoted in Rappard, 1979, p. 117) and, understanding *Wahrnehmung* literally as *Wahr-nehmung* (taking-for-real), Brentano claimed that "mental phenomena are those phenomena which alone can be perceived in the strict sense of the word" (Brentano, 1973, p. 9). A phenomenalism dangerously bordering on solipsism would appear to be lurking here not far beneath the surface.

Yet Oskar Kraus (Brentano, 1973, p. 94, note 16) reminds us that such a conclusion would be "completely mistaken." "Brentano," Kraus maintains, "was always phenomenalism's most determined opponent." The assertion that Brentano was in fact a realist would not be hard to document: It was his explicitly acknowledged understanding of himself. But his realism was an *indirect* realism, not unlike that of John Locke who held that we cannot know external bodies directly, but only indirectly by means of the impressions those bodies make upon our senses (Locke, 1959, Bk II, Ch. IX). He is therefore plagued with all the thorny problems of that position. He rejected the skepticism of David Hume and Alexander Bain, yet fell back on the weakest of all possible arguments for his realism, the observation that "the belief in the real existence of physical phenomena outside our presentation ...(has)... achieved the most general dissemination, been maintained with the utmost tenacity, and, indeed been shared for a long time by the most outstanding thinkers" (Brentano, 1973, p. 93). Oskar Kraus appears to be fully justified in labeling Brentano's realism as "blind" (Brentano, 1973, p. 94).

This Lockean indirect realism with its latent, though disavowed, phenomenalism in Brentano's thought is one source of the difficulty in resolving the problem of the status of the intentional object. The specific nature of the difficulty is revealed by an examination of the theory of perception that is part and parcel of this position, namely representationalism. Brentano could treat the presumed actual thing as epistemologically insignificant because it was not what formed, or could even possibly form, the object of a mental act. Only the representation of the thing was important. This meant for Brentano that there could be no essential difference between the object of perception and the object of cognition, and this is evidenced throughout the *Psychologie,* in which cognitive and perceptual terms are constantly interchanged. For instance, the reflexive apprehension of mental acts was called inner perception; it was also called inner consciousness and inner cognition. There are many passages in which the terms perception and cognition were alternated in virtually the "same breath" (e.g., Brentano, 1973, p. 160). In addition, inner perception was regarded as the truest perception. Any theory that thus disables itself in making the distinction between the thing-as-perceived and the thing-as-thought-about is crippled from the beginning, and must, to retain any credibility at all, escape into something like linguistic analysis. It will, however, never resolve the ontological problem, never really clarify the status of the object of mental acts like thinking.

Methodological Problems

A second source of difficulty for Brentano is methodological. Brentano began his analysis in typical idealist fashion, i.e., with the subject, and then moved outward through the object to the thing. The problem is that the analysis can proceed up to the so-called image or sensation of reality, but is utterly unable to penetrate to reality itself. The abstraction of reality is confronted before that from which the abstraction has been made, and we are then required somehow to derive or deduce the thing from its abstraction. History and logic clearly show that this is not possible. Thus approached, the abstraction, the image, the sensation become impenetrable barriers.

Surely three hundred years of philosophical failures - stemming from this method, based on the Cartesian certainty of self, of proceeding from the inside toward the outside - provide compelling proof of its incorrectness. Recent scientific psychology has provided overwhelming evidence of the falseness of the Cartesian thesis, from Freud's demonstration of the intentional unconscious to more recent demonstrations of dramatic introspectional failures in cognitive psychological investigations.[1] What we have learned about conscious and unconscious cognitive processes in the last three-quarters of a century has come largely from the application of procedures adapted from those already proved successful in the development of our knowledge of external physical things. In addition, the history of scientific development is well known to have begun with the physical sciences. This was followed in an apparently orderly, logically necessary way by the biological sciences, and only then by the social and psychological sciences.

The Materialist Approach to Intentionality

An alternative to the idealist Cartesian methodology is to proceed in the opposite direction. Descartes was right to demand that we begin with that which is most certain. He was mistaken to think that to be the *subject* of thought. Certainty begins with the things around us, and only gradually moves inward as our understanding of things increases. In the quest for clarification of the intentional object an important instance of the application of this alternative, materialist methodology, is that of the ecological theory of perception with its direct realist epistemology. The most notable contributor to this line of development was, of course, James Gibson (e.g., 1966).

Gibson and the Object of Perception

Gibson's methodological strategy has been characterized by the phrase, "what, how, who," which stresses its point of departure in the object and subsequent movement toward the subject. As Michaels and Carello (1981, p. 157) have expressed it: "...an explanation of the richness with which animals (human and otherwise) know their environments begins with the information to perceptual systems." According to the Gibsonian ecological analysis this information is energy structured by ob-

---

[1] I have in mind here a number of recent investigations showing that people do not know or are mistaken about how cognitive functions are performed and even about the contents of their cognitions. A brief discussion of some of these findings and their significance can be found in Flanagan (1984, pp. 192-198).

jects. This means that the analysis begins with a study of what Gibson would call the "animal-relevant" physics of objects, i.e., the ways in which objects, through their structural and transformational invariants, structure energy so as to inform animals about that which is ecologically important to them.

For Gibson the physics of objects cannot be taken as independent of considerations of the animal. The two form a unity in an animal-environment system which is evolutionarily based. According to Michaels and Carello:

> Ecological theories not only assume that organisms *exist in* a rich sea of information about their environments, but also that they *evolved in* a rich sea of information. Consequently it is supposed that the structure and function of the perceptual systems have become tailored to the available information. (1981, p. 15)

This means that the investigations of the "what" of perception has a second part, which Gibson calls "affordances," i.e., the ecological significance of physical invariances for particular animals. In short, the object within the animal-environment system must be understood both "in-itself" and "for-the-subject."

There are two additional points to be made here. First, the ecological theorist claims that the object of perceiving a horse is the horse, i.e., the actual, physical, mind-independently existing animal, not Brentano's contemplated horse.

A second point should be made about the object in traditional theories of perception. Their emphasis on the "how" of perception must presuppose something of the "what." Understanding of the "what" has been based, however, on what appears to be given or present in the receptor organs, e.g., retinal patterns, which are, in turn, taken to be correlated with the abstract results of traditional physical analysis, such as wave lengths and amplitudes. The end result is an impoverished representation of the world, the full richness of which must be restored (or, according to some accounts, invented) by constructive processes. The direct realism of the ecological theory sets itself off sharply against this indirect realism (and the phenomenalism into which it not infrequently degenerates). For the former the object of perception is the actual horse with all its informational richness. Nothing needs to be restored or constructed. One enormous advantage of the ecological theory of the object

of perception is that it provides the necessary background for a successful
clarification of the object of cognition.

Leont'ev and the Object of Cognition

A. N. Leont'ev's general methodology was the same as Gibson's,
but his treatment of cognition was more completely developed. His analysis of the object of cognition began with the object of perception.
When we perceive an object like a hammer, we are dealing with more
than just the physical energy which this object structures for us. It is not
a mere object but, as Gibson would say, it is an "affordance." We perceive the hammer as a "hammer." We know what it is, how it is used,
indeed, how to use it. As Leont'ev has expressed it:

> ...conscious reflection of reality is not just sensory exper-
> ience of it. Even simple perception of an object is reflec-
> tion of it not only as possessing form, colour, etc., but at
> the same time having a certain objective, stable signifi-
> cance as, for example, as food, as a tool, etc. (Leont'ev,
> 1981, p. 218)

It is this significance or meaning, which is present in perception and
which is detachable from the object as such, that is the principle object
of thought. Leont'ev speaks of meaning as "that which is objectively revealed in an object or phenomenon, i.e., in a system of objective associations, relations, and interactions" (1981, p. 225). The concept is sufficiently important to the theory to warrant an extended quotation:

> Meaning [writes Leont'ev] is the generalization of reality
> that is crystallized and fixed in its sensuous vehicle, i.e.,
> normally in a word or a word combination. This is the
> ideal, mental form of the crystallization of mankind's so-
> cial experience and social practice. The range of a given
> society's ideas, science, and language exists as a system of
> corresponding meanings. Meaning thus belongs primarily
> to the world of objective, historical phenomena and that
> must be our starting point.
>
> Meaning, however, also exists as a fact of the individu-
> al consciousness. Man perceives the world and thinks
> about it as a social, historical entity; he is armed and at
> the same time limited by the ideas and knowledge of his
> time and his society. The wealth of his personal

experience....He assimilates the experience of preceding
generations of people in the course of his life; that happens precisely in the form of his mastering of meanings
and to the extent that he assimilates them. Meaning is
thus the form in which the individual man assimilates generalized and reflected human experience. (Leont'ev, 1981,
p. 226)

Implications for Brentano's Thesis

It is clear that both Gibson and Leont'ev agree that perception is
intentional in the sense that it must take an object. It is less clear that
they would agree with Brentano's criterion of inexistence in as much as
both assert a mind-independent existence of the object as such. But, as
we have seen, Gibson and Leont'ev both insist that an essential moment
in the process or act of perception is the object-for-the-perceiver. This
is expressed in the "affordance" of Gibson and in the "meaning" of
Leont'ev. These quite unambiguously "inexist" in the act of perception
considered within the context of animal-environment system. And since,
according to Leont'ev, it is meaning that is the object of thought, meaning clearly inexists in the intentional act of thinking. Thus both Gibson
and Leont'ev can be understood as offering confirmation and further development of the fundamental truth of Brentano's thesis.

Leont'ev and the Evolution of Consciousness

As Chisholm has remarked: "The problem for the proponent of ...
this thesis is not so much that of showing that mental phenomena *are* intentional as it is that of showing that physical phenomena are *not* intentional" (1967, p. 203). Certainly the recognition that all things are essentially related to something else, i.e., do not exist in isolation, would seem
to blur the distinctiveness of intentionality as relation to an object. An
evolutionary account can help to clarify this issue.

According to Leont'ev, human consciousness, which we have seen
to be distinctly intentional in Brentano's sense, is the end result of a
series of evolutionary developments beginning in the activity of physical
matter. In the reciprocal action of two inorganic bodies it is impossible to
specify which is acting on the other and the result of the action is such
that each body, if not immediately annihilated and converted into another
body, will have been moved toward that end. The only way for an inorganic body to be preserved is to remain inactive.

With the evolution of organic bodies, the situation is qualitatively changed. It now becomes quite clear which of the two bodies is acting upon the other. The normal result of the interaction is the annihilation of the body acted upon and the preservation of the acting body. Indeed the organic body is of such a nature that it must interact if it is to be preserved. The emergence of this essential asymmetry is the origin of the subject-object relationship, and thus also of intentionality.

From this point onward, the evolutionary sequence can usefully be viewed as an evolution of the "object content" of activity. The most primitive organisms are active with respect to the simple physical or chemical properties of things which are of direct vital significance for them. A more advanced stage is achieved when the organism becomes active with respect to relations among properties. This arises with primitive locomotory capacity and results in the ability to use properties that have no direct vital significance as signals for those which do. Daphnia, for example, have evolved responses to light owing to its stable relation to that animal's food source.

In the next stage relations among properties merge into distinct things. This allows the development of a new activity component that Leont'ev calls an operation, a form of activity directed at the conditions in which the object of activity is found, as distinct from the object itself. This is possible because the conditions, such as an obstacle, are perceived as separate from the object, i.e., they are distinct things. As a result the animal develops a repertoire of operations within its object-oriented activity.

The highest subhuman development is found in the apes which display a broad and rapid transfer of operations across activities, accompanied by a highly differentiated object-content which is that of integral situations, complexes of things and their relations. All of this entails an important development in the structure of the animal's activity. Operations are easily transferred because they have become distinct structures which Leont'ev now calls actions. They have acquired many of the qualities of object-activity itself, e.g., their conditions emerge as distinct goals, although they remain components of that activity. Operations, as such, now are directed at the specific conditions of the goal-oriented action. The most familiar example is that of Köhler's chimpanzees who used sticks to rake in a banana. The activity of the apes organized around the food object has a distinct two-phase structure. The first is a preparatory action directed at the stick, the second is a consummatory action directed at the banana. It is the essence of animal intellect, or problem solving ability, that activity can be organized around an intermediate object or goal independently of the final motivating object. That is, the development of a distinct preparatory phase is key to problem-solving, use of instruments, and the comprehension of an integral situation. With this the groundwork has been laid for a distinctly human conscious, intentional activity.

Emergence of Meaning in Human Activity

What marks the transition to human activity is, according to Leont'ev, the "exarticulation" of separate actions within object-oriented activity by means of a social division of labour. He uses the example of a primitive hunt to illustrate this. The focus of the example is a "beater," whose job it is to frighten a herd of animals, sending them toward others who will make the kill. This is homologous with the preparatory action or phase in the example of Köhler's apes, but is, at the same time, significantly different. For one thing, the action of frightening the game has absolutely no biological sense, and, second, the consummatory phase is completed by other individuals. What binds the phases together for the chimpanzee is the physical situation. What holds the phases together for the primitive hunters is social relations. What makes this possible? According to Leont'ev:

> For man to take on the function of a beater it is necessary for his actions to have a relation that connects their result with the outcome of the collective activity; it is for this relation to be subjectively reflected by him so that it becomes "existent for him;" it is necessary in other words for the sense of his action to be revealed to him, to be comprehended by him. Consciousness of the sense of an action also comes about in the form of reflection of its object as a conscious goal. (1981, pp. 213-214)

In short, the beater must be conscious of the *meaning* of his own activity, i.e., of its location within the "system of objective associations, relations, and interactions" (Leont'ev, 1981, p. 225).

With the emergence of meaning itself as object, it becomes possible to think, to plan, to invent, and to create. A new form of evolution, cultural evolution or history, becomes possible and eventually transcends the limits of the merely biological.

Summary

Brentano was undoubtedly correct to assert intentionality as a distinguishing attribute of the mental, but his theory of intentionality was
unsatisfactory in a number of ways. Many of its difficulties were traced
here to a latently phenomenalist representationalist theory of perception
and to an idealist methodology. It was argued that a materialist methodology with a direct realist theory of perception overcomes the difficulties
of Brentano's theory. The materialist approach allows a clear and unambiguous distinction between the objects of perception and of cognition,
and with the aid of evolution theory provides an account of the nature of
the cognitive object and its relation to the object of perception. According to this account it is *meaning* that constitutes the intentional object of
cognitive acts. This is the object, which in accord with Brentano's original insight, is both distinguishing of the mental and most clearly "inexistent" in mental acts.

References

Brentano, F. (1966). *The true and the evident.* London: Routledge & Kegan Paul.

Brentano, F. (1973). *Psychology from an empirical standpoint.* London: Routledge & Kegan Paul.

Chisholm, R. M. (1967). Intentionality. In P. Edwards (Ed.), *The Encyclopedia of Philosophy.* New York: Macmillan.

Flanagan, O. J. (1984). *The science of mind.* Cambridge, Mass.: MIT Press.

Gibson, J. J. (1966). *The senses considered as perceptual systems.* Boston: Houghton-Mifflin.

Leont'ev, A. N. (1981). *Problems of the development of the mind.* Moscow: Progress Publishers.

Locke, J. (1959). *An essay concerning human understanding.* New York: Dover (originally published 1690).

Michaels, C. F. & Carello, C. (1981). *Direct perception.* Englewood Cliffs: Prentice-Hall, Inc.

Mohanty, J. N. (1972). *The concept of intentionality.* St. Louis: Warren H. Green, Inc.

Rappard, H. V. (1979). *Psychology as self-knowledge.* Assen, Holland: Van Gorcum.

Current Issues in Theoretical Psychology
Wm J. Baker, M.E. Hyland, H. Van Rappard, A.W. Staats (Editors)
© Elsevier Science Publishers B.V. (North-Holland), 1987

THE CONCEPT OF DEVELOPMENT AND THE STRUCTURE OF

DEVELOPMENTAL THEORIES

Paul Van Geert

University of Groningen
Groningen, The Netherlands

SUMMARY: Theories of development often use very different meanings of the word 'development' (cf. Overton, 1984). In this paper, I shall present ways to analyze some of the conceptual differences covered by the term 'development,' and by related terms such as 'learning.' I shall also give an example of how the structure of a developmental theory can be explained starting from the theory's definition of development (a more elaborate statement of the present ideas can be found in van Geert, 1986a, 1986b).

The Concept of Development

Development is a word widely used in ordinary language, and much of its ordinary language meaning is conserved in the technical, theoretical use of the term. Etymologically, 'development' stems from the Latin 'evolutio,' which originally meant the unrolling of book rolls (Trautner, 1978). This original concept of unrolling or unfolding is still at the basis of some of the major developmental theories. The epigenetic theories, such as Erikson's theory of identitiy development (Erikson, 1950), or Werner's differentiation theory (Werner, 1948), imply the notion of a developmental programme which, in one way or another, is built into the structure of the organism, and unfolds itself as time proceeds, provided that the necessary and sufficient environmental 'triggers' are present. In order to investigate how the word 'development' is presently used in theories of development, I shall present three forms of concept analysis, namely syntagmatic, paradigmatic, and system theoretic analysis.

Syntagmatic Analysis. In this type of analysis one tries to find the properties of all possible X's in the expression 'the development of X.' More specifically, one tries to find the properties which make an X a semantically acceptable argument of the predicate 'the development of.' If one analyzes a number of X's, such as 'child,' 'photograph,' 'animal spe-

cies,' 'idea,' 'prototype,' 'Volkswagen,' etc., there appear to be two ways
in which the word development can be used. It can be used in a retrospective sense, that is, one starts from a final state and looks back at the
preceding process, trying to understand the process in light of its end
point. The word can also be used in a prospective sense, that is, one
starts from an initial state and looks ahead, in an attempt at discovering
the possible endpoints that may be achieved. We shall see, however, that
the more technical use of 'development' in theories requires a third sense,
which I shall call topological *sensu stricto*.

The rules governing the use of the first type of X are as follows:

A process P is adequately called 'the development of X_1' if

    1) X_1 is the name given to the final point or final state of P,

    2) if the states of P are ordered, given the properties of X_1

    3) if it is possible to define a non-trivial initial state of P, given
       the properties of X_1.

With regard to X_1, the developmental process is retrospectively defined.
The rules governing the use of the second type of X are as follows:

A process P is adequately called the development of X_2 if

    1) X_2 is a name which can be given to all states of P,

    2) if the states of P are ordered, given the properties of X_2,

    3) if it is possible to define a non-trivial final state of P, given
       properties of X_2.

With regard to X_2, the development process is prospectively defined. The
third type of X is used according to the following rules:

A process P is adequately called the development of X_3 if

    1) X_3 may occupy any of a set of states reified in some form or
       another,

    2) if the states are ordered according to some reified criterion,

3) if P implies a progression according to the criterion.

The set of reified states may be called a set of 'places' or topoi. With regard to X_3 the developmental process is topologically defined. Since prospective and retrospective theories are also topological in the general sense, I shall call the third developmental conception 'topological *sensu stricto*.'

An example of an X which can be used in an X_1 meaning, as well as in an X_2, is 'animal species.' Figure 1 represents an imaginary evolutionary tree according to the non-gradualist conception of biological evolution. The figure shows that the nature of the processes discerned is clearly different. The final state or initial state of the process depends on the distinctive characteristics that have been employed to define the species in question.

Most of the classical development theories are retrospective. Piaget, for instance, was basically interested in how formal operational thinking, the thinking found in logic or science, comes about in the course of the individual life span. In view of this final stage, the initial state of development at birth is defined in negative terms, i.e., the absence of properties characteristic of formal operational thinking. In the last part of this paper, I shall demonstrate how Piaget's theory of developmental stages may be inferred starting from his conception of the final state.

There are several classical and modern prospective theories of development. Werner's orthogenetic differentiation theory (Werner, 1948, 1957) describes development as the differentiation of originally syncretic, diffuse structures in perception, cognition etc. Wohlwill's theory (Wohlwill, 1973) provides a model of developmental dimensions. A developmental dimension, perceptual constancy for instance, is defined and its initial state, e.g., at birth, is described. Finally, the changes in the developmental dimension are traced, as long as the dimension keeps its proper identity (e.g., as long as perceptual constancy processes have not turned into conceptual processes). A distinction between retrospective and prospective theories is that prospective ones tend to be gradualistic, while retrospective processes frequently take a stepwise form. The distinction is typical, not essential.

Finally, the third type of development notion is employed when the predicate X denotes some specific person or group. Development then concerns successive stages in socialization processes. The social system is conceived of as a set of places or topoi ordered along a temporal dimen-

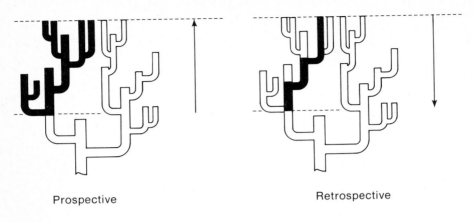

Prospective   Retrospective

Fig. 1. An imaginary evolutionary tree according to the non-gradualist conception
of biological evolution.

sion corresponding with the human life span. Examples of such sets of
places or topoi are roles or statuses in a specific society, a set of professions, types of scholarly knowledge, various developmental 'tasks' as in
Havighurst's theory (Havighurst, 1953). The topoi (statuses, professions, etc.) should be ordered according to some explicit criterion, defining relations of hierarchical similarity and subordination (e.g., a structure
of school types available to children of the same age, versus the structure
of successive scholarly achievements). In principle the set of topoi is
contingent, i.e., it is not based on some strong underlying logic. The topological conception is typical of theories that view development mainly
as a socialization process, e.g., the successive fulfillment of social roles
associated with specific ages. It is also possible to have a topological
theory *sensu stricto* which is not based on a set of social topoi. Freud's
theory of developmental stages, for instance, is based on two sets of biological topoi, namely a set of bodily functions consisting of the oral, the
anal, and the phallic function, and a binary set consisting of the self on
the one hand and the other person on the other hand. The first stages of
development can be conceived of as a sort of travel through various fields
of the body. The implicit order of these fields is biologically determined.
Finally, it should be stated that topological theories *sensu stricto* are the
least genuinely developmental conceptualizations of processes of psychological change.

Paradigmatic Analysis. In paradigmatic analysis we want to know
how the concept of development is related to concepts such as 'learning,'
'evolution,' 'acquisition,' 'change,' etc. That is, we assume that there is

a semantic field, for instance the semantic field covered by the term 'psychological change.' We want to know how this field is divided into subfields, and by which terms this dividing is done.

A very important relationship exists between 'development' and 'learning.' Many classical issues in developmental theory are rooted in the badly defined conceptual boundary between these two terms. In order to outline the distinction between these related terms, that is, in order to determine which parts of the semantic field of psychological change they are covering, we may compare their syntagmatic contexts. The question we shall ask is: what properties do X_1 and S_1 versus X_2 and S_2 take in the expressions 'the learning of X_1 by S_1' and 'the development of X_2 in S_2.'

The first distinction lies in the prepositions: They suggest that learning is an activity of S_1, while development is something that occurs to S_2. It should be noted, however, that prepositions have only very limited value in determining conceptual distinctions between terms. So, let us try some lexical specifications of 'X' and 'S.' 'Logical thinking,' for instance, can be used in both contexts. The distinction between 'developing' and 'learning' of logical thinking is that, in the first case, the acquisition of the thinking is viewed as the goal of intentional acts carried out by the learner while, in the second case, the acquisition is a non-intentional result of activities of the subject. The acquisition is the result of something that occurs in the subject, provided that a number of conditions are fulfilled. Thus, the first property of a 'learnable' X is that X has such properties that its emergence in the subject can be the result of intentional action by the subject, by a tutor, or by both.

If we compare X's that are incompatible with X's that are compatible with a 'development of' context, we observe a second distinction between learning and development. 'Learning' implies that the content which is to be learned is present, in one form or another, at the beginning of the learning process. The content can be present in the form of a tutor, a book, or list of instructions, or in the form of a representation in the learner. For instance, one might say "the learning of the alphabet by Ernie from Sesame Street" (since there is an alphabet which Ernie might learn), but not "the development of the alphabet in Ernie," unless one wants to give a very specific meaning to the expression 'the development of the alphabet.' On the other hand, it is normal to say "the development of the alphabet in Phoenicia" or even "the development of the alphabet by the Phoenicians." The first sentence makes a statement about the development of Phoenician culture, exemplified by the development of the alphabet. The second sentence tells something about the development of the alphabet, e.g., its gradual expansion, which is something the Phoenicians brought about.

Many discussions on learning versus development, for instance, the discussion on the learnability of formal thinking, or conservation, are not based on empirically decidable issues. It depends on how formal thinking is defined, for instance, whether the question of whether or not formal thinking can be learned is meaningful.

System Theoretic Analysis. The third form of concept analysis consists of a formalist approach. In contra-distinction with the ordinary language approach previously discussed, the formalist method tries to provide a definition of a technical concept 'development,' in terms of a formal process-language (see also Gosling, this volume). 'Development' is a member of the set of processes. Systems theory provides a technical instrument for dealing with multi-variable processes. A developing subject, a collection of subjects, or a single aspect or part of the subject, can be defined in terms of a finite series of variables. These variables are conceived of as necessary and sufficient for the description of the developmental state of the subject at any possible moment.

The nature and number of variables used to characterize the developmental process is the first criterion for distinguishing various theories. Take, for instance, Piaget's theory on the one hand, and a typical learning theory on the other hand. The learning theory will discern a set of variables that describe explicit educational properties of the environment. It is often assumed that Piaget rejects the importance of the educational environment, for instance, because Piaget would have claimed that education should follow development. It is simply untrue, however, that Piaget thinks that the environment has no definite effect on the course of development. More precisely, Piaget conceives of the set of environmental variables that are effective with regard to developmental progression as a function of the set of variables that describe the internal cognitive state of the subject. Thus, it is not necessary to introduce the environment as an independent explanative variable in the developmental system. This is not to say that the environment has no influence on development, that it is not necessary, or that any environment is as good as any other.

A very important subsystem of the system of developmental variables consists of the set of variables that describe internal properties, such as the subject's knowledge, memory span, etc. Psychological development can be represented in terms of this sub-space by specifying the temporal succession of internal states. We have already seen that the set of states should be ordered and limited (which is not to say that the number of states should be finite). We do not know, however, why or how the transitions from one state to another take place.

With regard to transition properties, the states, conceived of as internal states of the subject, may be located along two dimensions. The first distinguishes internally stable from internally unstable states (i.e., states in equilibrium versus states in non-equilibrium). The second dimension describes a distinction between open and closed states, i.e., states that are either sensitive or not to variables from outside the system.

Closed, internally stable states characterize 'steady state' theories, such as Chomsky's theory of an innate Universal Grammar (Chomsky, 1972), or Fodor's theory of innate concepts (Fodor, 1981). These theories are stable and closed with regard to the innate component, not with regard to the actual expression of the innate knowledge in behaviour. The latter requires the presence of so-called 'triggers' in the environment, for instance, a language spoken by the caretakers. With regard to the expression of the innate properties in behaviour, these theories are semi-closed, that is, they are open to only an extremely specific external influence, namely the 'trigger.' At the initial state, they are in instable equilibrium, which turns into stable equilibrium as a result of the trigger. Internally stable, open states are typical of classical learning theories, although there is probably not a single theory which claims that states are completely closed and stable. Closed, internally unstable states characterize maturation theories. Development is not caused by shaping external influences, but by a rule of development of an inherent form. Again, there is no theory which claims absolute closedness. Finally, internally unstable, open states form the building blocks of interactionist theories, such as Piaget's or Bruner's theory of cognitive development, or Erikson's theory of identity development. This kind of theory is the genuine developmental theory, that is, it corresponds most closely to the conceptual requirements made with regard to prospective and retrospective concepts of development. Theories from this collection may differ as to the nature and amount of internal instability and openness.

The Structure of Development Theories

Existing Views. In the past, several forms of developmental theory analysis have been put forward. Bromley (1970), for instance, provided an analysis of disengagement theory based on Toulmin's concept of a theory as a set of nested claims, supported by data and modified by qualifiers, warrants, etc. (Toulmin, 1958). Bromley's analysis conceives of developmental theories as sets of statements of various structural types. It does not provide an account of the factors that make a developmental theory truly developmental.

Various authors (see, e.g., Overton, 1984) have adopted Pepper's concept of basic metaphors, resulting in a classification of developmental theories into a group of organismic theories, and a group of mechanistic theories. The basic metaphor approach specifies the concepts of development which underly various theories, and the nature of the associated concepts and conceptual rules. It does not explain how specific models of development can be inferred by employing these concepts and rules.

Van den Daele (1968, 1972, 1976; see also Riegel, 1972; and Meacham, 1980) described developmental theories in the form of graph-structures, based on three independent dimensions (e.g., the dimension "unitary versus multiple progression"). The graph approach specifies the set of possible developmental process models, but it remains rather obscure about the relation between the underlying concept of development and the resulting process model.

A Generative Approach. The present writer has tried to provide an explanative account of the structure of developmental theories (see Van Geert, 1986b). A theory is viewed as a specific set of statements describing a model of development which are generated on the basis of some - usually tacit - grammar or set of generative rules. The present type of theory analysis requires that one specifies the generative rules, the concepts to which the rules are applied, and the resulting models of developmental processes. In the section on the concept of development, we have distinguished three types of development. Each type is associated with a specific set of generative rules (e.g., 'looking back' rules). In order to illustrate the present approach to structural analysis, I shall use Piaget's theory of cognitive development which is a major retrospective theory of development. For the sake of brevity, I shall deal only with the top structure of the theory, namely, the theory of the major developmental states (see Van Geert, 1986b for the analysis of the three types of development, and for some additional examples of retrospective theory analysis).

According to our findings from syntagmatic analysis, we should start the reconstruction of the developmental process at the final state. How can this reconstruction be carried out in practice? We need to introduce some further constraints:

1. All developmental states should be described as a finite set of binary variables, that is, A or non-A variables, e.g., $(A, \bar{B})$, $(\bar{A}, B)$ ...

2. The minimal distinction on one variable, therefore, a developmental state transition, consists of the substitution of a value of one and only one variable, e.g., $(\bar{A}, \bar{B}) \rightarrow (A, \bar{B})$.

3. The maximal distinction between states consists of different values on all variables, such distinction corresponds with the final state/initial state contrast e.g., $(\bar{A}, \bar{B}) \rightarrow (A, B)$.

In Piaget's theory, the states may be described by three binary variables. The final state takes the values *internal* (cognitive processes occur internally), *operational* (cognitive processes are formally equal to operations in logical systems), and *formal* (cognitive operations operate on abstract contents, for instance, the operations themselves).

The initial state, then, is characterized by maximal contrast, i.e., by the opposite values of the three variables. In Piaget's terminology, these opposite values are *external* (cognitive processes take place in the form of overt activities), *actional* (cognitive processes are actions, i.e., they are not reversible and do not form a logical system), and *concrete* (the contents of cognitive operations are concrete). By replacing one value at a time, we obtain the following structure of state transitions (see Figure 2). This structure is much more extensive than Piaget's actual stage theory. However, Piaget's variables are subject to a set of conceptual constraints. For instance, the predicate *operational* is conceptually incompatible with the predicate *external* (compare, for instance, with the *corner* of a *circle*). By their very nature, operations cannot take place but in the form of internal cognitive processes. The constraints can be written in the form of an implication relation, namely:

$$F \rightarrow O \rightarrow I$$

According to this constraint, four state descriptions should be deleted because they are conceptually impossible. What remains is a set of four successive stages, whose descriptions exactly correspond with Piaget's sensory-motor, pre-operational, concrete operational, and formal operational stages.

It should now be questioned why there is cognitive state transition anyway. For instance, we know that if the present state is pre-operation-

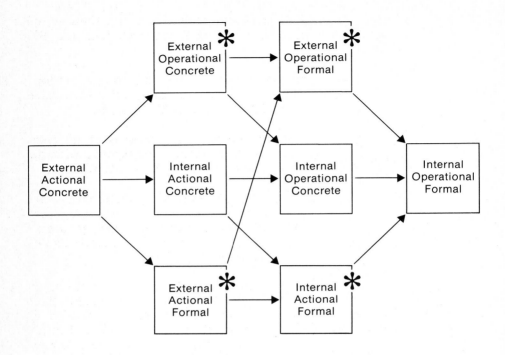

Fig. 2. The structure of state transtions.

al, the next state must be concrete operational by conceptual necessity. But why does the transition take place at all, why doesn't the system remain in the pre-operational state forever? Moreover, why is formal operational thinking the final state? Why aren't state transitions continuing as long as the subject lives? These questions require first a conceptual answer, which consists of making explicit the theory's transition rules. These transition rules are part of the concept of developmental state as it is employed in the theory in question.

In Piaget's theory, the rules are as follows:

1. a state is either in equilibrium or in non-equilibrium;

2. the transition from equilibrium to non-equilibrium is a state transition, transition from non-equilibrium to equilibrium is a state consolidation;

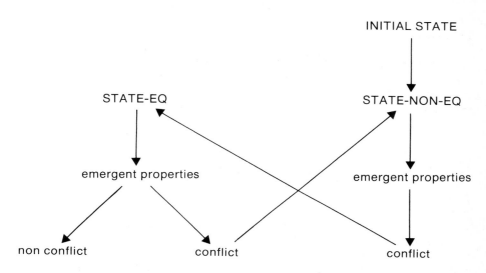

Fig. 3. Transition rules for Piaget's theory.

3. properties of the cognitive state call forth properties of the environment, that is, emergent properties;

4. emergent properties of the environment are either in conflict with cognitive state properties or not;

5. only if in conflict, emergent properties cause change of equilibrium state.

These rules can be summarized in the form of a flow chart (see Figure 3).

    If emergent properties are not in conflict with properties of the cognitive state, then the state remains in its equilibrium state, that is, state transitions will no longer occur. Emergent properties are no longer in conflict with the cognitive system if the latter consists of an adequate conceptualization of the nature and properties of reality. Such adequate conceptualization is formal operational thinking, a thinking which is logical and scientific. Thus, if formal operational thinking has come to its equilibrium state, cognitive developmental state transitions will no longer occur. The final state is reached.

Summary

The main goals of this paper have been to demonstrate, first, that an analysis of the concept of development reveals relevant underlying conceptual differences between various theories of development, and second, that insights into the concept of development may contribute to better understanding the structure of existing developmental theories.

The analysis of the concept of development proceeded along three different lines. In syntagmatic analysis, three types of developmental concepts have been found, namely a retrospective concept, *looking back* from an end point, a prospective concept, *looking ahead* from a starting point, and a topological concept, describing development as a predetermined voyage along various developmental *locations*. We have seen that existing developmental theories can be classified easily according to this conceptual tripartition. In paradigmatic analysis, the conceptual distinction between *learning* and *development* has been demonstrated, showing that various discussions on the relative contributions of learning and development to psychological change are not empirical but conceptual. In system theoretic analysis, we concentrated on the question of developmental transition. A two-dimensional framework has been employed, dividing developmental states according to their open-versus-unstable nature.

The structure of developmental theories has been analyzed according to a *generative* method developed by the present author. The method employs the three types of development discerned on the grounds of syntagmatic analysis. Piaget's theory, a retrospective theory still occupying a very important position in developmental psychology, has been used to demonstrate two types of generative rules, namely the rules generating the ordered set of developmental states, and the rules generating the conditions for actual state transition.

The present approach is mainly descriptive. It remains to be investigated whether or not it may provide grounds for deciding on the logical and conceptual consistency of theories, and their heuristic or generative value.

References

Bromley, D. B. (1970). An approach to theory construction in the psychology of development and aging. In L. R. Goulet & P. B. Baltes (Eds.), *Life span developmental psychology: Research and theory.* New York: Academic Press.

Chomsky, N. (1972). *Language and mind.* New York: Harcourt, Brace, & Jovanovich (Enlarged edition).

Erikson, E. H. (1950/1963). *Childhood and society.* (2nd ed. rev.) New York: Norton.

Fodor, J. A. (1981). The present status of the innateness controversy. In J. A. Fodor (Ed.), *Representations.* Hassocks: Harvester Press.

Gosling, J. (this volume). Systems, causality and time. A framework for the integration of theories of schizophrenia. Paper presented at the Founding Conference of the International Society in Theoretical Psychology, Plymouth, England, August 1985.

Havighurst, R. J. (1953). *Human development and education.* New York: Longmans, Green & Co.

Meacham, J. A. (1980). Formal aspects of theories of development. *Experimental Aging Research, 6,* 475-487.

Overton, W. F. (1984). World views and their influence on psychological theory and research, Kuhn - Lakatos - Laudan. In H. W. Reese (Ed.), *Advances in child development and behavior.* (Vol. 18). New York: Academic Press.

Riegel, K. F. (1972). Time and change in the development of the individual and society. In H. W. Reese (Ed.), *Advances in child development and behavior.* (Vol. 7). New York: Academic Press.

Toulmin, S. (1958). *The uses of argument.* Cambridge: Cambridge University Press.

Trautner, H. M. (1978). *Lehrbuch der Entwicklungspsychologie. Band 1.* Göttingen: Verlag für psychologie.

Van den Daele, L. D. (1968). Qualitative models in developmental analysis. *Developmental Psychology, 1,* 303-310.

Van den Daele, L. D. (1972). Infrastructure and transition in developmental analysis. *Human Development, 17,* 1-23.

Van den Daele, L. D. (1976). Formal models of development. In K. F. Riegel & J. A. Meacham (Eds.), *The developing individual in a changing world* (Vol. 1). The Hague: Mouton.

Van Geert, P. (1986a). The concept of development. In P. Van Geert (Ed.), *Theory building in developmental psychology.* Amsterdam: North Holland.

Van Geert, P. (1986b). The structure of developmental theories. In P. Van Geert (Ed.), *Theory building in developmental psychology.*

Amsterdam: North Holland.
Werner, H. (1948). *Comparative psychology of mental development.* New
    York: International Universities Press.
Werner, H. (1957). The concept of development from a comparative and
    organismic point of view. In D. B. Harris (Ed.), *The concept of
    development.* Minneapolis: University of Minnesota Press.
Wohlwill, J. E. (1973). *The study of behavioral development.* New York:
    Academic Press.

Current Issues in Theoretical Psychology
Wm J. Baker, M.E. Hyland, H. Van Rappard, A.W. Staats (Editors)
Elsevier Science Publishers B.V. (North-Holland), 1987

MAN-MACHINE ANALOGS AND THEORETICAL MAINSTREAMS

IN PSYCHOLOGY

Pieter A. Vroon

University of Utrecht
Utrecht, The Netherlands

SUMMARY: Introspection is an imperfect research tool because many aspects of affective as well as cognitive processes are, as a rule, inaccessible to both the subject and the experimenter. Philosophy and psychology have tried to solve this problem by comparing the mind metaphorically to several technological constructions cultures have produced, for example: time pieces, steam engines, radios, radar systems, and computers. These metaphors and their corresponding theories are briefly described. It is posited that during any particular time period, psychology uses several different metaphors. These metaphors have three functions: didactic, heuristic, and theory-constitutive. It is argued that the latter function particularly leads to scientific disunity. Since metaphors, theories, methods, and data are tied together, psychology consists of more or less separately operating intellectual 'circuits.' It is also suggested that there is disunity in historical perspective: the conceptual framework of a new metaphor sometimes leaves hardly room for the assimilation of facts from the past. As a consequence, findings may be lost along the way.

Introduction

A recurrent theme in the literature consists of dissatisfaction with psychology's lack of unity (see Staats, 1983, and Vroon & Draaisma, 1985, for an overview). Two types of disunity have to be distinguished. We define *synchronic disunity* as the fact that psychology consists of theoretical mainstreams such as psychoanalysis, behaviorism, and cognitive psychology. *Diachronic disunity* refers to breaks in communication in the sense that more recent investigators are hardly aware of the facts or theorems established by earlier investigators. We shall argue that these two types of disunity can be partly described and clarified on the basis of the technological metaphors psychology uses to study mental processes and behavior.

This paper is organized as follows. We start with some problems connected with introspection; subsequently, we discuss viewpoints on the use of metaphors, and the question of how far they dictate research. The following sections present an overview of various metaphors, such as the clock, the steam engine, radio and radar, and the digital computer. Finally, we discuss both types of disunity mentioned.

The Inaccessibility of the Mind

During the period 1875-1920, psychology studied mental life, primarily on the basis of introspection. It was felt that humankind differs from the animal world by claiming to possess consciousness and rationality. To an important degree, our actions flow forth from thinking, and frequently we have to give account of and justify our behavior from a rational point of view. This general idea implies that we have considerable access to our intellectual and emotional processes. For a long time, introspection was considered to be the best method for the exploration of the mind.

However, high expectations in this respect led to disappointment (Flanagan, 1984). At the affective level, it is likely that our existence is profoundly influenced by an unconscious, and cognitive processes also function largely at an unconscious level (Neisser, 1967). Studies of multiple personalities, hypnosis and the 'hidden observer' (Hilgard, 1977), and the strange behavior of split-brain patients (Wittrock, 1980) are some examples. It appears that there is not only a distinction between the conscious and the unconscious, consciousness itself is divisible and, as a rule, hardly accessible. We know *that* we are able to perform tasks, but not *how* we perform them.

As far as the relationship between motives and behavior is concerned, motives described by persons have often more to do with an unconscious retrospective justification of behavior than with factual motives (Nuttin, 1975; Nisbett & Ross, 1980). Also in this respect, introspection is frequently unable to reveal what is going on in mind and behavior.

Behaviorism is a school that has tried to bypass this problem by saying that it is not necessary to study mental processes. For behaviorists, unlike behavior, the mind is not open to observation. Consequently, why should we postulate two realities since the supposed mental states and processes are little more than 'behavior suspension?' A person is called musical when he or she shows the ability to play Beethoven. According to behaviorism this explanation is tautological in the sense that the same thing is said in two different ways, i.e., somebody plays well *and* is musical.

The position of cognitive psychology concerning introspection is somewhat different. Neisser (1967) contends that introspection is an inappropriate method because only the results of mental processes are consciously given. However, contrary to behaviorism, the aim of cognitive psychology is to unravel the mechanisms of the mind. On the basis of experiments and fragmentary personal statements of the subject the psychologist hypothesizes or constructs them. Mandler (1975) summarizes this as follows: "Thinking or cognition or information processing for the psychologist is a term that refers to theoretical processes, complex transformations on internal and external objects, events and relations. These processes are not conscious; they are, in the first instance, *constructions* generated by the psychological theorist" (p. 231). In order to make such constructions, the psychologist needs sources of ideas or inspiration. Only incidentally, such as in the study of thinking, does the cognitive psychologist use extensive introspective protocols (Resnick, 1976). The solution to the mind's inaccessibility has been sought in doing experiments with a marginal use of introspection and by using metaphors of the mind (Ortony, 1979; Hoffman & Nead, 1983).

Metaphors and Their Origin

Metaphors resist literal descriptions. They have been defined as 'feature filters,' 'mirrors of the world,' 'ways of seeing the world,' 'ornaments of language,' analogy mappings,' 'puzzles to figure out,' 'masks of the truth,' and so on. According to Aristotle, a metaphor means that different meanings are ascribed to the same words in a different context. Features of objects and the relationships between them are generalized on the basis of supposed similarity. We say that a ship ploughs the sea, because the movement of the water is reminiscent of the farmer's plough in action.

The origin of metaphorical expressions lies perhaps in synesthesia (Marks 1978, 1982) and in the transition from perception to language in the development of children (Billow, 1977). When having dinner, information from several senses is combined. A description of a meal implies that the meaning of these sensory impressions is condensed into a few words. As a consequence, the connotation of concepts referring primarily to one particular sense is extended to other senses (a warm colour, a light wine, a clear tone, a sharp sound). It is conceivable that relationships between objects are made in the same way: objects with unknown or hardly known characteristics are studied and described with the help of objects we are familiar with. The metaphor points then to (seemingly) identical properties and relationships, with the analogy-reasoning at the core. If we did *not* use metaphors, we might have to develop a new language for each new situation, and the acquisition of knowledge would become virtually impossible.

Pepper (1942) distinguishes several types of metaphors in science. Philosophical theories and world views are based on four incompatible *root metaphors,* e.g., 'the world is a machine' or 'the world is an organic process.' In psychological research, a metaphor is usually a gross comparison of the mind to a machine such as a computer. Such metaphors can also be very specific. An example is the idea of a 'switch' that takes a certain amount of time to 'change channels' in attention (Broadbent, 1971).

Philosophical Viewpoints in the Use of Metaphors

Philosophers have differing attitudes about the metaphorical use of language in general. Anderson (1964), Draaisma (1983) and Urban (1939) summarize several positions.

Jeremy Bentham (in Draaisma, 1983) says that because the mind is immaterial, we can only speak about it by using material analogs. The concept of 'person' is, in fact, physical (*persona,* mask). According to Bentham, all communication between persons about mental processes is only possible through physical reality, observed by all. Private (mental) events are only accessible through public, physical events. The mind belongs to the 'fictitious entities' about which we can only speak by pointing to 'real entities.' Bentham draws support for this from the way in which psychological processes are described by means of spatial and visual metaphors. The intellect has been considered as 'the natural light' (lumen naturale). We 'see' solutions; someone is 'brilliant,' has a 'dull' mind or a 'broad' mind; we have a 'view' point; we 'keep' something in mind; an argument is 'beyond' comprehension, and so on. Psychological processes are in some way or another projected into physical or public space.

Nietzsche (in Draaisma, 1983) even maintains that all (scientific) concepts are metaphorical. Acccording to him, we have in general, no direct contact with reality and have no choice but to resort to anthropomorphisms, metaphors, and even personifications (compare the latter with Hesiodus' cosmology as described in the *Theogonia,* in which numerous natural phenomena are presented in human form). Nietzsche posits that knowledge is hardly more than the exchange of old metaphors for new metaphors.

Not all philosophers shared this position, however; at the time of the scientific revolution (1550-1700), Aristotle's view that sensory qualities existed as such in nature was heavily attacked. Empiricists such as Galileo and Locke distinguished primary and secondary qualities. The latter were considered projections of the mind. In his *Novum Organum* Bacon criticized the Aristotelian tradition by saying that the mind had made a mixture of its own qualities and those of nature. Bacon opposed metaphors because many of the current examples were anthropomorphisms. He regarded metaphors as *idola fori*, 'village talk.' Other empiricists such as Hobbes even objected to the expression that a road leads to a town on the grounds that a road does not lead. According to Locke, the use of metaphors belonged to the field of rhetoric, which he described as an instrument of error and deceit. Ironically, Locke himself used a well-known metaphor in saying that the mind of a newborn is white paper, void of all characters (which is often incorrectly cited by speaking about a *tabula rasa,* an expression used by Leibnitz to describe Locke's position).

Nevertheless, experimental psychology as well as philosophy have abundantly used metaphors of some type or another. Psychology not only uses metaphors, but also defends them on the basis of what is known on information processing. For example, according to Paivio (1979), it is advantageous to derive scientific metaphors from technical products such as clocks, steam engines, and computers. In this case well known structures are chosen that are understandable and open to inspection. Objects consist of a collection of related characteristics, concrete and predictable. Such objects are easier and more readily understood than abstract concepts, and pictures are better remembered than words (Baddeley, 1976). In psychological terminology, metaphors of this type contain many chunks of quickly processed information. Finally, the internal representation of objects involves dual coding in the form of words or concepts, as well as images, so that they are easily retrieved and used.

Metaphor, Theory, Method, and Facts

In scientific research, technological metaphors have three more or less distinguishable functions: *didactic, heuristic,* and *theory-constitutive* (Ortony, 1979). An example of the didactic function would be to explain Boyle's law about the relationship between the volume and the pressure of a gas by showing a person a spring. The heuristic function refers to the value of a metaphor in doing research. It implies that the metaphor serves as a source of inspiration; it generates ideas, gives direction to questions, observation, and understanding. The theory-constitutive function of the metaphor means that its structure and related concepts are reflected in theories describing how the mind works.

Metaphors are neither right nor wrong; they are more or less *fruitful*. Theories sometimes disappear when their predictions turn out to be false; metaphors disappear because a new one promises to answer more questions. Pascal said that humankind is a thinking reed. This metaphor was not used in psychology because the characteristics of a reed are inappropriate for studying our intuitions about mental processes. Conversely, the computer proved to be more fruitful in this respect. These metaphors are tied to theories, and theories are tied to methods and data.

We suppose that psychology starts with the choice of a metaphor that appears to be relevant and attractive. Differences of opinion about the fruitfulness of a metaphor will cause a chain reaction: when questioning the metaphor, not only the corresponding theory may be rejected, but also the method and the 'facts.' For example, a behaviorist who uses a telephone exchange or a clock metaphor believes that the psychoanalyst's steam engine metaphor is not fruitful or relevant. Consequently, the theories, methods, and data are (mutually) rejected or at least seriously questioned. This results in *synchronic disunity,* which means that psychologists during the same period of time create more or less separate 'intellectual circuits,' hardly having contact with each other. Hoffman and Nead (1983) say that, according to the Kuhnian tradition, any paradigm or general approach to psychology - be it behaviorism, Gestalt psychology or whatever - will determine what *counts* as a worthwhile experiment, what *counts* as data, and what will *work* as theory. What counts is determined by different and often incompatible metaphors about the nature of human beings.

Psychology also seems to show *diachronic* disunity. When there is a succession of basically differing metaphors, parts of the empirical material may submerge because the 'old' facts no longer fit the language of the new metaphor. An example is the work of the German biologist Richard Semon (Schacter, 1982). In the 1920's, Semon wrote several books on memory in which he said that forgetting was not caused by 'trace decay' but by the inability to retrieve the information. This idea has now become accepted thanks to the computer metaphor. Because the memory metaphors current at Semon's time left no room for these findings, his work was consigned to obliviion and remained there for 60 years.

The next sections will describe several of the influential metaphors that play or have played a role in psychology. In this same framework we shall discuss the synchronic and diachronic disunity of the field.

Metaphors in Ancient Times

Technologically inspired metaphors were hardly used in Greek philosophy and psychology. There are several reasons for this. Aristotle's world view contained many anthropomorphisms, and the technology of the ancients as manifested in the use of levers, water organs, and catapults offered insufficient inspiration for comparisons with the mind. Another possibility is that tools and equipment were made by slaves and artists, persons with whom the intellectural Greek preferred not to be associated. Moreover, most tools did not function automatically - they demanded the constant presence of someone to supervise and steer them.

To a certain extent, metaphors of the mind were derived from the water supply of cities and irrigation works. Herophilus (300 BC) located the soul in a large water barrel, for which he chose the fourth and largest cerebral ventricle. Later, psychological functions were divided up and localized in the different ventricles. The nerves were believed to be tubes through which substances, such as water, steam, air, and fire could flow.

The Greeks used some clearcut metaphors to describe memory. Plato wrote in the dialogue *Theaetetus* that we can consider memory as a piece of wax, the size and hardness of which differs from person to person. These differences reflect those between people. What is engrained is remembered, and what is forgotten is wiped out or has melted away. Aristotle pursued this matter further and suggested that in older people the wax became more moist and pliable, so that new impressions are not retained. He described old people by saying that their memories are like a seal, pressed on water.

Akin to the spatial representation of memory is Cicero's loci-method as a means of memory training. One can imagine memory as a house or a landscape in which the details are located at different places. In recall, or during a speech, one imagines the house and oneself walking through it. Later St. Augustine draws parallels in his *Confessions* with nature and describes memory as "innumerable fields and caves filled with all varieties of innumerable things" (Book 10). By and large, however, the structure of the mind was rarely described in technological terms.

The Clock

Several conditions have to be fulfilled before a human product can be used to describe the mind (Vartanian, 1973). The technological analogs must contain an inbuilt element of automation and purpose. Furthermore there has to be an intellectual climate in which the immaterial soul can be brought under discussion. As long as the mind is considered as an immaterial, free entity, any comparison with material objects is blasphemic. These conditions were fulfilled partially in the 17th century, but mainly in the 18th century (Draaisma, 1983; McReynolds, 1980), when the Inquistion was abandoned in Europe and a rather liberal intellectual climate came into existence.

In the 16th century and onward, human beings were, thanks to the anatomist Vesalius, considered as consisting of organs meaningfully interconnected as the parts of a clock. Harvey's discovery of the blood circulation drew attention to the fact that the heart works automaticaly as a pump, ticking almost like a clock. One of the main problems in making clocks was not the driving mechanism, but rather how to construct a clock that worked regularly and with precision. The invention of the regulating mechanism was the most important piece of the puzzle. Once it has been wound, a clock tells time according to plan and structure, without continual human intervention. The attraction of the clock metaphor was that it allowed no room for chance and caprice. The clock was able to indicate time better than human beings. This also meant that a *mental* concept (time) could be indicated by a *material* device.

Descartes made analogies between bodily functions and the working of a clock and, in so doing, he became the father of the *bête machine* doctrine. This implied that animals and the human body (but not the mind) behaved mechanically. Others who used the clock metaphor for various purposes were Leibniz, Geulincx, and Kepler. Kepler compared the clock to the movements of the celestial bodies, and Leibniz saw the world as a divine clock, *le monde est l'horloge de Dieu*. The Dutch philosopher Geulincx clarified viewpoints with regard to the body/mind problem on the basis of relationships between two clocks directing each other, functioning independently from the outset, and so on.

What kind of influence had the clock upon conceptions of the mind? After Descartes proposed that the human body was a clock-like machine, Comenius did the same for the mind, but only by using the clock metpahor for didactic purposes. He said that the will forms the most vital wheel of the clock, the weights constitute desire, and reason is the regulating mechanism. The idea that a person as a whole *was* clock-like gained momentum not earlier than the 18th century, mainly in the writings of La Mettrie, d'Alembert, Diderot, and Cabanis.

La Mettrie said that the mechanical character of the clock could easily be applied to the mind. A difficulty with this idea was that springs do not wind themselves up. La Mettrie tried to solve this problem by referring to the *perpetuum mobile*, or by saying that food is for bodies what springs are for clocks. Persons are machines, winding themselves up. In answer to the question posed by his opponents "can matter think?", La Mettrie replied by asking the question "can matter indicate time?" In this way, the doctrine of the *bête machine* expanded to become *l'homme machine* (Thijssen, 1982).

The clock metaphor still functions in psychology. An implicit example is the behaviorist who is not interested in processes taking place in the organism. Although clocks are assembled in many ways, they all tell the same time. Behavior is like a clock-face which we can observe, driven by hidden mechanisms, about which, strictly speaking, we need to know nothing. An explicit example concerns the study of time and psychological and biological rhythms. In the field of time experience, Treisman (1963, see also Vroon, 1970) hypothesized that the accelerations and, decelerations of psychological time were caused by an internal clock or pacemaker. According to Michon (1967) and many others this clock even *ticks*: it generates 'time quanta,' each being 50-100 msec long. The clock metaphor is also applied to research on biological rhythms. Human beings are supposed to have a number of clocks in their brains, each being responsible for a particular rhythm. These rhythms are considered as the wheels of a clock; when the rhythms function independently of each other, there is 'desynchronization' which may lead to certain types of mental disturbance.

This short overview of the history of the clock metaphor draws attention to an important point as far as synchronic disunity is concerned. It is not true that psychology only uses the most *advanced* technological analog: several metaphors may function during the same period of time, and they are directed to different aspects of human functioning.

The Steam Engine

During the period of Romanticism (1780-1850), the mechanistic approach was more or less left behind in the physical sciences (Bem, 1985; Russelman, 1983). The Romantics objected to the way humankind and nature were viewed from the standpoint of the Enlightenment. Extreme rationalism was regarded as cool and mechanical. As far as the mind is concerned, opposition developed against faculty psychology with separated thinking, feeling, willing, and other functions. A synthesis was desired with respect to psychological structures, the relationship between mind and body, and our bond with nature. The 18th century had many adherents to the idea of a static *scala naturae*. Conversely, the Romantic biologists saw nature not as a machine but as an organism, characterized by continuous change. Herder (in Russelman, 1983) said that life is a continuum governed by invisible and powerful forces. Everything in reality is essentially alive. There exists a general life force, going beyond matter (vitalism).

In the natural sciences of this period, theories about atoms and anonymous mechanical forces underwent a shift towards ideas about more continuous or liquid-like phenomena. The corpuscular theory of light was replaced by a wave theory. Goethe opposed Newton's theory of the discrete, spectral colours, and the battery of Volta showed that there was a relationship between electricity and magnetisim, and it was discovered that heat could produce force (the steam engine). A general climate of thinking developed, characterized by universal forces that were considered to be indestructible, inter-related, and fluid-like.

Psychological forces were also distinguished, such as mental activity, self-realization, and creative power. We can see this in the work of Schopenhauer whose concept of 'will' embraced both mental and physical forces. The forces from which nature emerged and took its shape were present in the body as well as the mind. According to Lavater and others (Bühler, 1933) physical stature, handwriting, and facial shape expressed the nature of the mind. In other words, a person was a whole, united with the body and with the general forces of nature. During this period, unconscious mental *processes* were first hypothesized by the Swiss physician Carus (1846). His book *Psyche* opens with the following words: "The key to understanding conscious mental life is to be found in the unconscious."

Around the time of Carus' book the law of energy conservation was discovered and declared to be applicable to both the physical world and psychological processes. So-called nervous energy was regarded as inde-structible. On the other hand, mental energy can be transformed and express itself physically, as in the case of hysterical paralysis. The use of hypnosis is a way of liberating the accumulated energy. In this connection, Freud spoke of inhibited affections that are able to be discharged, and of 'abnormal connections' leading to conversion symptoms. This metaphor gave rise to a new method: the catharsis therapy (Breuer & Freud, 1895).

There are many connections between Freud's ideas and technical developments related to Romanticism, i.e., the steam engine. An important feature of the steam engine is that movement is made possible by a combination of a diffuse driving force and a regulating force needing only limited energy. It costs little effort to release steam opening valves. In the steam engine, the energy source and the regulating mechanism are *separated*. In addition, the energy is diffuse and has no particular direction. This invention was very important from a conceptual point of view: Da Vinci's designs for flying machines were equipped with double-functioning flapping wings, responsible for the supply of energy as well as for determining the direction. In Freud's work the diffuse energy source is the Id, with the Ego as a separate regulating mechanism. The non-directional and single form of energy consisted of blind drives, hardly distinguishable from each other in the Id. Freud used the steam engine metaphor explicitly in his work, for example: "We try to define the Id on the basis of analogy reasoning; we call it chaos, a kettle filled with boiling drives" (Freud, 1940, Vol. 15, p. 80). Other connections between Freud's theorizing and the steam engine are the following. The level of activity and stimulation in the central nervous system should be kept constant. In this respect Freud refers to the constant energy flow of a steam engine. Earlier we mentioned the 'abnormal connections' in the nervous system, which are comparable to a shunting-yard. Psychological activity has to obey similar rules. Finally, it seems clear that ideas about the transition of energy into different forms are related to the defense mechanisms. Sexual energy, for example, may find its way out as intellectualization and rationalization.

Freud was not the only psychologist to use a steam engine model of human beings. We also find traces of this in ethology. as is evident in the Dutch translation of a book by Lorenz in 1965. The flap reads: "One can compare aggression to steam in a kettle, that in some way or another has to find an escape route if an explosion is to be avoided. Nature has provided us with exhaust valves so that fatal consequences of this build-up of pressure can be prevented" (Lorenz, 1965).

The steam engine metaphor shows that different analogs of the mind are used simultaneously, and that they are directed towards different psychological phenomena. The steam engine metaphor made it possible to study motivation in a certain way, and the clock metaphor inspired research on time perception and rhythms.

Radio and Radar

Metaphors based on detection and communication equipment became very influential in the years between 1945 and 1965 (Broadbent, 1958, 1971). During the Second World War, army units were separated by long distances. The radio was indispensible for communication purposes, radar was important for the detection of enemy aircraft and ships, and many psychologists were involved in the use and the development of these systems. The primary purpose of radio and radar is to transmit information, but not to perform tasks. The radio and radar metaphor implied that much attention was paid to the way information is handled by the organism. In this view, human beings are more or less passive, limited capacity *transmission* systems, and not *processing* systems. Broadbent (1958) describes this metaphor clearly: "A practical analogy may be found in a radio receiver designed to eliminate impulse interference and so to present a signal to the listener free from such interference" (p. 41).

Research concentrated on the concept of information, channel capacity, redundancy of messages, the extent to which a signal can be detected in noise (signal to noise ratio), and selective attention. First and foremost, the radio (as well as a radar system) must be able to detect and transmit information. The question as to what extent persons can carry out detection tasks became the basis of signal detection theory. The performance of the observer was expressed as a 'receiver operating characteristic,' which reflects the analogs of the radar and radio.

As far as the transmission of information is concerned, much work was done on serial processes, presumably because a radio is tuned to one station at a time. Generally speaking, human functioning was mainly studied in terms of the input and the first stages of information transmission, namely the characteristics of stimuli, perception, and attention, but not thinking, memory, and imagining. It was hypothesized that the visual stimulus was responsible for the apparent conversion of vague pictures into steaks when a person is hungry (Broadbent, 1971). Stress was supposed to be determined by stimuli and circumstance, and not considered as a function of internal coping mechanisms. Along similar lines Witkin, Lewis, Herzman, Machover, Meissner, and Wapner (1954) introduced the 'new look in perception,' and they showed that personality differences are reflected in perceptual phenomena.

The information transmission models of this period consisted of discrete stages with few feedback loops. The system was considered to be *data driven* and *conceptually driven,* i.e., determined by higher cognitive processes.

The Computer

The last decades show a domination of the computer metaphor in (cognitive) psychology. Turing (1950) asked the question of whether or not it would be possible to distinguish between a person and a computer, if both were taking part in a written question and answer game. Simon (1957) described the 'general problem solver,' which later became the kernel of artificial intelligence. Cognitive psychology, however, only started to take shape in the 1960s (Neisser, 1967).

The reasons for the shift to the computer metaphor were at least twofold. There was stagnation of the research in the framework of the radio metaphor, and the widely available linear digital computers showed stronger analogs to human functioning. Persons not only pay attention to objects, they also store them in their memories, reflect on them, calculate odds, make decisions, and act accordingly. The shift from information transmission to information processing meant that the interaction between stimulus, memory, and many other processes was taken into account. It would be pertinently wrong to say that the new metaphor was *chosen.* First, models were made that did not fit the radio metaphor any longer. This state of affairs was *legitimized* by using the analog of the digital computer, and *subsequently* the computer was used as a heuristic means to continue the research.

The field of cognitive psychology is defined as the study of all processing dealing with the perception, storage, retrieval, and use of information (Neisser, 1967), and its jargon stems directly from the computer: programs, subroutines, procedures, flow schemes, and so on. Shifts with regard to the radio metaphor are that much more attention was given to later stages of information processing, which also influence early stages. If we maintain the radio analogy, motivation is not so much concerned with the features of stimuli, but rather with characteristics of the processing system. Stress is not, in the first place, a feature of stimuli or circumstances, but has to do with the way in which the individual handles these.

Another difference between radios and computers is that a computer can carry out several tasks simultaneously. A radio is always tuned to one station at a time. This parallel processing of information was soon found to exist in individuals. An important development in memory research, which is clearly related to the computer, has been that forgetting is not always due to trace decay, but that the information is sometimes no longer retrievable (Baddeley, 1976).

A current and theoretically interesting area with respect to the relationship between metaphors and the mind is artificial intelligence. The computer can deliver solutions to problems. In addition to being able to play chess, for example, some computers can also read, translate, draft a summary, and even speak and make decisions. Many hold the view that artificial intelligence only succeeds in demonstrating that computers can do the same things as people (Searle, 1981). It does not follow, however, that a computer is able to solve a problem in the same way as a human being. Several optical illusions have been explained in neurophysiological terms (lateral inhibition), whereas the computer accurately describes the perception of some illusions on the assumption that we continuously perform complex mathematical calculations (Fourier analysis) when viewing contrasts (Cornsweet, 1971). These alternative explanations or descriptions illustrate the inaccessibility of the mind and the fact that incompatible metaphors are sometimes able to explain the same phenomenon.

From Radio to Computer: Publication Trends

The transition from the radio metaphor to the computer metaphor can tentatively be studied by counting the number of publications using them. Forrester (1984) has shown that during the period of the radio metaphor relatively few papers were published in memory, which is rather understandable. Radios have no memory. In the course of the 1960s, this number increased considerably.

Another approach to the question in which respect publication trends have changed is that we count some relevant key words in the *Psychological Abstracts*. We compared the years 1958, 1959, and 1960 with 1978 and 1980 (not all data of 1979 were available). Correcting for the larger number of publications in 1978 and 1980 we find the following figures (Table 1). A value of 1.00 would mean that the proportion of publications on a certain topic is equal in both periods. A value greater than 1.00 indicates more frequent occurrence in the later period.

Table 1

Ratios of Numbers of Publications in the Period 1978-1980
to Those in 1958-1960

Subject	Ratios
Effects of Noise on Information Transmission	0.16
Subliminal Perception	0.21
Communication and Information	0.22
Selective Attention	0.62
Decision Making	1.68
Memory	2.37
Imagining	4.64
Cognitive Processes and Problem Solving	5.28

Some differences are clear. Concepts and problems related to the first stages of information processing attract much less attention in favor of higher cognitive processes. The same seems to be the case when handbooks are compared. Around 1965 about 40 percent of the chapters were devoted to higher cognitive functions. Around 1980 this percentage is about 90.

A good example of the transition from the radio metaphor to the computer metaphor involves the study of time. The experience of time is subject to accelerations and decelerations. Until 1970 these variations were almost exclusively ascribed to the intensity and the speed with which stimuli succeeded each other. The term time *sense* was widely used to describe an hypothesized sensory organ for time which belonged to the information transmission metaphor, and it determined the speed of an internal clock. In the 1970s the time sense was replaced by time *experience*. The problem was brought into line with the computer metaphor by considering subjective time as an *internal* byproduct of cognitive processes such as memory and thinking (Ornstein, 1969; Vroon, 1972, 1974; Block, 1979).

Disunity

It stands to reason that these data should be considered with care because they contain indirect evidence, just like those published by Forrester (1984). At first sight, there appears to have been not only a metaphor shift, but also some diachronic disunity. It seems that 'old' facts, theories, and topics are hardly referred to, not because they are wrong or not applicable, but because they do not fit the most recent influential metaphor. The debate about early models of attention was not stopped around 1965 because the issues were settled, but because research along the lines of the digital computer seemed more promising. Information theory is a very strong example, in the sense that the data were not even *incorporated* in later theories. The same holds for many findings in the field of time perception, and the new look in perception was completely left behind.

Finally, the data should also be cautiously considered because it is conceivable that research continued under different headings. This holds possibly for parts of the research on subliminal perception, which is in recent times more or less back under headings such as automatic facilitation, late selection, pre-conscious processing, and blindsight. Careful search of the literature and citations have to show in which respect and to which degree there is diachronic disunity that can be related to metaphor shifts.

Nevertheless, this short overview suggests a possible cause of diachronic disunity: 'old' data does not always match the conceptual framework of a new metaphor. The synchronic disunity of psychology may be explained along similar lines. Behaviorists, cognitivists, and psychoanalysts form more or less separated intellectual 'circuits' because they are inspired by quite different technological metaphors, tied to specific methods and data. Finally, it becomes clear that psychology is not, as a whole, inspired by the most complex metaphors that are available in a certain period. To an important degree, the choice of the metaphors is determined by (implicit) ideas about relevant and 'fitting' aspects of human functioning. The connection between psychological systems and metaphors is also defended by Gentner and Grudin (1985): "Thus, there does appear to be a correlation between changes in metaphoric domains and changes in the dominant schools in psychology" (p. 189). Also, these authors show that the newness of technology is neither a necessary nor a sufficient condition for the use of a system in mental metaphors. Metaphors of highly differing technological levels may function at the same time, and they contribute to the accumulation of knowledge as well as to disunity.

Memory Metaphors and the Homunculus

The function of technological metaphors in psychology can also be illustrated by a specific subject such as memory. Roediger (1980) and Hoffman (1980) give a comprehensive overview. Descartes proposed a variation on Plato's wax tablet when he suggested that memory was like a piece of cloth in which holes were pierced in order to allow fluids to flow through. At the turn of the 20th century, the spatialization of memory became apparent in the work of Freud and William James, both of whom used the house as a model. Memory has been described as a grammaphone record, and more recently as a tape recorder. Near the end of the 19th century it was advocated that memory could be compared with a collection of identical records. This idea had to do with the discovery that many functions showed degrees of deterioration proportional to the amount of damaged brain tissue. This phenomenon has been observed many times since then, and later gave rise to the hologram analogy (Pribram, 1971). Such memory metaphors present a problem. There is no room for the well established fact that people know immediately that they do *not* know something. Within the framework of a spatial memory metaphor we would need much time for searching memory in this case.

More importantly there is the problem of the homunculus in all technological metaphors. The homunculus is based on a logical error (*petitio principii*), i.e., the fact that the theory postulates the process that has to be explained. As far as memory is concerned, does a homunculus read the piece of wax? Who interprets the grammaphone record, walks through the house, consults the book index in the library, and so on? How does the 'librarian' know where to find the book? Does he or she remember where it is? Has the homunculus a library in his head?

These questions can also be applied to the computer metaphor. How valid are statements that cognitive schemes have a 'purpose,' that comporators 'compare' quantities, that representations of reality 'enable' us to act, and that a central processor 'scans' memory? The logical flaw is that rationality is inplanted in us as a postulate. This same postulate cannot then be used to explain behavior, and intentional statements like this do not apply to machines. Dennett (1978) has tried to solve the problem of the person in the machine. As time goes by, the homunculus drifts deeper into the mechanism. According to Aristotle, perception takes place in the eye itself, while Descartes localizes the homunculus somewhere near the pineal gland. Dennett says that ideally there is no general homunculus, but rather an 'army of idiots' each of which is capable only of carrying out mundane assignments so that they might be replaced by machine components or new machines.

Concluding Remarks and Some Speculations

We assume that disunity in psychology has to do with the fact that each metaphor has its own heuristic value. This leads to the existence of theoretical schools, operating in relative isolation. As far as synchronic disunity is concerned, current schools study different aspects of behavior or mental life. Roughly speaking, these are conditioning, motivation, and higher cognitive processes. Staats (1983) says that these systems do not have sufficient contact with each other, which is true. On the other hand, it is possible that the general theories or approaches parallel the organization of psychology's *object*. Koestler (1967) argues that the human brain developed very fast, and is divided into three systems with relatively autonomous functions, namely, a reptilian, a primate mammalian, and a higher mammalian brain. According to Koestler, these systems are particularly involved in primitive forms of learning, emotion and motivation, and cognition, respectively. If this idea is correct, and there are several indications in this direction, and if the three mainstreams of psychology direct themselves particularly to these assemblies of functions, human nature is 'accidentally' reflected in three metaphors, and in three theoretical systems. Disunity is not bad if the object is divided along corresponding lines, and if this very general theory proves to be valid and productive.

Secondly, there is some diachronic disunity, which means that in psychology knowledge accumulates relatively slowly. In physics metaphors are also abundantly used as didactic and heuristic principles, but hardly for theory-constitutive purposes: abstract theories are built in which the metaphors are completely or, for the greater part, abandoned. Psychology, however, stays close to the metaphor so that general theories embracing vast amounts of material are not constructed. A consequence of this strong connectedness to metaphors is 'scientific amnesia,' which is a rather serious phenomenon. Schacter (1982) says that there is no reason "to lead one to conclude that the insights of the past have been thoroughly digested by contemporary practitioners. The relevant past in psychology seems to be defined in terms of a decade or two: Events occurring prior to the onset of the latest research trend are too often regarded as ancient history, and ancient history is dead history ... Psychology cannot yet be characterized as a *cumulative* science" (pp. 262 and 264). However, Schacter is not able to explain *why* this happens. We believe that studying metaphors may throw light on these phenomena and problems. In this sense the present analysis is an attempt to characterize the nature of psychology as a science. We can see, in this analysis, differences from the natural sciences - a point also made in considering the disunity of psychology and the unity of the natural sciences (Staats, 1983). Apart from the conceptual frameworks dictated by the characteristics of the chosen metaphors, different methodologies related to the metaphor may also be a contributing factor in the unity-disunity difference, a possibility that asks for further exploration of handbooks and publication trends.

Finally, the computer metaphor marks an interesting change in psychology. In the past, psychological research was influenced by the characteristics of the chosen metaphor or parts of it. The most recent history, however, shows that the construction and the software of computers is changed to theories about the way the mind works. This means that there is now a *circular* relation between psychology and its metaphors that poses new problems and opens new perspectives.

References

Anderson, C. (1964). The psychology of metaphors. *Journal of Genetic Psychology, 105,* 53-73.

Baddeley, A. D. (1976). *The psychology of memory.* New York: Harper & Row.

Bem, S. (1985). *Het bewustzijn te lijf.* Meppel: Boom.

Billow, R. M. (1977). Metaphor: a review of the psychological literature. *Psychological Bulletin, 84,* 1, 81-92.

Block, R. A. (1979). Time and consciousness. In G. Underwood & R. Stevens (Eds.), *Aspects of consciousness* (pp. 179-217). London: Academic Press.

Breuer, J., & Freud, S. (1895). (Ed. 1970). *Studien über Hysterie.* Frankfurt am main: Fisher Bücherei.

Broadbent, D. E. (1958). *Perception and communication.* Oxford: Pergamon.

Broadbent, D. E. (1971). *Decision and stress.* London: Academic Press.

Bühler, K. (1933). *Ausdruckstheorie.* Stuttgart: Fischer Verlag.

Carus, C. G. (1846). (Ed. 1975). *Psyche, Zur Entwicklungsgeschichte der Seele.* Darmstadt: Wissenschaftliche Buchgesellschaft.

Cornsweet, T. N. (1971). *Visual perception.* New York: Academic Press.

Dennett, D. C. (1978). *Brainstorms: philosophical essays on mind and psychology.* Hassocks: Harvester Press.

Draaisma, D. (1983). *De geometrie van de geest.* Groningen: Groningen University Press.

Flanagan, O. J. (1984). *The science of the mind.* London: Bradford.

Forrester, W. E. (1984). Publication trends in human learning and memory: 1962-1982. *Bulletin of the Psychonomic Society, 22,* 2, 92-94.

Freud, S. (1940). *Gesammelte Werke.* London: Imago Publishing Company.

Gentner, D., Grudin, J. (1985). The evolution of mental metaphors in psychology: a 90-year retrospective. *American Psychologist, 2,* 181-192.

Hilgard, E. R. (1977). *Divided consciousness: multiple controls in human thought and action.* New York: Wiley.

Hoffman, R. R. (1980). Metaphor in science. In R. P. Honek & R. R. Hoffman (Eds.), *Cognition and figurative language* (393-422). Hillsdale, NJ: Erlbaum.

Hoffman, R. R., & Nead, J. M. (1983). General contextualism, ecological science and cognitive research. *The Journal of Mind and Behavior, 4,* 4, 507-560.

Koestler, A. (1967). *The ghost in the machine.* London: Hutchinson.

Lorenz, K. (1965). *Over aggressie bij dier en mens.* Amsterdam: Ploegsma.

Mandler, G. (1975). Consciousness: respectable, useful and necessary. In R. Solso (Ed.), *Information processing and cognition (pp. 228-238)*. New York: Wiley.

Marks, L. E. (1978. *The unity of the senses*. New York: Academic Press.

Marks, L. E. (1982). Bright sneezes and dark coughs, loud sunlight and soft moonlight. *Journal of Experimental Psychology, 8,* 2, 177-193.

McReynolds, P. (1980). The clock metaphor and psychology. In T. Nickles (Ed.), *Scientific discovery: case studies* (pp. 97-112). Dordrecht: Reidel.

Michon, J. A. (1967). *Timing in temporal tracking*. Assen: Van Gorcum.

Neisser, U. (1967). *Cognitive psychology*. New York: Appleton Century Crofts.

Nisbett, R., & Ross, L. (1980). *Human inference, strategies and shortcomings of social judgment*. Englewood Cliffs: Prentice Hall.

Nuttin, J. M. (1975). *The illusion of attitude change*. New York: Academic Press.

Ornstein, R. E. (1969). *On the experience of time*. Baltimore: Penquin Books.

Ortony, E. (Ed). (1979). *Metaphor and thought*. Cambridge: Cambridge University Press.

Paivio, A. (1979). Psychological processes in the comprehension of metaphor. In A. Ortony (Ed.), *Metaphor and thought* (pp. 150-171). Cambridge: Cambridge University Press.

Pepper, S. C. (1942). *World hypotheses*. Berkeley: University of California Press.

Pribram, K. H. (1971). *Languages of the brain*. Englewood Cliffs: Prentice-Hall.

Resnick, L. B. (Ed.) (1976). *The nature of intelligence*. Hillsdale, NJ: Erlbaum.

Roediger, H. L. (1980). Memory metaphors in cognitive psychology psychology. *Memory and Cognition, 8,* 3, 231-246.

Russelman, G. H. E. (1983). *From James Watt to Sigmund Freud*. Deventer: Van Loghum Slaterus.

Schacter, D. L. (1982). *Stranger behind the engram*. Hillsdale, NJ: Erlbaum.

Searle, J. R. (1981). Minds, brains and programs. In D. R. Hofstadter & D. C. Dennett (Eds.), *The mind's I* (pp. 353-373). New York: Basic Books.

Simon, H. A. (1975). *Models of man*. New York: Wiley.

Staats, A. W. (1983). *Psychology's crisis of disunity*. New York: Praeger.

Thijssen, W. Th. M. (1982). *De mens-machine theorie.* Meppel: Krips Repro.

Treisman, M. (1963). Temporal discrimination and the indifference interval: Implications for a model of the internal clock. *Psychological Monographs, 77,* Whole No. 576.

Turing, A. M. (1950). Computing machinery and intelligence. *Mind,* 433-460.

Urban, W. (1939). *Language and reality.* New York: MacMillan.

Vartanian, A. (1973). Man-machine from the Greeks to the computer. In P. P. Wiener (Ed.), *Dictionary of the History of Ideas.* New York: Scribner.

Vroon, P. A. (1970). Divisibility and retention of psychological time. *Acta Psychologica, 32,* 366-376.

Vroon, P. A. (1972). *Some psychological and cognitive aspects of the time sense.* Utrecht: Utrecht University Press.

Vroon, P. A. (1974). Is there a time quantum in duration experience? *American Journal of Psychology, 87,* 237-245.

Vroon, P. A. & Draaisma, D. (1985). *De mens als metafoor.* Baarn: Ambo.

Witkin, H. A., Lewis, H. B., Herzman, M., Machover, K., Meissner, P. B., & Wapner, A. (1954). *Personality through perception.* New York: Harper & Row.

Wittrock, M. C. (Ed.).(1980). *The brain and psychology.* New York: Academic Press.

AUTHOR INDEX

Page numbers refer to text citations. Italicized numbers refer to the
reference lists at the ends of the papers.